The New Local Government Series

No. 26

THE NATIONAL WORLD OF LOCAL GOVERNMENT

The New Local Government Series
Series Editor: Professor Peter G. Richards

THE NATIONAL WORLD
OF
LOCAL GOVERNMENT

R. A. W. RHODES
University of Essex

London
ALLEN & UNWIN
BOSTON   SYDNEY

Allen & Unwin (Publishers) Ltd,
40 Museum Street, London WC1A 1LU, UK

Allen & Unwin (Publishers) Ltd,
Park Lane, Hemel Hempstead, Herts HP2 4TE, UK

Allen & Unwin, Inc.,
8 Winchester Place, Winchester, Mass. 01890, USA

Allen & Unwin (Australia) Ltd,
8 Napier Street, North Sydney, NSW 2060, Australia

First published in 1986

British Library Cataloguing in Publication Data

Rhodes, R. A. W.
    The national world of local government. − (The New
    local government series; no. 26)
    1. Local government − Great Britain − State
    supervision 2. Great Britain − Politics and
    government − 1964
I. Title   II. Series
354.4108′3   JS3137
ISBN 0−04−320170−9

Library of Congress Cataloging-in-Publication Data

Rhodes, R. A. W.
    The national world of local government.
    (The New local government series; no. 26)
    Bibliography: p.
    Includes index.
    1. Local government − Great Britain.
    2. Intergovernmental fiscal relations − Great Britain.
I. Title.   II. Series.
JS3137.R49   1986   352.041   85−15103
ISBN 0−04−320170−9 (alk. paper)

Set in 10 on 11 point Times by
Mathematical Composition Setters, Salisbury
and printed in Great Britain by
Biddles Ltd, Guildford, Surrey

For Cyn, Edward and Bethan

By the same author:

Intergovernmental Relations in the European Community
  (with C. Hull)
Training in the Civil Service (editor and contributor)
Public Administration and Policy Analysis
Control and Power in Central–Local Government Relations
The New British Political System (with I. Budge *et al.*)

CONTENTS

LIST OF TABLES AND FIGURES

Tables

List of Tables and Figures

Figures

ABBREVIATIONS

ACC	Association of County Councils
ACT	Association of Charter Trustees
ACCE	Association of County Chief Executives
ACE	Advisory Centre for Education
ACPO	Association of Chief Police Officers
ADC	Association of District Councils
ADCT	Association of District Council Treasurers
ADS	Association of District Secretaries
AEC	Association of Education Committees
ALA	Association of London Authorities
ANC	Association of Neighbourhood Councils
ALACE	Association of Local Authority Chief Executives
AMA	Association of Metropolitan Authorities
AMC	Association of Municipal Corporations
BACT	British Association of Conference Towns
BRA	British Resorts Association
BEC	Business Education Council
CACFOA	Chief and Assistant Chief Fire Officers' Association
CASE	Confederation for the Advancement of State Education
CBI	Confederation of British Industry
CCA	County Councils Association
CCLGF	Consultative Council on Local Government Finance
CEOS	County Education Officers' Society
CFBAC	Central Fire Brigades Advisory Council
CIPFA	Chartered Institute of Public Finance and Accountancy
CLEA	Council of Local Education Authorities
COHSE	Confederation of Health Service Employees
COSLA	Convention of Scottish Local Authorities
CP	Council for the Principality
DE	Department of Employment
DEP	Department of Employment and Productivity
DES	Department of Education and Science
DHSS	Department of Health and Social Security
DoE	Department of the Environment
DPCP	Department of Prices and Consumer Protection
DTp	Department of Transport
ESGE	Expenditure Steering Group (Education)

FBCA	Federation of British Cremation Authorities
FBU	Fire Brigades' Union
FSC	Field Studies Council
GLC	Greater London Council
GMWU	General and Municipal Workers' Union
HMIs	Her Majesty's Inspectors of Fire Services
ICSA	Institute of Chartered Secretaries and Administrators
ILEA	Inner London Education Authority
ILGA	Institute of Local Government Administrators
IMTA	Institute of Municipal Treasurers and Accountants
INLOGOV	Institute of Local Government Studies (University of Birmingham)
JACOLA	Joint Airports Committee of Local Authorities
LACOTS	Local Authorities' Coordinating Body on Trading Standards
LACSAB	Local Authorities' Conditions of Service Advisory Board
LAFBs	Local authority fire brigades
LAHEC	Local Authorities' Higher Education Committee
LAMIT	Local Authorities' Mutual Investment Trust
LAMSAC	Local Authorities Management Services and Computer Committee
LAOSC	Local Authorities Ordnance Survey Committee
LBA	London Boroughs Association
LEAs	Local education authorities
LGTB	Local Government Training Board
MAFF	Ministry of Agriculture, Fisheries and Food.
MHLG	Ministry of Housing and Local Government
MSC	Manpower Services Commission
NAFO	National Association of Fire Officers
NALC	National Association of Local Councils
NALGO	National and Local Government Officers' Association
NAPC	National Association of Parish Councils
NATFHE	National Association of Teachers in Further and Higher Education
NBPI	National Board for Prices and Incomes
NFER	National Foundation for Educational Research
NIAE	National Institute for Adult Education
NILGOSC	Northern Ireland Local Government Officers Superannuation Committee
NJC/JNC	national joint council/joint national council
NJC for APT & C	National Joint Council for Administrative, Professional, Technical and Clerical Staffs

NJC for LAFBs	National Joint Council for Local Authority Fire Brigades
NUPE	National Union of Public Employees
NUT	National Union of Teachers
PES/PESC	Public Expenditure Survey/Public Expenditure Survey Committee
RDCA	Rural District Councils Association
RPI	Retail price index
RSG	Rate support grant
SACLAT	Standing Advisory Committee on Local Authorities and the Theatre.
SCS	Society of County Secretaries
SCT	Society of County Treasurers
SEO	Society of Education Officers
SLCC	Society of Local Council Clerks
SMT	Society of Metropolitan Treasurers
SOCPO	Society of Chief Personnel Officers
SOLACE	Society of Local Authority Chief Executives
TAC	Theatres Advisory Committee
TGWU	Transport and General Workers' Union
TUC	Trades Union Council
UCATT	Union of Construction, Allied Trades and Technicians
UDCA	Urban District Councils Association
WACTC	Welsh Association of Community and Town Councils
WCC	Welsh Counties Committee

ACKNOWLEDGEMENTS

The origins of this book lie in the work of the Social Science Research Council's Panel on Central–Local Government Relationships. The panel not only invited me to produce a framework to guide their research initiative (Rhodes, 1979 and 1981a), but its subsequent report stimulated an extensive research programme on central–local relations (SSRC, 1979). This programme explored variations in the relationship depending on policy, function and area. It aimed to develop an understanding of intergovernmental relationships, policy-making, implementation and accountability. The panel was set up in 1978 and the first research projects were commissioned in 1979. This study of the national world of local government formed part of this first phase. The fieldwork was completed in October 1982 and the preliminary results published in a series of discussion papers during 1982 and 1983 (Rhodes, 1982; Rhodes, Hardy and Pudney, 1982a, 1982b, 1982c, 1983a, 1983b, 1983c and 1983d). Self-evidently, therefore, I owe a considerable debt of gratitude to the SSRC. Without their financial support, this research would not have been possible. Additionally, individual members of the panel provided advice and assistance, as did co-researchers on other projects commissioned by the panel. My thanks to them all.

Inevitably, working in the same field for five years, I have accumulated debts. Pride of place must go to my two research officers, Brian Hardy and Kevin Pudney. Brian took the 'lead' in collecting the data on the structure and functions of the individual organizations within the national community and for the case study of pay negotiations. Kevin took the 'lead' for the case study of the Consultative Council on Local Government Finance. Without their enthusiasm and willing 'workaholism', the study would have been far more limited in scope.

A number of other colleagues provided advice and criticism above and beyond the call of duty. My thanks to Michael Goldsmith (Salford), George Jones (LSE), John Stewart (INLOGOV), David Marsh (Essex), Ed Page (Hull) and Pat Dunleavy (LSE). Practical help was provided by John Gyford, Marie James and a number of students at Essex – Andrew Flynn, Philip Gibson, Tony Moulder and Mel Read. Initially Pat Caplin, Judith Monk and Janet Isley coped with voluminous manuscripts and impossible deadlines. Their work was ably and speedily completed by Noel Finney and Carol Snape. I am grateful to them all. And the list can only be reduced to its present length by thanking *en masse* all those individuals who have commented on particular papers either at seminars and conferences or in writing. The help was appreciated and I trust they will accept the need for brevity. Finally, Caroline Cunningham provided invaluable help in proof-reading and preparing the index.

I have left until the end perhaps the most important acknowledgement of all. Without the willing support of the ACC, ADC and AMA (and, of course, all the other national organizations of local government) this study would have been, literally, impossible. Similarly numerous central departments (most notably the DoE) and professions (especially CIPFA and SOLACE) co-operated willingly. Convention dictates that officials are not named and I must respect the wishes of my numerous interviewees and informants. But I insist on one exception: Len Roberts at the ACC. He provided the usual assistance but, in addition, he was interested in the research! Consequently, I possess his 'collected letters' criticizing the project and I benefitted generally from his advice. I hope he will forgive not only his explicit identification but, for the first time in three years, the use of his Christian name. I often felt that his blend of friendly interest and formality captured part of the soul of the ACC.

I cannot believe that any of the organizations analysed in this book will agree with, or even like, its contents. I trust they will accept that the criticism herein is disinterested criticism − I am grinding no axe, supporting no one protagonist in past or present controversies − and that I consider their co-operation over the past three years a model of its kind. To say I am grateful is to resort to typical English understatement.

As ever, the responsibility for any remaining mistakes and shortcomings is mine alone.

R. A. W. RHODES
July 1984

Chapter 1

———————◆———————

INTRODUCTION

OBJECTIVES

The phrase local government conjures up a picture of the parish pump, of mundane if essential services. Unlike a Cabinet minister the local councillor belongs to a prosaic world encompassing, if one is to believe television series, both graft and corruption on building sites and the 'do-gooder'. Not for him the great affairs of state, the policy which guarantees a place in the history books. Local government is local and parochial. Similarly, relations between central and local government are seen as the relations between central and local *departments*. The relationship is not seen as between units of government such as occur within the European Community. Local authorities are all too frequently seen as the agents of central departments, implementing services to national standards within national guidelines. But local government is an actor on the national stage: its national representatives live in the village that is Westminster and Whitehall, meeting with ministers and civil servants on a virtually routinized basis. The objective of this book is to describe and analyse this 'national world of local government' (Stewart, 1983, pp. 11–12).

To be more precise, the book has four objectives:

- to describe the national community of local government and to assess its effectiveness;
- to locate this community within the national local government system and to describe its roles and relationships within that system;
- to explore the changing relationship between the national government environment and the national local government system and to assess the impact of these changes on the national community of local government; and
- to explain the changes in the national world of local government which occurred between 1970 and 1983.

This chapter introduces these themes or objectives as well as providing a synopsis of the book's structure.

The National Community of Local Government

It would be misleading to suggest that there was no awareness or knowledge of local government's role on the national stage. The local authority associations are not newcomers to political theatre. Each type of local authority has its own national representative organization or pressure group to protect and foster its interests. Thus, the county councils are represented by the Association of County Councils (ACC); the metropolitan districts and counties, the Greater London Council (GLC) and the London boroughs are represented by the Association of Metropolitan Authorities (AMA); and the county districts are represented by the Association of District Councils (ADC). These three organizations were established following the reorganization of local government in 1974 but their origins go back much further. The AMA's predecessor organization, the Association of Municipal Corporations (AMC), was created in 1873, the County Councils Association (CCA) was created in 1888 whilst the Rural District Councils Association (RDCA) and the Urban District Councils Association (UDCA) were created in 1895. Most students of the relationship between central and local government would agree that these associations have been, and continue to be, important actors. Thus Griffith suggests that:

> Any description of central and local public authorities in Britain would be incomplete without some mention of the role of the local authority associations. It is difficult to exaggerate their importance in influencing legislation, government policies and administration and in acting as co-ordinators and channels of local authority opinion. (Griffith, 1966, p. 23)

Belying this assessment, however, there have been few studies of the associations.[1]

Paucity of knowledge could simply be a reflection of the esoteric nature of the subject. There are many facets of British government of interest only to the specialist. The associations do not fall into this category. Even the ubiquitous man-in-the-street is aware, in a vague way, that local government is a 'problem'. Throughout the 1970s there has been legislation affecting the structure, functions and finance of local government and the associations have been in the firing line for all these developments. To examine the role of the associations is to examine a highly turbulent policy area which has been in the forefront of British politics and shows little sign of abating.

But what is the role of the associations? They can be seen as just another pressure group, articulating the interests and demands of their member local authorities. From this standpoint, it is obviously important to explore their effectiveness. Thus, it will be necessary to examine the links between the associations and their members to see if they accurately reflect the latter's views. It will also be necessary to assess their success in influencing government policy and to describe their tactics for the various stages of the policy process. And any such account must consider the constraints which limit effectiveness.

All of these topics are the traditional subject-matter of case studies of particular pressure groups but no study of the national world of local government can restrict itself to them. The scope of the analysis must be extended to the changing nature of the network of relationships within which the associations are embedded. This standpoint requires an examination of the range of organizations speaking for local government at the national level and not just the associations. This set of organizations is referred to as the national community of local government. The shift of emphasis represented by the use of this phrase is away from a focus on individual organizations to a focus on the relationships between them: to an examination of the network.

The national local government system
The national community is not the only network in which local government is embedded. For example, several local government professions have close ties with their appropriate central service department, for example, education and fire. These functional networks, or policy communities, are also channels of communication for local government. The phrase 'national local government system' refers to the range of networks in which local government is embedded. It refers to 'the set of organisations and actors which together define the national role and state of opinion in local government as a whole' (Dunleavy, 1981, p. 105). It encompasses the national community of local government but it is not limited to this network, encompassing also the policy communities. It also refers to ideas and values shared by the several institutions and professions – to such influential notions as 'best professional practice'. Any exploration of the national world of local government must involve a description and analysis not only of relations within the national community but of relations between that network and the policy communities. The 1970s saw the attempt to create an intervening tier of representation at the national level through which individual local authorities funnelled all their contacts with the centre. The origins, development and ultimately setbacks to this attempt to consolidate and strengthen the position of the national community cannot be studied in isolation. Not only did the national community try to increase its influence over the policy communities but the aspiration towards being *the* channel of communication for local government was encouraged and supported by central government. The position of the national community and changing relationships within the national local government system were moulded by central interventions. It is essential, therefore, to examine the national government environment.

The national government environment
The national local government system is embedded in a national

government environment composed of central government institutions (and their environment) concerned with local government. The term refers, therefore, to the context within which intergovernmental relations are conducted: to the changing interventions of government and to the social, economic and political factors which prompted those interventions. (The terminology is modified from Stewart, 1983, pp. 11–12 and 65–8.) The national world of local government refers to the sum of the national local government system and the national government environment. This terminology will be developed below (see Chapter 2) but a brief discussion at this stage makes it clear that the focus of the book is centre–centre relations not centre–local relations. Individual local authorities only feature in this book as members of their appropriate national representative organization. Their separate links with central departments are not of prime concern, important though they may be.

The major objective of this book is to describe and analyse the tumultuous times of the national community of local government within the national local government system. There are, however, two subsidiary objectives. First, the study of intergovernmental relations has had a markedly normative bias and it has been studied from a public administration, or a legal-institutional, perspective. Only rarely has the subject drawn upon or related to theories and issues of concern to the social sciences more generally. (For a review of the literature see Rhodes, 1981a, ch. 2.) This book does not attempt to set the world to rights nor, with the exception of Chapter 3, does it provide a great deal of institutional description. Rather it describes the actual behaviour of participants in central–local relations and it draws upon neo-pluralist accounts of industrial societies (for example Lindblom, 1977) in an attempt to explain that behaviour.

Second, in order to provide such an account of the national world of local government, this study makes extensive use of case studies. This particular methodological tool has been heavily criticized, primarily on the grounds that each case study is unique and inhibits generalizations. Such criticism assumes that case studies are chronological accounts of single issues. This book attempts to demonstrate that case studies which trace the development of issues over a period of years and which explicitly explore the utility of concepts for understanding the events portrayed are an invaluable tool for analysing intergovernmental relations: they can be 'theory-laden'.

STRUCTURE

The book has three main sections. Part One provides the basic building blocks by providing both the theoretical framework and a description of the organizations being studied. Part Two examines these organizations 'in action', focusing on the relationship between the national community of local government and the national government environment. Part Three explores the other relationships within the national local government system.

Any analysis and assessment of the national world of local government will vary with the spectacles worn for viewing the subject. As Allison (1971, p. 245) has argued, conceptual models:

> are more than *simple* angles of visions or approaches. Each conceptual framework consists of a *cluster* of assumptions and categories that influence what the analyst finds puzzling, how he formulates his question, where he looks for evidence, and what he produces as an answer.

This study is no exception to Allison's comment. It is important, therefore, to explain 'the cluster of assumptions and categories' which will be used. Chapter 2 undertakes this task. Because the focus of the study is somewhat unusual, and as much attention is placed on the network as on individual organizations, the unit of analysis is defined rather more formally than earlier. Subseqently, a framework is presented which encompasses:

- the micro-level of the behaviour of individual organizations within a network (that is, within the national community);
- the meso-level of the interactions between networks (that is, between policy communities and the national community in the national local government system); and
- the macro-level of the effects of the national government environment on the national local government system.

Some readers may be more interested in the description of the national community at work. This chapter has provided a brief summary of the major concepts and the more formal account in Chapter 2 could, at a pinch, be 'skipped'; although readers will find Figure 2.3 a useful guide to the rest of the book. More important, the final section of the chapter discusses the constraints and cleavages which limit the effectiveness of the national community. The constraints include the multiple interests which the national community has to represent, the voluntary nature of membership, the resources available, the functional nature of British government, the influence of the professions and the direct and indirect controls of national government. The cleavages include type of authority, party political allegiance, competition between service interests and the conflict between national and local priorities. In short, it describes the multiple criteria necessary for an assessment of the effectiveness of the national community.

Many of the organizations discussed in the bulk of this study will be totally unfamiliar to the majority of readers. Indeed, many will feel that their obscurity is wholly deserved. None the less, it will be helpful to describe their structure and functions. More important, each organization, however obscure, is a constituent of the national community of local government. If the behaviour of this network is to be understood, it is crucial to determine which organizations are central and which are peripheral. Accordingly, Chapter 3 presents a *comparative* description of the national organizations of local government which serves the dual function of introducing the actors and mapping the network's terrain.

Part Two of the book examines the national community 'in action' and the choice of case studies is a direct product of the earlier discussion. Chapter 2 identifies three major sets of relationships and Part Two focuses on the first set of relationships, namely, those between the national government environment and the national local government system (see Figure 2.3). Chapter 2 also argues that the major interests of the national community of local government in its relationships with the national government were grant negotiations, pay negotiations and the reorganization of local government. Chapters 4, 5 and 6 present case studies of each of these policy areas. The individual chapters concentrate on describing the events and the behaviour of actors. Interpretation is reserved for the overall conclusions to this study. And it is worth repeating that these case studies are 'theory-laden': they *will* permit generalization and the critical appreciation of theoretical issues.[2] The 'stories' (Rein, 1976, pp. 75–7) which follow may or may not be intrinsically interesting but they do generate explanations of the changing role of the national community. Equally, it is not being claimed that the 'stories' admit of only one interpretation. Although the phrase is a dangerous one for anybody specializing in the study of public administration, these stories are 'thick descriptions': that is, they are told in detail, encompass the different views of events held by the participants and permit (even require), therefore, several different interpretations. The interpretation presented here can, I hope, be challenged using my description of events, the actors and their motives and behaviour. If, at times, the detail seems excessive, it is the necessary price of case studies which aim to generate explanations.[3]

The 'stories' refer primarily to local government since the reorganization of 1972 but attention is not limited to this period. For example, it is necessary to say something about the associations immediately prior to reorganization. Equally, the impact of the 1979–83 Conservative government on local government has been dramatic and cannot be ignored. Effectively, therefore, this study covers the period 1970–83. No attempt has been made to provide a descriptive guide to current affairs. This book is an analysis of the changing role of the national world of local government and the conclusions drawn are *not* specific to a particular government or a particular policy. The sense of urgency and immediacy, not to mention secrecy, which surrounds the study of current affairs can hamper the appreciation of the context of particular developments. For the tumultuous years of the 1970s such a sense of perspective is particularly important.

Whilst the relationships between the national government environment and the national local government system are of key importance, they are by no means the only relationships relevant to understanding the changing role of the national community. Part Three explores, in a series of additional case studies, the relationships within the national local government system and between that system and member local authorities (see Figure 2.3).

Chapter 7 explores relationships within the national local government system. It examines the links between the associations and between the associations and 'their' joint bodies. Although earlier chapters examined the relationship between the ACC, ADC and AMA, the smaller associations were touched on only in passing. Attention is now turned on the Welsh and London associations and their relationship with both the major associations and the national government environment. For the joint bodies, after a general review of the formal pattern of relationships, the link between the associations and LACSAB is further explored in a case study of LACSAB's 'constitutional crisis'.

Chapter 8 focuses on the links between the national community and the policy communities. It describes the major actors and patterns of *formal* participation by the national community in the education and fire services. Attention is concentrated on the role of the national community – and not, for example, on the trade unions or central departments – and the objectives are to demonstrate the existence of distinct policy networks, to determine the extent of the national community's involvement in these networks, and to assess the extent to which the policy communities constrain the issue scope of the national community.

Chapter 9 explores the links between the associations and their member local authorities, focusing on who participates in association business (members *and* officers), the patterns of contact, the dissemination of information and evaluations of the role of the associations. If earlier chapters have focused on centre–centre relationships, this chapter redresses the imbalance by examining one facet of central–local relationships.

The final chapter explores the patterns of relationships within the national world of local government, describing the phases in the relationships between the national government environment and the national local government system, and changes in relationships within the national community. Finally, the constraints on the national community are reviewed and I present an overall assessment of the effectiveness of the national community as one of the legitimate or even dignified parts of the structure of government.

NOTES AND REFERENCES: CHAPTER 1

1   The associations rate no, or the most perfunctory, mention in many general histories and introductory texts. See, for example, Buxton, 1970; Hasluck, 1949; Jackson, 1966; Laski *et al.*, 1935; Maud, 1932; and Redlich and Hirst, 1958. Brief descriptions of the associations can be found in Isaac-Henry, 1980a; Griffith, 1966; Keith-Lucas and Richards, 1978; and Richards, 1980. Their role in the reorganization of local government is described by Brand, 1974; Isaac-Henry, 1975, 1980b; Richards, 1975; and Wood, 1976. Even with the addition of unpublished theses (for example Barnhouse, 1972; Beck, 1971; and Cross, 1954) and 'in-house' histories (for example AEC, 1953, and AMC, 1972) there is still precious little material available on the associations.

2   A variety of means were used to study the changing role of the national community of local government. The sources of information included: published statistics, questionnaires, case studies, unobtrusive measures, primary, documentary sources (for example, files), semi-structured interviews and secondary sources (for example, books and articles). For a more detailed discussion see Rhodes 1982, pp. 3–16.

3   On 'theory-laden' case studies see Geertz, 1973, ch.1; and Eckstein, 1975. On the strengths and weaknesses of case studies see the exchange between Miles, 1979, and Yin, 1981. On the compilation of case studies see Barzun and Graff, 1970.

   In order to capture the several meanings accorded to events by participants, the research methods should have included participant observation. For the study of national policy-making, this form of access is not available. The sources for the 'thick descriptions' were interviews and primary documents. Clearly, these sources are less than ideal and limit the comprehensiveness of my account of the participants' interpretations.

Part One

THEORIES AND ACTORS

Chapter 2

UNDERSTANDING INTERGOVERNMENTAL RELATIONS: POWER-DEPENDENCE, POLICY COMMUNITIES AND INTERVENTION

The objectives of this chapter are to define public interest groups and the national community of local government; to describe the framework for interpreting the changing role of the national community; and to specify the criteria for assessing the influence of the national community.

It cannot be assumed that the associations are just another pressure group. There has been some recognition of the distinctive nature of the associations by earlier studies. Thus, Mackenzie (1969, p. 274) comments:

> the Association of Municipal Corporations and the County Councils Association . . . have achieved unofficially a status which makes them something like sub-parliaments. . . Their terms of reference are so wide, their respectability so great, that they have become channels of pressure rather than pressure groups. (See also Isaac-Henry, 1975, p. 9, and Stewart, 1958, p. 83.)

Accordingly, the Associations are described here as 'public interest groups' in recognition of their distinctive characteristics.

The term 'public interest group' is of American origin, where it is used to refer to the national associations of chief executives – for example, the International City Management Association, National Governors' Conference (Haider, 1974; Wright, 1978). In the British context, the term refers to the national organizations representing the interests of subnational units of government in their interactions with central institutions. This definition obviously encompasses other units of government besides local government – for example the nationalized industries (Tivey, 1982) – but the following discussion focuses on the distinctive characteristics of local government's public interest groups (cf. Rhodes, Hardy and Pudney 1981).

First, public interest groups are distinguished by their 'officiality':

> The designation 'official' is the sign manifest that the bearer is authorised by social understanding to exercise against all groups and individuals certain powers which they may not exercise against him. (Latham, 1952, pp. 33–5)

The simple point is that the members of public interest groups are elected units of government. For example, in contrast to private sector organizations, they are subject to public accountability – to control by elected representatives, with concomitant requirements of obeying the law, equity and financial and moral probity (Dunsire, 1975, p. 169). Because their membership is distinguished by being part of the structure of government, public interest groups are *legitimated*.

Second, and a logical corollary of their legitimate status, public interest groups have extensive *access* or a privileged position in consultations and negotiations with central institutions. As with any other pressure group, the *raison d'être* or prime function of public interest groups is 'to influence the decisions of public bodies' (Mackenzie, 1969, p. 263) or to articulate demands 'that the authorities in the political system ... should make an authoritative allocation' (Kimber and Richardson, 1974, p. 3). But many 'private' groups experience difficulty obtaining the access necessary to exercise such influence. Not so public interest groups, and indeed the associations have been described by Duncan Sandys, then Minister of Housing and Local Government, as 'virtually... a part of the constitution of the country' (cited in Griffith, 1966, p. 33).

Third, public interest groups are *'topocratic'*. The word 'topocrat' refers to the authority deriving from place and thus 'topocrats' promote or defend the interests of particular geographical areas (Beer, 1978, pp. 9, 21). They are not primarily concerned to promote specific policy programmes as are the 'technocrats' or professional programme specialists. The interests of the 'topocrat' are limited only by the geographical area of the governmental unit from which they are drawn, whereas the interests of the 'technocrat' are narrowly defined by their professional expertise. Thus the 'topocrats' promote and protect local government and local democracy and the interests of particular types of local authorities; their interests span several policy or functional areas.

Finally, local government's public interest groups comprise an intergovernmental lobby or *a national community of local government*. An exclusive focus on the local authority associations is potentially misleading. There is a set of organizations at the national level serving the interests of local government and it is as important to explore the relationships between these organizations as it is to explore the role of any particular organization. In short, local government's public interest groups form a national network.

There is a variety of public interest groups at the national level corresponding to the variety of interests in local government. They can be classified by organizational type – local authority association, joint body, independent association and professional societies – and by number of functions – single or multi-function. The associations represent the interests of particular types of local authority and cover a range of functions. However, the associations do not hold a monopoly in the representation of local government's interests: a number of function-specific bodies have been set up jointly where the associations have a shared interest (for example, LAMSAC, LACSAB, LGTB). At the very least these joint bodies indirectly represent local government by providing advice to the associations and their role is not necessarily so limited. In addition, some local authorities with a common interest in a particular function have formed their own organization independently of the associations (for example, the British Resorts Association and the British Association of Conference Towns). Finally, some professional societies do not limit their activities to their specific service interests. They provide advice and expertise across a range of policy areas; their members are wholly or substantially employed in local government; and they have formal organizational linkages with public interest groups – that is, they have a *de jure* right of representation on, or a formally prescribed role within, a public interest group (for example, the nomination of

Table 2.1 *Public Interest Groups: by Constitutional Type and Number of Functions (1978/9)*

		Single Function/Service	Multi-Function/Service
Local Authority Associations (10)[c]	England and Wales		[a]1 Association of Charter Trustees (ACT) 2 Association of County Councils (ACC) 3 Association of District Councils (ADC) 4 Association of Metropolitan Authorities (AMA) 5 National Association of Local Councils (NALC) [b]5a Association for Neighbourhood Councils (ANC)
	London[d]	6a Inner London Education Authority (ILEA)	6 Greater London Council (GLC) [e]7 London Boroughs Association (LBA)
	Wales		8 Council for the Principality (CP) 9 Welsh Association of Community and Town Councils (WACTC) 10 Welsh Counties Committee (WCC)

Continued

Table 2.1 *(Continued)*

		Single Function/Service	Multi-Function/Service
Joint Bodies (9)		11 Council of Local Education Authorities (CLEA) 12 Joint Airports Committee of Local Authorities (JACOLA) 13 Local Authorities' Coordinating Body on Trading Standards (LACOTS) 14 Local Authorities' Conditions of Service Advisory Board (LACSAB) 15 Local Authorities' Mutual Investment Trust (LAMIT) 16 Local Authorities Management Services and Computer Committee (LAMSAC) 17 Local Authorities Ordnance Survey Committee (LAOSC) 18 Local Government Training Board (LGTB) 19 Standing Advisory Committee on Local Authorities and the Theatre (SACLAT)	
Independent Associations (3)		20 British Association of Conference Towns (BACT) 21 British Resorts Association (BRA) 22 Federation of British Cremation Authorities (FBCA)	
Professional Societies (10)			23 Association of District Council Treasurers (ADCT) 24 Association of District Secretaries (ADS) 25 Chartered Institute of Public Finance and Accountancy (CIPFA) ^e26 Institute of Local Government Administrators (ILGA)

Table 2.1 *(Continued)*

	Single Function/Service	Multi-Function/Service
Professional Societies (10) Total 32		27 Society of Chief Personnel Officers (SOCPO) 28 Society of County Secretaries (SCS) 29 Society of County Treasurers (SCT) 30 Society of Local Authority Chief Executives (SOLACE) (including Association of County Chief Executives (ACCE)) 31 Society of Local Council Clerks (SLCC) 32 Society of Metropolitan Treasurers (SMT)

Notes

^a The Association of Charter Trustees encompasses 36 *former* cities and boroughs.

^b At the time of the survey of public interest groups, the Association for Neighbourhood Councils was discussing a federation with the National Association of Local Councils, hence its inclusion.

^c The numbers attached to each category do *not* imply that the various organizations are of equal significance: the numbers have been included to show the distribution of the various types of public interest groups, not their relative importance.

^d Those public interest groups listed under the subheadings 'London' and 'Wales' are also members of other local authority associations. Thus, ILEA, the GLC and the LBA are members of the AMA; the members of the Council for the Principality are also members of the ADC; and the members of the Welsh Counties Committee are also members of the ACC. In each case, separate organizational arrangements have been made to allow the particular class of authority to speak for their interests where issues primarily concern them. Although the GLC is a local government unit and would not normally be described as a local authority association, it is commonly treated as such by central government and the associations themselves because of the special nature of the capital city. (See Chapter 7.)

^e There have been a number of changes since this list was compiled. The LBA split in 1983 and the Association of London Authorities (ALA) was established. (See Chapter 7.) ILGA no longer exists. It was merged in 1981 with the Institute of Chartered Secretaries and Administrators (ICSA). The Association of Councillors did not reply to any inquiries and had to be excluded, although it now 'seems' to be 'active' again. Where relevant, any changes in the list since 1979 are noted in the text.

advisers to association committees). The obvious examples of such professional groupings are the various accountancy associations and the Society of Local Authority Chief Executives (SOLACE). Table 2.1 lists all the public interest groups within the national community of local government in 1978/9 (as well as translating the plethora of acronyms). At this juncture, it is only necessary to define and name local government's public interest groups. The individual organizations will be described in the next chapter. It is now necessary to provide a framework for understanding the role of public interest groups and the national community.

A FRAMEWORK FOR ANALYSIS

The framework employed here has its roots in the 'power-dependence' model of intergovernmental relations outlined in detail in Rhodes, 1981a, and modified in Rhodes, 1983d. Accordingly, a relatively brief summary is provided here and the emphasis falls on three concepts: power-dependence, policy communities and intervention.

Any attempt to explain the changing role of the national community of local government confronts the problem that the study of intergovernmental relations cannot be separated from the effects of the political system of which they form a part. And yet it is not the objective of this book to provide a theory of the changing nature of British government. It is important, therefore, to distinguish clearly the different levels of analysis in this exploration of the national world of local government. First, it is necessary to examine the roles of particular organizations, most notably the local authority associations. This task is referred to as the micro-level of analysis and is covered by the section on 'power-dependence'.[1] Second, there are recurrent patterns of interaction both within the national community of local government and between the national community and other central networks. The exploration of these networks of organizations constitutes the meso-level of analysis and is covered by the section on the national local government system and 'policy communities'. Finally, the relationships between the networks and national government constitute the macro-level of analysis and will be discussed in the section on the national government environment and 'intervention'. This section will identify those features of British government of particular relevance to the study of the national community. It will necessarily be selective but it will relate intergovernmental relations to the larger system.

'Power-dependence'
Until recently, the study of intergovernmental relations has abounded in misleading metaphors. Thus, local authorities have been said to be either the agents or the partners of central government (Rhodes, 1981a, pp. 14–21). Neither description is accurate and the alternative characterization of 'power-dependence' has been proposed. Thus, it is argued, both central departments and local authorities are inter-

dependent and no matter how powerful central government may seem it is always dependent upon local authorities to some degree. Rather more formally, the 'power-dependence' framework contains five propositions:

(a) Any organization is *dependent* upon other organizations for *resources*.
(b) In order to achieve their goals, the *organizations* have to exchange resources.
(c) Although decision-making within the organization is constrained by other organizations, the *dominant coalition* retains some discretion. The *appreciative system* of the dominant coalition influences which relationships are seen as a problem and which resources will be sought.
(d) The dominant coalition employs *strategies* within known *rules of the game* to regulate the *process of exchange*.
(e) Variations in the degree of *discretion* are a product of the goals and the relative power potential of the interacting organizations. This relative power potential is a product of the resources of each organization, of the rules of the game and of the process of exchange between organizations (Rhodes, 1981a, pp. 98–9).

Thus, relations between the associations and central departments in particular, and central–local relations in general, are characterized by bargaining for resources. Five resources, or means for supplying the needs of public sector organizations, are central to this bargaining: authority, money, political legitimacy, information and organization.

(a) Authority (or legal resources) refers to the mandatory and discretionary rights to carry out functions or services commonly vested in and between public sector organizations by statute or constitutional convention.
(b) Money (or financial resources) refers to the funds raised by a public sector organization from taxes (or precepted), from service charges and from borrowing.
(c) Political legitimacy (or political resources) refers to access to public decision-making structures and the right to build public support conferred on representatives by the legitimacy deriving from election.
(d) Informational resources refers to the possession of data and to control over either its collection or its dissemination or both.
(e) Organizational resources refers to the possession of people, skills, land, buildings, material and equipment and hence the ability to act directly rather than through intermediaries.

(This list of resources draws upon Rhodes, 1981a, pp. 100–1; Hood, 1983, pp. 5–6; Benson, 1975, p. 232.)

Less formally, the balance of resources between centre and locality is illustrated by Figure 2.1.

The relationship between the national community of local government and central departments takes on the aspects of a 'game', therefore, in which both sides manoeuvre for advantage, deploying the resources they control to maximize their influence over outcomes, and trying to avoid (where they can) becoming dependent on the other 'player'. Each organization, be it local or central department or association, will pursue its own goal or policies but in so doing it will face a number of constraints. These include not only the past decisions of the organizations but also the political nature of decision-making within organizations. Goals are the product of bargaining within organizations and out of this process emerges a dominant coalition with an agreed set of temporary goals. The perceptions of the dominant coalition will influence the choice of goals, the definition of the problem and the identification of needed resources. These perceptions are described here, following Vickers (1965, ch. 2), as the decision-maker's 'appreciative system' or that combination of factual and value judgements which describe the state of the world or reality. The emphasis on the exchange of resources suggests a mechanistic model of relationships and it is particularly important, therefore, to stress the influence of the decision-makers' interests, expectations and values (or ideology) on the process of exchange.

The resources of an organization constitute a potential for the exercise of power. Whether that potential is realized depends upon the effective deployment of resources: on the rules of the game and the

Central government	*Local government*
• control over legislation and delegated powers	• employ all personnel in local services
• provide a large part of local service finance under block grant	• local knowledge and expertise
• control of capital expenditure	• control of policy implementation and key knowledge about how to administer policy
• sets standards for and inspects some services	• independent power to raise taxes (rates) to finance services
• party control of House of Commons	
• national electoral mandate	• local electoral mandate

Figure 2.1   *The resources of centre and locality.*

Source: Dunleavy and Rhodes, 1983, pp. 113–14.

choice of strategies. The rules of the game are the less formal or conventional rules which 'largely define the institutions of society... they
set the approximate limits within which discretionary behaviour may
take place' (Truman, 1951, pp. 343–4). Strategies are the means for
imposing upon other organizations an organization's preferences concerning the time of, the conditions for and the extent of the exchange
of resources. An organization which effectively deploys its resources
will maximize its room for manoeuvre (or discretion) and be able to
choose amongst various courses of action or inaction.

Some of the rules of the game are relatively obvious. For example,
Heclo and Wildavsky (1974, pp. 14–21) have pointed out that 'trust',
or reliability, is an essential component of the Whitehall 'village
community' concerned with public expenditure. This study will
demonstrate that a variety of rules existed for the period and policy
areas under study. However, as the rules are 'conventional' and set
approximate limits to discretionary behaviour, they are not immutable. Some of the rules operated for all of the 1970s but others
were discarded and even the rules which persisted varied in their
relative importance. The effect of changes in the rules of the game
upon the national community of local government will be explored in
some detail in the case studies.

In exactly the same manner, this study will identify the strategies
available to the participants. For example, consultation has been the
preferred strategy for the bulk of the postwar period, with government initiating discussions with local authorities but not committing
itself to any modifications to policy. As before, a wide range of
strategies can be identified which vary in their relative importance. It
will be important to explore, therefore, the conditions under which the
strategies can be deployed.

Implicitly this picture of intergovernmental relations suggests a continual conflict of goals with attendant manoeuvring for advantage. In
fact, decision-makers in central and local government can agree on
policies and on their respective roles. An appreciative system may not
be specific to any one organization but common to a set of organizations. The focus on the exchange of resources draws attention to the
variations in the relationships between organizations; it does not simply substitute bargaining for the metaphors of agency or partnership.
Central and local government have different interests but the outcome
is not perpetual conflict but a shifting mosaic of relationships.[2]

This picture of intergovernmental relation is, of course, an over-
simplification and a number of important caveats must be noted
immediately.

First, it is important to distinguish between

resources as prizes and resources as weapons. The resources which
are bargained *for* may not necessarily be the same as the resources

which are bargained *with*: after all, at the gaming table there is a distinction between the chips and the cards. (Gyford and James, 1982, p. 27)

Moreover, no resource is always the prize and the prize of one round of bargaining may well be the weapon in another round: a point which highlights a related feature of resources – their variable, transmutable quality. As Simeon (1972, p. 201) has argued, resources are 'predominantly subjective', depending upon the beliefs and perceptions of individual decision-makers, and 'their distribution is highly variable and relative to both the issues and the time'. No list of resources can be comprehensive, objective or finite. Indeed, every resource could be seen as a species of political resource. Equally, the distinctions between the resources can become hard to sustain. For example, the personnel and skills of local authorities are structured by departments which also possess and control information. The resources of organization and information are fused in the person of the professional. But it is analytically possible to control the resource of organization without possessing financial or legal resources (Hood, 1983, p. 6). Thus, central departments are non-executant agencies: they do not have direct control of service provision although they do have considerable control of financial and legal resources. Noting these problems does not, however, remove the need for a classification of resources. It simply cautions that any such list should be seen as a starting point for analysis and that due care and attention should be paid to the variability of resources. The list provided here is not comprehensive and other resources will be noted at various junctures. However, it does identify the *major* resources relevant to an analysis of the national community.

Second, as Page (1982, pp. 328–30) has argued, an emphasis on bargaining and resources can divert attention away from the fundamental inequalities in a relationship of interdependency.

The relationship between central and local government is not so much a variety of 'different' types of relationship, but rather one relationship between a constitutional superior and subordinate in which the centre has a differential disposition and ability across different services and activities to set parameters varying in their tightness and consequently varying in the discretion they permit local government actors. (Page, 1982, p. 332)

There is a persistent asymmetry in the relationship, with the centre possessing a virtual monopoly of legal resources. The centre can exercise 'hegemonic leadership' or restructure the rules of the game. Such hegemonic power exists when one state is powerful enough to maintain the essential rules governing inter-state relations, and willing to do so. In addition to its role in maintaining a regime, such a state can abrogate existing rules, prevent the adoption of new rules that it opposes or play the dominant role in constructing new rules. (Keohane and Nye, 1977, p. 44)

In short, bargaining is not between equals and the centre can unilaterally alter the rules of the game.

Third, to focus on 'power-dependence' − on the exchange of resources between central departments and local authorities − is to focus on the 'figure' and to disregard the 'ground' or the context of such interactions. Intergovernmental relations operate in a political system characterized by a strong executive tradition and can be no more divorced from the effects of the larger system than any other facet of British government. As Griffith (1966, pp. 506−7) pointed out:

The two sides are not equal. The departments are stronger and make far more of the important decisions. They promote the new laws, including those which confer new powers on local authorities. Governments are, at the political top, single party machines having party policies which they will implement. No discussion of the relationship between central departments and the local authorities is real which fails to recognise that the Government will seek to ensure that its policies are carried into effect.

In short, analysis needs to be extended to encompass such key features of the British political tradition as non-executant central departments and elite fragmentation. These characteristics will be discussed below but it is important to emphasize that this comment on the limitations of a focus on the 'figure' should not consign the topic to oblivion. For a study of the national community of local government, the concepts of resources and bargaining are essential tools for exploring the relationships between public interest groups. The conflict between the associations is said to be extensive and to reduce their effectiveness when bargaining with central departments. And yet, as we will see, there is extensive exchange of resources within the national community and considerable joint activity and mutual support. A focus on the 'figure' will permit a realistic assessment of the degree of co-operation and conflict within the national community. Nor can it be assumed that all member organizations of the national community are equal. It is important to explore, for example, whether the various joint bodies are creatures of the associations or whether they are a separate channel of representation for local government. And, whilst it may seem self-evident that the associations are the key actors within the national community, it would be as well to establish their pre-eminence. In short, the power-dependence framework permits a comparative study of the public interest groups within the national community of local government.

It also raises important questions about the relationship between the national community and central departments. Even if central departments have a monopoly of legal resources, they are not wielded on all occasions. Bargaining does take place and the power-dependence framework facilitates an exploration of the conditions under which it occurs and provides concepts for an analysis of the process. It also poses the question of precisely whom the national community is representing. It could articulate the interests of member local authorities; or it could have developed its own appreciative system and articulate its own interests; or, finally, through long association with the centre, it could share the centre's appreciation of problems, and articulate the interests of the centre to the local authorities. In short, the 'figure' is a necessary but not a sufficient component of any attempt to understand the role of the national community of local government. In addition, it is necessary to explore *changes* in the distribution of resources and in the rules of the game. Central to an understanding of the 'ground' is the concept of 'policy community'.

Policy community

In their study of budgeting in British government, Heclo and Wildavsky (1974, p. xv) identified an expenditure community or network of 'personal relationships between major political and administrative actors – sometimes in conflict, often in agreement, but always in touch and operating with a shared framework'. The concept of a policy community is an extension of Heclo and Wildavsky's personal network to organizational networks based on the major functional divisions of government. Following Benson (1982), a policy network can be defined as

a ... complex of organisations connected to each other by resource dependencies and distinguished from other clusters or complexes by breaks in the structure of resource dependencies.

A policy community is, in the context of British government, a policy network with the following characteristics:

1 *functional interests*: that is, the organizational networks are based on the service interests – that is, departments – in central and local government;
2 *extensive membership*, encompassing a variety of 'private' interest groups – most notably the 'technocratic' professions and trade unions – and quasi-government/quasi-non-governmental organizations as well as public interest groups;

3 *vertical interdependence*: that is, a non-executant role for central departments which are dependent, therefore, on other organizations/groups for the implementation of policies for which, none the less, they have service delivery responsibilities; and

4 *compartmentalized horizontal structure*: extensive internal organizational span focused on the 'lead' central department coupled with rigid horizontal articulation of policy-making; that is, the network is insulated from, and often in conflict with, other policy communities.

Policy communities are relatively stable with continuity of membership. Decisions are taken within the communities and this process is substantially closed commonly to other communities and invariably to the general public (including Parliament). Policy communities are, therefore, stable integrated policy networks.

Attempting to characterize policy-making for particular services is no easier than describing policy-making in British government as a whole. Not only does the attempt raise the intractable issue of the distribution of power in British society but the choice of metaphors is embarrassingly wide. It is important to discuss, therefore, the metaphor of policy communities in more detail in order to assess its strengths and weaknesses relative to other available metaphors – for example, sectoralization (Wildavsky, 1980), issue networks (Heclo, 1978) and corporatism (Schmitter, 1978), to mention only three.

A similar attempt to apply the metaphor of policy communities to British government is to be found in Richardson and Jordan (1979). They argue that

> policy-making is fragmented into sub-systems, and that the main boundaries are between sub-systems rather than between the component units of the sub-system. There is a breaking down of conceptual distinctions between government, agencies and pressure groups; (Richardson and Jordan, 1979, pp. 43–4)

> The policy-making map is in reality of series of vertical compartments or segments – each segment inhabited by a different set of organised groups and generally impenetrable by 'unrecognised groups' or by the general public. (Richardson and Jordan, 1979, p. 174)

These subsystems or segments are termed policy communities and Richardson and Jordan (1979, pp. 48–57 and 103–5) identify the varieties of consultation processes – for example tripartism, group sub-government and clientelism – and the rules of the game which regulate negotiations – for example, conflict avoidance, secrecy. Thus policies are

made (and administered) between a myriad of interconnecting, interpenetrating organisations. It is the relationships involved in committees, the *policy community* of departments and groups, the practices of co-option and the consensual style that perhaps better account for policy outcomes than do examinations of party stances, of manifestoes or of parliamentary influence.

The policy communities metaphor has a number of advantages over other available metaphors, most notably corporatism. Over recent years, an extensive literature both advocating and criticizing corporatism has emerged. The concept has been variously defined but an essential element in any definition is the integration of different sectors of society (for example, public and private sectors) or different tiers of government (for example, central and local) by means of formalised bargaining between central government and the outside organizations to be controlled. Policy-making is no longer characterized by free-wheeling interest group activity and open access for any affected group. Instead, the government recognizes a few powerful outside interests – a process known as aggregation – which are co-opted into government decision-making – a process known as incorporation – and in return this privileged group (or peak association) controls or regulates its membership on behalf of government. The peak association is no longer solely concerned with representing its members. It has the dual role of both representing and regulating members and, consequently, a system of interest intermediation is said to exist: that is, literally, the group 'comes between' members and government.

It is impossible to provide a definitive characterization of corporatism and it is the very elusiveness of the concept that has fuelled much criticism. It is necessary to distinguish between corporatism as a classification of 'a form of state' and corporatism as 'a theory of the state'. The former has the more limited scope of providing a model of government-interest groups whereas the latter is a theory of power, explaining changes in the structure and role of British government (Marsh, 1983, pp. 1, 12). At this point it is relevant to ask whether or not corporatism has identified a distinctive change in the pattern of interest-group–government relations. Unfortunately, the characteristics of corporatism such as aggregation, licensing of groups, monopoly of representation and regulation of members by group leaders are rarely found in unsullied form (Marsh and Grant, 1977; Cox, 1981). This state of affairs has prompted adjectival proliferation – for example neo-corporatism, liberal corporatism, bargained corporatism. Indeed Jordan (1981, p. 110) objects to 'the trick of so altering the definition to make it fit' because 'it leads to [corporatism] losing its essential corporateness' and argues that it is 'merely pluralism in a new environment'. He concludes that

The nature of British politics has certainly changed, – but not towards anything which could be identified with any rigorous definition of the corporate state. If one looks at the major works which have popularised the corporatist tag one finds surprising reluctance to apply the term without reservation ... The order that they see in British politics is the order of segmentation, inter-sectoral bargaining, limited access, voluntary groups: is there a need to conjure up corporatism with its distinctive associations?

Corporatism suggests hierarchy and unambiguous relations. Its vocabulary is of command, order, discipline, authority. In contrast the more useful kind of image would appear to be the network. (Jordan, 1981, pp. 113 and 121)

In sharp contrast to the 'corporatists', Heclo has coined the metaphor of 'issue networks', which

comprise a large number of participants with quite variable degrees of mutual commitment or of dependence on others in their environment; in fact it is almost impossible to say where a network leaves off and its environment begins ... Participants move in and out of the networks constantly ... no one, as far as one can tell, is in control of the policies and issues. (Heclo, 1973, p. 102)

This atomistic picture contains an ambiguity: there is order in the network. Participants evolve a common language, there is interchange of personnel and the logic of the policy process creates pressures for stable relationships. If corporatism presents a too rigid metaphor, then issue network is too unstructured: the metaphor of policy communities is an attempt to bridge the gap. However, as with most other discussions of the concept,[3] my account to this point has a number of limitations. It has been used solely as a metaphor and has limited explanatory value. A detailed discussion of the concept will help both to develop it further and to facilitate its application to the national community of local government and the specific policy areas discussed below. The most important topics to be considered are issue scope, the role of central government, the comparison of policy areas, strategies of regulation, the level of explanation and policy outcomes.

Issue scope If policy communities are the dominant feature of policy-making in Britain, presumably they are a dominant feature of all key policy areas. However, as Jordan (1981, p. 112) comments in his criticisms of corporatism:

If anything there is an inverse relationship between the importance of an issue and the degree of corporatism. Corporatism demands either (a) the imposition of governmental values, or (b) a degree of consensus on values. Both of these are progressively more difficult to achieve in important areas of economic life.

But policy communities also require a degree of consensus on policy values and presumably, therefore, are of lesser significance in important areas of economic life. Here Lindblom's (1979, p. 523) distinction between 'ordinary' and 'grand' issues is relevant:

> Let us divide policy issues into two categories: those on the ordinary questions of policy, and those that constitute the grand issues pertaining to the fundamental structure of politico-economic life. The grand issues include those on the distribution of income and wealth, on the distribution of political power, and on corporate prerogatives. On the first set, the ordinary issues, partisan mutual adjustment is active (though not without defects of inequality in participation and disturbing tendencies towards corporatism). On the grand issues, partisan mutual adjustment is weak or absent. The treatment in politics of the grand issues is governed by a high degree of homogeneity of opinion – heavily indoctrinated, I would add. As has often been pointed out, the grand issues are ... simply left off the agenda.

Lindblom's argument suggests that policy communities will only be a distinctive feature of policy-making on ordinary issues: their issue scope is limited.

The role of central government   Central government is more than *primus inter pares* in the policy process. It cannot be treated as but one more group. Whilst the government can and does specify, unilaterally, substantive policies, it also has the key ability to control access to policy communities, the agenda of issues, the rules of the game surrounding consultation and the timing and scope of consultation. Whilst it may prefer 'to create a nexus of interests so that co-operation flows from a sense of mutual advantage' (Richardson and Jordan, 1979, p. 105), it retains the option of coercion. Indeed, the choice of strategies open to government (see below) is not limited to coercion. Through the substantial resources it controls, the government has the luxury of choice between the many available strategies, including bargaining, incorporation and direction. And, if these indirect controls over policy communities fail, the government can impose its preferred policy. Policy communities are not, therefore, a constraint on government necessarily but can be manipulated by government in its own interests. Any account of policy communities must be predicated on the asymmetrical relationship between government and other actors.

The comparison of policy areas   The preceding section used the conventional shorthand of 'government' to refer to a collection of departments with discrete interests. The departments not only have discrete interests. It is possible also to identify distinct 'styles', or policy processes, within the several policy communities. It is important, therefore, to compare policy areas and to avoid assuming that there is a dominant policy style. There are a number of interlinked strands to this argument.

First, and continuing the argument of the preceding section, styles within the policy communities are a product of the central department's 'departmental philosophy' or the 'store of knowledge and experience in the subjects handled, something which eventually takes shape as a practical philosophy' (Bridges, 1971, p. 50). This observation is unremarkable but it is difficult to explain such variations in style if the central department is but one of many actors. Moreover, if the era of the 'giant department' (Clarke, 1971) has passed, none the less large, multifunctional departments persist. Thus, the Department of the Environment (DoE) is composed of major divisions, including (at various times during the 1970s) water, transport, local government, housing, planning and construction. By no means all of these divisions are at the heart of a function-specific network but, equally, there is no single DoE policy network. It is inadequate, therefore, to search for *a* departmental philosophy. It is also necessary to search for variations within departments to determine whether or not a single department has several distinct styles – a possibility rendered all the more probable when it has been created from several previously separate departments. The separate organizational arrangements devised for transport and construction during the 1970s attest to their distinctiveness. The term 'central government' has to be understood, therefore, as shorthand for a diverse collection of departments *and* divisions.

It is only to be expected that this diversity is matched by the range of interests within central government. At its simplest, it is possible to distinguish between the 'guardians', or the Treasury, concerned to restrain public expenditure and 'advocates', or the service, spending departments (Wildavsky, 1975, p. 7). In the national world of local government, however, a further two distinctions are necessary. The 'advocates' comprise those departments (and policy communities) which have a direct involvement with the services of local government and those which have no such involvement. The latter will be at least neutral in, for example, any argument with the Treasury involving local expenditure and, more probably, they will have a healthy interest in local authorities bearing the brunt of any reductions in expenditure. Last but by no means least is the DoE, which, as the 'lead' department for local government, acts both as 'guardian' in the negotiations about government grant and as 'advocate' for spending on those services for which it has responsibility. And this characterization of the interests within central government is a general one: it ignores the more specific interests associated with particular policies, institutions or professions. To the range of policy networks, therefore, it is necessary to add a parallel and profuse range of interests.

Second, the analysis of policy communities presupposes that they have a key impact on policy content. However, as Lowi (1972) has argued, the 'politics determines policy' axiom can be turned on its head: 'policies determine politics'. It is no mere coincidence that the Home Office, responsible for policies on police, fire and prisons, should be repeatedly characterized as authoritarian, secretive and directive. Lowi's reversal of conventional axioms has the virtue of pungent argument but the problem of overstatement: policy is both a dependent and independent variable. But, leaving such complexities to one side, it is clear that the analysis of policy communities cannot be limited to an analysis of process: it must encompass policy content.

Third, the concept of policy community presupposes a relatively high degree of integration between the organizations in a network. This assumption may be inappropriate for some policy areas – for example, leisure and recreation. Not only is there an enormous range of actors in leisure and recreation but there is no obvious central nexus for a policy community. Indeed, as Laffin (1982, pp. 7–17) has argued, it may be advisable to employ different labels for each type of policy network, and leisure and recreation may be best viewed as an 'issue network' rather than as a policy community. Whatever label is adopted, it is clear that different policy areas must be compared if variations in the degree of integration are to be identified and explained. This study uses the concept of the policy community because it is the most appropriate metaphor for the networks described below. None the less, the existence of diffuse networks must be recognized. Comparative analysis would not only help to identify variations between policy networks but it would inevitably raise the question of why policy communities exist in one policy area and not others: that is, comparison would facilitate explanation (see below).

Fourth, many discussions of British policy-making see it as 'humdrum' and recognize the unintended consequences of many policy decisions (Hayward, 1974; Richardson and Jordan, 1979) but they do not offer an adequate explanation of what I would term 'policy messes' – that is, the non-correspondence of policy systems and policy problems. It is possible to identify at least three major forms of non-correspondence. First, the policy system can be over-structured: that is, the policy community is tightly compartmentalized. Consequently, complex policy problems are simplified to the extent that they have few or none of the intended effects but generate a series of side-effects within the policy area such that the most undesired outcomes are attained and the problem becomes ever more intractable for future policy decisions which will, in all probability, simply repeat the cycle.

Second, the policy system can be under-structured: that is, the policy problem spans a number of discrete policy communities but there is no articulation between these communities. Consequently policy messes are generated both by problem simplification within each community and by problem interdependence between the communities. Finally, the policy system can be de-structured: that is, there is no set of interlocking organizations and consequently there is no coherent policy but a series of discrete reactions to particular events. Examples of policy messes would include legislation on industrial relations, the block grant system for central grant to local authorities and high-rise housing policy (for examples see Rhodes, 1984; Dunleavy, 1981b; and Dunleavy and Rhodes, 1983). Any explanation of policy failure would have to include not only relatively obvious factors such as resistance by the implementors but also the extent of compartmentalization, the lack of articulation between policy communities, the absence of such policy systems and the tension between the interdependence of participants within policy communities on the one hand and authoritative decision by central government on the other.

In sum, it is important to explore the effect of central departmental style and policy content on the policy process, the varieties of policy systems and the effect of such variations for policy outcomes. Only a comparative study of policy systems would repair these problems. Moreover, a comparative study requires a more detailed conceptualization of policy communities and here the link between power-dependence theory and policy communities is essential. If policy networks are seen as networks of resource-dependent organizations, they can be distinguished by their structures of dependencies. Thus, leisure and recreation differs from education in that the relevant organizations have a limited degree of resource dependence. The concepts of resources, exchange, strategies, rules of the game and appreciative systems are relevant, therefore, for the analysis of relationships *within* policy networks. Policy communities will have distinctive structures of dependencies. Moreover, variations in the distribution of resources and the pattern of exchange will be central to the explanation of variations in the behaviour of actors within communities. The characteristics of policy communities identified earlier can now be seen as a general characterization of *the structure of dependencies* within policy networks, covering the interests of the network (that is, function); membership of the network (that is, public and/or private); interdependence within the network (that is, vertical interdependence); and interdependence with other networks (that is, horizontal interdependence). Any comparison of policy networks *and* policy communities will involve, therefore, a comparison along these four dimensions.

For the sake of clarity, it should be noted that the concept of policy communities will be used in three related ways. Primarily, it will refer to relatively stable structures of resource dependencies and the power-dependence framework will be used to generate explanations of the behaviour of actors within particular functional areas. Additionally, the concept will be used as a metaphor for a policy-making style in British government: it is a convenient, shorthand description of the policy-making process. Finally, and more important, the concept is used to explain policy-making in Britain. In other words, the very existence of policy communities causes certain policy-making processes and outcomes. For example, it will be argued that the policy communities had a vested interest in, and helped to fuel, the continued expansion of the welfare state. Policy communities do not provide a complete explanation of policy-making in British government. The concept does not explain, for example, changes in the salience of particular policy areas. Accordingly, it is necessary to explore the context of policy communities: the distribution of resources, shared appreciative systems, the policy content and the issue scope of policy communities cannot be treated as 'givens'. The origins and development of policy communities have to be explained.

Strategies of regulation   Some care should be taken not to dismiss corporatist theory out of hand. To begin with, many corporatist theorists share with other commentators the objective of identifying significant changes in Western liberal democracies and the common ground is both considerable and ably summarized by Schmitter (1978, p. 15):

> (1) the growing importance of formal associational units of representation; (2) the persistence and expansion of functionally differentiated and potentially conflicting interests; (3) the burgeoning role of permanent administrative staffs, of specialised information, of technical expertise and, consequently of entrenched oligarchy; (4) the decline in the importance of territorial and partisan representation; and (5) the secular trend towards expansion in the scope of public policy and (6) interpenetration of private and public decision arenas.

It is precisely these developments that the concept of policy communities attempts to explore and the differences between neo-pluralism and neo-corporatism are, at least descriptively, frequently differences of emphasis, no more. Clearly, identifying the changes in British policy-making is more important than the particular label used to capture them. However, too premature a rejection of corporatist theory creates two problems: first, it limits the range of strategies considered; and, second, a focus on interest groups devalues the underlying explanatory theory in corporatism. In this section, I focus on strategies, returning below to corporatism as a theory of the state.

If the asymmetric nature of relationships within policy communities is accorded insufficient attention, the government's potential capacity to manipulate the communities will be devalued. This manipulative capacity includes the ability to create and strengthen policy communities and not just to obtain preferred policy outcomes. A distinct strand in the corporatist literature is its emphasis on the constitutive role of government: the deliberate attempt to aggregate interests. It would be incorrect to claim that this role was 'discovered' by corporatist theorists (see Jordan, 1983) but they have elevated it to some prominence. However, belying claims to the contrary, aggregation (and incorporation) do not amount to a corporatist *system* of interest intermediation. It is distinct from consultation, subgovernment or clientelism, because it is a means for establishing such forms of group–government relations. But it is still only one strategy in the arsenal of central government.

This discussion of the constitutive role of government still tends to emphasize the institutional and procedural aspects of group–government relations. Thus, to simplify its relationships with and to integrate the several interests, government devises or employs various procedures (formal rights to and forms of consultation) and institutions. But integration can be generated in other ways and Dunleavy (1981a) has coined the phrase 'ideological corporatism' to cover integration based on a 'unified view of the world': on common ideas, values and knowledge. He has also stressed the role of professions in generating such ideological integration and argued that their interventions in policy-making are a distinct strategy to be distinguished from corporatist or bureaucratic interventions. The most concrete application of this form of integration is to be found in Dunleavy's (1981b) parallel analysis of the national local government system and mass housing in Britain. He argues that the national local government system is not only a key means by which local government can convey a wide variety of different views to Whitehall; it also provides a framework within which any individual local authority can situate their own problems, concerns and strategies. Local authority actors (both councillors and officers) do not decide policies for their areas in isolation; instead they often look to the national local government system for guidance about what standard of service to provide, for ideas to imitate or to avoid, for ways of tackling common problems, and for justifications or philosophies of particular strategies. Some councils are innovators across a wide field of policy, but they are rather exceptional. Most councils most of the time follow national trends in the local government world, or national trends in their kind of authority facing their kind of general problem under their kind of political control. Each of them will innovate from time to time in one issue area or another, adding their own small contribution to the national picture. But most of the time local decisions are made within nationally defined parameters of what counts as good policy, rather than helping to redefine those parameters. The policy communities are the constituent units of this national local government system, reflecting the all-pervasive functionalism in the organization of British government.

Dunleavy's analysis clearly demonstrates that integration need not be a product of the procedural and institutional aggregation of interest groups and that the professional is a key actor in policy communities. Once again, it is important to recognize the range of variations in relations between central departments and their policy communities. The choice of strategies encompasses bureaucratic, incorporative and consultative strategies as well as professionalization (or ideological corporatism). Similarly, the role of the professional varies. Not only can the values of particular professions display considerable diversity – they can be a source of conflict as well as consensus – but professional influence varies between policy communities and from issue to issue. Policy communities are *relatively* stable and *relatively* structured networks.

Level of explanation   The question of why policy communities have become the dominant style in British policy-making is rarely answered in detail. Such factors as 'the increased scope of governmental objectives', 'the interdependence of problems' and 'the "logic" of the policy process' are commonly accorded the greatest importance (Richardson and Jordan, 1979, pp. 14, 140 and 171). Corporatist theory offers a more comprehensive theory of the state. For example, Schmitter (1978, p. 24) argues that corporatism is a response to the 'basic imperatives or needs of capitalism to reproduce the conditions for its existence and continually to accumulate further resources'. To this macro-hypothesis, he adds a number of specific imperatives – for example, concentration of ownership, competition between national economies, expansion of the role of public policy. Whilst many criticisms can be offered of the explanatory bases of corporatism (for example, Panitch, 1980; Jessop, 1978), the central point is that 'the imperatives of rationalisation and planning' (Cawson, 1978, pp. 196–7) are but one, certainly not the sole, strand in an explanation of corporatist trends. Similarly, any account of the emergence of policy communities limited to government intervention and interdependence will be incomplete. The centre needs some overarching, representative body for a variety of reasons. It is dependent on the resources controlled by other organizations – including information, legitimation and control – for effective policy-making. But such an explanation does not account for variations in intervention both over time and between policy communities. This macro-level of explanation must also include an account of the changing socioeconomic context of government – a point developed further in the final section.

Policy outcomes   This discussion of policy communities has focused on variations between service delivery systems. Very little has been said about what differences arise from such variations. The policy outcomes and distributional consequences — the effects of variations in service delivery systems for the consumers of the service — have not been explored. It is possible to identify some of these consequences.

First, given the need to accommodate the different interests within a policy network, one would expect incremental changes: that is, marginal changes in policy and expenditure. This pattern will be reinforced by the relatively impervious nature of policy communities: they are insulated from outside demands, whether from other policy communities or from non-legitimated groups in the populace at large. To employ Wildavsky's (1980, ch. 3) felicitous phrase, 'policy becomes its own cause'; current initiatives are a response to the policy community's previous initiatives and its own structure of interests. Policy-making in policy communities serves to sustain, even reinforce, therefore, the existing distribution of power.

Second, the insulation of policy communities, as noted earlier, will generate policy messes. It is too easily assumed that a discussion of policy outcomes is a discussion of the degree of success in attaining stated objectives. In fact, such outcomes may bear little or no relationship to the initial objectives and will invariably encompass a number of unintended consequences.

Third, and more speculatively, policy communities can create and sustain 'sectoral cleavages'. Dunleavy (1980, pp. 70 and 74) has argued that:

> The most important implication of the growth of the public services has been the emergence of sectoral cleavages in consumption processes, by which we may understand social cleavages created by the existence of public and private (broadly speaking collective and individualised and often also service and commodity) models of consumption.

And, in order to explain how consumption locations affect political alignments, he suggests that:

> powerful (national) ideological structures ... socially created and sustained by dominant classes, groups or institutions ... make available to individuals in different social locations particular perceptions of their interests *vis-à-vis* state policies and the interests of other social groups.

The national local government system can be viewed as a national ideological structure and the networks of resource exchange that constitute the several policy communities as the dominant groups and institutions sustaining that structure. In short, policy communities can be seen as a key mechanism in the distribution of resources between classes and interests. If the concept of policy communities has been used in the past primarily as a tool for exploring group–government relationships, its utility is by no means limited to this task. If related to an analysis of the context of government, it is capable of exploring a range of phenomena. This broader context or macro-level is explored in the next section. This section has attempted to clarify the concept of policy communities.

In sharp contrast to both pluralist and corporatist approaches, the analysis of policy communities requires the comparison of policy areas. Thus, the corporatist approach is far too inclusive: it provides a single characterization of all government–interest-group relations. Such relationships are far too complex for the corporatist model to provide anything but a rough approximation to reality. An approach based on the concept of policy communities demonstrates that it is possible to develop an analytical framework which takes the variety of relationships as its starting point. Above all, it stresses the importance of detailed, longitudinal case studies of several policy areas. And, although the case studies presented here focus on local government, this approach can be generalized to other policy areas. My characterization of policy communities incorporates a dynamic element. Varying structures of dependence, asymmetric relations within communities, distinct departmental styles, the varied roles of professions and differences in policy content all suggest why differences exist between policy communities.

By now it should be obvious that the national community of local government is another label for the local government policy community. As indicated at the outset, the phrase can be justified because the national community has a number of highly distinctive features. Employing the four dimensions of interdependence specified earlier, these features are:

1 *shared general interests* of local government, most notably in grant negotiations, the structure and functions of local government and local government pay negotiations;
2 *exclusive membership*, limited to the DoE and the representatives of elected units of government.
3 *limited vertical interdependence*, that is, there are extensive exchanges of finance and manpower as well as considerable formal and informal contact between national organizations which have *no* executive service delivery responsibilities;
4 *externalized horizontal structure*: limited internal organization span coupled with flexible horizontal articulation; that is, the community itself is focused on the associations, joint bodies,

topocratic professional societies and the DoE but penetrates a wide range of functional policy communities.

The national community of local government has its own distinct interests *but* it also spans policy areas – it is composed of 'topocratic' organizations with access to a range of policy communities. The function-specific policy communities have no equivalent access to each other or to the national community. Indeed, the national community deliberately excludes one major class of participants, the trade unions. The difference in terminology serves to focus attention on these contrasts.

Just as the power-dependence framework facilitates a comparison of individual organizations, the focus on policy communities facilitates a comparison of the networks. The material in subsequent chapters compares the national community with other policy communities to highlight the former's distinctive characteristics. But the focus on policy communities also raises a number of more specific issues. For example, given the competition for scarce financial resources, conflict between the policy communities is to be expected. But the national community has an interest in resource allocation which spans policy communities and, accordingly, extensive conflict with them can be anticipated, paralleling the conflict between 'topocrats' and 'technocrats' in American intergovernmental relations. In addition, attention is focused on the capacity of central departments to manipulate, even constitute, the national community, the nature and extent of ideological integration within the national community, the role of the 'topocratic' professions and the causes of variations in the national community's relationships with other policy communities – indeed, the range of issues discussed for policy communities in general.[4]

However, if the focus on policy communities extends analysis beyond the level of the individual organization, it still does not encompass the changing nature of the relationships between policy communities. The salience of policy areas varies, sometimes dramatically. The rules of the game are not immutable. To explain these changes it is necessary to relate intergovernmental relations to a broader analysis of the changing nature of British government.

Intervention

That British government has been subject to numerous stresses and strains over the past decade is an unremarkable statement. The precise nature of the changes, their causes and consequences, is a matter of heated debate.[5] This section does not attempt either a detailed analysis of the changes or a survey of the debate surrounding them. Rather, attention is focused on trends, processes and the national local government system.

Earlier the national local government system was said to comprise the set of organizations which defined the national role of local government and the policy communities (including the national community of local government) were said to be the constituent units of the system.[6] In addition, the national local government system is part of a larger national government environment (Stewart, 1983, p. 65). Changes in this national government environment affect the national local government system. Those actions by central government which impinge on the system are called 'interventions', that is, the actions do not necessarily achieve central purposes (Stewart, 1983, p. 61). These interventions changed dramatically during the 1970s. This study will identify three distinct *trends* in intergovernmental relations: bargaining, incorporation and direction.

The first trend was the tail end of a long-standing bargaining-consultation pattern of relations which existed for the bulk of the postwar period and which still survived under the Heath government. The term 'partnership' was used to describe relationships based on a series of expectations about consensual dealings between Whitehall, the national community and local councils.

When Labour came to power in 1974 on a tiny Commons majority, the government adopted a strategy of incorporation as part of its policy of containing local expenditure. There was a sustained effort to introduce a kind of top-level integration in the government's dealings with local authorities. Through the creation of the Consultative Council on Local Government Finance, local government was co-opted into central decision-making on expenditure.

By contrast, the Thatcher government elected in May 1979 had little faith in such 'corporatist' devices. It attempted to restructure central–local relations, unilaterally changing the rules of the game and imposing policies on an increasingly polarized and oppositional local government system. Central direction was the means for controlling the expenditure of individual local authorities.

This study will document the trends in intergovernmental relations but description is only the first part of the exercise. It is also necessary to explain these transformations. The most obvious cause was the continuing economic decline of the United Kingdom but it was not the only factor of significance. Three *processes* are important for understanding both the changes and the contradictory results of government action: economic decline, fragmentation and the tradition of executive authority.

Economic decline   So much has been and is still being written on Britain's economic decline that a further excursion into this territory must be undertaken with both brevity and caution. At the most general level, it is sufficient for the purposes of this book simply to note that for the governments of the 1970s the 'problem' was compounded of high inflation, high unemployment, declining productive capacity and a lack of international competitiveness. Local expenditure is a significant proportion of total public expenditure and, as a result, its reduction has been a prime objective of both Labour and Conservative governments. Whether or not local expenditure was out of control and whether or not (allegedly) high public expenditure had a deleterious effect on Britain's economic performance remain matters of heated debate. Whatever the merits of the various arguments, the definition by successive governments of Britain's economic problems required stringent controls of public expenditure. The consequences for local expenditure included a substantial reduction in capital expenditure and various means for controlling current expenditure which varied in their effects.

Such retrenchment or the several attempts to control local capital and current expenditure is not specific to Conservative or to Labour governments. Nor is it being implied necessarily that the expenditure on particular services was reduced. The term encompasses actual reductions in expenditure and, crucially, changes in the expectations of, and aspirations to, incremental service expansion (Stewart, 1980). This associated 'ideology of retrenchment' – the belief on the part of local politicians and officers that the size of, and especially the rate of growth of, local expenditure should be curtailed in deference to central government's responsibility for, and its stated views on, the management of the economy – has become a pervasive component of local government's 'responsibility ethic' (Bramley and Stewart, 1981, p. 60). This ethic has been articulated most cogently by the Treasury with support from both the topocratic professions and the national community of local government.

Fragmentation A distinctive feature of policy-making in British government is its fragmentation in the form of policy communities. This functional differentiation in government produces a set of professional-bureaucratic complexes, each of which has personnel sharing an ideology, expertise and a career structure and spans the boundaries of government institutions, national and subnational. In sharp contrast to the usual view of Britain as a unitary state centred on a supremely authoritative body, the Cabinet, able to command both Parliament and the Civil Service, I have suggested that the centre is fragmented and executive authority is dispersed. The phrase 'central government' is convenient shorthand but potentially misleading because it accords the centre a unity it does not possess. But fragmentation and dispersion should not be treated as equivalent to decentralization. Fragmentation refers to fragmentation at the centre. Dispersion refers to the distribution of authority between policy communities and not its redistribution away from central departments. Fragmentation *and* centralization coexist at the centre. Thus, with the extension of functional differentiation, there has been an extension of national policy programmes, the emergence of centrally defined services and standards and the movement of decision-making power from small to larger – that is, central – jurisdictions.

Key actors in this development have been the professions. The obvious example is the role of the medical profession in the National Health Service (Haywood and Alaszewski, 1980) but the list of examples is extensive (Dunleavy, 1980, pp. 110–19). Quite obviously, professional influence varies between policy communities and from issue to issue within a given policy community.

There is also the distinction between the 'technocratic' and 'topocratic' professions (see above) and the emerging role of the latter constituted an important challenge to the more widely appreciated influence of the 'technocrats'. However, irrespective of such variations. the institutionalization of professional influence has to be seen as a major process in British policy-making of the postwar period.

The consequences of functional differentiation and fragmentation are not specific to the professions or to central government. There have also been marked effects on local political elites. It is quite common for such effects to be described as the 'nationalization' of local politics (Grant, 1977) and the 'insulation' of national from local elites (Ashford, 1982). The role of the national parties in local elections and the domination of such elections by national factors has led some to criticize the liberal-democratic justification of local government as a representative institution (Dearlove, 1979). However, the 'nationalization' of local politics refers more to the spread of the national party *label* than party policies. Marked divergences of interest remain between national and local levels within each party (Gyford and James, 1983). Similarly, it can be concluded that national politics is insulated from local politics if attention is restricted to the *cumuls des mandats* or the number of politicians who hold, concurrently, political office at national and local levels. Local government interests can be articulated, however, through a variety of channels – intra-party, professional-bureaucratic and the national community. An examination of all these channels suggests that the degree of insulation is more apparent than real. None the less, there has been a change in the channels for articulating local government interests. With the increase in the complexity of the policy process and in its own dependence on other actors for the implementation of policy, the centre has sought to restrict the number of interests to be consulted for any given policy by aggregating them. Consequently, there has been a movement of access to the process of decision-making from local political elites to the national community of local government which forms an intermediate tier of representation. This marginalization of local political elites has been a central feature of the changing role of the national community and the emergence of an intermediate tier of representation will be explored in detail in later chapters.

As policy-making becomes increasingly differentiated, the 'logic' of the process generates imperatives to co-ordinate. This logic has been cogently explained by Hanf (1978, pp. 1–2):

> Territorial and functional differentiation has produced decision systems in which the problem solving capacity of governments is disaggregated into a collection of sub-systems with limited tasks, competences and resources, where the relatively independent participants possess different bits of information, represent different interests, and pursue separate, potentially conflicting courses of action. At the same time, however, governments are more and more confronted with tasks where both the problems and their solution tend to cut across the boundaries of separate authorities and functional jurisdictions ...
>
> A major task confronting political systems in any advanced industrial country is therefore that of securing co-ordinated policy actions through networks of separate but interdependent organisations where the collective capabilities of a number of participants are essential for effective problem solving ...

Indeed, Richardson and Jordan (1979, pp. vii, 14, 140 and 171) have seen the emergence of policy communities as the dominant 'style' of British policy-making as a response to this logic of the policy process.

In contrast to many Marxist interpretations of the 'state' this picture of fragmented elitism refuses to see government either as a unity or whole, serving the interests of a particular class (for example, Cockburn, 1977), or even as acting necessarily in the interests of one faction of capital in the long-term interests of capital. (See Saunders, 1980 for a review of the relevant literature.) In contrast to conventional pluralist accounts it also refuses to see government as the arbiter or referee between competing group claims acting in the public interest. Rather, without denying that government can and does act to sustain the existing socioeconomic structure, it quite clearly implies that government has a range of functions – for example regulatory, productive, allocative, legitimative – amongst which are the interests of the individual policy communities with their own needs for maintenance, growth and power. In short, the 'state' is not primarily a tool of the capitalist class or a neutral referee but

> an independent entity with organisational needs of its own, thus serving as a broker between the capitalist class and other classes and meeting its own needs for growth and power in the process. (Perrow, 1979, p. 215)

The consequences of this conception of government for policy-making are that values and interests institutionalized in policy communities are a crucial constraint on policy initiatives. Organizational inertia constrains policy initiatives.

But implicit in this account is the notion that someone at the centre wishes to co-ordinate the activities of policy communities and to take initiatives which impinge upon one or more policy communities. With the emphasis on fragmentation, there is the danger that British government will appear wholly directionless and uncoordinated. The changing scope of executive authority is the final process to be considered.

Executive authority   As Birch (1964, pp. 243–4) has noted:

> Another and most important tradition of British political behaviour is the tradition that the government of the day should be given all the powers it needs to carry out its policy.

In short, leaders know best and this facet of British political tradition, coupled with the centre's monopoly of legal (legislative) resources, underpins the structural power of central government. As with other central features of British government, there is little agreement on how executive authority is exercised. This book does not rehearse the arguments about the relative power of the Prime Minister, the Cabinet and Parliament. These 'chestnuts of the Constitution' (Heclo and Wildavsky, 1974, p. 341) will be treated as inedible. Three points only are relevant for the analysis of intergovernmental relations.

First, with the ever-increasing functional differentiation of British government the tradition of 'leaders know best' has *not* been supplanted. Rather the exercise of executive authority has become constrained and its effectiveness reduced:

> because the number of dependency relationships in which government is involved has increased substantially, and because the incidence of acts of non-compliance by the other participants in these relationships has also increased substantially. (King, 1975, p. 290)

As a result, there is a tension between executive authority on the one hand and the interdependence of centre and locality on the other. If authority is unilaterally exercised and bureaucratic, directive strategies adopted, then governments have to confront unintended consequences, recalcitrance, instability, ambiguity and confusion. If compliance is sought and a more conciliatory mix of strategies preferred, then governments have to confront 'slippage' or the adaptation, at times substantial, of policies in the process of implementation as well as 'policy messes'. And yet it is precisely such slippage which provides the incentive for unilateral action. The tension between executive authority and interdependence has remained to plague all governments of the past two decades irrespective of political complexion – to use Anthony Crosland's phrase it induces ministerial 'schizophrenia' (Kogan, 1971, p. 171) – and it has been a recurrent feature of relationships between the national community and government.

Second, the source of executive authority resides neither in prime ministers nor is it exclusive to political leaders. As the foregoing account of policy communities clearly implies, decision-making is fragmented with sporadic prime ministerial interventions in particular policy areas, most notably defence and foreign affairs and management of the economy.[7] Ministers responsible for domestic departments operate in distinct spheres from the prime minister – to a substantial degree, they are 'sovereign' in their own 'turf' – and co-ordination is achieved and conflicts resolved in and by the Cabinet and its multifarious committees. However, co-ordination at the political level is supplemented by bureaucratic mechanisms. In this study, the most important mechanism is the Treasury. Its guardianship role in the co-ordination of public expenditure is crucial and it was and remains a substantial counterweight to the expansive proclivities of spending departments and the policy communities of which they are an integral part. Other means of bureaucratic co-ordination include interdepartmental official committees, the Cabinet Office and the official committees which 'shadow' ministerial Cabinet committees. However, it is *not* being argued that such bureaucratic mechanisms for co-ordination bypass departmental ministers and undermine policy initiatives (cf. Sedgemore, 1980). The precise consequences of such official arrangements vary from policy area to policy area. It is being argued that the fragmentation of British policy-making has generated a concern about the 'central capability' of government and called forth a variety of co-ordinating mechanisms and networks of varying effectiveness.

Finally, the increasing awareness of the limits of executive authority has had a number of partisan consequences. Numbered amongst these is the concern to develop the policy-making capacity of the political parties whilst in opposition. Manifestos, it has been suggested, should contain policies which have been worked out in detail, thereby facilitating their effective implementation. Of greater concern in this study is the resurgence of ideological politics.

The resurgence of ideological politics has been ably documented by Plant (1983). In brief, the postwar consensus on the welfare state and the mixed economy managed by Keynesian techniques has foundered on the end of economic growth, fears about the deleterious effects of an enlarged and increasing public sector on the private sector, and disenchantment with the ability of governments to realize their stated policies. The response of the Conservative Party has been to reject all corporatist solutions and to assert the virtues of social market liberalism: the belief that economic recovery depends upon restricting the role of the state and expanding the scope for market forces in the allocation of public goods. This economic strategy has a marked political component which has led some commentators (for example, Hall and Jacques, 1983) to talk of a political strategy of restructuring the welfare state. Certainly, the belief in the minimalist state has been manifested in the atttack on public expenditure, although the consequences for the welfare state are mixed. A paradoxical corollary is that the limited state required decisive state action for its realization and the tradition of leaders knowing best received its clearest expression for many years in the Conservative government of 1979–83. The ideological debate about the role of the state in British society has occupied centre-stage in British politics and the Conservative resolution of the problem of state intervention has fed and reinforced the desire for decisive government action.

Changing patterns of relationships   The interrelationships between the trends and processes are complex and they have generated numerous changes in relationships. It is possible to identify four sets of changing relationships: the national government environment and the national local government system (especially the national community of local government); the organizations within the national community; the national community and other policy communities; and the national community and its members. These relationships form the core of this study. Additionally, the relationship between the policy communities and the national government environment also changed. These relationships are not explored directly in this study and, consequently, they will only be described briefly.

The changes in the relationships were not caused by any one process or combination of processes. Rather, the tensions between the processes led to a series of contradictory developments with, for example, the centre at first supporting the national community and then bypassing it. These contradictions arise from the conflicts between executive authority and interdependence and between the institutionalization of professions in policy communities and economic decline. These tensions and related changes in relationships will be explored in considerable detail in subsequent chapters. In brief, just as relationships between the national government environment and the national local government system shifted from bargaining through incorporation to direction, so relations within the national community changed from being disconnected through integration (or the attempt to create an intermediate tier of representation) to fissure (or conflict). Equally, relations between the national community and the policy communities changed from insulation through involvement (of the national community in the policy communities) to disengagement. Finally, the remote relationship between the national community and its members became characterized by member discontent. And the actual consequences of these changes were often unintended. For example, the Conservative government's policy explicitly rejected incorporation and bypassed the national community in favour of direct control. But direction ignored the problem that the government was dependent on local government for the delivery of services (including 'cuts' in the services). The agreement of local councils had not been sought by the government and it was not forthcoming. As a result, local current expenditure increased in real terms. When executive authority confronted interdependence, the government found that it could declaim about, but not deliver, its policies.

This introduction to the trends and processes in intergovernmental relations completes the framework for understanding the changing role of the national community of local government and its relationship with national government. Against this backcloth it is now possible to assess the effectiveness of the associations.

CRITERIA OF EFFECTIVENESS

There is an extensive literature on the effectiveness of pressure groups. Eckstein (1960) argues that the effectiveness of a group is a function of the group's characteristics (for example, resources, size); the characteristics of the policy (for example, the skills and information required for a policy); the characteristics of the governmental decision-making structure (for example, the degree to which power is dispersed, the character of the administrative structure); and the group's 'operative attitude' (that is, its ability to mobilise opinion). Beer (1966, pp. 320–30) suggests that a group's effectiveness is a function of the government's dependence on it for advice, approval and acquiescence on policy. It is possible to refine further these lists by distinguishing the various forms of access – for example, statutory consultation, clientelism – or by more detailed description of one or other criterion. For example, one of the more comprehensive listings of factors affecting the power of groups can be found in Finer's (1973) discussion of the political power of trade unions. He identifies seven variables: density of membership, wealth, prestige, militancy, organization, voting power and socioeconomic leverage. This last characteristic refers to the power of a group to disrupt society because the exercise of that function cannot be constrained by force or fear. Such listings can be helpful, although Finer refers primarily to the group's characteristics and a broader range of characteristics would seem desirable. Moreover, for present purposes, it is particularly important to assess the success of the group in influencing the decisions of public bodies. Although some writers on pressure groups would stress the articulation of a demand rather than actual impact on a decision (Kimber and Richardson, 1974, pp. 2–3), the ability to exert influence on government remains a crucial element in the *raison d'être* of pressure groups. None of the criteria are intrinsically unsatisfactory. Rather, the problem is the range of criteria which can be employed coupled with, in the case of influencing government decision, the intangible nature of a key criterion. Quite clearly, the effectiveness of a group cannot be reduced to a simple dichotomy between whether it does or does not influence government decisions. We need to know how much influence the national community exerted relative to other actors, at what stage in the policy process, over what range of issues, and how its influence changed over time. To further compound the problem, the changing role of the national community in the 1970s gives the discussion of effectiveness some special features. There was a clear trend in the 1970s to build the associations into 'peak associations' or *the* representative channel of local authorities – a policy which required an integrated national presence.

Other commentators have noted the trend towards aggregation. Thus, Alexander (1982, p. 164) comments that since the formation of the CCLGF:

> it has virtually displaced the direct contacts on policy between departments and individual authorities that were fairly common before reorganisation. Almost all such contact between local authorities and the government is now channelled through the Associations, whether it is on general matters that are the direct concern of the CCLGF or on specific matters where discussions with an individual department are appropriate.

> Some chief executives and leading members see dangers to individual local authorities in channelling all approaches to government through the Associations, largely because they believe that the need for an Association to form a view may obscure the special needs of specific areas.

Nor was this trend the product of the hidden hand of group–government bargaining processes: it was the deliberate intent of both sides. The associations actively sought closer links on grant and pay negotiations and their view that they are the key channel of communication has not changed. Any assessment of the effectiveness of the associations must encompass, therefore, the attempt to strengthen their role and create peak associations. It is not the only necessary step. The associations are a part of the national community and their claim to speak for local government could be undermined if there were extensive competition and conflict between the national community's constituent organizations. In other words, integration within the national community facilitates a strong central presence and any assessment must examine the attempt to improve links between members of the national community.

There are, therefore, multiple criteria for assessing the effectiveness of the national community. It is possible to select from the range of criteria, however, using the framework outlined above. In brief, it will be necessary to examine effectiveness at the levels of the individual organization and the policy process as well as in relation to the structure of government. Analysis at each of these levels will be approached through an exploration of the constraints (and associated cleavages) upon the national community of local government. They are described as constraints because they limit:

1 the effectiveness of the constituent organizations of the national community in (i) representing the interests of member local authorities and (ii) influencing the decisions of public bodies;
2 the extent of integration within the national community; and
3 the attempt to create 'peak associations' representing the interests of local government.

At this juncture the several constraints and cleavages are simply identified and related to the framework of analysis. They will be described in more detail in the following chapters.

There are five major constraints on the national community of local government. First, there is the constraint of 'representation' which refers to the multiple constituencies of the national community and the range of interests to be represented. Second, there is the constraint of 'members', which refers to the voluntary nature of membership of the national community, contact with members and the capacity of the national community to control or regulate members. Third, there is the constraint of 'organization', which refers to the resources of the national community and its capacity to deploy those resources in its relations with central government. These first three constraints constitute primarily, if not exclusively, the micro- or organizational level of analysis. Fourth, there is the constraint of 'policy communities', which refers to the relationship between the national community and the single-function policy communities and between the 'technocratic' and 'topocratic' professions. This constraint constitutes the meso- or network level of analysis. Finally, there is the constraint of the 'national government environment', which refers to the direct (for example, statutory) and indirect (for example, ideological) controls exercised by central departments over the national community of local government. This constraint constitutes the macro level of analysis.

Each of the constraints has its roots in one or more cleavages within the national community. As before, only a brief summary is presented at this stage. First, there is the cleavage of 'type of authority' which refers to the different interests of the various classes of local authority in the English local government system. These interests encompass the functional or service interests of each class of authority but extend to the preservation of that class of authority as a whole. Second, there is the cleavage of 'political party' which refers, rather obviously, to the variations in party control and associated interests (for example, differences in policy). Third, there is the cleavage of 'urban–rural' which refers to the differences in the socioeconomic environment of local authorities and the consequent differences in the need for services between for example, densely populated metropolitan areas and sparsely populated county areas. The first three cleavages are primarily if not exclusively related to the micro-level constraints of representation, members and organization. For example, the national community is constrained by the need to represent the interests of each type of authority, the major political parties and urban and rural areas. Fourth, there is the cleavage of 'functional diversity', which refers to the service-specific interests within central and local government and the competition between them, most commonly for resources. This cleavage is not only apparent in conflict between the national community and policy communities but also in conflict within particular organizations. It is primarily related, however, to the constraints imposed on the national community by the policy communities. Finally, there is the cleavage of 'national–local priorities', which refers to the ever-present conflict between local authorities making and adapting policies to local circumstances and a central government concerned with the management of the national economy and uniformity in the provision of services. This cleavage underpins the constraints arising from national government environment and comprises the macro-level of analysis.

This introduction to the constraints and cleavages within the national community of local government completes the discussion of effectiveness. The range of criteria involved at each level of analysis will preclude any simple assessment but should permit an appreciation of the contradictory demands made upon the national community and its, at times, inconsistent and incompatible responses.

CONCLUSIONS

This chapter has covered a lot of ground and introduced some unfamiliar terminology. A brief résumé is, therefore, in order. Figure 2.2 presents a synopsis of the three levels of analysis and their associated unit of analysis, key concepts, constraints and cleavages. However, this summary is static: it omits the dynamic or causal sequence. It has been argued that the processes of economic decline, fragmentation and executive authority have generated a shift in the relationship between the national community and central government. In the initial bargaining phase, the national community of local

Level of Analysis

	Micro ORGANIZATIONS	*Meso* NETWORKS	*Macro* INTERVENTION
Unit of Analysis	Public interest groups	National community of local government	National local government system
Key concepts	Resources: authority money political legitimacy information organization Rules of the game Strategies Appreciative system	Structures of interdependence (dimensions): Interests Membership Vertical interdependence Horizontal interdependence	Trends: bargaining incorporation direction Processes: economic decline fragmentation executive authority
Constraints on Effectiveness	Representation Members Organization	Policy communities	National government environment
Cleavages	Type of authority Political party Urban–rural	Functional diversity	National–local priorities

Figure 2.2   *The framework of analysis: a summary statement.*

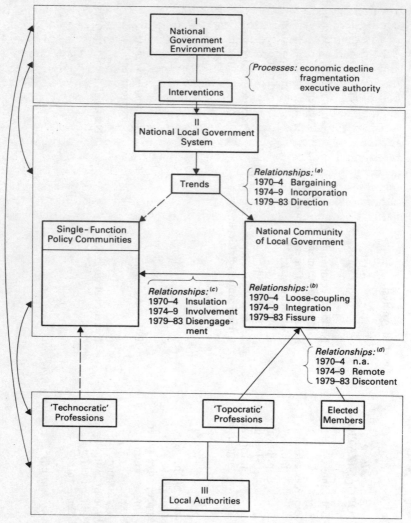

a   Relationships between the National Government Environment and the National Local Government System
b   Relationships within the National Community of Local Government
c   Relationships between the National Community of Local Government and the single function Policy Communities
d   Relationships between the National Community of Local Government and its member local authorities
→   Relationships directly explored in this study
⇢   Relationships indirectly explored in this study
n.a. No data available

Figure 2.3 *Changing patterns of relationships in the national local government system, 1970–83: a schematic outline.*

government existed only in incipient form: it was a 'loosely coupled' competitive structure. In the incorporation phase, the deliberate intent of the centre was to create a strong central presence and the period 1974–9 can be seen as the era of local government's 'peak associations' and the heyday of integration. Subsequently, in the direction phase, the national community has fissured under the impact of executive authority, revealing its own inherent weaknesses. Figure 2.3 presents a simplified, schematic outline of these changing relationships.

The remainder of the book documents the twists and turns in the fortunes of the national community, entering a variety of qualifications and a deal of detail to the bare arguments of this chapter. This account is structured around Figure 2.3. Thus, Part Two explores the relationship between the national government environment and the national local government systems, focusing in particular on the national community. Part Three explores the other relationships, especially within the national community, and between the national community and policy communities. The argument proceeds from the centre downwards, although it should be stressed again that this book is a study of centre–centre, rather than central–local, relations. The national world of local government is not the whole of central–local relations but it provides a key to understanding the dramatic transformations of the past decade.

NOTES AND REFERENCES: CHAPTER 2

1   For the more general analysis of central–local relations, the micro-level of analysis will be negotiative behaviour and the internal political processes of organizations. See Barrett and Hill, 1982. In this study, the appropriate micro-level of analysis is relationships between the organizations within the national community.

2   This section is a brief summary of Rhodes, 1981a, ch. 5. The reader interested in a more detailed discussion should consult that chapter and Rhodes, Hardy and Pudney, 1983d.

3   The progenitors of the concept in the UK are Heclo and Wildavsky (1974). Its potential utility has been argued in a number of places, including Grant, 1982; Hogwood, 1979; Raab, 1982; Rhodes, 1981a; and Richardson and Jordan, 1979.

4   The associations do not deliver any services and, accordingly, this study cannot explore the effects of variations in service delivery systems for the consumers of services.

5   The interpretations of recent trends in British government which have had the greatest influence on this account include Cawson and Saunders, 1983; Budge *et al.*, 1983; Schmitter, 1978; Jessop, 1978; Sharpe, 1979; and Rose, 1983. In addition, belying their years, Beer, 1966, and Birch, 1964, remain relevant.

6   Although they do not figure prominently in this study, it is important to note that the national local government system also contains organizations established by central government which influence both local government's views of its role and the state of opinion in local government. The most prominent of such organizations are the Audit Commission and the Commission for Local Administration in England.

7   I know of no systematic statement of the fragmented view of central co-ordination. The nearest approximations can be found in Budge, McKay, Rhodes, *et al.*, 1983, and

Dunleavy, 1983b. On the sporadic interventions of prime ministers and their pre-eminent concern with foreign affairs, defence and economic management see Wilson, 1974. On departmental ministers and 'turf' protection see Crossman, 1975. The 'conspiracy theory' of bureaucratic co-ordination can be found in Sedgemore (1980). The co-ordinating role of the Treasury is clearly demonstrated by Barnett (1982) and Pliatzky (1982). Reliance on such anecdotal, and invariably self-interested, sources of data is intrinsically unsatisfactory but inevitable given the restrictions on access for the study of central decision-making.

Chapter 3

THE STRUCTURE OF THE NATIONAL COMMUNITY OF LOCAL GOVERNMENT: ACTORS, RESOURCES, CONSTRAINTS AND CLEAVAGES

INTRODUCTION

The objectives of this chapter are to describe and compare the various public interest groups and to identify the constraints and cleavages originating *within* the national community. I provide the descriptive building blocks for subsequent analysis. The basis for this exercise is the 'power-dependence' (or micro-) level of analysis in the framework: that is, I analyse the distribution of resources within the national community. [1]

Given the large number of organizations within the national community, it would exhaust the patience of both reader and writer to describe each and every one. The first step, therefore, is to compare the organizations in order to determine their relative importance. Five indicators are particularly useful for this purpose:

1	*Size*	number of members;
2	*Total income*	the total of funds available irrespective of their source;
3	*Source of income*	percentage of income from independent (for example, subscription) sources;
4	*Staff*	number of full-time staff (including full-time equivalents) employed.
5	*Political composition*	percentage of Labour Party (LP) representation;

It is not necessary to use a more extensive list of indicators because, as can be seen from Table 3.1, the indicators selected distinguish clearly between public interest groups. [2] Thus, the societies tend to be relatively large, with a small, independent income, employing no staff and untouched by party politics. The independent associations similarly have a small, independent income and are non-party, but they employ a small number of staff and are smaller than the societies. For both the joint bodies and the associations, there is a split. A substantial minority of both are small, with a large income, large staffs and strong political organization. The majority are similarly small but have a small income (if any), few staff (if any), and weak or no party organization. There is one significant difference between the joint bodies and the associations – three joint bodies have 50 per

Table 3.1   *Selected Indicators of the Distribution of Resources Between Types of Public Interest Groups*

	Associations[a] (N = 9)	Joint bodies (N = 9)	Independent Associations (N = 3)	Societies (N = 10)
1 Size				
> 1000	1	—	—	2
250–1000	1	—	1	3
< 250	6	9	2	5
[b]NR	1	—	—	—
2 Income (£000s)				
> 500	3	3	—	1
50–500	1	—	—	—
< 50	5	3	3	9
0	—	3	—	—
3 Source				
100%	5	—	2	10
50–100%	1	1	1	—
< 50%	—	2	—	—
0	—	6	—	—
[b]NR	3	—	—	—
4 Staff				
> 50	2	3	—	—
10–49	2	—	—	1
< 10	3	3	2	—
0	—	3	1	9
[b]NR	2	—	—	—
5 Political composition				
> 50% LP	2	—	—	—
10–49% LP	3	6	—	—
< 10% LP	—	1	—	—
Non-party	1	2	3	10
[b]NR	3	—	—	—

Notes
[a] Excludes GLC, ILEA, and ANC. See notes to Table 2.1.
[b] NR means no response to questions on this item.

cent or more of their income from independent sources. However, Table 3.1 does not bring out the magnitude of the differences. As Table 3.2 clearly demonstrates, the distribution of resources in the national community of local government is highly unequal, with financial, staff and political resources concentrated on the four 'big' associations (ACC, ADC, AMA and LBA) and three joint bodies (LACSAB, LAMSAC and LGTB).

And this disparity in resources is paralleled by the centrality of the

Table 3.2 *The Distribution of Resources within the National Community of Local Government*

	Size		Finance (£000s)		Staff[b]	
	Total	%	Total	%	Total	%
ACC	47	0·2	845	12·1	97	15·1
ADC	333	1·4	587	8·4	48	7·5
AMA	77	0·3	939	13·4	74	11·6
LBA	33	0·1	69	1·0	22	3·3
Totals	490	2·1	2440	34·8	241	37·6
LACSAB	7	*a*	822	11·7	81	12·6
LAMSAC	9	*a*	743	10·6	102	15·9
LGTB	5	*a*	1658	23·7	138	21·5
Totals	21	0·1	3223	46·0	321	50·1
CIPFA	10 806	46·8	942	13·4	45	7·0
ADCT	325	1·4	5	*a*	—	—
SCT	140	0·6	—	—	—	—
SMT	91	0·4	0·3	*a*	—	—
SOLACE	531	2·3	20	0·3	1	0·2
Totals	11 893	51·5	967	13·8	46	7·2
TOTALS	12 404	53·7	6630	94·6	608	94·9
NCLG	23 102	100	7010	100	641	100

Notes
a less than 0·1.
b Total includes both part-time staff and advisers converted to full-time equivalents. For details see Rhodes, Hardy and Pudney (1982b), pp. 157 and 173.

associations in the overlapping membership of the governing bodies of public interest groups, within the national community of local government. The extent of such 'interlocking' is shown in Table 3.3.[3] Quite clearly the officers and members of the ACC, ADC and AMA dominate the pattern of interlocks, accounting for 73 per cent of the total. In addition, although the raw data is not presented here (see Rhodes, Hardy and Pudney, 1982c), LACSAB, LAMSAC and LGTB account for 51 per cent of the linkages.

The conclusions of this brief comparative exercise are as straightforward as they are crucial for subsequent analysis. The various public interest groups are linked together by both overlapping membership and the exchange of resources (see below). In addition, this network is dominated, in terms of control of resources, by a relatively small number of organizations: namely, the 'major' associations and the 'big three' joint bodies. Consequently the following comparative

Table 3.3   *Interlocking within the National Community of Local
Government*

No.	ACC		ADC		AMA		Other	Total
	M	*O*[b]	*M*	*O*	*M*	*O*		
0	127	—	101	—	223	—	271	722
1	38	61	20	47	32	52	1	251
2	5	8	2	3	2	2	1	23
3	3	1	3	—	2	—	—	9
4	—	1	—	—	—	1	—	2
Total	177[a]	71	126	50	259	55	273	1011[a]

Notes

[a] Total includes 4 missing cases.

[b] In the case of Treasurers, membership of both CIPFA and either SCT or ADCT or SMT is virtually inescapable and, if counted separately, the number of interlocks would be inflated. Accordingly, membership of CIPFA has been discounted.

analysis focuses on the resources of these actors, in particular on the distribution of authority, money, organizational resources, information and legitimacy.[4]

AUTHORITY

The authority or legal resources of local government's public interest groups falls into two broad groups. First, constitutional resources, which refer to the authority allocated by statute or 'those laws which regulate the structure of the principal organs of government and their relationship to each other and to citizens, and to determine their main functions' (Wade and Phillips, 1975, p. 5). Second, 'charter' resources, which refer to the allocation of authority within (and between) a group (groups) or the rules which regulate the composition and functions of public interest groups (Pugh and Hickson, 1976, p. 37). The demarcation line between these two species of authority is not precise. All aspects of charter will be influenced by the constitutional status of local government. None the less, the distinction is essential, if at times opaque, because there is an enormous difference in both kind and degree in the authority (statutory and internal) of public interest groups.

Constitutional resources

Little work has been done to clarify the constitutional nature and context of intergovernmental relations (Elliott, 1981). None the less, it is possible to identify three specific facets to the constitutional resources of public interest groups.

Elliott (1981, pp. 100–1) has argued that local government's constitutional status can be summarized in four propositions. Thus, and in brief, local government is subject to Parliament; the executive may exercise coercive power over local authorities, and both levels of government should be accountable for the exercise of their powers. Most important, and in full, Elliott suggests that:

> The administrative processes by which central–local relations are habitually carried on should be informed by the principle that each side has the right to put its arguments for any desired action, know the arguments against such action, and know the reasons for a decision between competing arguments. The process of argument and discussion should continue until agreement has been reached; if no agreement is able to be reached, the centre may legitimately take a decision on its own.

The associations are key channels through which 'the process of argument and discussion' is conducted and this proposition can be said to provide the underpinning for the claim that they are part of the constitution.

The second facet of constitutional resources is, in a manner directly comparable to individual local authorities, the statutory basis of the associations' work. For example, the Local Government, Planning and Land Act 1980, s. 54(4), stipulates that:

> Before determining the amount available for grant ... the Secretary of State shall consult with such associations of local authorities as appear to him to be concerned ...

Finally, as the representative organizations of governmental units, the associations are affected by the variations in the powers of their members. Thus, the internal organization of the associations reflects the differences in the allocation of functions between local authorities. The ACC's composition, functions and committees are directly influenced by the statutes designating county councils.

In sum, the constitutional resources of public interest groups are directly conferred by statute and indirectly conferred by the constitutional status of local authorities. And, whilst these resources are primarily reserved to the associations, they are not their exclusive preserve. Some joint bodies, most notably LACSAB, acquire constitutional resources via the constitutional status of their member local authorities.

Charter resources
Important though constitutional resources may be, they are only part of the picture. I now turn to examine the composition and functions

Table 3.4 Composition of the Major Public Interest Groups (1979)

Associations	Established (re-established)	Total	Membership type/ Constituent bodies	Sovereign body (size)	Governing body (size)	Representation on governing body
ACC	1974	47	County councils in E. and W.	AGM (177)	Executive council (177)	Pop. < $\frac{1}{2}$ million : 3 reps / $\frac{1}{2}$–1 million : 4 reps / > 1 million : 5 reps
ADC	1974	333	Non-met. district councils in E. and W.	AGM (333)	Council (106)	Dist. pop. > 190th. : 1 rep. / County pop. < 400th. : 1 rep. / 0·4–0·8 million : 2 reps / 0·8–1·2 million : 3 reps / > 1·2 million : 4 reps
AMA	1974	6 / 36 / 1 / 1 / 1 / 32	Met. CCs / Met. DCs / GLC / City of Lon. / ILEA / London boroughs	AGM (231)	Quarterly association meetings (231)	Each authority – 3 reps and 1 vote
LBA	1964	32 / 1	London boroughs / City of London	AGM (99)	Special committee (5)	Each council : 3 reps and 1 vote
JOINT BODIES						
LACSAB	1948 (1974)	5	ACC / ADC / AMA / COSLA / NJCs	AGM (28)	Council of the board (28)	ACC 5 / ADC 5 / AMA 6 / COSLA 1 / NJCS–APT & C 3 / Manual 3 / Fire 1 / Scottish councils 1 / Police 1 / Burnham 2
LAMSAC	1968 (1974)	5	ACC / ADC / AMA / COSLA / LACSAB	The four associations	The committee (23)	ACC 6 / ADC 6 / AMA 6 / COSLA 2 / LACSAB 3

				AGM (43)	The board (43)		
LGTB	1967 (1974)	3	ACC ADC AMA	AGM (43) (all members)	The board (43)	ACC	6
						ADC	5
						AMA	6
						NJCs	3
						NALGO	4
						NUPE	3
						TGWU	5
						GMWU	3
						UCATT	1
						Education members	4
						Government assessors	3
SOCIETIES							
ADCT	1974	325	Chief officers of non-metropolitan district councils and New Towns in England and Wales	AGM (all members)	Executive committee (25)	Society officers	5
						Members	20
CIPFA[a]	1885	10 806	*Inter alia*, any local authority in UK	AGM (all members)	Council (27)	Society officers	4
						Members: (a) elected	16
						(b) co-opted	7
SCT[b]	1974	140	Chief officers of non-metropolitan and metropolitan county councils (including GLC)	AGM (all members)	Executive committee (18)	Society officers	6
						Members	12
SOLACE	1974	531	Chief officers of any local authority in UK (except local councils)	AGM (all members)	Executive council (61)	Society officers	7
						County councils	8
						Met. districts	4
						Non-met. districts	8
						GLC	4
						Branches	20
SMT	1974	91	Chief officers of met. ccunties and districts, L3s GLC	AGM (all members)	Executive committee (16)	Society officers	4
						Met. counties	2
						Met. districts	6
						GLC	1
						LBs	3

Notes

[a] Formerly the Corporate Treasurers and Accountants (1885) and the Institute of Municipal Treasurers and Accountants (1901) before becoming the Chartered Institute of Public Finance and Accountancy (1973).

[b] Reconstituted upon the reorganization of local government.

of the 'major' associations, the 'big three' joint bodies, and the 'topocratic' professional societies.

Composition Public interest groups represent elected units of government. Their membership vests the authority to act in them and determines the conditions under which authority is exercised. Differences in membership account for many of the differences between public interest groups. Two aspects of composition are of prime importance: type and number of members.

Table 3.4 shows some of the more obvious differences between the *associations*. Their members vary both in terms of the functions exercised and geographical area covered. The associations vary in terms of membership size and representation. The associations with a large number of members tend to limit the size of their sovereign and/or governing bodies, the exceptions being the ACC and the AMA. Those associations with a varied membership have equally varied representative arrangements, with larger local authorities having more representatives. In the case of the ADC, geographical location and population size are combined to determine the number of representatives (if any) from an individual local authority, with only the very largest automatically represented. The AMA and LBA have the organizational equivalent of 'one man, one vote', in the other associations 'some are more equal than others'. In all the associations final or sovereign authority is vested in an AGM or equivalent. Frequently, this body is deemed to be too large for regular executive action and a small governing body is constituted, although the AMA and the ACC do not follow this practice. The precise division of responsibility between sovereign bodies, governing bodies and committees varies greatly, and it will be discussed in more detail later.

The memberships of the *joint bodies* are also elected local government units, although in this case the link is not a direct one, their composition being predominantly some permutation of the associations. However, their composition is not limited to the English and Welsh associations: collectively their constituency is both geographically broader and more diverse. Thus the Convention of Scottish Local Authorities (COSLA), which represents all Scottish regional, islands and district authorities, is a member of LAMSAC and LACSAB. In one case, LAMSAC, another joint body (LACSAB) is a member separately from the associations. LACSAB itself is significantly different from the other joint bodies in that it represents local authorities through two different channels. On the one hand, local authorities are members of LACSAB via the associations' representatives on the board. On the other hand, they are represented via provincial council nominees to the national joint councils (NJCs). The NJCs are the major bodies for negotiating local government pay. They are composed partly of appointees from provincial councils which, in turn, are composed of individual local authorities.

These variations in membership point to important variations in the locus of authority (see below). Thus, the associations are the determinant authority for CLEA, and share authority with one other organization for LAMSAC, but for the LGTB and LACSAB there are several other important members of the sovereign/governing bodies. As a result there are variations in the ability of the associations to hold the joint bodies to account.

The membership of the *societies* is significantly and obviously different from the other public interest groups in being composed of individuals. The societies divide into two distinct groups, CIPFA and the rest. In CIPFA membership is given to those who attain the requisite professional qualification, as determined and granted by the institute, irrespective of type of employing authority or their position in that authority. Of the other societies, none exist to confer professional qualifications and all are restricted to chief officers (and their deputies in a few cases). The membership of the majority is further restricted by type of local authority and/or by geographical area. SOLACE is an exception because it spans the range of local authorities and has a membership which is not restricted to English and Welsh authorities. SOLACE, like CIPFA, has Scottish members and since 1980 members from local authorities in Northern Ireland. Without exception the sovereign body of the societies is the AGM, composed of all members, whereas executive action is delegated to a significantly smaller governing body. Finally, in spite of their different composition compared with the associations and joint bodies, the membership of the societies is distinctive compared with 'private' groups: it is restricted to individuals employed in the public sector, predominantly (and, in the vast majority of cases, exclusively) local government.

Functions

> Our whole aim is to represent the views of the counties in membership and to represent those views to central government or anywhere else with any other organization who might be interested in it ... everything we do stems from that representational role.[5]

This quote serves to emphasize the simple point that the primary function and duty of the associations is to further their sectional interests. For all public interest groups, especially the associations, representing the interests of their members is the *sine qua non*.

The position of the joint bodies is more complex. Their memberships are broader than those of the associations, and there are corresponding differences in the interests represented. Although it can be argued that the joint bodies represent a range of local authorities on a single service and that the associations represent a single type of local authority on a range of services, the distinction is misleading in a number of ways. First, not all the associations represent only one type of authority: the AMA represents six types. Second, the services provided by LAMSAC, LACSAB and the LGTB are so extensive and wide-ranging that it is misleading to classify them with the obviously single services represented by JACOLA, CLEA and SACLAT.[6] Third, LAMSAC, LACSAB and the LGTB provide services explicitly for local government in general – that is, for all types of local authority (except parishes). JACOLA, CLEA and SACLAT, however, represent a narrower range of authorities because not all types of local authorities are education authorities or control municipal airports or municipal theatres. Finally, LAMIT, LAOSC and, in particular, LACOTS[7] represent a broad range of local authorities and provide a very specific service. Although the interests to be represented vary, the majority of joint bodies are constitutionally required to act in the general interests of local government, with the caveat that this 'general interest' is defined by the associations as employers.

THE ASSOCIATIONS   At the meeting in 1872 at which the decision was taken to form the AMC the local authorities sent a letter to the Prime Minister protesting that the 1873 Act was 'inconsistent with the first principle of local self-government'. When it was formed later that year the AMC's stated objectives were: 'by complete organisation, more effectively to watch over and protect the interests rights and privileges of municipal corporations' (AMC, 1972). In other words, in contrast to the letter, they stressed the threat to municipal corporations and not to local democracy. None the less, the AMC frequently equated the two because claims to be acting in the general interest of local government aided the protection of its own sectional interests.

The element of sectional protectionism can be found in the original constitutions of the CCA, the UDCA and the RDCA. The associations have been criticized repeatedly for protecting their own interests at the cost of the broader interests of local government (for example Robson, 1966; Barnhouse, 1972). The criticisms are not just that the associations should have considered the interests of local government first and foremost, but that by failing to do so they progressively weakened not only the more important general interests but also their own interests. This argument was often voiced during the protracted debate about the reorganization of local government and it recurred, more recently, over the ACC's accommodation with the government which ended the associations' united opposition to the Local Government, Planning and Land Act 1980.

The first instance of a broader concern being *explicitly* adopted as an objective of an association was the NAPC's constitution of 1947, which stated one aim as being 'to promote good local government'.

This objective is restated in the NALC's constitution. With the reorganization of local government, the sectional protectionism of the other associations' constitutions was diluted and the constitution of the ADC and ACC now also refer respectively to joining where appropriate with other associations 'to promote the interests of local government in general'. Indeed, the ACC constitution goes so far as to call for 'the setting up of a single organisation to speak for and represent local government in England and Wales'.[8] The AMA makes no reference in its constitution to furthering the general interests of local government because, according to Sir Robert Thomas (last chairman of the AMC and first chairman of the AMA), it is taken for granted that this is automatically done by the AMA pursuing its own interests.[9]

The associations tend to regard it as self-evident that whatever furthers their own interests cannot be to the detriment of local government's general interests. Their *raison d'être* always has been, and remains, to represent the interests of their members by protecting and promoting their rights, powers and privileges, and advising and informing them. The pursuit of these objectives has typically been subject to two constraints, each reflected in the associations' constitutions and organizations. First, that the associations recognize and accommodate both the diversity of members' interests and the differences in their size. Second, that the associations shall have neither executive power nor the powers to commit or to compel members. None of the associations claims to represent the views of individual member authorities — whether to central government or elsewhere — except on those issues concerning the class of authority as a whole.

This description of the functions of the associations has been very general but it is possible to specify the policy areas of prime concern to them. Rather obviously, the associations will defend their members against attempts either to abolish them or to remove functions. As Griffith (1966, p. 49) has noted, it would be a rather strange representative body which did not so defend its members. The reorganization of the structure (that is, boundaries) and functions of local authorities is, therefore, a key issue for the associations.

As a former chairman of the AMA said, there are 'two bodies whose work is fundamental to local government — the CCLGF and LACSAB'. In a similar vein, a former secretary of the AMA commented that '*the* one major thing which local government decides nationally for itself is pay' (Poole, 1978, pp. 69–70). In short, the negotiations over the level and distribution of central grant and over pay and conditions of work for local government employees are key issues for the national community. And, given the requirement that each association concern itself with matters affecting its class of authority *as a whole*, these are the very matters which one would expect to be of prime importance.

Webb and Wistow (1982, p. 14) have distinguished between governance, resource and service policies. Governance policies concern perceptions of the role of the state and the relationship between its constituent units. Resource policies concern the desired level of financial, staffing and capital inputs. Service policies concern the needs of client groups. Given that the national community has been described as 'topocratic', it follows that its prime interests will lie in governance and resource policies. The interests of the national community (and, most directly, its member authorities) do extend to service policies but local government's structure and functions, grant and pay negotiations are the hard core of the national community's interests and functions.

Protection is not, however, the all-dominant function of the associations. A secondary function is to provide advice and information to individual member authorities, as well as a forum for collective discussion of matters of common interest. In acting as channels of information the associations are two-way conduits between members and central departments. In this capacity the associations have been referred to as 'efficient clearinghouses or post offices midway between their members and central government' (CPRS, 1977, p. 37). Some of the associations (for example, ADC and WCC) have been criticized by member authorities for allowing themselves to provide 'free' services for central government. The associations contend that they are careful to avoid this position. However, the smaller associations (for example, the WCC) claim that it is difficult to object for fear of jeopardising normal consulting procedures on more important issues. [10]

One notable exception to the essentially defensive and non-executive role of the associations is the LBA. The LBA's general role is 'to protect [the boroughs'] interests and part of their interest is their autonomy; their right to make their own decisions on things like expenditure'. [11] However, a distinctive feature of its activities is its limited executive powers: it distributes grants to voluntary bodies; exercises quasi-executive powers in running an inter-borough housing mobility scheme; mounts the London Youth Games; and determines London borough representation on AMA committees.

The other semi-executive function of the LBA, and the only one also performed by the other associations, is the distribution of capital allocations. Under present RSG arrangements, following the Local Government, Planning and Land Act 1980, capital allocations for 'the other services' and 'transport' blocks are shared amongst the associations for distribution to their members. Prior to the 1980 Act locally determined sector monies (the predecessor to the 'other services' block) were similarly shared between the associations for distribution by them. [12]

The LBA is able to perform a broader range of executive functions because – unlike the other associations – it has a limited geographical area and a relatively small number of members: the boroughs are broadly similar in area and population and simple geography allows easy communications. Nevertheless, the LBA can perform such functions only where the boroughs are prepared to concede them, and 'there are pretty limited individual bits where they are happy for [the LBA] to do it. We can only do this with permission [and] so long as we retain interest from boroughs'.[13] The LBA is the only association with such executive powers and is also the only association to refer specifically in its constitution to the fact that it 'shall not have the power to bind or commit a constituent council'. Though not made explicit by other associations, the same rule applies to each.

THE JOINT BODIES Two features distinguish the functions and duties of the joint bodies from those of the associations. First, collectively they have a variety of duties and individually perform a wide range of executive and advisory functions. Second, they serve diverse constituents.

LAMSAC was formed to provide a co-ordinating and advisory service and not a fully operational consultancy service. By 1970, however, there was a growing number of requests from local authorities for a consultancy service and the constituent bodies agreed to an extension of LAMSAC's terms of reference provided the work was done on a self-financing basis. The advisory service was funded half by the associations and half by the government whereas the consultancy service is paid for by the local authorities using the service.

LAMSAC's advisory service consists of both general guidelines and answers to specific questions on all aspects of management, computing and purchasing. LAMSAC keeps a register of management services arrangements in local authorities; maintains an index of computer applications within authorities; produces performance profiles for different types of computer installations; collects and disseminates details on performance standards for a range of tasks; and provides, in co-operation with the LGTB, training in management services and computing. The consultancy service is tailored to the requirements of individual local authorities. The claimed benefits include the provision of specialised disciplines and techniques not available in local authorities; an unbiased view, independent of local factors and loyalties; a satisfactory way of meeting peak workloads within the local authority; and a function (on a retainer basis) which smaller local authorities could not justify providing on a full-time basis.

Up until local government reorganization in 1974 the LGTB's function was to provide general advice on training principles. The board sought to guide and support the training programmes of local authorities and not take over the authorities' responsibilities. Thus, it identified employee groups whose training needed improving, carried out investigations and issued advice on appropriate training programmes. If necessary, this was supplemented by the production of training material, the organization of short courses and some limited assistance by the board's own officers.

The board's original aims were simply:

(i)   To increase the efficiency of local government by ensuring that sufficient training of the right type and quality is given to the staff and employees of local authorities at all levels;

(ii) To operate a system of training levies and training grants so as to ensure that the cost of this training is spread fairly and evenly amongst all local authorities. (Lofts, 1970, p. 92)

The levy system sought to redistribute costs while the grant system sought to influence the quality and quantity of training and indeed stimulated a notable increase in training facilities provided by local authorities for their employees. As the board's job grew, it became involved not just in advice to individual authorities about their training needs but in implementation of training recommendations. The board paid large grants towards the cost of the salaries of local authority training personnel and also on the provision of training centres. It encouraged staff development programmes and post-experience training through grant-aided block-release and sandwich courses at universities and polytechnics.

The board also supported training costs for a range of initial qualifications and has always conducted a range of examinations of its own (for example, Diplomas in Municipal Administration and Trading Standards). The board also administers, on an agency basis, the examination of the Fire Service Central Examinations Board and the Police Promotion Board. There are, therefore, two aspects to the LGTB's work: it operates as a training and research body, and as an examination and qualifying body. Research is commissioned both internally and externally (including studies from LAMSAC). Similarly, in the area of management development, part of the board's advisory work is carried out by its own staff in local authorities, and a major part of the actual training is carried out in grant-aided courses at INLOGOV and the Administrative Staff College.

It is a notable feature of the LGTB that, alone amongst the public interest groups, it is partly composed of trades unions. Although employers dominate membership of the council and committees, the board is nevertheless required to issue advice and undertake training on behalf of employee groups.

The functions and duties of LACSAB have remained basically unchanged since its establishment in 1948. They are:

to co-ordinate the activities of the *employers'* sides of local government wage negotiating organisations, to provide a joint secretariat for those bodies to maintain liaison with other employers and to obtain and disseminate information on service conditions (emphasis added).

LACSAB sits at the apex of complex negotiating machinery. There are forty-two wage negotiating organizations covering the local government service, most operating on the established Whitley principle of joint employer–employee councils, variously described as national joint councils (NJCs) and joint national committees (JNCs). The two NJCs representing the largest employee groups – the NJCs for Administrative, Professional, Technical and Clerical Staff (NJC for APT and C) and the NJC for Manual Workers – each have a number of provincial councils – thirteen in the case of the NJC for APT and C and fourteen in the case of the NJC for Manual Workers. Each of these twenty-seven provincial councils covering England and Wales has the same Whitley pattern of joint employer–staff sides as the national councils and committees. There are also similar provincial councils covering Scotland and Northern Ireland. The employer sides of the provincial councils are composed of elected members from the local authorities within the area of the council. Each provincial council, as with the national council, has employer and employee secretaries. In the employees' case these are usually local full-time union officials. The employer side secretaries are shared in the case of some provincial councils. The employer secretaries liaise both with the relevant officers in the local authorities within their area and with the secretary of the employers' side of the national councils. The secretary of the employers' side of all the national negotiating bodies is one person – the secretary of LACSAB. It is his duty to ensure that the employers' sides of all forty-two national negotiating bodies are properly briefed; in the case of the two largest NJCs this is principally through contact with the employers' side secretaries of the twenty-seven provincial councils.

The secretariat of LACSAB is required to provide both a professional negotiating service and a general advisory service on manpower and industrial relations to the council of the board (the secretariat's employers); the associations; the forty-two national wage negotiating councils and committees; the provincial councils; and individual local authorities. The board's council meets quarterly and, on the advice provided by the secretariat, seeks to maintain an overview of local authority manpower policies in order to provide all the bodies and authorities listed above with guidance on the staffing, industrial relations and pay implications of government policies. In pursuit of this aim the board maintains a register of industrial tribunal decisions affecting local authorities; publishes guides to relevant Acts and advisory bulletins on legislation affecting local authorities as employers;

and publishes a monthly journal. Since its inception in 1975 LACSAB has also collated quarterly information from local authorities for the Joint Manpower Watch.

Decisions of LACSAB are implemented either by the board alone or, more often, on a joint basis with the associations; the latter 'on occasion reinforce or supplement the advice to member authorities within their respective associations' (LACSAB, 1978, pp. 11–13). The board may offer advice to any or all of the negotiating bodies. Although not mandatory, this advice, according to LACSAB would never be lightly disregarded.

Ostensibly, then, LACSAB's role is purely advisory, with responsibility for actual negotiations resting with the various employers' sides. In practice, however, the secretariat

> with their day-to-day contacts with trade unions, local authority associations, government departments and local authorities, play an influential part in the conduct of negotiations. (Poole, 1978, p. 79)

Moreover, it is conceded by the employers that this is necessarily the case because of the time scale and practicalities of negotiations.

THE SOCIETIES   The societies share two important characteristics: their constitutions are phrased in terms of promoting general not sectional interests; and their primary function is to confer upon ... discuss ... promote and exchange knowledge in ... advance the art and/or science of ... improve the efficiency of ... their particular profession and service. In pursuit of this function as learned societies, the societies all undertake research and training and hold conferences and seminars.

The societies differ primarily in terms of the geographical areas within which particular services are performed, and in the beneficiaries of their services. Thus, for the ADCT, discussion of local government finance focuses on its effects on district councils; whereas CIPFA's concerns extend to all public sector bodies; whilst the SCT is concerned with local government in general and county councils in particular.

The constitutions of the societies do not refer to the interests of their individual members. For example, CIPFA's constitution states that 'it is not directly concerned with the advancement of the personal interests of its members'. Only SOLACE refers to its members' interests. Its constitution refers to considering 'in particular the role and responsibilities of Chief Executives' and to doing whatever is 'in the interests of the body of members, as chief executives of local authorities'. However, it also speaks of the society taking a lead 'in matters of fundamental importance to the health and future of local government'; SOLACE will continue 'to play its part in defending the concept of local democracy' and will provide 'leadership and commitment to the ideals of local government'. Such statements prompt the suggestion that SOLACE is the quintessential public interest group. It is important to remember, therefore, that SOLACE was and remains concerned to promote a wide-ranging conception of the role of the chief executive.

According to their constitutions the other societies exist only to promote the interests of particular services in particular areas. Any furtherance of the interests of individuals consequent upon these promotional activities is regarded as incidental. It is important, however, to distinguish sectional interests related to the functions of particular types of local authority from 'trade union' matters, that is, pay and conditions of service. All societies clearly distinguish between 'trade union' and 'other activities' by entrusting the former to separate organizations, for example, the Association of Local Authority Chief Executives (ALACE). Nevertheless, on their own admission, the societies necessarily, even if incidentally, pursue sectional interests.

In addition to being learned societies it is a common function of most of the societies to provide advice to the associations and also to government departments. Two societies, CIPFA and SOLACE, have no such reference in their constitutions. Amongst the others, one aims to advise only one association (ADCT for the ADC). The remaining societies, SCT and SMT, aim to advise any or all of the associations as well as government departments. Although the wording and the tone of the constitutions are generally similar when referring to the advisory function, there are some differences. For example, the ADCT constitution is notably diffident, seeking

> to take every opportunity to approach the ADC, with a view to collaborating with and providing advisory services for the Association: in particular to consider and report upon any matter which they may refer to this body.

It is a truism in political science that constitutions are an inaccurate guide to political behaviour. It is as true of the societies as it is of governments. The constitutions of the two societies which have closest links with the associations make *no* reference to such a purpose. SOLACE's membership is unique because it covers all types of local authority in the United Kingdom and because its members are senior advisers to every committee of each association. The relationship between SOLACE and the associations is indubitably a close one. It has been described as 'desperately important that there should be a good relationship and an understanding between them'. SOLACE is 'part of the local government family . . . we have got to work with the local authority associations'. Nevertheless, SOLACE's primary function is to seek to further the broadest local government interests. When the interests of the associations radically differ, SOLACE is placed in a difficult position. On the issue of 'organic change', for example, the society 'acknowledged the fact that the work of the chief executives in that area was going to be done through professional associations'.[14]

The clearest formal recognition of different interests, and of the need for SOLACE to distance itself from them, is the existence of a separate and semi-autonomous branch, the Association of County Chief Executives (ACCE). This association was formed (in 1974) principally to perpetuate the traditional relationship of the Society of County Clerks to the CCA. Thus ACCE, and not SOLACE, is responsible for nominating officer advisers to the ACC. Membership of ACCE is conditional upon membership of SOLACE, and ACCE studiously avoids asserting an 'independent' voice:

> it is very rare for ACCE to express any view at all. If it's a matter affecting all chief executives we would endeavour to express it through SOLACE; if it was a matter affecting county government we would act through the ACC.[15]

Such a statement summarizes the advisory function of most societies.

FINANCIAL RESOURCES

Income
The most tangible and readily identifiable resource of public interest groups is their income: amounts of income are obviously one measure of relative size and potential power; source(s) of income are a measure of relative independence (see Rhodes, 1981a, p. 101).

Amongst the associations, the ACC and the AMA have the largest income, totalling some £845,000 and £939,000 respectively in 1978/9. At the time the ADC's income was £587,000 and the LBA's totalled £69,000. In the AMA and the LBA subscriptions are levied on a flat rate for each member: £11,250 per authority in the AMA. In the ACC and the ADC subscriptions are based on population and total rate and grant-borne expenditure. Thus, in 1978/9 ACC subscriptions ranged from £4,500 to £33,800 per authority.

A detailed description of the societies' income serves no useful purpose. The most obvious fact about the societies is the enormous disparity between the income of CIPFA and all the others: indeed, CIPFA's 1979 income of £941,000 is larger than all of the other public interest groups except the LGTB. Of the chief officer societies, SOLACE has an income comparable with the smaller associations. However, all other societies have extremely small incomes, reflecting the simple fact that their members are individual officers and not local authorities. CIPFA is also distinctive in the small percentage of its income (22 per cent) which it derives from membership subscriptions

— by far the smallest percentage of any public interest group. The largest proportion of CIPFA's income comes from its various services (for example, the financial information service), conferences and seminars; it also derives a substantial income from its own training activities. In contrast to CIPFA, the associations are dependent on their member authorities for virtually all their income: in effect it is 100 per cent in the cases of the ACC, AMA and LBA, where 'miscellaneous income' constitutes interest on investments made with subscription monies.

In terms of source of income the joint bodies divide into four groups:

1   Directly funded by 'user' local authorities (LAMIT);
2   Association funded (a) and separately accounted (CLEA);
                            (b) but not separately accounted (JACOLA, LAOSC, SACLAT);
3   Section 2(7) funded (LACOTS);
4   50 per cent or less Section 2(7) monies (LACSAB, LAMSAC, LGTB).

The source of funding is particularly important in the case of the joint bodies and particularly those bodies funded by section 2(7) monies. This shorthand phrase refers to that section of the Local Government Act 1974 which allowed for the deduction of money from the total of the needs element (of the rate support grant) for payment to bodies providing services to local authorities and specified in regulations made under this section of the Act. The Local Government, Planning and Land Act 1980 allows similar deductions from the total of block grant in regulations made under Section 56(9) of the Act.

It was in 1978 that the three main associations set up a joint sub-committee (the S2(7) subcommittee) of the policy committees of each association to consider submissions from each approved body and to advise their respective policy committees on the amounts to be agreed for each. Since 1978 this joint subcommittee has been constituted annually and meets in September to consider submissions from each approved body. It is the policy committees which decide upon the bodies to be financed via this procedure, although proposals for deductions must be approved formally by the Department of the Environment. The associations' criteria for choosing bodies is that:

the more related the service to the whole of local government or to some important sector of it then the better the claim for inclusion in the Section 2(7) procedure. Equally, the less related the service to the main operation of local government as a whole or a particular sector, then the greater the presumption against inclusion.

Moreover:

> This latter presumption should be particularly strong if in addition
> the body is providing a service, for example, in the form of con-
> sultancy or training courses, for which charges to finance the body
> could be made.

The S2(7) subcommittee meeting is not a mere formality for the
specified bodies: it follows a detailed screening process during which,
as LAMSAC's director said, the bodies are fully apprised of the
associations' requirements. Submissions for 1979/80, for example,
were required to be on the basis of nil growth in real terms; and for
the following year the ACC took the view that

> strict proof of need must be shown, both for any increases re-
> quested above the 1979/80 level and for the maintenance of grant
> at that level for 1980/81.[16]

Without doubt the associations control the amounts received from
S2(7) monies by the relevant bodies, notwithstanding the fact that the
associations can only make recommendations which the DoE must
then ratify – something it has not yet failed to do. With the exception
of LACOTS, however, S2(7) monies are not the sole source of income
for the relevant joint bodies.

The LGTB's accounts 'show that the greater part of the Board's
financial transactions are now undertaken on behalf of the Training
Services Division of the Manpower Services Commission'.[17] In
1978/9 the board, 'following its policy of seeking funding from central services to benefit local government . . . acted as the administering
body for a number of schemes mounted by the MSC, through the
Training Services Division. In addition the MSC provided funding for
some aspects of the Board's work'. However, the board refers in the
report on its accounts to 'its own work programme', thereby
distinguishing between work initiated by the MSC and administered
by the board on an agency basis. Nevertheless, it would be incorrect
to describe the board's administrative role as purely that of a conduit:
it is not merely implementing schemes over which it has no control.
On the contrary, the board and the MSC regularly liaise about the
nature of the schemes. If the £3·5 million of MSC monies are not
treated as income, then S2(7) monies would represent 79 per cent of
a total board income of nearly £2 million.

In the case of LAMSAC the grant from the DoE matches the
amount 'provided' by the associations via S2(7). Thus the DoE has a
potentially powerful voice in settling LAMSAC's programme of work
– both by ratifying the amount which the associations recommend
should be provided via S2(7) and by agreeing to match this amount
itself.

LACSAB also has sources of income other than the associations. The negotiating bodies (and their provincial councils) have a (potentially) powerful voice in the conduct of LACSAB because they provide 46 per cent of the board's total income of £822,000, whereas the associations provide 41 per cent through S2(7).

Expenditure

As might be expected, the dominant items of expenditure for all types of public interest group are salaries, accommodation and administrative expenses. Given the Section 2(7) monies system, it is scarcely surprising to note that there is little evidence of financial transfers between public interest groups. Similarly, groups (for example, JACOLA, SACLAT) with no income are unlikely to have high levels of expenditure! In spite of the eminently predictable nature of the expenditure patterns, however, there are a few points of interest. First, the extensive involvement of the associations in the 'grant industry' is reflected in their expenditure. It accounts for between 2 and 6·5 per cent of the expenditure of the AMA, ACC and ADC. Second, this expenditure on grant negotiations encompasses fees to other organizations, most notably to CIPFA for its technical support service. Third, the distinctive functions of the LGTB are obvious from the fact that it is the only public interest group disbursing grants – an activity which accounts for 41 per cent of its expenditure. Finally, the expenditure of the societies suggests that their prime function is that of 'learned society' for members and not that of providing advisers for the associations.

ORGANIZATIONAL RESOURCES

The term 'organizational resources' encompasses, for example, the people, buildings, material and equipment of the public interest groups (Hood, 1983, p. 6). In this section it also encompasses the formal division of authority and responsibility, the councils and committees and the procedural rules within public interest groups. In other words, it covers how the organizational resources are structured and managed by the groups.

The secretariats

All the associations and the large joint bodies are located in central London and, for those so inclined, within walking distance of Westminster and Whitehall. Whilst there may be some dispute about the relative architectural merits of Old Queen Street (AMA) and Sloane Square (ACC), the physical proximity of the associations to central government is indisputable and important because it facilitates communication and interaction. Given the nature of their work, materials and equipment are not key organizational resources of the associations. Over and beyond the inevitable reams of A4 paper, filing cabinets and typewriters, only access to computing facilities has been a material constraint (see chapter 4, below). The prime organizational resource of the associations is their secretariats.

The number and type of personnel employed by the associations and joint bodies are shown in Table 3.5, which suggests a number of straightforward conclusions. First, the AMA and ACC are much larger than the other associations. Second, the administrative staff of the ACC is much larger than the professional staff. Third, the AMA, ADC and ACC employ relatively few professional staff – a combined total of fifty. Fourth, the total staff of the associations is small when compared with the joint bodies. LACSAB, LAMSAC and the LGTB all have full-time staffs larger than any of the associations, and LAMSAC and the LGTB employ more professionals each than the associations together. The other joint bodies, however, have extremely small staffs (and none at all in the case of JACOLA, LAOSC and SACLAT). Amongst the societies only CIPFA has any full-time professional staff (and more than either the ACC or ADC) and of all the other societies only three have any paid staff – all part-time secretarial staff. The societies in general are run by honorary officers who undertake the duties in addition to their normal local authority duties.

Perhaps the most striking aspect of Table 3.5 is the small number of professionals employed by the associations – a measure of their reliance upon officer advisers or local government professional officers who, on a voluntary basis, provide information and advice to the associations (see below, pages 83–5).

Table 3.5   *Personnel of the Major Public Interest Groups (1979)*

Association	Professional		Secretarial/Admin.		Professional Advisers	
	Full-time	Part-time	Full-time	Part-time	Paid	Unpaid
ACC	15	0	59	9	0	160
ADC	13	0	27	2	0	66
AMA	22	0	37	0	0	136
LBA	5	7	5	4	0	50
Joint Bodies						
LACSAB	24	0	54	5	0	0
LAMSAC	80[a]	0	c	c	0[b]	200
LGTB	59	0	79	0	0	0
Societies						
CIPFA	20	0	24	1	0	0

Notes
[a] 13 on consultancy service.
[b] Omits consultants used on *ad hoc* basis.
[c] No figures available.

In each of the main associations prior to local government reorganization the secretariats' primary function was administrative and they were staffed almost entirely by generalists or, to be more precise, lawyers. In 1968 all six of the AMC's professional staff were lawyers. Prior to reorganization the main task of the secretariats was to seek, collate and present to committees advice from professional advisers in member authorities. At meetings between the associations and civil servants it was the advisers who would present and argue an association's case, supported by members of the secretariat; since reorganization the position has been reversed – at such meetings it is the advisers who support members of the secretariat. Similarly, the associations' secretariats and not the advisers now usually initiate policy documents; the advisers are now used much more as sounding-boards. Their views, on whatever documents (from whatever source), are collated by the secretariats, who prepare reports for committees. But these reports are not mere précis of advisers' views (although they may be this too) but will contain the advice of the secretariat themselves. The latter do not regard themselves as mere middle men or post offices. They are in a position to present only those views of advisers which they think suitable or necessary.

This change since reorganization is not simply a change in emphasis: it is closely related to the associations' policy since reorganization of recruiting their own specialists. This trend is in fact denied by the ACC:

> I don't know that we've become more specialized except in so far that we have one or two specialist officers on the staff that we didn't have in the past.

These two specialists were an education officer and an under secretary for finance; in each case they were deliberately appointed for their appropriate professional background. But in general 'the man who has been looking after planning this week might be looking after social services next week ... we see ourselves primarily as generalists not specialists'.[18] The advantages of 'getting your real professional technical advice from the ground' have been described by an ACC secretary as being 'up to date, it has accountability ... you have not only to do something but to live with it'.[19] He conceded nevertheless that as issues become increasingly complex it was essential for the generalist secretariat to develop a sufficient technical expertise to be able to cope with the 'real professionals'.

In the case of both the AMA and ADC there has been a deliberate policy of appointing specialists. In the ADC this decision was taken in order to develop close links between the secretariat and professional colleagues, although the association still claims to rely predominantly upon advisers to provide advice on best professional practice in various fields. As grant negotiations especially became more complex and time-consuming it was regarded as essential to have an internal specialist. Similarly, when the AMA withdrew its support for CIPFA's statistical information service and this source of advice was denied to all the associations, the ADC decided to appoint its own full-time statistician.

In the AMA the decision to appoint specialists to the secretariat followed the appointment of a new secretary in 1976. Shortly after his appointment he wrote that 'the AMA can only survive and make any contribution if we get changes in the organization and the staffing'. He proposed, therefore, a 'modest expansion' in the staff. On reorganization the AMA had a staff of thirty-seven, increasing to forty-two in 1976. Following the new secretary's proposal, it was increased to fifty-eight in 1977. The reorganization entailed the creation of a number of sections within the association, each servicing one of the association standing committees and each headed by an under secretary (paralleling the Civil Service not just in title but also in pay scales – unlike the remainder of the staff, whose pay scales are related to equivalent local authority grades). The under secretaries for finance, social services and housing have all been recruited from local government. The relationship of these specialists with advisers and professional colleagues obviously differs from those of the non-specialist under secretaries: there are, for instance, no firemen or policemen on the AMA staff; therefore, there is a necessarily greater reliance upon advisers in these fields, notwithstanding the 'specialist' expertise of the members of the secretariat responsible for these services.

Internal organization

The internal organization of public interest groups is based on three principles:

1 *Locus of authority*: to so allocate authority and responsibility as to fully involve and allow adequate representation to the whole membership;
2 *Representation*: to accommodate differences in size and interests, most notably between geographical areas, political parties and type of authority;
3 *Specialization*: the need to reflect the range of functions and duties carried out by members.

And it is important to note the potential for conflict between these principles. For example, the locus of authority can and does conflict with specialization, full involvement leading to either excessive numbers *on* committees, or excessive numbers *of* committees, or both. Such conflicts are long-standing: in 1945 the AMC noted that 'despite all theories of management structures' there had been an inevitable increase in the membership of the council and standing committees 'to ensure so far as possible that representatives from a large proportion of the member corporations play an active role in the affairs of the Associations at one level or another' (AMC, 1972).

The locus of authority In general the public interest groups have three formal organs of management: annual meeting, executive council, and committees. For each of the associations and societies, the annual general meeting is the sovereign body. All members of the group are entitled to attend (except in the case of NALC) and only at this meeting can the group's constitution be altered. For the joint bodies, either the annual meeting is the sovereign body (LACSAB and the LGTB) or the respective constituent associations (for example, the AMA and ACC) are sovereign.

The function of the AGMs is to receive annual reports and accounts and, in the case of the associations and societies, to appoint honorary officers. Typically, AGMs are not policy-making bodies: resolutions concerning the group's policy may be introduced but generally do not bind executive councils.

The most important exception to this rule was the AMC. The composition of the association's council sought both to accommodate the two types of authority represented (county boroughs and non-county boroughs) and to reflect the varying strength of the county borough members. The six county boroughs with the largest populations, together with the City of London, had automatic representation. The remaining sixty-eight county boroughs (including the London boroughs) served in rotation for two years. Since 1890 the two types of authority had parity of representation – a recognition that although the number of non-county boroughs far exceeded the number of county boroughs (three-quarters of the total of approximately 350) the population represented by the county boroughs was far larger. The AMC's constitution stated that the council 'shall have power generally to conduct the business of the Association' (Rule 7); nowhere, however, was it specified that the council was the association's sovereign body. According to Cross (1954), ultimate power in fact resided not in the council but in the association's annual meeting, in so far as the latter expressed the will of a simple majority of the whole membership. The local authorities represented at annual meetings did not initiate policy but the power to do so was there and served 'as a check against acts ... open to challenge as not being in the general interest of municipal corporations'. Nevertheless, Cross argues, the council managed the association and formal power resided with the council: no decisions were effective until adopted by the council. This account, however, introduces a spurious note of precision into its description of the locus of authority. Whether the annual meeting or the council was sovereign was a matter of dispute within the AMC. Thus a former chairman, Sir Mark Henig, asserted that the council was supreme and denied that decisions at annual meetings were binding on the council, whilst his successor, Sir Frank Marshall, argued the exact opposite. (Isaac-Henry, 1980b)

With the reduction in its membership to seventy-seven, the AMA has dispensed with a council and meets as a whole to receive committee reports; it is now spared disputes about the location of sovereign power. In fact, the AMA's constitution does not specify the precise division of responsibility. Although the purpose of the association's quarterly meetings is described as receiving reports from committees, they perform more than a residual or ratifying role in policy-making. The association itself maintains that policies are determined by the quarterly meetings, by the policy committee and by the other eight standing committees.

The question of divisions of authority and responsibility within public interest groups becomes important when members are under-represented, and even more important when some members are unrepresented on the main policy-making bodies. It is insufficient merely to have representation on the sovereign body when AGMs are typically non-executive bodies. It is not a problem for those associations small enough for each member to be represented on all decision-making bodies (for example, the LBA). Neither is it a practical problem for the societies, which face the problem of persuading individuals to take an active part in their work. Nor is this problem an acute one for the AMA because the sovereign body and governing body are one and the same. There is, however, the problem that not all authorities are represented on the AMA's policy committee. Three types of authority are guaranteed representation: the GLC, ILEA and the metropolitan counties. But at any one time the majority of metropolitan districts and London boroughs are excluded, although they do have a guaranteed majority of the total number of seats on the committee.

In the ACC, membership of committees is determined by the executive council (which is responsible for the management of the association) upon recommendations of the selection subcommittee of the policy committee. Membership is determined partly by party – the minority is always represented on the policy committee and the selection subcommittee – and partly by geography. The ACC's unwritten rule is that all county councils are represented on either the policy committee or the finance committee, the two main committees of the association. In fact, ten county councils have never been represented on the policy committee, which is without doubt the association's principal committee.

The question of non-representation – of exclusion from principal policy-making bodies – arises mainly in those associations with the largest memberships, the ADC and NALC. In each association a number of member authorities are always excluded from the two principal policy-making bodies – the council and policy committee (or general purposes committee). Most public interest groups are managed by executive councils which commonly are responsible for appointing committees and working officers and for ratifying committee decisions. The ADC is managed by such a council and representation is determined on a county basis, varying according to population (see Table 3.4). Consequently many authorities are not represented. The one significant exception to this population rule concerns district councils with a population of 190,000 or more, which have a representative on the council as of right. This exception recognizes that the so-called 'big eleven' district councils, former large county boroughs, should be accorded a special position commensurate with their status. Although collectively the big eleven districts have no formal committee recognition within the ADC, they do frequently meet and operate informally as a separate group. The practical effects of county-based boundaries are extremely significant in the ADC's case – a point returned to below.

Representation: geographical area, type of authority and political parties The AMA's constitution (Rule 3) recognizes the need to allow the various types of authority in membership to express their views – although there is no rule debarring the AMA from speaking in the event of a dispute. If a subject is primarily of local concern, the class of authority concerned speaks for the interests it represents and the AMA can speak only for its other members, and only then if the issue has implications for these other members. If a subject is one which concerns local government in general, but in the opinion of any of the various types of authority affects them in particular, then they can speak for their own interests irrespective of whether the AMA speaks for the other members. Finally, in matters affecting local government in general, or concerning all member authorities, the AMA speaks for all its members.

The LBA acts on behalf of the London boroughs in accordance with the terms of this rule, which it describes as a 'friendly arrangement' aimed at ensuring:

1　that the interests of the London boroughs are fully protected and that their views are expressed with maximum effect;
2　that the work of the AMA and LBA is not necessarily duplicated and that the possibility of friction is avoided.

The constitutions of the ACC and ADC (each of which has English and Welsh local authorities in their membership) also provide for the expression of distinct interests – in each case to acknowledge the distinctiveness of Welsh affairs and to accommodate their Welsh member authorities. In the ADC this is done ostensibly through both its Welsh committee and the CP.

In addition, each major association contains 'informal' groupings of local authorities. For example, within the AMA there are regular meetings of the chief executives and majority party leaders of the metropolitan counties on matters of common concern. Similarly, within the ACC there is the North of England County Councils Association – which has submitted, for example, evidence to parliamentary committees (House of Lords Select Committee on the European Communities, 1981). And, of course, the ADC contains the 'big eleven' and 'the twenty-two' (see Chapter 6).

The AMA is the only association with more than one type of member authority (see Table 3.4) and care is taken to represent each type of member on the association's nine standing committees. Where six seats are allocated to the metropolitan counties, one member is appointed by each county council. Where twelve seats are to be allocated, two members are appointed by each metropolitan county. Each metropolitan district council and each London borough council is entitled to representation on at least two and not more than four standing committees. The representation of each type of authority on the various committees corresponds to functions performed: metropolitan counties are not responsible for education or social services. Metropolitan districts and London boroughs are not responsible for police and fire; whereas the City of London is responsible for its own police force. There are two noteworthy features about the distribution of seats within the AMA. First, the interests of London are well represented with a large number of seats allocated to the LBA, GLC and ILEA. Second, the committees are large to ensure that every member authority is represented.

Of all the associations, only the ADC, in the view of some members, does not adequately accommodate party political differences between constituent authorities.[20] The county area basis to ADC representation has marked effects on its political complexion. A previous minority (Labour) leader of the association has said that:

> the ADC can never claim to be as valid as the ACC and the AMA are, where every authority is represented: the ADC can't have that claim to be representing district councils.

Moreover:

> the method of election of the council will almost always ensure a Conservative majority. ... what you get in an average normal county is two highly urban areas and a whole variety of rural areas all having one vote each. So what will happen is that the rural areas, never mind the population, will totally out-vote the urban areas.[21]

As a result, in certain counties, approximately one-third of the population may be in Labour-controlled urban districts, but all representatives to the ADC will be Conservatives from rural districts. In this situation, Norwich, for example, is unrepresented on the ADC council.

Norwich is one of the twenty-two medium-size authorities within the ADC which have been pressing for improved representation within the ADC. Unlike the 'big eleven', 'the twenty-two' are not a semi-formal group within the ADC; nor do they have the representative rights accorded to the 'big eleven'. By 1983, several attempts to rectify such non-representation had borne no fruit. Thus, at the ADC's annual conference in 1980, two resolutions were proposed by Norwich that attempted to rectify this situation. The first proposal, to lower the population figure at which a district would have the right to a place on the ADC council, was rejected. The second resolution, which was passed, required the council to bring to the 1981 annual meeting a scheme providing thirty-six additional places (nine extra places on four committees), to be filled by representatives from authorities not represented on the ADC council. When brought before the annual meeting in 1981 this scheme was rejected. Nevertheless, the composition of committees is decided on the basis of proportional representation between parties and the leader of the minority group is entitled, *ex officio*, to sit on all other committees. In addition 'there is a tradition of inviting minority groups to participate in deputations and committees'. [22] However, in 1979, eighteen of the twenty members on the association's policy committee represented Conservative-controlled districts. Of the two Labour members one was a member of the committee by virtue of being chairman of the Council for the Principality and the other, who was a co-opted member, was the leader of the Labour group.

The proportional representation of parties applies also to the committees of the ACC, AMA and LBA, but only in the AMA and LBA is the rule explicitly in the constitution. LBA and metropolitan district representatives on the committees of the AMA are selected by the LBA (since 1976), and each of the districts in each county area respectively. In so deciding, 'the LBA and districts concerned shall pay regard to the principle of proportional representation of party interests'. Alone amongst the associations the AMA commonly has had minority party chairmen of committees, in part because of this rule and in part because of the proportional allocation of seats amongst types of local authority.

The LBA determines borough representation on AMA standing committees by agreeing a political division of seats for each committee and holding separate elections amongst majority and minority parties. [23]

Representation in the joint bodies and the societies is straightforward. Thus, all societies distinguish between full members, who are entitled to representation on governing bodies, and honorary or retired members, who usually have no voting rights. Party political factors are deemed irrelevant by the societies. It is surprising, however, how little party political considerations impinge upon the joint bodies. Most associations appoint representatives on a proportional basis from majority and minority parties but the extent of party organization in the joint bodies remains limited. This discussion of political parties has not covered such topics as the effect of party organization on decision-making. This and associated topics will be discussed in the description of the political resources of the public interest groups.

Specialization: committee structures   The committee structures of the ACC, AMA and ADC reflect the structures of their member local authorities. Each association has a policy committee and standing committees for the major services. The large number of committee places in the ACC and AMA ensures participation by representatives from all member authorities but results in large committees: the average size is thirty in the ACC and thirty-two in the AMA. The ADC has fewer committees and fewer members on committees. Indeed, it is wholly impractical for representatives from each member authority to participate. Some restrictions are essential. The average size of ADC committees is nineteen.

The LBA has four standing committees: general purposes, housing and works, social services, and education. The average size of the committees is thirty. Membership of the education committee is restricted to the outer London boroughs, each nominating one representative. The three other committees have one representative from each London borough. The association chairman, vice-chairman, deputy chairman and honorary treasurer, together with the majority and minority party whips, are *ex officio* members of each committee. The LBA also has a special committee composed of the leading representatives of the association, and their role on the committee 'is to speak for London as a whole and not on behalf of their individual authorities'. The special committee differs from the general purposes committee because individual authorities are not represented as such.[24]

The structure of association committees reflects the range of services for which member authorities are responsible; the size of committees reflects the need to fully involve the whole membership – except in the ADC, where this is a practical impossibility.

In the joint bodies the size of committees similarly reflects the need to maintain the proportional representation of constituents. LACSAB has no committees as such, but it is the umbrella body for the employers' sides of the forty-two wage-negotiating committees and councils. Up to 1979 LAMSAC had two principal subcommittees – a technical advisory subcommittee and a purchasing subcommittee – with a large number of panels and working parties, made up of local authority officers and trades union representatives, working to each committee. Since 1979, LAMSAC has had only a purchasing subcommittee and has rationalized the panels and working parties.

The LGTB has five main committees and three qualifying councils: for example, the Training Resources Committee, Personnel and Administration Committee and Housing Service Training Committee. The average size of each committee is 21·5. On the principal committees, the employers (associations and employers sides of NJCs) collectively outnumber the trades unions. Only in the personnel and administration committee do the two sides have parity of representation.

The committee structures of the societies generally reflect their roles as additional resources for the associations and also their wish to involve as many members as possible. The SCT seeks to ensure that all its members have a role to play by establishing *ad hoc* groups on particular issues. The society has no formal mechanism to support ACC advisers. Other than its executive committee, the society's only standing committee is the professional committee (previously the statistics committee), which is responsible for compiling financial statistics. The ADCT has no committee structure; apart from the executive committee, there is only the 'inner cabinet' of an executive subcommittee, consisting of the association's four senior officers, which meets informally to discuss matters of an urgent or confidential nature. The SMT has three subcommittees of its executive committee, one for each of the three groups of authority in membership (metropolitan counties, metropolitan districts and London).

SOLACE operates through a combination of *ad hoc* national working parties and panels (for example, on central–local relations, and public relations) and through sixty-four branches (counties) combined into twelve territorial divisions. The latter divisions produce working papers and arrange their own seminars. There is, however, no formal policy-making structure beneath the society's executive council except the president's advisory group, which acts as a steering group initiating discussions and taking action. Initiatives from individual members, however, do not have to be referred up to executive council via branches; they can be referred directly.

The committee structure of CIPFA is complex, reflecting the society's extensive activities compared to chief officer societies. In general terms there are four central committees (for example, policy, disciplinary); seven executives, each covering a functional area (for example, health, water, local government); and eight panels on such topics as audit, financial data processing and education and training.

The executives report direct to the institute's council, whereas the panels report to the public finance central committee.

Specialization: departmental structure Each of the three main associations now has a number of sections headed by under secretaries; although the ADC resisted 'any trend towards having self-contained sections' until 1983.[25] The three secretariats are very similar and to avoid repetition only the AMA will be described. It has six main functional sections, each headed by an under secretary: education, manpower, planning and transportation, policy and finance, housing and public works, social services, and legal, general, police and fire. Each section reports to one or more of the association's standing committees. The AMA's sections are more numerous and do not have as many responsibilities as some of the ACC's and most of the ADC's sections.

Only the LGTB, LAMSAC and LACSAB of the joint bodies are sufficiently large to require any division of responsibilities. The LGTB's three sections – Training, Examinations, and Finance and Administration – correspond to the board's principal functions. Similarly, LACSAB's sections correspond to different employee groups: namely, APT and C staff, manual workers, education, police and fire. In addition there is a section for research, statistics and surveys and one for LACSAB's 'domestic' needs – accounts, printing, reception. LAMSAC's organization is structured to serve a large number of panels and working parties, which themselves are composed of local authority officers, trade-union officials, consumer groups and others. (See Rhodes, Hardy and Pudney, 1982c, for a more detailed description of the organization structures.)

None of these public interest groups had any formal corporate management structure, although regular informal meetings of secretaries with under secretaries or assistant secretaries are common and may be described, as by the ADC, as management team meetings. The LGTB, which is the largest of all the public interest groups, has a management team of the director and the three department heads; but there is no equivalent to the local authority chief executive management meeting:

> we try to see that there is a day in every week when the three of us . . . get together . . . and that tends to turn into a pretty informal management group day . . . and we don't have anybody sitting there taking notes, we don't keep records . . . it's very informal.

The total number of staff employed by public interest groups is small – even the largest would be no larger than many local authority departments (particularly non-metropolitan county councils and metropolitan district councils) and the associations' secretariats would barely constitute the equivalent of a section within these same local authority departments. Their small size tends to ensure that there is not the same rigid departmentalism that characterized local authorities, and for which corporate management was the professed cure. Within the largest section of the largest public interest group, for example (the LGTB's training department), 'senior training advisers and training advisers are treated ... as a pool of talent ... they are put together in teams to do a particular project'.[26]

Amongst the societies, CIPFA is the only one large enough to require any major division of responsibilities, once again emphasizing the distinctively broad nature of the institute's functions as compared with the other societies.

The LBA's secretariat differs from those of the other associations in two ways: first, although centred on Westminster (because the honorary secretary traditionally is the chief executive of this borough), the association has no single headquarters, but is spread around the boroughs (one full-time employee in each of five boroughs); second, none of the members of the secretariat is employed by the LBA as such – they remain employees of their boroughs and the LBA reimburses the boroughs for their services in proportion to the time spent on association business – now 100 per cent in most cases.

There is one notable omission from this description: the GLC. There are at any one time many joint GLC-LBA officer working parties, particularly in the fields of housing, planning and transportation; the GLC usually supplies the secretariat for these working groups. The LBA and GLC also work 'very closely' on RSG grants working groups and the London Working Party. Indeed, the latter was originally composed of the DoE and LBA but the GLC became involved and was welcomed by the LBA 'because of their facilities for doing technical work'.[27]

INFORMATIONAL RESOURCES

Professional information and expertise is available to public interest groups from four sources:

internal advisers: appointed, officially or otherwise, from the public interest group's membership on a voluntary basis;
societies: the local government professional societies;
secretariats: the public interest groups own employees who can be paid or unpaid, full-time or part-time, and administrative or professional;
external advisers: appointed from outside the national community of local government and from outside membership of the public interest groups – for example, paid consultants.

And this list omits such sources as central departments and 'private' interest groups, which can also provide information, although more intermittently. Obviously, as noted initially, professional and organizational resources are virtually coterminous in the local government context. Analytically, however, there is a clear distinction and, in this section, attention is focused on the information and expertise provided by local government's professional officers both individually (advisers) and collectively (the societies).

Internal advisers

Whether it is an official or an informal appointment, internal advisers will generally be unpaid, part-time and (invariably) professional. There are some important exceptions to this general rule. The ACC uses county council officers as full-time specialist 'consultants' to their secretariat; the officers remain employees of their local authority but the ACC pays the respective county council for their services. This resource has been used to provide detailed technical and computing support in RSG negotiations; it also enables the association to obtain expertise on matters such as superannuation.

Official advisers are almost without exception chief officers. Unofficial advisers typically will be senior employees of local authorities who either provide a specialist expertise on an *ad hoc* basis to various association or joint body committees, or provide detailed back-up to their chief officers who are 'official' advisers, or act as a personal secretariat to elected members. A number of senior local authority politicians (leaders of majority and minority groups) use individual officers within their local authority in such a way – in some cases virtually full-time.[28] It is not uncommon for these members to use officers employed in other local authorities. Thus elected members from small district councils use the expertise of Bristol City's officers. Other members also have friendly arrangements with officers in neighbouring, usually larger, local authorities, who similarly offer assistance.[29]

Whilst this particular practice is peculiar to the associations' political leaders, the use of 'unofficial' advisers for general advice is commonplace not only among elected members but also among the associations' secretariats and official advisers. The 'official' advisers are expected to provide a distillation of the experience and expertise within their departments and their professions. However, since both their time and expertise are limited, they naturally seek advice from their own staff and from senior colleagues in other departments. For example, the major associations appoint chief executives and treasurers to each of their service committees. When asked for advice by the associations' secretariats, the chief executive advisers commonly ask for comments from the chief officer for that service within their own local authority. In this sense, it is possible to describe the

Table 3.6   *Officer Advisers to Association Committees (1978/9)*

Association (No. of committees)	ACC (14)	ADC (7)	AMA (9)	Total	(%)
Profession					
Chief executives	31	16	25	72	20
Treasurers	19	12	22	53	15
Others	110	38	89	237	65
(No. of professions)	(24)	(10)	(19)		
Total	160	66	136	362	

collective skills of local government as a resource of the associations. And such informal arrangements are reinforced by the practice of appointing advisers from a range of member authorities, thereby ensuring that no more than one officer from each authority will be an 'official' adviser to the same committee. As Table 3.6 shows, a wide range of professions advise the associations but the most striking feature is the dominance of the 'topocratic' professions — chief executives and treasurers. These two professions are represented, uniquely, on every committee of all the associations. They comprise 32 per cent (ACC), 42 per cent (ADC) and 35 per cent (AMA) of all advisers in each association. Another notable feature is the large number of advisers appointed for each committee — averaging eleven (ACC), nine (ADC) and fifteen (AMA).

The ADC refers to the sixty-six committee advisers as senior advisers' although, in common with the ACC and AMA, the most senior advisers are the advisers to the policy committee. The ACC's senior advisers comprise the officers advisory group, twelve of the twenty-two members of which (in 1978) were also policy committee advisers. The officers advisory group meets prior to the policy committee meeting and acts as a broader source of advice for its members who subsequently advise the policy committee. In all the associations the advisers participate in committee discussions but in none, except NALC, can they vote.[30]

In the case of the joint bodies, officer advisers are appointed by the associations and, therefore, by the professional societies at one remove. The directors of LAMSAC or the LGTB, when they want advisers for one of their working parties or panels, will approach the associations in the first instance. (See Chapter 9 for an analysis of the links between the associations and their advisers.)

The societies

As is evident from their constitutions, the majority of the societies exist in varying degrees to assist the associations. The assistance given is of two main kinds. First, the societies provide lists of suitable advisers to the associations. In most cases this is a list of names, but in some of the county societies (for example, ACCE) the number of names corresponds to the number of advisers which the ACC requires. In such cases the society is, *de facto*, appointing, not nominating, advisers; and the associations are only 'selecting' them *de jure*. Second, the societies may provide additional advice to the associations either directly or by acting in a supporting capacity for the association advisers.

The practice of formally asking the societies to nominate suitable officer advisers is common to all the associations except the AMA, which claims to jealously guard its right to choose its own advisers. In fact, all the other associations profess the same right, each one emphasizing that nominees are not automatically appointed. Invariably, the nominees are appointed, but the associations nevertheless stress that the final choice is always theirs. In the ACC's case there are historically close links with the county officer societies and a long tradition predating local government reorganization of the association's selection committee annually inviting nominations from the societies. There is also a tradition of accepting these nominations, although if any committee had a leading member from a particular county the association would rarely appoint an adviser from the same county to that committee. In the ADC the practice of asking the societies for nominations was not formally introduced in 1974, but it is now a developing convention. Nor is the AMA's position as clearcut as professed. The SMT nominates treasurers;[31] the rule that the association makes the ultimate choice is, therefore, a proviso, albeit an emphatic one.

On one point all the associations (except the LBA) and societies concur: officer advisers are appointed as individuals on the basis of their expertise, experience and integrity. As individuals they necessarily reflect the position and problems of their local authority and are similarly expected to reflect the views of their professional society. This latter role involves keeping the associations aware of best professional practice. In no sense are they mandated by their societies. This fact is fully and officially accepted by the societies themselves and, on practical grounds alone, it is difficult for the societies to act in any other way. The time scale on which the associations require responses from their advisers is generally very short.

A number of the societies have topic-related working parties which may initiate proposals or consider matters referred to them by their executive councils. In turn these matters *may* have been referred to the executive council by the associations.

Association advisers are certainly not required (or even expected) to accept and forward any recommendations their societies may make. At most, the societies expect reports, oral or written, from the association advisers. SCT expects no reports from advisers. There are also cases where advisers do not report back to their society, contravening the latter's expressed wish (for example, SMT). The problem with reporting back for some of the societies lies in their mixed metropolitan and non-metropolitan membership. In effect, the advisers would be reporting back the proceedings of one association to officers employed by local authorities which are members of another association. The attendant problem of confidentiality has resulted in some mixed-membership societies having poor links with the associations compared with single-membership societies. The problem is rare in the ACC, with its long-established county societies.

It is rare for the associations, when choosing advisers, to take account of the party in control of the officer's local authority; it is even rarer to take account of the officer's own political persuasions. Factors which are taken into account are geography, type of authority, the individual's special interests, relevant experience, other work being done for the associations or joint bodies, and continuity. The importance attached to the last factor varies amongst the associations and is balanced against the desire to rotate officers periodically. In the ACC and AMA, advisers are appointed annually; in the ADC for two years. In each case, as with the other associations, advisers are seldom moved until they resign.

Although this discussion of professional resources has focused on the contribution of the 'topocratic' professions, it is important to remember that the 'technocratic' professions are an important source of information and expertise. The procedures for their appointment are predominantly the same as for the 'topocratic' professions, although their remit is commonly limited to their functional area. Advice is rarely provided to more than one association committee. Moreover, the standing of some 'technocratic' professions is not particularly high and they have to establish their credentials with the associations – for example, housing managers (Laffin, 1982, ch. 5). Nor do the 'technocratic' professions owe the same allegiance to the national community of local government. They have alternative channels of access to central government through membership of the service-specific policy communities – for example, education (see Chapter 8 below). Indeed, the 'topocratic' professions are not the exclusive resource of the associations. For example, CIPFA provides a great deal of statistical information for the associations – and on occasion (for example, the technical support service) it has provided information exclusively for them – but it also makes the selfsame expertise available to individual local authorities and to central departments. In part, CIPFA's high standing stems from the *range* of organizations which value its services.

The advice of individual local authority officers is obviously an invaluable resource for the associations and joint bodies. Authorities invariably allow chief officers to take on these duties but, for senior advisers especially, the time and cost involved in being 'on loan' can be considerable – even more so if time spent on their society business is also taken into account. An analysis of the diary of one senior association adviser revealed that in one year 3 per cent of all his meetings were on joint body business; 6 per cent on association business; and 22 per cent on professional society business (over half of which – and 12 per cent of all meetings – were for three public interest groups). The percentage of time spent at meetings will not be equivalent to the total time spent on association business: it disregards, for example, all advisory work done by correspondence. None the less, the time spent at meetings alone is considerable, especially for advisers – as in this example – who have to travel to London where the majority of association, joint body and even professional society business is conducted. Furthermore, not all local authorities unconditionally approve of the time spent by chief officers on association business. Members in a number of authorities have expressed their concern about the amount of time some advisers spend in London.

The informational resources of the associations are clearly an invaluable supplement to their organizational resources. However, the resource is not without constraints. The dual allegiance of the 'technocratic' professions and the demands on the time of the individual officer are but two examples of the way in which the usefulness of these resources is limited. There are other constraints, which will be described and discussed when exploring the national community 'in action'.

POLITICAL RESOURCES

The discussion of political resources has been left until the end not because they are of limited importance but because, in one sense, they encompass all the other resources – money, information and authority can all be counters in the process of bargaining. Party membership, access to government, public campaigns/support and legitimacy can be seen, however, as specifically political resources and this section focuses on them.

Political composition and organization
The first attempts to organize party activity in the associations were made by the Labour Party, following a resolution at its annual conference in 1952 that use be made of the associations' annual conferences to hold meetings of Labour representatives. Thereafter:

it became the custom to hold group meetings for Labour representatives on the AMC and the CCA prior to their quarterly meetings in London, as well as meetings for Labour delegates to the annual conferences of the AMC and the Association of Education Committees (AEC). (Gyford and James, 1982, p. 171)

Similar delegate meetings were held at the UDCA and RDCA annual conferences in 1957 but were abandoned the next year because of poor attendances. They were revived in 1962, lapsed two years later and were resumed again in 1967. Although by 1967 the Labour Party organized some of the activities of Labour representatives on the associations, this fell far short of any attempt to secure political control of the associations. It was the Conservative Party that in 1967 first sought, and gained, such control.

Isaac-Henry (1980b, p. 329) refers to:

the new development in the relationship between Central Office and the Conservative groups on Local Authority Associations which began in the latter part of the 1960s.

He describes the view of Lord Brooke (a former Minister of Housing and Local Government) that:

this new relationship ... was one in which Conservative groups were expected to adopt policies consistent with the Conservative Party as a whole ... [and] a good example of the workings of this new relationship was the removal from the Chairmanship of the AMC of the Labour Alderman, Mark Henig, in 1967 when the Conservatives gained control of the Association.

Lord Marshall (former Conservative group leader and AMA chairman) inaugurated the new era with the comment:

We had won hundreds of new seats all over the country and I wasn't going to have so many Conservatives on the AMC and still have some Labour Party chairmen. That would have been ridiculous and no one else would have put up with it either. (Cited in Gyford and James, 1982, p. 179)

The Conservative Party did not attempt, however, to exercise the same control in the CCA, UDCA and RDCA, which were dominated by independents and seen by the party as not 'politically political'.

In the CCA prior to reorganization 'there was no party structure whatever'.[32] This is not to say that there were not identifiable political differences between members:

if the association or the executive council had ever had to go into lobbies and there were only two ... and there was a lobby for independents ... then 90 per cent of them would have gone into that.

but if there had only been two lobbies, Conservative and Labour, 80 per cent or more would have gone into the Conservative lobby.

Nevertheless, in the CCA,

the four major committees were chaired by men who had Labour Party labels round their necks — but didn't behave as such.

When the ACC was formed, however,

chairmanships would all clearly now be members of the majority party ... at reorganization ... the political parties moved in in a big way to those areas where there had not been politics before.[33]

Or, to put it another way:

The CCA had chairmen on seniority and general ability; the ACC had it on seniority and general ability of the leading party.[34]

In spite of this, after reorganization some county councils initially appointed one of their three or four members from a minority party on their council, a practice which had ceased by 1981.

According to its last secretary the UDCA, like the CCA (and indeed the RDCA), 'was entirely non-political; you would never have known the politics of elected members'.[35] John Potter, who was the leader of the Labour group on the ADC from 1974 to 1977, and had previous experience of the UDCA, described the latter as a 'typical club affair rather than a real vehicle for political change'. He also claims that:

the first three years [of the ADC] were unique in that it wasn't politicized ... it was all seen in terms of the old UDCA and RDCA that we must have that [local] authority because it's a big authority and never mind the political complexion.

One result of this was that 'at the inception stage we were only two short of a majority'.[36] This situation changed dramatically in 1977 when the Labour Party did very badly in the local elections: the ADC Labour group fell to fourteen; after rising to twenty-two in 1979 it was down again to twenty-one, in 1981.

Table 3.7 indicates the present dominance of the Conservative group in the ADC and their unbroken control of the ACC. The AMA, by contrast, has been Labour-controlled for all but two years since 1974. In the AMA the election procedures since 1979 allow for changes of control, where necessary, to follow soon after the local elections in May; prior to 1979, changes could not be put into effect until the beginning of the following year.

Table 3.7 *Political Composition of the Major Local Authority Associations 1974–83*

ACC	Conservative	Labour	Independent	Liberal
1974	88	65	21	0
1977	141	23	11	2
1981	99	61	12	7

ADC	Conservative[b]	Labour		
1974	45	43		
1977	90	14		
1981	85	21		

AMA	Conservative	Labour	Liberal	
1974	25	51	1	
1975	27	49	1	
1976	33	44	0	
1977	38	39	0	
1978	43	33	1	
1979	39	38	0	
1980	32	44	1	
1981	27	49	1	
1982	33	43	1	
1983	30[a]	44	2	

LBA	Conservative	Labour	No overall control	
1974	13	19	0	
1978	17	14	1	
1982	16	11	5	

Notes
[a] One Conservative-controlled London borough resigned from the AMA.
[b] Figures supplied by the ADC included independents in the total for Conservatives. Where the total is less than 106, the party affiliation of the 'missing' representatives is not known.

In all the associations there is some form of internal party organization, that is, group meetings (minuted), before council and committees and the election of officers. None of the associations have party groups formalized to the extent of having model standing orders; and in only two associations, the AMA and the LBA, are party groups formally recognized in the associations' constitutions.

On the joint bodies there are no party groups across the associations:[37] association representatives 'go as local authority representatives ... [they] don't have any sort of pre-meeting at political level'.[38] The following assessment of LACSAB also applies to other joint bodies:

it tends to get as representatives from political parties people who are specifically interested in that particular subject, have been there for a long time, and there is an attitude ... that's my subject and why the hell should I be responsible to a lot of grotty councillors who don't understand the subject as much as I do.[39]

In fact, although there are no party group pre-meetings on LACSAB they do take place prior to meetings of the negotiating bodies. For the board itself, there are group pre-meetings but they comprise representatives from each association not of each party.

In brief, representatives to the joint bodies are not appointed on a strict, proportional party basis. Indeed, only the AMA adheres to such a rule and the majority parties on the joint bodies do not always take all chairmanships.[40]

Access

The effects of party composition on the internal organization of the joint bodies may be limited but the overlap of party political membership between the association and the joint bodies is none the less extensive. Access to the joint bodies is not the only, or even the most important, form of access open to the largest associations. Access to the national political parties and to Parliament are of some significance.

The party groups on the associations are represented on both the Labour Party's NEC Regional and Local Government subcommittee and on the Conservative Party's National Advisory Committee on Local Government (NACLG). On the former each of the Labour groups on the ACC, ADC, AMA, and LBA has one seat — four out of a total of forty seats. The Conservative groups on these four associations also have one seat on the party's NACLG, as do the Leader and Deputy Leader of the GLC — six out of a total of fifty-four seats. The local government officers of both Labour and Conservative parties liaise with their respective party groups on the associations, in the case of the Labour Party acting as secretary to the Labour groups. Because both local government departments are relatively small, they are very rarely used in a research capacity by the associations. They do, however, advise the various party groups on respective party policies.

The links between the associations and Parliament take the form of parliamentary vice-presidents (MPs and peers) appointed by the AMA (40), ADC (53) and NALC (6). Their function is to advise the associations and promote the associations' interests in Parliament, either by supporting, or seeking to amend, proposed legislation or by introducing private members' Bills on the associations' behalf. The vice-presidents are appointed for their general sympathy towards the association and the class of authorities in membership: frequently they have had previous experience as local councillors.

In the CCA and ACC vice-presidents were, and are, appointed solely in honour of their long service to the association. In 1978 the association had no vice-presidents; in 1981 it had two, one in the House of Lords and one in the House of Commons.

Public support

The associations have rarely concerted demonstrations of public support in order to persuade the government of the day to change its mind. The reasons for this reluctance are many and varied. It is because public campaigns are antithetical to their consultative style, because the impact of campaigns can diminish with their frequency, and because disagreements between the associations on major issues prohibit joint action. However, there have been some campaigns. The RDCA launched a substantial campaign against the report of the Royal Commission on Local Government in England (Wood, 1976, p. 78). Mr R. E. Mote — the Bulldog Billie of the local government world — cost some £40,000. More recently, the AMA launched a campaign — under the slogan 'Keep it Local' — against Mr Heseltine's attempts to control local expenditure and rate increases (see *Municipal Review*, October 1981, pp. 105–6; and November 1981, pp. 125–6). Less spectacularly, both the AMA and the ACC have improved their public relations activities; an example is the ACC launch of the newsletter 'Accent'. As the chairman of the AMA forcibly stated:

> We are proposing to spend money reminding people of what local government is about, what it does and why it is important that local decisions continue to be made by locally elected councils ... [it was] right and proper and with good precedent that public money should be spent to ensure that the public at least realises what the issues are and what is at stake.

Furthermore:

> if this country is to go still further down the road to total central control, then it must not happen because no one told the public which way the signposts were pointing.

In spite of these developments, however, the attempts of the associations to engender public support can be most accurately described as low-key.

Legitimacy

Legitimacy can be described as simultaneously the most intangible and most important of all the political resources of the associations. The associations represent elected units of government which together encompass all the parliamentary constituencies in England and Wales. It is from this elective basis that the associations derive their political legitimacy. Cross (1954) described how the AMC's claim to speak for a large section of the population was legitimated by the nature of its representation:

> it is representation having its roots in the elective principle with a line of accountability and having its ultimate source of authority in practically speaking the whole of the adult population of England and Wales.

By convention central governments have accepted that the claims of the associations (and the joint bodies) to represent local authorities are legitimate and, in a few cases, most notably grant negotiations, this has been enshrined in statute.

The legitimacy of the associations is bolstered by the 'quality' of their membership (Grant and Marsh, 1977, pp. 34–6): the lower the percentage of potential members actually in membership, the less plausible is the group's claim to speak for that group. The relationship between high membership rates and a group's legitimacy affects the claims of SOLACE to speak for chief executives, as well as the claims of the associations to speak for their members. SOLACE's voice is authoritative not just because it represents chief officers of local authorities but because it represents virtually all (95 per cent) of them. Seven of the associations have 100 per cent of their potential membership. There are, however, a number of caveats to these figures. First, constitutionally, the ACC's potential membership includes all non-metropolitan and metropolitan county councils (fifty-four) whereas in fact there are forty-seven members. Since its formation, no metropolitan county councils have joined the ACC, although South Yorkshire took part in framing the association's constitution. Second, the ACC, ADC and AMA all have members who belong to more than one association. All eight members of the WCC are also members of the ACC. All thirty-three members of the LBA are also members of the AMA. All thirty-seven members of the CP are also members of the ADC. Finally, the associations have lost members in recent years. For example, in September 1981, Derbyshire County Council resigned from the ACC. Similar resignations have occurred in the AMA, LBA and ADC. These reductions in an association's membership rate may only slightly reduce its authority but they reveal the stresses and strains confronting the associations in the 1980s (see Chapter 9 below).

CONCLUSIONS

This chapter has identified the major public interest groups and provided detailed information on their resources. It is perfectly clear that the national network of local government is dominated by a relatively small number of organizations and subsequent chapters will supplement this description with an analysis of these organizations 'in action'. However, this chapter has identified three constraints within the national community of local government – namely, representation, members and organization – and these limits to an integrated network remain to be summarized.

First, it is clear that the national community encompasses a wide range of interests. Each association does not speak for one type of local government and, if agreement within an association can sometimes prove elusive, agreement between the associations can often seem like a will-o'-the-wisp. Nor is the diversity of interests limited to type of authority. Since reorganization, the divisions within the national community have been complicated by the extension (*not* the arrival) of party politics. Even that redoubted stronghold of the independent member, the CCA, re-emerged after 1974 not only with a new acronym but under Conservative control and with party group meetings. The increasingly prominent position of the political parties has served to complicate internal and external relationships. There is, therefore, an ever-present potential for conflict between the sectional interests of the associations (be it type of authority or political party) and the need to represent coherently local government's interests.

Second, the description of the national community's relationship with its member local authorities underscored the *voluntary* nature of membership. The associations are not mandated by members but equally they can neither commit members to particular policies nor compel them to pursue certain courses of action: they cannot regulate members.

Finally, the way in which the public interest groups organize themselves can limit effectiveness and this chapter has identified a number of organizational constraints. At this juncture, four issues require further exploration. First, the scale of resources available to the national community is often said to be limited, especially by the secretariats and leading members. For example, the associations employ relatively few professionals and rely heavily on the, in the main, part-time assistance of officer advisers. However, compared with other major pressure groups such as the CBI and TUC, the associations could be described as relatively affluent (see Grant and Marsh, 1977, pp. 33 and 37; Taylor, 1980, pp. 24 and 90). Whether or not their resources are commensurable with the tasks to be carried out is a matter to be explored further. Second, the associations are reluctant to deploy the resources at their disposal – for example, in public campaigns. Again, therefore, it is necessary to explore whether such self-imposed constraints reduce their effectiveness. Third, it is not clear that the internal organization of the associations facilitates their work. For example, their structure emphasizes functional or service specialization whereas their strategic capabilities – for example, long-term policy development or corporate planning – seem unduly limited. Finally, the joint bodies – ostensibly a 'joint' resource of the associations – in fact serve multiple constituencies. *In toto* the associations may be the major source of funds for joint bodies but for key bodies – for example, LACSAB – they are not the major let alone sole source of income. The capacity of joint bodies to act independently of the associations could further constrain the latter's effectiveness.

All of these constraints will be explored in more detail in subsequent chapters. This chapter has provided a formal, static description. This description helps to pinpoint potential weaknesses in the national community of local government. But the key phrase is 'potential weaknesses'.

The chapter has shown that the national organizations of local government are closely linked by both the exchange of monies – for example, Section 2(7) funding – and of personnel – for example, interlocking committee membership. Such linkages suggest that it is plausible to talk of a national *community* of local government. But equally there are limits to the degree of integration. It is now essential to explore the national community 'in action' and determine whether or not potential constraints are actual constraints. Part Two of this book undertakes the task by presenting case studies of policies central to the interests of local government – namely, grant, pay and reorganization.

NOTES AND REFERENCES : CHAPTER 3

1   This approach has two limitations. First, the comparison is formal. I do not explore the actual behaviour of public interest groups, a task deferred to later chapters. Second, depth of analysis for a particular organization has been sacrificed to increase the scope of coverage. No attempt is made to provide a comprehensive history of each organization. The advantage of this approach is that, for the first time, it is possible to compare systematically local government public interest groups.

2   For a more detailed discussion of these indicators see Rhodes, Hardy and Pudney, 1982b, pp. 156–64. Their importance is also demonstrated by the following, more detailed description of public interest groups.

3   For a more detailed discussion of the methodology (and its limitations) see: Rhodes, Hardy and Pudney, 1982c, pp. 49–51; Giddens, 1974; and Rhodes, 1982, pp. 3–16. I would like to thank Andrew Flynn for his help in analysing the extent of interlocking.

4   For a detailed description of *all* local government's public interest groups see: Rhodes, Hardy and Pudney, 1982b. Where necessary, the 'minor' groups will be described briefly in the footnotes. The base year for comparison was 1979 but major changes up to and including 1983 have been included.

5 Interview with secretary, ACC, transcript.

6 JACOLA was established as a forum for discussing matters of common interest to local authorities which either operated or had an interest in airports. The committee's work is intermittent: it meets four or five times a year and regularly considers such recurrent items as airport charges and fees. JACOLA's work involves responding to, for example, Civil Aviation Bills or plans for a third London airport. Because it has no staff of its own, the committee's role is necessarily a reactive one. Its principal function is to provide a single point of contact for municipal airports; to ensure that they are consulted on matters affecting them; and to co-ordinate their response.

CLEA's function is to act as the body through which all local education authorities discuss matters of common interest. The council is responsible for negotiating terms and conditions of service with teachers; for undertaking joint discussions with government departments (principally DES); for liaising with a range of educational organizations (for example, the Committee of Directors of Polytechnics) and for co-ordinating information and advice to member education authorities. The latter is done in part via an annual CLEA conference and in part by frequent circulars to chief education officers and chief executives. The council's remit is highly circumscribed. The education committees of the two associations are responsible for all across-the-board policies involving other functions and CLEA is empowered to act only within its designated limits and only when there is unanimity between the two associations. Where there is a difference of opinion on the council the matter must be referred back to the two association education committees. (See Chapter 8.)

SACLAT acts as a forum for discussions between theatre interests and local authorities and provides the latter with an advisory and information service. It holds two seminars a year, and since 1980 has produced a twice-yearly broadsheet. Its work can be summarized as small-scale, intermittent and essentially limited.

7 LAMIT provides an investment advisory service to individual local authorities but principally it is responsible for the investment and day-to-day management of local authority superannuation funds.

LAOSC seldom meets more than twice a year and the agenda comprises highly technical and specialized matters – hence the officer composition of the committee. LAOSC represents members' views to government and it is essentially a liaison body. Collectively, local authorities are the Ordnance Survey's biggest customer and this customer relationship makes LAOSC's links with central government unique amongst the joint bodies: it is the only body which is composed, in part, of representatives from a government department.

LACOTS is the point of reference for central government in its general dealing with local authorities on technical trading standards matters. It attempts to ensure that EEC requirements on trading standards are effectively operated and to modify new proposals where necessary.

8 The functions of the small associations – WCC, CP, LBA, etc. – are described in more detail in Chapter 7 below.

9 Interview with Sir R. Thomas, Labour group leader and chairman, AMC/AMA, transcript.

10 Interview with honorary secretary, WCC, transcript.

11 Interview with deputy secretary, LBA, transcript.

12 In the ADC's case, for example, the methods used to distribute the blocks for 1982/3 were as follows:

(i) other services: 'based on 40% population, 25% 1981/2 allocation (excluding any specific allocation for derelict land), 25% 1980/1 outturn and 10% housing starts, with a safety net related to cash allocations'.

(ii) transport: based on 'planned expenditure for those district councils with a bus undertaking'. (Correspondence with authors, 21 May 1982)

In the AMA's case, for the 'other services' block the 1982/3 allocation is based on 'a split between counties and districts by reference to the past three years' spending and then, within each group, a 75% past spend/25% population formula'.

LDS was split between counties and districts in the ratio of $26\cdot5:73\cdot5$. (Correspondence with authors, 28 June 1982)

13 Interview with Deputy Secretary, LBA, transcript. See also Chapter 7 for an account of recent developments in the LBA.
14 All preceding quotes from interview with honorary secretary, SOLACE, transcript.
15 Interview with honorary secretary, ACCE, transcript.
16 All preceding quotes are from Association of County Councils, *Brief Outline of the Activities of the Committees of the Associations, 1978/79* (London: ACC, 1979), pp. 8–9.
17 LGTB, *Report and Accounts, 1978–9*, pp. 19 and 4.
18 The preceding quotations are from interviews with two deputy secretaries of the ACC, transcript.
19 Interview with secretary, ACC, transcript.
20 Interviews with J. Potter, Labour group leader, ADC, and C. Booler, Labour group leader, ADC, transcripts.
21 Interview with J. Potter, Labour group leader, ADC, transcript.
22 Interview with C. Booler, Labour group leader, ADC, transcript.
23 The City of London is the only member council of the LBA with representatives who take neither party whip.
24 The one exception to this rule is the City of London, which was granted non-voting membership of the special committee in 1979.
25 Interview with deputy secretary ADC, transcript. In April 1983, the ADC created four policy divisions each headed by an under secretary.
26 Both quotations are from an interview with director, LGTB, transcript.
27 Interview with deputy secretary LBA transcript. See also Chapter 7, below.
28 Interview with J. Potter, Labour group leader, ADC transcript.
29 Interview with C. Booler, Labour group leader, ADC transcript.
30 Until 1949, advisers at the AMC could vote in committees. In the 1920s officers – usually town clerks and their deputies – outnumbered elected representatives at annual and council meetings; and the AMC's principal committee, the law committee, was until 1939 composed entirely of town clerks. After 1939, the general purposes committee, with elected representatives in the majority, became the principal committee but up to 1949 member authorities could still be represented on standing committees by either officers or elected members. Currently, 19 of the 44 members of NALC's council are officers and they can vote.
31 Interviews with honorary secretary, SMT, transcript.
32 Interview with secretary, ACC, transcript.
33 The preceding quotations are from an interview with Sir M. Whittaker, chaiman, ACC, transcript.
34 Interview with secretary, ACC, transcript.
35 Interview with secretary UDCA, transcript.
36 Interview with J. Potter, Labour group leader, ADC, transcript.
37 JACOLA resolved in 1980 that henceforth the chairman should come from the majority party.
38 Interview with Dame E. Coker, chairman, ACC, transcript.
39 Interview with J. Potter, Labour group leader, ADC, transcript. The selfsame point was made in an interview with the director, LGTB, transcript.
40 Interview with the director LGTB, transcript.

PART TWO

THE NATIONAL COMMUNITY 'IN ACTION'

Chapter 4

GRANT NEGOTIATIONS AND THE CONSULTATIVE COUNCIL ON LOCAL GOVERNMENT FINANCE

INTRODUCTION

The Consultative Council on Local Government Finance (CCLGF), belying its unprepossessing title, was one of the most important innovations in central–local relations between 1974 and 1979:

> The one major innovation of 1975 was the creation of the Consultative Council ... It was a powerful engine through which central government persuaded local government to do what it wanted. But there was a price to be paid for such an arrangement. Just as in order to secure TUC and CBI co-operation on issues which central government regards as vital, those bodies have gained the right to be listened to on other matters and very often to blackball what they do not like, so corporatism in the relations between central and local government has reduced central government's freedom to introduce reforms.
>
> A major result of the growth of this consultative apparatus has been to enhance the influence of the local authority associations. (Foster, Jackman and Perlman, 1980, pp. 3 and 351)

As with most innovations, assessments of its merits differ markedly: to some people 'if it did not exist, local government would have to invent it'; others regard it as a 'confidence trick designed to sell the "cuts" to local government'. Such disparities are to be expected. Throughout the CCLGF's existence local government's finance has been a controversial 'problem' and no institution in the public expenditure process could hope to remain untouched by this controversy.

In spite of its importance, there have been few studies of the CCLGF and none of them is comprehensive. (See Barnett, 1982, pp. 75–6; Harris and Shipp, 1977; Pliatzky, 1982, pp. 116–17; and Taylor, 1979). The first objective of this chapter is to describe and analyse its origins, development and demise. However, the work of the council cannot be understood in isolation from developments in the rate support grant (RSG) and public expenditure survey (PES) systems. Accordingly, the case study presents more than a simple history of an institution. The second objective is to outline the trends in local government expenditure which at first fostered the CCLGF and then eroded its pre-eminence. It will be argued that the period 1970–83 saw a shift from bargaining through incorporation in the CCLGF to direction under the exigencies of economic decline and cuts in public expenditure.

THE ORIGINS AND ESTABLISHMENT OF THE CCLGF

Context

Interviews with local government politicians, association secretariats and professional advisers identified four general accounts of its origins. The most widely held belief, particularly amongst local politicians, is that the council merely formalized the political level meetings initiated by the Secretary of State for the Environment, Anthony Crosland, in 1974. The second account sees the council primarily as a response to the evidence to and recommendations of the Layfield Inquiry, which sat from August 1974 and reported in May 1976. The third account regards the council as an evolution and extension of the existing RSG machinery, which had expanded, particularly since 1970. The fourth and least articulated account sees the council as a result of the 'hidden hand' of the Treasury responding to a changing economic climate. Before examining these accounts, it is necessary to explore the context in which the CCLGF originated – that is, the early rounds of RSG negotiations; formal changes in the grant system, most notably the Local Government Act 1974; and PES.

Grant negotiations before 1975/6   The importance of grant negotiations is difficult to overestimate. They have become *the* forum for fixing both the total expenditure of local government, running at its height at £14·8 billion in 1975/6 (constant prices) and for deciding the total and distribution of central grant to local government, amounting to some £8·4 billion annually. Yet most accounts of these negotiations are, at best, formalistic. There are two main reasons for this state of affairs. First, until recently, little was known about the consultative council within which the negotiations took place: in its first year, meetings and papers were secret. Second, many decisions crucially affecting grant negotiations formed part of PES and were taken in Cabinet (and in Whitehall) in the autumn of each year, preventing access from local government and interested observers alike. As a consequence the dominant tendency has been to treat the negotiations as a formal and almost technical process in which the grant totals are largely non-negotiable but determined on professional and technical criteria. The emphasis is laid on the plethora of committees working on a variety of technical systems for assessing the need to spend of local authorities; on the financial and service specialists from both levels of government producing joint forecasts of expenditure and policy consequences; and on the technical aspects of the methods for distributing grant between the different types of local authority. To place so much emphasis on this formal aspect, however, is misleading because it downgrades the effects of politics and bargaining, and tends to ignore conflict between and within the two levels of government. Indeed the history of RSG is the history of conflict over not only the total and distribution of grant but also the level of local expenditure. To recognize these conflicts implies a shift of focus from the technical aspects of the grant system to bargaining on the level of local expenditure (including central grant). But care must be taken not to overstate the extent of bargaining. It is as important to analyse the constraints on strategic behaviour as it is to describe the strategies and tactics.

The RSG negotiations are best viewed as a bargaining process subject to a set of well defined rules which constrain the participants. The participants adopt strategies according to their objectives, bargaining position and available resources; *but* changes in the political complexion of the government (or an association) and in the national economy can lead to dramatic transformations in the rules of the game. These points can be illustrated by looking at grant negotiations prior to the formation of the CCLGF (for further details, see Rhodes, Hardy and Pudney, 1982a, pp. 22–34).

In bare outline, negotiations began with the deliberations of the grants working group and its various forecasting subgroups. Their task was to prepare authoritative estimates of 'relevant expenditure' – that is, the current expenditure (net of income from trading services) deemed eligible for grant. These official meetings culminated in the statutory meeting with ministers at which the decision on grant was formally taken. It was only at this meeting that the associations' elected representatives became involved in negotiations. The government announced the level of grant in an 'RSG order' with 'increase orders' used to compensate for any increases in the level of prices (or pay) and for any additional expenditure arising from new legislation.

In reality, this ostensibly simple process was complex. Delays in the circulation of information and the cancellation of meetings were regular events which prompted much criticism by the associations. They were seen as a central ploy, designed to weaken the associations' bargaining position. Rather, they were the inevitable product of negotiations involving the Department of the Environment (DoE), the associations, the Treasury and those spending departments with a direct budgetary interest in local services (for example, education, social services). The DoE was (and remains) the 'lead department' in the negotiations, involved in numerous 'bilaterals' as well as Cabinet and Cabinet committee meetings. This standard feature of the public expenditure (and grant) process is well illustrated by Joel Barnett's (1982, p. 81) account of one 'bilateral' between himself as Chief Secretary to the Treasury and Tony Crosland, (then) Secretary of

State for the Environment:

> he came in with all his officials and almost before we had started offered to accept my proposals, amounting to £1 billion in respect of roads and other environmental services. But he then refused to given an inch over housing. We thus ended our meeting without agreement on my housing proposals ... I eventually obtained cuts in housing, but only after a struggle over the Cabinet table.

> Some time later, Tony Crosland asked me for my opinion on the outcome of this particular exercise. He had worried about his tactics ... I was bound to tell him that ... His agreeing easily to make cuts did not prevent my pressing strongly for further cuts in his housing programme. I told him that if he could have been as unreasonable on every penny of his programmes as Barbara Castle certainly would have been, he might well have got away with smaller cuts.

Grant negotiations are not limited to negotiations with the associations but also involve reconciling the diversity of interests within central government. Such a reconciliation often proved difficult. With some justification the associations regarded the final subgroup reports as more than an 'opening bid' to the negotiations: the government's decisions could now be based on realistic projections of local expenditure. Unfortunately for the associations, the departmental representatives on the subgroups had not received Cabinet instructions – based on the PES review – when agreeing the estimates of expenditure. The results of the PES deliberations could be considerably different from the subgroup recommendations, requiring a substantial reassessment of the level of local expenditure. This point is all too clearly illustrated by the progress of the negotiations for 1971/2.

After six months of assessment, the subgroups reported a forecast increase in relevant expenditure of around 5·8 per cent for 1971/2. On 19 October 1970 the associations' negotiators and advisers met to consider the reports, and amended forecasts, recommending a 5·8 per cent increase, were communicated to the then Ministry of Housing and Local Government (MHLG) on 26 October. However, on 4 November the association received a paper containing the government's proposals on the rate of growth of local authority revenue expenditure, which expressed the view that 'the rate of growth of local authority expenditure will in future be brought more into line with the general rate of growth of the economy'.[1] The paper proposed a 3·8 per cent increase. In subsequent meetings between the associations and departmental representatives, the associations acknowledged that the state of the economy required restraint but argued that the claim for 5·8 per cent was not arbitrary. In reply the government admitted that 5·8 per cent was reasonable for local government, but not in the national context, where local authority expenditure was growing faster than the economy as a whole. Nevertheless, in negotiations between officials, the government amended its initial offer and the statutory meeting confirmed a 4·6 per cent increase.

This compromise, however, rang hollow for the associations. In the White Paper of 27 October 1970, *New Policies for Public Spending* (Cmnd 4515, HMSO, 1970), the government had proposed a variety of cuts in local authority expenditure which were to be achieved by savings on school meals, increases in further education fees and 'improved efficiency'. After these modifications, the RSG settlement increase stood at 3·7 per cent – a figure remarkably similar to the government's original 3·8 per cent offer – and the proposed 1 per cent increase in grant had been reduced to ½ per cent. In other words, RSG negotiations were inextricably linked with and constrained by the government's views on the state of the national economy. Indeed, as the Treasury commented:

> the Government through its relations with local authorities and the mechanism of the rate support grant is able to exercise a strong influence over the rate of growth of current expenditure.[2]

But, equally, increasing involvement with local government had created limits to this influence. Growth rates or cuts now had to be tempered by a recognition that the data on the spending plans of local authorities were increasingly accurate.

This pattern of negotiation continued up to 1975/6. The timetable continued to be tight in the final stages of negotiation and appeared to be largely dictated by the interests, parliamentary and departmental, of the government. Important proposals were circulated too late for association negotiators to study fully the implications – for example, the government's proposals on the level of relief to domestic ratepayers were not disclosed until the statutory meeting itself in the 1973/4 negotiations. The approved relevant expenditure figures continued to be far more consonant with government's PES figures than with either the associations' claims or the subgroup forecasts. Disagreements persisted on a range of issues but were most intense on the annual proposals to restrict severely the growth of relevant expenditure. The government did not hold all the cards; certainly it made the decision on the level of grant, but local government's capacity to raise income through the rates meant that, in aggregate, it exceeded PES ceilings. It was essential, therefore, for central government to bargain for local government's compliance. Through grant it could influence, but not determine, the level of local expenditure.

By 1975 it was apparent that relations between central and local government on finance were deteriorating markedly. The government objected to local authority expenditure rising faster than the rate of growth of gross domestic product, and to local government ignoring its responsibility towards the management of the national economy by overspending the limits set out in the PES White Papers and (indirectly) RSG settlements. In four of the five years between 1971/2 and 1975/6 the outturn of local authority relevant expenditure exceeded the government's expenditure plans.

In reply, the associations criticized the PES system, on which the RSG settlements were largely based, for being inaccurate, for ignoring the views of local authorities by excluding them from the procedure, and for using figures incompatible with local authority budgetary processes. The associations also complained of increasing government controls of expenditure. They claimed that the grant negotiations were being manipulated to control all local government revenue, not just the government's contribution, and that the procedure for approving capital expenditure – known as 'loan sanction' – was being misused to limit such expenditure. Moreover, the sudden announcements (without sufficient, or at times any, consultation) of cuts in forecast expenditure had disruptive effects because they disregarded the practical difficulties faced by local authorities, not to mention the right of local authorities to adjust their expenditure to local needs. These problems were compounded by the regular contradictory advice issued by different departments – some urging financial parsimony whilst others advised, encouraged or even legislated for the development of services. The gulf between central and local government had clearly reached sizeable proportions.

It would be misleading to suggest, however, that the source of dissatisfaction lay in the procedures for determining central grant. The context within which grant negotiations took place had changed. The Heath government (1970–4) had been elected with a clear commitment to restricting the role of government and stimulating the private sector. This 'Selsdon man' image took a number of hard knocks, however (see Blackaby, 1978). Within two years the ubiquitous U-turn took place and the government used increases in public expenditure to counter rising unemployment. This resort to Keynesian macro-economic management tools simply helped to fuel inflation. Thus began an era of high inflation, adverse balance of payments, an escalating public sector borrowing requirement (PSBR), a declining GNP and rising (and high) unemployment. The intensification of economic decline, and crucially of inflation, coincided with the reorganization of local government. It was a source of some debate whether or not the unprecedented rate increases were caused by inflation or by the profligacy of the retiring councils. It is clear, however, not only that public expenditure as a whole was rising rapidly but that local government's share of the total was rising even more quickly

(Pliatzky, 1982, Appendix 1, p. 212). The rate rises which attended the reorganization of local government were the catalyst to action on the financial relationship between central and local government. The problems of the grant system, which had been tolerable in an era of expenditure growth, now became major irritants. The initial reaction was appointment of the Layfield Committee to investigate and make recommendations on the system of local government finance. But governments and their problems can rarely wait for the results of the deliberations of a committee of inquiry. Before the Layfield Committee had reported, 'cash limits' had been introduced and the creation of the consultative council had been announced.

Formal changes in the grant system   If the impact of economic decline on the financial relationship between central and local government has been widely appreciated, other ostensibly technical changes occurred in 1974 and 1975 which had a substantial effect on the subsequent years' negotiations: the introduction of multiple regression analysis as the basis for distributing grant between local authorities and the introduction of 'cash limits'.

The first change was embodied in the Local Government Act 1974, which sought to make a number of changes in the financial system to coincide with the reorganization of local government. The grant system contained, at this time, three components: the resources, needs and domestic elements. The resources element aimed to equalize the rateable resources of local authorities. Thus, poor local authorities (that is, those with low rateable values) had them made up to a 'national standard rateable value per head of population'. The domestic element aimed to lessen the rate burden on domestic ratepayers and was, in effect, a subsidy for individual ratepayers. The needs element aimed to redistribute resources to those local authorities which faced the greatest problems or need to spend per head of population. For example, a local authority with a high proportion of schoolchildren (or old people) resident in its area would have a greater need to spend than an authority with a low proportion of these groups. The distribution of the needs element between local authorities depends upon the accurate measurement of differences in the need to spend. Multiple regression analysis was introduced to improve the basis for distributing the needs element (approximately two-thirds of total grant) between local authorities. (For a more detailed description see Hepworth, 1976; Layfield, 1976, annexes 27 and 28.)

The AMA, the main beneficiaries of the new system of distribution, thought that its introduction stemmed from

what has come to be called the revolt of the cities in 1973 against the inadequate representation of the need to spend in urban areas of the 1966 version of RSG. That is why the government of the day moved to the 1974 version for RSG which took as its basis a measure of need to spend being represented by national patterns of actual expenditure.[3]

The ACC and ADC, however, the main losers of the system, saw the change as being 'steamrollered' through by a government which was taking advantage of the upheaval of local government. The issue was not new; it had been discussed in the grants working group over the previous two years. With reorganization the associations, already lacking in specialist staff, were in no position to give detailed consideration to the issue, but the usual consultation procedures were followed. At the time, the associations were preoccupied with the reorganization of local government and this concern relegated changes in RSG procedures to the sidelines. Moreover, the complaints gained in intensity only after the consequences of multiple regression analysis became clear. And these consequences were to prove dramatic.

Equally important was the introduction of 'cash limits' in 1975 for the 1976/7 negotiations. Thus, the government placed a fixed ceiling, in money (or cash) terms not real terms, on the amount that would be paid under increase orders. The government proposed that cash limits apply only to central grant and were not intended to control local government's total spending directly. Cash limits have come to be regarded by local government, however, as a means for making real grant (and expenditure) cuts because they have been set at levels which severely underestimate the true rate of inflation, especially the size of wage settlements in the public sector. If such unexpected increases in costs are not paid for by increases in grant (through increase orders), then local authorities have either to build up their balances (or savings), to increase rates (by levying, for example, a supplementary rate), or to cut services. If the level of expenditure is maintained, then grant falls as a proportion of relevant expenditure and its real value or purchasing power is eroded by inflation. From their inception to the end of the period of study, cash limits were a key weapon in the government's armoury for controlling grant and local expenditure.

The Public Expenditure Survey (PES)   Although PES can be viewed as part of the formal machinery and procedures for determining grant, it is of such importance that it will be considered separately.

Long before the CCLGF was envisaged, it was made plain that RSG negotiations were considered in the broadest macro-economic context. As Peter Walker, then Secretary of State for the Environment, stated in the House of Commons on 10 December 1970: 'in coming to our consideration of the total [of RSG] the Government have three major matters to take into account': first, present expenditure and general forecasts; second, population changes and changes in demand; and 'the third consideration is the general economic situation and the total of the grant is always made within that context'. Indeed, another former Secretary of State for the Environment, Peter Shore, referred to his position as that of a 'mini-chancellor'.[4] PES was central to RSG decisions and, although local government was aware of this fact, its reaction has frequently been ambiguous.

PES was designed to provide regular surveys of public expenditure for five years ahead, taking into account the resources available. The survey itself took no decisions but it provided the Cabinet with a picture of the present and future cost of current expenditure levels and the implications of any change. The survey covered all the expenditure of central and local government along with the capital expenditure of nationalized industries and the plans were in constant price terms – that is, costs were assumed to remain the same for the five years covered by the survey (see Heclo and Wildavsky, 1974; Else and Marshall, 1979). For local government, PES became significant in 1969 when the White Papers announcing the government's decisions on public expenditure became annual documents. The White Papers based on PES thus became the government's primary macro-economic decision-making tool, determining the level of public expenditure and covering both central and local government. A second development, in 1970, further emphasized the relevance of PES to local government: the Department of the Environment was created as *the* department responsible for co-ordinating the government's relations with local government. It was to introduce a note of economic realism into central–local fiscal relations by breaking down the rife departmentalism over bids for available resources.[5] It was to be assisted in this task by the Treasury and the PES process.

Local government, however, appeared remarkably unconcerned about PES. For example, the forecasting subgroups merely provided a factual basis for discussions and did not consider economic analyses. Indeed the groups, by disaggregating, prevented any overall perspective on the national economy emerging from the associations. After the establishment of the forecasting groups the associations were even less inclined to produce general assessments of the financial and economic conditions confronting local government. The associations did not accord the White Papers any importance until 1971, and the individual local authorities regarded the White Papers as irrelevant for their working until 1975 (Blackburn, 1978). Local government's interest in PES can be dated, however, from the circulation of internal AMC paper in May 1971 which sketched a brief and simple history of PES and its timetable. The paper saw difficulty in linking PES to the RSG negotiations, except as a source of background information, and did not suggest any possible involvement by the associations in PES. Later that month the ACC's secretary wrote to the DoE suggesting 'a closer association of the local authority asssociations with the development of public expenditure policy'.[6]

By March 1972, it had been agreed that reconciliation tables between RSG and PES figures would be produced, that the departments would arrange discussions on White Paper capital expenditure figures with the associations, and that the subgroups should extend their forecasting to three years. However, the associations were not convinced that the discussion of current expenditure in the RSG negotiations did constitute an adequate input to the equivalent discussion in the PES process. In particular, the CCA complained about inadequate information both on the distribution of expenditure between services and on the disparity between local authority figures on current expenditure and the government's figures. The CCA wanted a separate document on local authority expenditure linked to RSG forecasts. While growth prevailed such disagreements were minor. The more exacting test of local government involvement in macro-economic decision-making occurred in May 1973, when the Chancellor announced a series of cuts totalling £80 million without consulting the associations, followed in December of the same year by a further £120 million reduction, again without consultation. The subgroups, which the associations had considered to be an input to PES as well as RSG discussions, were used to evaluate the policy implications of the cuts for local government services. As a DoE letter noted, 'it is not the function of the sub-groups to negotiate about the figures'.[7]

After a slow but encouraging beginning the associations found that their sought-after involvement in PES was more illusory than real, a product of a period of rapid growth when local government was the prime beneficiary. However, the exact nature of local government involvement in PES was always unclear and vague generalizations served to conceal a clear misunderstanding by local government of its nature.

PES can be looked upon as a set of formal procedures and techniques – as a decision-making tool – but such a characterization omits a key element. Underlying the formal expenditure process is 'a community united by ties of kinship and culture' (Heclo and Wildavsky, 1974, p. 36). The shared assumptions of this 'village' or expenditure community (see Kellner and Crowther-Hunt, 1980, p. 69 and pp. 272–3) have exercised a marked influence on the appreciative system of the national community. To central departments PES was not a decision-making process but a structured, internal and substantially closed review of existing commitments which collected information on public expenditure to present to ministers. The decisions were made in Cabinet. Local government participation would improve the quality of the information and advice presented to Cabinet. The invitation to participate in PES was intended to involve precisely and only the provision of information. Local government, in so far as it thought involvement was desirable, envisaged a more direct link between information and decision than was ever recognized by central government, hence the disillusionment over 'minimal' involvement. The Treasury may have wanted local government's involvement but it was to be strictly confined, and its objective was to restrain local expenditure, not to enhance local authority influence.

Such differences highlight the schizophrenic world of the *national* community of *local* government. On the one hand, the *raison d'être* of its constituent parts is to represent their members: on more than one occasion doubts were expressed about the wisdom of any involvement in PES, such matters being regarded as the exclusive concern of central government. Thus, an AMA chairman felt that the associations had been 'neutered very, very considerably'[8] and one of his predecessors at the AMC opined 'that sort of emasculating exercise is very good for central government but not good for the influence of the various local government Associations'.[9] Nor was this involvement with the centre at the behest of the associations' membership. Indeed, the distance between the associations and their members could be said to have facilitated incorporation. As one secretary of the ACC commented (unfavourably), his staff were too willing to define the interests of members rather than asking them what they wanted.[10] Involvement served, therefore, to distance the associations from their members. On the other hand, continuous contact with central government develops an awareness and understanding of the impact of PES and the government's view of the economy.

To disregard PES, therefore, is to abrogate one's responsibility to one's members; but, at the same time, involvement in PES courts the dangers of an oversensitivity to the government's problems and of creating a gulf between the association and its members. To become involved in PES for a minimal pay off is the worst of all possible outcomes. It is the classic dilemma of respectable pressure groups and it was a very real one for the national community of local government. The national community had not been absorbed into the 'village community' but the invitation had been made, the allure of the centre proved highly tempting and involvement generated both tensions and disappointments. But, if the hopes of the national community were unrealistic and, ultimately, unrequited, the importance of PES for grant negotiations remained a constant. Indeed, the impact of PES on local government was to become more immediate and direct.

Origins and establishment
Against this backcloth, it is now possible to examine the four accounts of the origins and establishment of the CCLGF.

The Crosland meetings   Until 1974, with the exception of the RSG statutory meeting, regular consultation and negotiation between central and local government was the domain of local authority officers and civil servants. Politicians from individual local authorities and the associations met ministers, but only on an *ad hoc* basis. In 1974 Mr Crosland was appointed Secretary of State for the Environment. At this time confidential, 'off the record' quarterly meetings were held between the secretaries of the associations and the permanent secretary at the DoE. Mr Crosland thought that there was a gulf between himself and the associations, particularly at the political level; therefore, in July 1974 he instituted a series of meetings with their senior politicians and secretaries.

The meetings were informal – often over lunch – with a limited number of participants and an unspecified agenda. In the words of one association secretary, the meetings amounted to little more than 'pleasant chats'.[11] Nevertheless, these meetings achieved the objective of 'breaking the ice' and bridging the political gulf between central and local government; at least one senior member has said that he preferred these meetings to the later meetings of the consultative council, which were more structured, more formal and larger – 'now you need the Albert Hall for a meeting of the Consultative Council'.[12] Some association participants, however, thought that the meetings with Mr Crosland were insufficiently structured and that something else was needed.[13] Within ten months of the first meeting, the CCLGF's creation was announced. Informing the associations' chairmen by letter on 11 April 1975, Mr Crosland proposed that the council should be set up on a formal and regular basis, continuing the 'exchanges between Local Authority leaders and Government Ministers [which] have developed over the past year'.[14] Although the Crosland meetings were not the origins of the CCLGF, they influenced the general climate of discussion concerning the problems of local government finance and may explain the receptiveness to the CCLGF of both the DoE and the associations.[15]

The Layfield Committee   The Layfield Committee of Inquiry into Local Government Finance was announced by Mr Crosland on 27 June 1974 with terms of reference 'to review the whole system of local government finance in England, Scotland and Wales, and to make recommendations' (Layfield Committee, 1976, p. iii). The inquiry was the first major comprehensive review of local government finance for over half a century (since the Kempe Committee on Local Taxation in 1911–14) and was established against a background of 'crisis in local government finance that ... was serious and complex, [and] symptomatic of lasting problems' (Layfield Committee, 1976, p. xxiii).

The Layfield Committee produced a wide-ranging report but of prime concern here are its deliberations on a forum similar to the CCLGF. In evidence to Layfield two of the three main associations declared a need for a body similar to the later-established council. The ADC called for a 'standing committee of local government service Ministers and representatives of the Local Authority Associations' (ADC, 1976, p. 110), while the AMA argued for a 'free inter-change of views between government ministers and representative local authority members', which might require the setting up of consultative machinery (AMA, 1976, p. 269). Taylor (1979, p. 11) reports that these ideas became familiar to central departments through the civil servants who appeared as witnesses to the Layfield Committee.

The Layfield Committee considered various proposals, none of which was identical to the CCLGF as it later emerged. In December 1974 a discussion paper entitled 'New procedures and new institutions for expenditure control' noted that:

> It could be argued that there is a case for an ongoing review body to appraise the continuing relationship between central and local government ... Such a review body would also take account of such other issues as Rate Support Grant negotiations.[16]

The following month, three options were discussed. The first option was a formal, continuing consultative and negotiating body composed of central and local government representatives. Its remit would cover RSG and other matters of joint concern – for example, local government's request to participate in PES, and the operation of multiple regression analysis for grant distribution. Through such a body local government would be offered the opportunity to be involved in formulating government policy on public expenditure. The second option was an independent review body to continue the work of the Layfield Committee and prepare annual reports reviewing central–local relations. Finally, they considered a body with the combined responsibility of the first and second above, with its agreed findings binding on both central and local government.[17]

Little was done to elaborate these proposals before the Chancellor of the Exchequer, Denis Healey, announced the government's intention to establish the CCLGF in his budget speech of 15 April 1975. Following this announcement, the Layfield Committee continued work on the 'forum', though clearly under the shadow of the new council:

> Although there were arguments for a new and completely independent institution to stand between central and local government in financial matters ... the group recognised that such a recommendation would be impracticable now that the Consultative Council had been established. The Committee should concentrate on strengthening the independence and authority of the Consultative Council's secretariat.[18]

The discussions on the forum continued in the Layfield Committee at least until October 1975, and a number of preferences were recorded. The forum's role would be that of a mutual advisory body, exchanging information, plans and priorities between central and local government to increase mutual understanding. It would be composed of ministers and the political leaders of the associations. Layfield's proposals, which differed from the (now established) council, included a strong independent secretariat, and the appointment of the Treasury as the sponsor and chair, recognizing its actual role in the determination of grant levels. The Layfield Committee's recommendations, which were regarded as a critique of the CCLGF rather than an extension of it,[19] were for a forum that would develop out of the CCLGF.

It is evident that the CCLGF did not originate in the deliberations of the Layfield Committee, although the committee's analysis heightened awareness of the problems of central–local relations in general and the finances of local government in particular. Indeed the forum proposals contained in the report of 1976 were opposed by central and local government, both preferring to continue and develop the council. Nevertheless, the evidence received by the committee may, as with the Crosland meetings, have provided some additional impetus towards the emergence of the CCLGF.

The extension of RSG machinery   A substantial part of the CCLGF machinery in 1975 had been in existence for a number of years and for some participants the CCLGF was merely an extension and a consolidation of the existing RSG machinery.[20] As one AMA financial adviser put it 'I don't think the machinery for RSG and all the other things changed wildly when the Consultative Council came in; it just put on top of the existing machinery two more bodies'[21] – namely the official steering group and the consultative council itself (see below).

Of the machinery comprising the CCLGF, the forecasting subgroups (responsible for joint forecasting of service estimates), the grants working group (concerned with grant distribution) and the statutory meeting with ministers all predate the CCLGF, as do a number of other working groups, for example on local government financial statistics. Much of the expansion of the RSG machinery occurred in 1970 and 1971, and the establishment of the CCLGF can be seen as an attempt to rationalize this disparate machinery in a comprehensive framework under more effective political direction. This view of the origins of the council does not explain, however, why such consolidation occurred at a particular time, or the source of the impetus for consolidation. For such explanations it is necessary to consider the fourth account of the council's origins.

The Treasury and the economic context This fourth, and usually vague, account (amounting to suspicion on the part of some local government representatives) sees the CCLGF as a creation of Treasury civil servants. From interviews conducted with senior Treasury and DoE officials of the mid-1970s, this account has been corroborated. However, it cannot be separated from the changing economic context of those years.

According to the architect of the council, a senior Treasury official, the seeds of the consultative council lay in the Heath government's economic policies and their consequences. It is important to sketch briefly *the perceptions of the Treasury officials at that time* to understand why a body like the council was thought to be necessary, and what it was hoped to achieve.

The Heath government of 1970 was elected with a mandate to cut public expenditure; it was noted that local government expenditure accounted for about 30 per cent of total public expenditure and over 50 per cent of its total growth. Restrictions on growth were implemented, but within a year the economy had begun to slump, with unemployment rising to 1 million. The government responded in mid-1971 with an increase in public expenditure, which had no effect on the level of unemployment, and then embarked on a policy of rapid reflation. For the Treasury a particularly worrying consequence of this reflation was the growth rate of local government spending: some services grew at rates of up to 10 per cent per annum, and over 5 per cent in real terms as a whole, compared with the small (2–3 per cent) growth rate of the national economy. Indeed, the increase in local government expenditure was equivalent to the entire DHSS budget, and, even when unemployment began to fall, local government expenditure continued to increase.

The architect of the CCLGF was, at this time, responsible for the PES system. He thought it was important to restrain the growth of local authority spending and, originally, restraint was to be achieved through the RSG negotiations and the use of loan sanction to control borrowing. But the sharp increase in inflation in 1972/3 made the PES target figures unattainable. Local government was also experiencing difficulty: personal social services, for example, had been encouraged to spend in the period of reflation and now were asked to cut back almost simultaneously. Reduced growth rates were reflected in PES figures and in central grant but local authorities, faced with high rates of inflation, made up any shortfall in grant by increasing rates, contrary to the government's counter-inflation policy. Central government's incompatible demands on local government were unpopular and unsettling, as the Layfield Committee (1976, p. 10) discovered:

The government was strongly criticised for a contradictory attitude, especially in recent years. On the one hand some government departments urged local authorities to develop and expand their services. Legislation was promoted, circulars were published and loan sanctions were granted, all designed to encourage expansion or improvement. Simultaneously, other branches of government were urging that local expenditure should be restrained and economy practised.

In short, public expenditure in general, and local government expenditure in particular, was rising much faster than GNP. By 1974/5 a substantial discrepancy was apparent in the government's planned expenditure:

> The discrepancy of several billions of pounds between the outturn for 1974/5 and that forecasted for that year in the Public Expenditure Survey of November 1971 came to light in a recent inquiry conducted by the Select Committee on Expenditure. The 'missing billions', as they became known, were the subject of debate in the House of Commons, and both there and outside in the press were seen as proof that public expenditure was out of control. (Wright, 1977, p. 148)

For the Treasury, which was attempting to control public expenditure, the 'situation was impossible'.[22] The contradictory advice proffered by central government was exacerbated by the lack of accountability at both levels of government. In the autumn of 1974 an attempt was made to control local capital expenditure by introducing 'cash limits', which set a prescribed limit on capital programmes. This method left the bulk of current expenditure (for example, wages) unaffected. Accordingly a new political initiative was required to convince *both* central spending departments and local government representatives – particularly the local politicians – of the severity of national economic problems and the need for restraint in local expenditure. But this 'had to be done by agreement';[23] the government simply did not have the powers to enforce its expenditure plans when faced with unconvinced local governments; nor did it feel that statutory controls would be the most effective way of dealing with the situation:

> I think the way we have our greatest successes is when we settle down and face the problem and try to understand it, with the two parties, or more parties if there are any, and on that basis to decide what is a prudent course and then to follow it ... I do not think we gain necessarily by having somebody imposing a settlement in the end, as the agreed method of procedure, as the law. (H.M. Treasury, 1976, pp. 301–2)

Against this backcloth, in autumn 1974, an internal memorandum – proposing new consultative machinery, with details of the objectives, membership and frequency of meetings – was discussed at permanent secretary level within the Treasury. This memorandum concluded that there were no existing satisfactory arrangements for discussing local government finance and the case for reform and new consultative machinery was quickly accepted within the Treasury. The matter was then discussed by a high-level interdepartmental group composed of the Treasury and the large spending departments in an *ad hoc* informal meeting. The group welcomed the idea, and the DoE in particular was most receptive.[24] The council was publicly announced in April the following year, a matter of six months or so after its conception.

From interviews with the architects of the council, a number of important points can be made about its origin and intended role. First, the Crosland meetings were not regarded by the Treasury officials as explaining the DoE's receptiveness to the proposals. The council was seen as a much more serious form of consultation, with extensive ramifications for the whole of central–local relations. Second, the Layfield Inquiry did not impinge on Treasury deliberations about a consultative council. Third, the associations played no part in the initiative – they were simply informed of the government's decision. Responsibility for local government lay with the DoE and other spending departments. The Treasury had no direct contact with the associations and did not wish to 'invade' the territories of other central departments. The DoE was the 'lead department' through which contact was made with the associations and, therefore, no approach could be made to consult the associations until the Treasury had secured the DoE's agreement. Moreover, the Treasury was keen to reinforce the 'lead' position of the DoE because its proposal was *not* directed solely at local government. An equally important objective was to counter the departmentalism of central government and prevent it 'speaking with two voices'. A clear understanding that the DoE was the 'lead department' was necessary to establish a coherent pattern of *central* responsibility. Fourth, the CCLGF was more than the consolidation of existing RSG machinery. The council itself was a *political* forum at which, for the first time, local politicians could meet *all* ministers responsible for local government services. Finally, the origins and objectives of the consultative council were inextricably linked with the problem of national economic management. The objective was to create an atmosphere of consultation and cooperation. The Treasury saw the new machinery as a way of involving local government in the public expenditure survey by explaining the national economic situation to local government and central departments alike and by working out the feasibility and consequences of economic adjustments. It was a means for winning agreement on cuts in public expenditure. There seems little doubt that all sides were seeking genuine consultation and a joint approach to solving mutual fiscal problems.

Reactions
After the acceptance of the council proposal by senior DoE officials and the secretary of state, the associations were consulted. The proposal was well received. In his letter to the association chairmen, Mr Crosland said that 'It would not of course be our intention to disturb the very necessary and continuing contacts between the Associations and central departments on a wide range of major issues'.[25] Four days later, on 15 April 1975, the creation of the CCLGF was announced by the Chancellor, Denis Healey, in his budget speech. Calling for cuts of £1,000 million in public expenditure, the Chancellor felt it was imperative that local authorities should have 'closer guidance and help from ministers'. The consultative council would facilitate the provision of such help 'on all matters of policy affecting local authorities which have major financial implications'. Thus:

> Through this new machinery central and local government should establish a closer mutual understanding of the constraints under which they have to operate. Each will be able to contribute, more directly and effectively than before, to the difficult but urgent policy decisions which will be necessary;

The day after the official announcement, the *AMA News* 'strongly welcomed' the proposal, as did the ACC. More cautiously the ADC opined that the council:

> Could become the vehicle for . . . partnership if it is allowed to grow beyond what, to the cynical at least, would appear to be a Treasury instrument to reduce and control more stringently local government expenditure with the apparent cooperation of the local authorities. (Marshall, 1975, p. 293)

Guarded optimism was the general theme in the local government press:

> The top level Consultative Council of Ministers and local government representatives is presented as a means of securing closer control of local expenditure – as though this was not fairly tight already; – all the same it may prove a convenient piece of machinery for discussing rate support grant and other central/local government financial matters.
> It will be welcome if it provides genuine consultation in which the

views of local government are given due weight, but not if it proves to be no more than an institution for noting what it says and then ignoring it. (*Local Government Chronicle*, 18 April 1975, p. 371)

One notable warning to local government came from Arthur Jones MP, who, both in the Commons and in a letter to the AMA, cautioned:

I cannot envisage a sensible relationship between the government and local authorities in a Consultative Council. The power lies with the Government. It is not fair to expect local authorities to join with the Government and take decisions which will be at their expense ...

Whenever were local government organisations listened to on the rate support grant settlement? It is not a dialogue. They are called in and told what the rate support grant will be.

To try now to shift this responsibility that central government must have for local authorities is a clever trick. Trying to suggest that local government should be instrumental in curtailing its own expenditure is the very negation of what local government is about.[26]

The internal AMA reaction to this warning is particularly interesting, and throws light on subsequent behaviour by the associations: 'There is some truth in what A. J. says *but can we see any better alternative*?'

This comment is a good summary of the position of the associations. Only a year after reorganization, they did not have the resources, unity or plans to initiate an alternative. They were under considerable central government pressure to reduce the rate of growth of local expenditure and were under no illusions about the consequences of repeated overspending, as the Treasury (1976, p. 327) evidence to Layfield made abundantly clear:

Through consultation and persuasion effectively done I hope we could get effective control. If we did not get effective control we could not remain in the position where there was not effective control, and therefore other measures would have to be considered.

Central government's offer of consultation therefore seemed to offer local government the most sensible way forward, especially when Whitehall estimates of local authority expenditure predicted that it would exceed the target by 4½ per cent. This excess caused the *Financial Times* (7 May 1975) to comment that 'the case for more effective central control over local government is now overwhelming'. Quite clearly, the national community of local government accepted this assessment. As an ACC secretary pointed out, it is 'a tradition that the Associations consistently, with any Government, accept the national position and do not argue'.[27] Such shared assumptions undoubtedly facilitated the arrival of the CCLGF. It is also relevant to note that involvement with central decision-makers does have a seductive appeal for local government, although it is nigh impossible to assess the importance of this factor in the acceptance of the CCLGF.

It was with a mixture of optimism and reservations that the associations attended the first consultative council meeting on 12 May 1975 to discuss its constitution and organization. Following the first meeting both sides expressed approval at the progress. Sir Robert Thomas (chairman, AMA) commented that 'the amount of cooperation was very surprising. Whitehall has opened its doors to us', and Mr Crosland was similarly pleased

> by the clear recognition by the local authority members of the Council of the gravity of the country's economic position and of the obligation on local authorities to play their full part in the Government's measures for dealing with it.[28]

Some reservations were expressed after the first meeting – the AMA's policy committee was concerned, for example, with 'ensuring that the council should not merely be a government-oriented consulting machine'[29] – but most of the problems encountered in the initial meetings concerned the right to attend and secrecy. Local government's fears were also lessened by the (obstensibly) new opportunities for involvement in the PES and those macro-economic decisions affecting local government. In his speech to CIPFA's annual conference, the Chief Secretary to the Treasury, Joel Barnett, said that he regarded the creation of the consultative council as the single most important development in central–local relations of recent years. He went on to say:

> ... we are seeking ... a greater sense of shared responsibility for the development of local government policies and their claim on the nation's resources ... central government must explain to the local authorities and their representatives the economic reasoning underlying its public expenditure plans and the nature of the competing claims on resources from the rest of the public sector, the private sector and the balance of payments ... Shared responsibility also means a greater degree of participation by local government at the formative stages of the public expenditure planning process and when individual proposals for new policies are being shaped.
>   ... What is required and what we are determined to create in the

Consultative Council is a confident and effective instrument of our common interests.[30]

Whether or not these hopes were to be realized remains to be seen.

THE EVOLUTION OF THE CCLGF

By far the most important and demanding work for the CCLGF in time and resources is, and always has been, the negotiations on the rate support grant. From much more humble beginnings in 1966, the RSG negotiations now represent the greatest demand on the associations:

> Negotiations with central government and with other outside bodies on behalf of all their member authorities is the most important function of the Associations. These negotiations obviously include the discussions on the level of local government expenditure and the rate support grant. The negotiations have almost become an industry.[31]

Certainly the CCLGF is regarded as part of this industry and its establishment in 1975 both encompassed previous RSG negotiating machinery and routinized it. Of course, the council's work encompassed more than grant negotiations (see Figures 4.1 and 4.2); but this section focuses on this most important of all its functions.

A Qualified Success : the CCLGF 1974–9
The architects of the CCLGF thought that it would encourage local government to participate, albeit in a limited way, in the allocation of resources and that it would ensure their co-operation by explaining why restraint was necessary. The purpose of the council was to control public expenditure but the style was to change from bargaining, which imposed little or no responsibility upon local government, to incorporation, which, it was hoped, would oblige local government to honour its agreements. Until the beginning of this new era, central government's style largely reflected the 'stop-go' features of the national economy, oscillating between consultation in times of growth, and ineffective dictation in the slump years. No structured system could be said to have evolved in the period from 1966 to 1975, but rather a series of pragmatic and often contradictory actions and reactions in the face of a changing economy.

The terms of reference which were discussed and agreed at the first consultative council meeting were deliberately general and wide ranging. Its purpose was the promotion of

> regular consultation and co-operation between central and local government on major financial and economic issues of common

concern, with special emphasis on the deployment of resources both in the long term and the short term. In this way local government can be associated with the process of settling priorities for the whole of the five-year public expenditure period and local government would be consulted at an early stage when individual proposals for new policies directly involving local government are being shaped.

Further, the council should be concerned with:

the general economic outlook, the level of local authorities spending in the short, medium and long terms, the broad balance between the main local services, developments in policy with major financial implications – including both changes in the management of the economy likely to affect local authorities generally and major alterations of policy for particular services – and the financing of the activities of local government. It is not intended that the Council should affect the existing relationship between departments and local government under which policy issues of concern to individual departments are discussed directly between that department and local government.[32]

After three meetings of the council a DoE paper was introduced reviewing the nature of business to be discussed by the council. The paper noted that although certain items for discussion had been wide-ranging, for example the general items on local authority expenditure, nevertheless, other items had been far more specific, for example 'Control of Pollution Act 1974 – implementation of part I'. The DoE noted that:

The general effectiveness of the Council will inevitably become blunted unless it confines its attention to matters of major import-ance which cannot be dealt with through other existing channels.[33]

It was suggested, therefore, that items considered for discussion should fall under one of two headings: 'strategic matters' and 'depart-mental/tactical matters'. The council was to focus on those matters with financial implications for all or many local authorities, or where consultation between central and local government goes beyond a single department or association. Quite clearly, the council's remit was to extend far beyond grant negotiation *per se*.

The structure of the CCLGF at this time is shown in Figure 4.1 and it is clear that the greatest proportion of working groups predate the CCLGF. The most important additions, excluding the council itself, were the official steering group (OSG) and the joint manpower watch group.

The former was the official committee, paralleling the council,

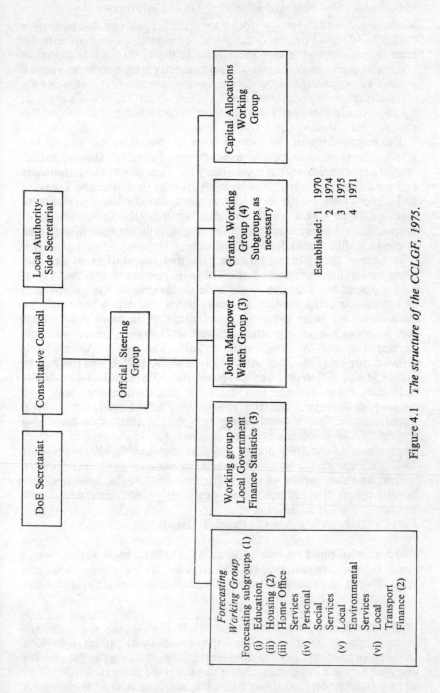

Figure 4.1 *The structure of the CCLGF, 1975.*

DoE Secretariat

Consultative Council

Local Authority-Side Secretariat

Official Steering Group

Working group on Local Government Finance Statistics (3)

Joint Manpower Watch Group (3)

Grants Working Group (4) Subgroups as necessary

Capital Allocations Working Group

Forecasting Working Group
Forecasting subgroups (1)
(i) Education
(ii) Housing (2)
(iii) Home Office Services
(iv) Personal Social Services
(v) Local Environmental Services
(vi) Local Transport Finance (2)

Established: 1   1970
              2   1974
              3   1975
              4   1971

which acted as the clearing house for the CCLGF agenda, preparing background and briefing documents. The decision to establish the joint manpower watch was announced in the 1975/6 RSG settlement and the objective was to review local authority staff numbers to guard against any expansion beyond inescapable commitments. It was subsequently consolidated into the CCLGF structure (see Chapter 5, below). And in these early days both sides had a secretariat serving the council and its groups.

The composition of the council from its inception reflected its key role in the control of public expenditure. Table 4.1 shows that all central departments with responsibility for local services sent ministers and senior civil servants. Most notably, for the first time, the Treasury had direct contact with local government. On the local government side (see Table 4.2), the most notable feature is the sheer number of representatives present at council meetings, reflecting the diversity of interests within the national community.

In spite of the changes, however, the first round of grant negotiations under the auspices of the CCLGF continued the pattern of earlier years. In 1975, there was little disagreement, the main bones of contention being the levels of cash limits and expenditure targets. Both sides were eager to take full advantage of the new opportunities for co-operation and mutual influence. However, there was one development of key significance in 1975. The White Paper *Public Expenditure to 1978–79* (Cmnd 5879, HMSO, 1975a) was the first to reconcile the different price bases of the PES and local authority estimates: thereafter the link between RSG settlements and PES became more direct; and the government issued guidance to local authorities on their expenditure plans. Within three months of this settlement the associations were pressing for the promised greater involvement in the PES procedure. The inescapable conclusion was that *local* expenditure was now part of the *national* public expenditure process and that greater involvement with PES was at least one way of attempting to influence the decisions which determined the outcome of grant negotiations.

In December 1975, Mr Crosland declared:

> We want to build on this advance by involving local authorities in our expenditure planning for future years, so that the previous gap in thinking and planning between central and local government can be narrowed still further. [34]

In the same month, the newly appointed local-authority-side secretary to the council, after consulting the associations' secretariats and advisers, drafted a paper for the associations outlining the reasons for involvement and suggesting that the matter be discussed quickly to allow participation in the formative stages of the next PES review. A

Table 4.1 *Consultative Council Statutory Meetings 1975–80 by Departments and Status of Representative*

	1975		1976		1977		1978		1979		1980	
	M	CS	M	CS	M	CS	M	CS	M	CS	M	CS
Dept of Environment	2	8	3	6	3	11	3	7	4	10	4	8
Dept of Education and Science	1	1	2	2	2	2	1	2	1	1	1	1
Dept of Health and Social Security	1	1	1	1	1	2	2	2	1	2	0	1
Treasury	1	1	1	1	1	1	1	1	1	1	1	1
Home Office	0	2	0	1	1	2	0	2	1	1	1	1
Welsh Office[a]	0	1	1	1	1	0	1	2	1	1	—	—
Dept of Transport	—	—	1	2	1	2	1	2	1	2	1	2
Dept of Prices and Consumer Affairs	—	—	1	1	0	1	0	1	0	—	—	—
Dept of Employment	—	—	1	1	1	2	0	1	1	1	0	1
Dept of Trade	—	—	—	—	—	—	—	1	1	0	—	—
Office of Arts and Libraries	—	—	—	—	—	—	—	—	0	1	—	—
Totals	5	14	11	16	11	23	9	21	12	20	8	14
Total central government	19		27		34		30		32		22	

[a] Welsh RSG now the responsibility of the Welsh CCLGF.

Table 4.2 *Consultative Council Statutory Meetings 1975–80 by Association and Status of Representative*

Association	1975			1976			1977			1978			1979			1980[b]		
	P	S	A	P	S	A	P	S	A	P	S	A	P	S	A	P	S	A
ACC	7	1	2	7	2	2	7	2	2	6	2	2	7	2	2	7	2	2
AMA	3	2	2	3	2	3	3	3	3	3	3	4	3	2	2	3	1	1
ADC	7	1	1	5	1	1	6	2	1	6	2	1	6	2	2	7	1	2
LBA	2	1	1	2	1	1	2	1	1	2	2	0	2	2	0	2	2	1
GLC	1	1	1	1	0	1	1	1	1	1	1	1	1	1	1	1	0	1
Totals	20	6	7	18	6	8	19	9	8	18	10	8	19	9	7	20	6	7
Total local government	33			32			36			36			35			33		

[b] Welsh RSG now the responsibility of the Welsh CCLGF.

Key to Tables 4.2 and 4.3
P   Politician
S   Secretariat
A   Adviser

Sources: Joint Association Reports on rate support grant negotiations, 1975–80.

draft paper for the official steering group was then circulated to the associations on 12 January 1976. Although no specific procedures were proposed, the paper asked the OSG to put the matter to the full consultative council, and outlined the case for local government involvement. It noted that 'the broad levels of expenditure on which the 1976/7 grant settlement is based were predetermined by Cmnd 5879 and the subsequent Budget reductions which local government had little opportunity to influence'; that the work of the expenditure forecasting subgroups was constrained by the White Paper figures; and that in order to prevent a widening gulf between central and local government the relationship 'would be assisted if local government were to make a contribution to the 1976 public expenditure review in its formative stages'. This paper also noted a number of reasons why local government involvement would be beneficial to both parties:

  (i)   local government accounts for around a quarter of annual total public expenditure;
  (ii) it would help to win the confidence and support of local authorities in pursuing national policies for local services;
  (iii) it would increase the efficiency and effectiveness of managing limited national resources for common objectives;
  (iv) central government needs local government information to improve the reliability of its forecasts;
  (v)   local government, as the implementor of government policies, is best able to judge their effectiveness;
  (vi) for local government, reconciliation of PES and RSG figures would assist in dispelling the widespread confusion about White Paper figures;
  (vii) local government would be assisted in preparation of their long term programmes.[35]

The paper was well received by the associations and, after minor amendments, submitted to the OSG, on 28 January 1976, where it was 'warmly welcomed', although the central departments had some reservations on details.

At this stage the associations were pressing for full and extensive involvement, making PES a joint exercise, and were encouraged when their revised paper was considered by the consultative council, under the new secretary of state, Peter Shore, on 12 April 1976. The government expressed sympathy with local government's objectives. It agreed that the 1975 settlement was a product of the decisions embodied in the previous White Paper and, as a result, PES had not benefited from local government's views on forward planning. The separation of PES and RSG negotiations was not conducive to local authorities keeping in line with government plans, nor for promoting a partnership between central and local government. Consequently, the council agreed to establish six new high-level steering groups (see Figure 4.2), which the associations regarded as an input to PES, discussing policy implications for local services over the years of the PES period. In the council, the associations would be able to express their views on relative priorities between services and on the total level of local expenditure. For its part, the government would seek to give a commitment on the acceptable level of local authority expenditure for more than a single year ahead. These arrangements were designed to allow local government to convey their full range of views to ministers before Cabinet reached its final decisions on public expenditure in the autumn.

The function of the subgroups remained basically the same, namely, to identify the trends in and to forecast the effects of present policies. The purpose of the steering groups, however, was to assess the implications of the subgroup forecasts. Their membership includes the negotiating spokesmen and service advisers from local government and the relevant government department, supported by key members of the subgroups. Thus, the subgroups assess the implications of containing expenditure on each service within PES White Paper figures whilst the steering groups use this information to identify the policy implications for services of adhering to White Paper targets.[36] The new steering groups began their work almost immediately – the first group (for personal social services) held its meeting only eight days after the consultative council meeting which established the new structure. Meanwhile, the associations were encouraged by the recruitment of the former principal finance officer of the DoE as secretary to the AMA in April 1976: he was strongly in favour of local authority involvement in PES.[37] An early review of the CCLGF by the AMA in November 1975 noted that 'there is a manifest need for machinery of a formal kind between central and local government and the series of meetings already held have certainly helped local government to express comprehensive views'.[38] If the style of negotiation was changing, the outcomes showed great similarity to earlier rounds. The relevant expenditure total accepted in the settlement was based on the totals contained in the 1975 White Paper (Cmnd 5879) as amended by the April budget. A 'standstill' was imposed on current expenditure, backed by cash limits on increase orders. Further, the proportion of relevant expenditure funded by the centre was reduced by 1 per cent (a loss of some £100 million). Nevertheless, the settlement was regarded by the associations as 'good in parts' and as providing the basis for greater involvement and co-operation in the future.

However, 1976 marked not only the beginning of a spirit of partnership in PES but also its end. Central government policies for managing the economy required a loan from the International Monetary Fund (IMF), which imposed restrictions on public expenditure. With hindsight many of the participants in the CCLGF regarded the IMF's

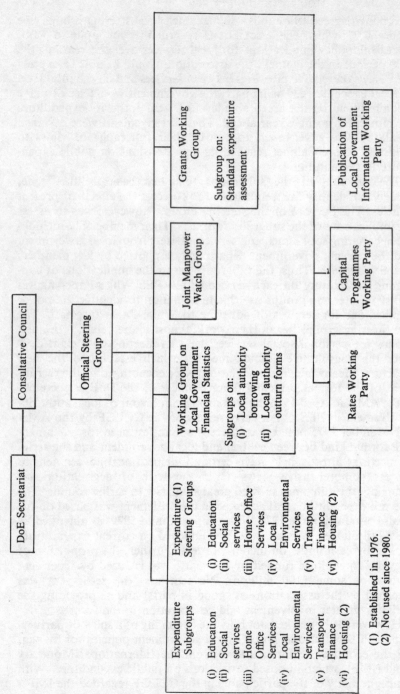

Figure 4.2 *The Structure of the CCLGF, 1980.*

Consultative Council

DoE Secretariat

Official Steering Group

Grants Working Group

Subgroup on:
Standard expenditure assessment

Joint Manpower Watch Group

Working Group on Local Government Financial Statistics

Subgroups on:
(i) Local authority borrowing
(ii) Local authority outturn forms

Expenditure (1) Steering Groups

(i) Education
(ii) Social services
(iii) Home Office Services
(iv) Local Environmental Services
(v) Transport Finance
(vi) Housing (2)

Expenditure Subgroups

(i) Education
(ii) Social services
(iii) Home Office Services
(iv) Local Environmental Services
(v) Transport Finance
(vi) Housing (2)

(1) Established in 1976.
(2) Not used since 1980.

Publication of Local Government Information Working Party

Capital Programmes Working Party

Rates Working Party

intervention as a turning point in central control of local expenditure. Local government involvement in PES was to be severely reduced from its already limited level and the next round of negotiations were to provide an exacting test for the CCLGF.

The 1976 settlement was made in the context of an 'extremely grave economic situation' and 'no settlement in the present economic situation can be anything but severe'.[39] The negotiations were notable in four ways: first, the reduction in the extent and scope of negotiations in determining the level of settlement; second, the increasing disagreement between the two levels of government over the details of the settlement and negotiating procedures; third, the growing dissension between the associations; and, finally, the rapid disillusionment of the associations with their involvement in PES.

As in the previous round, the outcome was substantially influenced by the PES conclusions. The White Paper *Public Expenditure to 1978/80* (Cmnd 6393, HMSO, 1976a), published in February 1976, announced the government's intention to reduce local government's total expenditure by 1½ per cent in both 1977/8 and 1978/9, and the reduction would be even greater if spending for 1976/7 exceeded the approved ceiling. In May 1976 this outcome looked likely, with estimates suggesting a £417 million overspend. The associations were clearly on the defensive, and a letter from the AMA secretary to the other associations, analysing the predicted overspend, noted resignedly that the forthcoming consultative council meeting would be a forum for the government to 'say what their action will be . . . we shall have no choice but to accept the Government's action'.[40] The letter also called for unity among the associations after the ACC had blamed London and other metropolitan authorities for the overspend. The government's action took the form of Circular 45/76, issued on 27 May, asking for revised budgetary estimates, and noting that

> The Government will assume that any excess resources authorities will receive in 1976/77 above that necessary to finance expenditure in accordance with the Public Expenditure White Paper (Cmnd 6393) figures has been put to balances and so will be available to finance expenditure in 1977/78. These additional sources of revenue will be fully taken into account in setting the level of grant for 1977/78.

The ACC and AMA, in particular, strongly objected to this circular claiming that it had not been discussed in the consultative council. The DoE, in reply, claimed that the issue had received some attention, albeit not exhaustive, and rejected the objections.

The associations recommended that their members co-operate with the government's circular. The revised estimates still showed a £243 million overspend beyond Cmnd 6393 levels and the government regarded this figure as too high. It seemed essential, therefore, for the associations to maintain unity, but hostility between them was increasing, particularly in the grants working group. A local authority side pre-meeting of the GWG noted 'that increasing differences of viewpoint between the Associations might lead the DoE to impose solutions and disband the Working Group'. [41] In particular the ACC and to a lesser extent the ADC were increasingly bitter about London's increasing share of grant. Because of its high rateable values, London can maintain a particular level of expenditure at a lower rate level than the rest of the country. Accordingly, the grant to London is reduced to correct for this advantage – a procedure known as 'clawback'. The ACC wanted to increase 'clawback'. For their part, the LBA were 'unhappy about too much dirty linen being washed in front of the Treasury' – and concerned that this bitterness 'might harm the negotiating position for local government as a whole'. As a counterattack the LBA suggested an attack on Wales and its higher subsidy for domestic ratepayers as 'tactics for dividing the ACC and ADC' and 'as a diversion to embarrass the ACC'. [42] But even within the AMA the issue of 'clawback' was contentious. The GLC and LBA were opposed to 'clawback' in principle, but the metropolitan districts outside London would suffer reductions in grant if this redistribution of resources was abandoned. The metropolitan districts were in favour of 'clawback', therefore, and indeed would have preferred it to be increased. A letter to the AMA secretary from an adviser noted: '. . . our desire for unity in the AMA may be reaching a stage where loyalty is being strained'. [43] 'Clawback' was, however, only one issue. The associations were also divided on, for example, the methods used for assessing the need to spend of local authorities, the indicators used for measuring this need, the distribution of the needs element, and the extent to which the technical means employed to distribute grant should be allowed to generate marked fluctuations in the actual grant income of individual local authorities. The GWG were unable to agree on a recommendation for grant distribution for 1977/8. In such circumstances, it was easy for central government to impose its own preferences. Indeed, although central government is frequently accused of using a 'divide and rule' tactic against the local government side, it is infrequently necessary either because the associations are rarely united or because the government can impose policies even when the associations are united.

The size of local government's overspend remained a matter of contention between the two levels of government. At the 27 July 1976 meeting of the consultative council, the secretary of state suggested a further £100 million saving in current and capital expenditure. Two days later the associations informed the DoE that they saw no scope for such savings on current expenditure and could not provide information on savings in capital expenditure. The associations felt that the whole issue was based on a misunderstanding. Central government's calculations about the scale of overspending were based on *estimates* of the previous year's expenditure. But this estimate was £100 million below actual expenditure. If actual expenditure formed the basis of the government's calculations the overspend was reduced to £150 million or 2 per cent. Further, £40 million of this overspend was on the police service at the government's request. The associations concluded, therefore, that there was no overspend or, if the predicted remaining £110 million overspend proved accurate, it was merely 1 per cent above target – a margin of error rarely achieved by central government.

The DoE were not impressed. They replied on 30 July stating:

> The overspend must be recovered. But the recovery can be spread over two years. What is not recovered in 1976/77 can – and will – be recovered in 1977/78.[44]

The method of recovery, however, was still not clear. One method was discussed in the local transport finance Steering Group, where it was reported that:

> the Minister was prepared, if necessary, to withdraw transport supplementary grant and to cancel the grant of key sector loan sanction in cases where individual authorities did not achieve the reduced level.[45]

A further circular was issued on 26 August specifying the cuts in capital expenditure of £50 million requested by the Chancellor on 22 July, and reducing the increase order by £50 million[46] The associations strongly criticized the circular for its lack of clarity and ambiguity – a view apparently shared by its authors. The local authority side secretary to the CCLGF wrote to the association secretaries on the circular, stating that:

> DoE officials are clearly embarrassed by their inability to give clear, helpful and positive advice to authorities at this crucial stage of the year before authorities get into detailed budget preparations for 1977/78. Informally they acknowledge first the near impossibility of achieving a reduction of some 3½% in the level of current spending from such an insecure starting point and second that Ministers by attempting to keep their options open until November on the total and distribution of RSG will lose even more of what chance remains to control the situation.[47]

Ironically, the outturn figures for the year show a £203 million *underspend*, by far the largest underspend since RSG was introduced in

1966. Certainly local authority expenditure had been controlled, but the co-operative style envisaged in consultative council negotiations did not seem to be much in evidence. Nevertheless, although the two levels of government strongly disagreed over the amount of over-spend, the associations accepted that there was a grave economic situation and that local expenditure must be controlled — a consensus rarely achieved before the establishment of the CCLGF. And this 'responsibility ethic' of local government (Bramley and Stewart, 1981, p. 60) undoubtedly played a major part in achieving the reduction in expenditure.

The proposals for the 1977/8 round of RSG negotiations were circu-lated in early November 1976 after the Cabinet had reached its decisions on overall public expenditure. They called for local authorities to use £250 million from their balances (or funds set aside for unexpected increases in expenditure); they reduced the proportion of relevant expenditure upon which grant would be paid from 65·6 per cent to 61 per cent; and they proposed a cash limit of between £495 million and £597 million. Despite strong association protests these measures were announced at the statutory meeting of 22 November. As the secretary of state noted at the meeting, 'the settlement is, therefore, in accord with the government's earlier declared intentions ... The government believe that a grant rate of 61% should be a strong influence for ensuring that expenditure is kept in line with government plans while avoiding the danger of widespread excessive rises in rates'.[48]

All the association chairmen complained to Shore about the lack of consultation before the cuts were announced. In reply to one AMA politician, Shore stated:

> I am anxious to hear the view of the Associations on these ques-tions, but I must make it clear once again that the Government will have to take its decision at the end of the day in the light of its own judgements of the effect of overspend.[49]

Not only was local government dissatisfied with the 1976 settlement but they were also disillusioned about their involvement in PES. An ACC adviser to the official steering group noted that the main con-straints on local government involvement in PES had been lack of time, lack of information and insufficient explanation of policies in the White Paper.[50] The local government side secretary to the council also noted that, as Layfield had advocated, there had been local government involvement in PES, but that 'the process in this first year has left much to be desired'. In particular he expressed dissatisfaction with the late publication of the White Paper, the preoccupation with short-term planning, the lack of access by the associations to PES working papers, and the protracted examination of the implications of the White Paper rather than joint forward planning. These deficiencies resulted in local authorities being unable to understand the meaning of the government's public expenditure plans or having time to act upon them. These problems were important because 'the economic constraints of the last few years have forced the Government to make much more explicit the relationship between public expenditure forecasts and the annual grant settlement'. The paper concluded its review of the involvement in 1976 by noting:

> Despite the concession from Government this year that the Associations should be consulted through the Consultative Council on the Cmnd 6393 figures before Ministers reached decision in the autumn on the next White Paper, the formulation of the content of the next Cmnd paper as regards local authority services remains firmly in Government hands.[51]

The same disillusion was shared by the members of the sub- and steering groups. A joint association meeting between the main negotiators and 'convenors' of these groups in October 1976 to review and discuss their work did not regard PES involvement as satisfactory. In their meeting

> it was made clear that local government had not yet achieved the involvement it considered necessary. Doubts were expressed about the validity of the amounts included in the PESC White Paper and also as to whether local government ought to disassociate itself from the whole exercise.[52]

And the limits to their involvement were made only too clear by the DoE. In its introduction to the first meeting to discuss the final reports of 1977 it noted that 'neither Ministers nor Members are of course in any way committed to the proposals which are put forward simply as a basis for discussion'.[53] At best local government's involvement in PES can be described as 'limited'.

The following two rounds of negotiations in 1977 and 1978 for the financial years 1978/9 and 1979/80 respectively were conducted in much improved economic circumstances and in the belief that local authority expenditure was now under control. The main procedures and features of negotiation were unchanged. Approved levels of relevant expenditure continued to conform with the PES White Papers, cash limits continued in accordance with the counter-inflation policies of the time, and the grant percentage remained stable at 61 per cent. Local government could expect little more, especially as the most objectionable aspects of the 1976 settlement – for example, the use of balances and reductions in increase orders – were not considered necessary. While certainly not partnership, the relationship between central and local government in RSG negotiations was 'as well as could be expected', and the settlements regarded as 'generally fair'. In other words, many of the more objectionable (to local government) means of control were a consequence of the economic crisis, and were withdrawn as the crisis receded.

Local government's involvement in PES remained limited. In 1977, the remits of the sub- and steering groups were taken from the latest White Paper, *The Government's Expenditure Plans* (Cmnd 6721, HMSO, 1977a). They were asked to assess the implications of further cuts of 2½ per cent and 5 per cent below the White Paper figures for later years. There was little scope, therefore, for the associations to influence PES even at the margins.

If the promised involvement had not materialized, it was not the only problem facing the associations in the CCLGF. First, the associations were disadvantaged in negotiations by their relative lack of resources. As the AMA secretary noted in a letter to the DoE, 'it is the representatives of Government departments who hold all the cards. You have both the staff and the detailed knowledge which we, with our limited resources, do not have.'[54] As a result:

> I don't think there is hardly anybody in a local authority association who ever initiates policy; you somehow never have time to initiate policies because you are always having to react.[55]

Whilst it is inaccurate to suggest that the associations *never* initiate policies, the comment does clearly illustrate the problems confronting them.

Second, the relationship between the associations had begun to deteriorate markedly. Conceivably, the appointment of a single, joint local government spokesman on the expenditure steering and sub-groups could have fostered co-operation but there is little evidence of any such improvement. The main rivalry was between the AMA and ACC, although these associations were often disdainful of the ADC's comments during meetings.[56] The local government view became simply the lowest common denominator of all the associations' views, and on occasion even this limited agreement was impossible.

In the opinion of the local government side secretary to the CCLGF, the inter-association disputes were the primary weakness of the consultative council. In particular, on the distribution of grant between the various types of local authority, the associations 'really tore themselves apart at times',[57] never more so than in the late 1970s. Indeed, the positions of the associations on RSG distribution were so entrenched and so well known that there was no basis for a compromise, nor could the grants working group make any recommendations from July 1978. Instead each association submitted its own views in a separate paper to the consultative council, and in the council meetings the associations came to an understanding not to discuss their positions as it would lead to embarrassing arguments in front of the ministers.

Without doubt the main cause of the disputes was the use (and consequences) of multiple regression analysis for distributing the needs element of grant. Although introduced in 1974, it was not until two years later that its effects began to cause comments. In March 1976, the ACC prepared a report for the official steering group noting the loss of needs element by the counties, despite their increase in population, and the corresponding shift of grant to the metropolitan authorities, a shift which was accentuated by the prevailing policies of financial restraint. The paper was presented to the OSG five days after initial circulation, giving the other associations little time to prepare a response. The OSG passed the paper to the CCLGF for 'noting' without discussion, recognizing that the paper's analysis was 'in some respects a partial one'.[58]

The ACC had five main objections. First, the method was based on the assumption that differences in present need could be measured by differences in past expenditure levels. But variations in expenditure have causes other than needs, including the different dispositions to spend of the political parties. Second, the whole method was too complex for all but the most expert to understand – a sentiment reiterated subsequently by Michael Heseltine:

No one in the country understands how regression analysis works. It is not defensible to have a system responsible for the allocation of billions of pounds a year under such circumstances. (*Local Government Chronicle*, 23 November 1979, p. 1245)

Third, the system was subject to a number of statistical problems and, as a result, there were dramatic fluctuations in the actual distribution of grant from one year to the next, generating large changes in grant for individual local authorities. To overcome this problem a number of techniques were used to limit year-to-year fluctuations, for example, 'freezing' the data, 'safety nets' and 'damping'.[59] All these modifications made the system more complex. Fourth, although one of the initial attractions of MRA was its 'objectivity', it quickly became apparent that there was a large subjective component and the technique was open to political manipulation. In particular, the choice of factors (or measures of need) was a political choice which was deliberately exercised by the Labour government between 1974 and 1979 to favour the urban areas at the expense of the shire counties. Fifth, the data were from the 1971 Census, which became more dated throughout the 1970s. In reply to these criticisms, the AMA/GLC/LBA argued that although the system was imperfect the 'regression analysis was the best means of needs assessment available. It required decisions to be taken on the indicators to be tested but the factors used in the distribution formula and the weights attached to them were selected on an objective basis.'[60] By 1977, ACC opposition to MRA had become total and it continued throughout the subsequent rounds of negotiations. The criticisms were both theoretical and practical, but were prompted by the loss of grant by ACC member authorities.

The AMA saw the shift of grant to their members as partially correcting the trend towards the counties of earlier years, and as reflecting the needs of urban areas. The Labour government from 1974 to 1979 was sympathetic to the AMA case, although it is impossible to assess whether or not the policy was the result of successful AMA bargaining. Faced by a totally divided local government side, the government could choose almost any distribution formula. The initiative on proposed formulae (that is, each containing different indicators of need) came from the DoE, and the exemplifications or test runs of each formula simply provided more ammunition for the associations to continue their arguments with each other. Nevertheless, the ACC's objections had some effect – hence the introduction of the various means to slow down the shift to the metropolitan authorities noted earlier (for example 'damping').[61] In addition, the government also agreed to establish a number of subgroups under the GWG to investigate other methods of needs assessment but the agreement of all the associations could not be obtained.

The growing tension between the associations also had an adverse influence on their joint activities. If the associations had limited resources, none the less they had tried to increase their capacity for servicing the grant negotiations. The ACC had recruited financial advisers from county councils on temporary secondments. Both the AMA and the ADC appointed additional, specialist staffs. The associations had also co-operated to increase their informational resources. They had appointed the local government side secretariat to the CCLGF, initially on a two-year contract renewable for a further three years. They funded CIPFA's technical support service (TSS) which provided statistical back-up and analysis for grant negotiations. But, with growing conflict, the interests of the associations demanded exclusive, not shared, technical back-up: each wanted advice specific to its own interests in the negotiations. Although the contract of the CCLGF secretariat was renewed, he subsequently left, relieving the associations of their need to abolish the post (as they would most certainly have done). No replacement was appointed. Similarly, the AMA withdrew its financial support from TSS, which effectively abolished the facility. Although there are many justifications for abandoning the joint ventures, including the need for the associations to save money in the era of 'cuts', the prime reason for these actions was the perceived need of the associations (especially the AMA) for direct line control of information and analysis. If the growing conflict between the associations did not inspire the demand for sole control of information resources, it gave the question of control added urgency and precipitated action.

Neither of these decisions was of cardinal importance but both illustrate the growing fissures within the national community – fissures which were muted in this period by Conservative control of all the associations. Certainly the Conservative-controlled AMA co-operated with the Labour government in making the 'cuts'. It is by no means certain that a Labour-controlled AMA would have had an equivalent relish for the task. The decision to adopt directive strategies by the Thatcher government may reflect, in part, their judgement that they would never enjoy equivalent support from a Labour-controlled AMA. Certainly, when conflicts arising from the interests of the different types of authority were reinforced by differences in political control, the fissures in the national community came to resemble ravines. But, before exploring the decline of the CCLGF experiment and the stresses and strains within the national community, it would be as well to specify what the CCLGF had achieved between 1975 and 1979.

The 'success' of the CCLGF and its contribution towards cutting local expenditure are not easy to discern. Some of the benefits were mixed blessings. On the one hand, improved co-ordination between central departments meant that local authorities were not subject to contradictory demands to increase expenditure on individual services whilst reducing total expenditure. On the other hand, local government's ability to negotiate individual service increases was impeded by the Treasury's improved ability to monitor departmental spending. However, there were some clear advantages. It improved the access of local government to ministers and, on occasion, allowed the associations to 'embarrass certain departmental ministers in front of the Treasury'.[62] It provided an early warning system for local government as issues and proposals were often raised initially at Council meetings: 'forewarned is forearmed'.[63] The consultative council also provided a means for local government at least to make their views known to both the Treasury and central spending departments. Any influence that the associations could exert may have affected changes only at the margin, but when the total volume is considerable, even small marginal changes can have major implications for service provision.

Perhaps its greatest contribution, however, was a symbolic one. It signalled to local government that the economic crisis was a grave one and that the government preferred a joint, co-operative approach to the problem of local expenditure. It also increased local government's awareness of the government's economic problems. But many members and officers in local government were totally unaware of the council and its deliberations. For them, 'cash limits' undoubtedly had a more important effect. Undoubtedly also, the government benefited from the simple acceptance by members and officers that the government knew what was best for the economy – local government's 'responsibility ethic'. Moreover, the mid-term swing to the Conservatives in the local elections brought into being councils more amenable to expenditure cuts than their Labour predecessors and the then Chief Secretary to the Treasury has explicitly acknowledged the beneficial effects of this shift in local control (Barnett, 1982, pp. 75–6). Nor was the Labour government reluctant to employ a wide range of controls when necessary. Thus, they issued guidance on local expenditure plans, used balances to compensate for over spending, called for revised, mid-year budgets and used the loan-sanction procedure to curtail capital expenditure as well as instituting cash limits. The council can only be seen, therefore, as a qualified success – as but a contributory factor in the reduction of local expenditure (see Table 4.3).

The council did have one significant consequence, however: it pushed the associations into prominence as the peak associations of local government. All policies of financial significance were now considered by the CCLGF and such a remit was scarcely narrow or confining. The route to government was clearly signposted: it was through the associations. The Central Policy Review Staff (1977, p. 38) had recommended that 'It would clearly be in central government's interest to help build up the status of the associations'. The advice had

Table 4.3   *Local Government Expenditure from 1975/6 to 1979/80*

		1975/6	1976/7	1977/8	1978/9	1979/80
Local Authority Expenditure[a]						
at current prices	£m	15,345	16,360	17,050	18,823	22,425
at 1975 prices	£m	14,790	13,979	13,021	12,995	13,536
percentage of GDP	%	15·5	14·3	13·1	12·8	13·2
percentage of public sector	%	31·1	30·4	29·9	28·2	28·3
Central Government Grant[b]						
at current prices	£m	8,360	9,041	9,524	10,386	11,845
at 1975 prices	£m	8,360	7,775	7,048	7,063	7,107
percentage of LA expenditure	%	63·1	59·9	58·4	56·9	54·0

Notes
[a] Capital and current expenditure, less debt interest.
[b] Current grant only, and current grant as a percentage of current expenditure.
Source: *Local Government Trends 1983* (London: CIPFA, 1984)
School for Advanced Urban Studies, *The Future of Democracy* (Bristol: SAUS, mimeo, nd).

been taken. The national community was an obvious ally in the Treasury's fight to restrain expenditure. It had no commitment to a particular service and could, at the very least, be expected to see the problems 'in the round'. The council marked, therefore, a shift of influence within local government away from the service specialists or technocrats towards financial managers and chief executives or topocrats.

This shift of influence was not limited to local government. As the AMA secretary noted:

> people get it wrong by thinking there is a national chasm between central and local government. The clash comes between our point of view and that of the Treasury, and these clashes occur within central government between the promoters of services and the controllers of finance. (*Local Government News*, November 1983, p. 3)

The Treasury as guardian of the purse strings was challenging the advocates of expenditure and the creation of the CCLGF and support for the national community were but elements of this broader strategy. Nor is this assessment produced with the benefit of hindsight. At the time it was explicitly argued that one of the benefits of the council was that it served 'to enforce a more corporate approach across Government departments in their dealings with local authorities'.[64]

The associations' new-found status was not without its problems. Involvement with the centre was one-sided. For the Treasury, the decision to establish the CCLGF contained an element of 'altruism' in its desire to engage the interest and enthusiasm of local government for macro-economic questions.[65] Similarly a DoE official described his department's attitude as 'paternalistic', claiming they tried to develop local government.[66] Above all, the associations courted the danger of co-option by the centre. Because so much of the associations' work is responsive to central government demands and initiatives, the associations' interests tend to be submerged, and, even though their staff and members are aware of the dangers of being assimilated to the appreciative system of central government, it becomes their normal environment and the sheer pressure of events dictates that the necessary accommodation is made. The distinction between a realistic response to an initiative and acceptance of the principles (if not the details) of that initiative is too fine a line to be drawn by busy administrators. It is too simple to suggest that the national community has been absorbed into the Whitehall 'village community' but it is clear that the pressures placed on the associations by successive governments caused them to speak not only for their members but also for the government. Perhaps the most distinctive feature of the appreciative system of the national community of local government is this contradictory amalgamation of national and local perspectives on local problems and interests.

If the CCLGF's contribution to the cuts in local expenditure is opaque, its defects are transparent. The associations cannot regulate their members and cannot, therefore, 'deliver' any policy. Moreover, the incorporation of the associations increased their distance from member local authorities, making the possibility of the associations representing effectively the interests of their members even more remote. Incorporation was an inherently unstable strategy based on the false premise that in talking to the national community the government was talking to local authorities. It was not, it did not and the government's own strategy ensured that it would be so. By 1979 criticisms of the council abounded but they focused on the conflicts between the associations, the size of meetings and the lateness of consultation – all of which could have been levelled at the grant system at any time in the past ten years. The inherent defects of the CCLGF were manifested, however, with the election of a new Conservative government and the problems which had so exercised participants in the CCLGF paled into insignificance.

An Unqualified Decline: the CCLGF, 1979–83

The foregoing analysis of the evolution of the CCLGF suggests that the government was more than an equal partner – particularly in times of economic trouble and when faced with divided associations. The advent of a new Conservative government and the 1979 RSG negotiations provide conclusive proof of the centre's ability to take unilateral action.

The joint association report for 1980 notes that 'negotiations on the level of expenditure to be provided in 1980/81 effectively ceased in July 1979' when the new secretary of state, Michael Heseltine, announced reduced target figures for 1980/1 and the current year 1979/80.[67] The new 1979/80 figures required a 3 per cent reduction in the RSG settlement figures and, for 1980/1, a 5 per cent reduction in the targets of the previous Labour government's White Paper, *The Government's Expenditure Plans, 1979–80 to 1982–83* (Cmnd 7439). These revised targets formed the basis of the RSG settlement and were incorporated in the preliminary White Paper, *The Government's Expenditure Plans 1980–81* (Cmnd 7746).

Furthermore, the government asked local government to advise it on how expenditure reductions would be achieved on a service-by-service analysis. These cuts severely constrained the work of the sub- and steering groups. There were no opportunities to comment on policy, only on the implications of the cuts. In a letter to the DoE in September 1979 the ACC secretary noted that 'there is probably no need this year for the substantial and detailed "final reports" of the Expenditure Steering Groups'.[68] This change of procedure was quickly adopted and for the 1980 negotiations only the interim reports were required.[69] (See Figure 4.2.) In addition, the housing sub- and steering groups had no formal meetings for the first time, reducing local government's PES input from the previously limited levels. For local government, the groups' remits had been narrowed, their discussions shortened and their reports largely ignored. The groups no longer assessed the requirements of services, but were given targets and asked to find ways of meeting them, that is, the groups were now instruments for cutting expenditure and little more. These changes were not uniformly criticized by the associations. With the change of government, the ACC's criticisms of the system for distributing grant were heeded and the shift of grant from the counties was reversed. But, if the ACC could find some consolation in the Conservative government's policy, it was as worried as the other associations by the proposal for a new grant system which penalized individual local authorities for overspending.

The proposals for a block grant system had been anticipated in the Layfield Committee's Report (1976, pp. 231–3) and in the Labour government's Green Paper, *Local Government Finance* (Cmnd 6813, HMSO, 1977b, para. 3.7 and appendix 1). These proposals for 'unitary grant' had been unanimously rejected by the associations and the Labour government did not legislate. At the time local government expenditure was seen as under control: both 1976/7 and 1977/8 saw local government underspending the approved targets of relevant expenditure (Greenwood, 1982, p. 257). The conditions in 1979 were very different. The government was committed to cutting public expenditure and the secretary of state was much exercised by 'the problem of overspenders':

This is a notoriously difficult area. But so great is the volume of public expenditure, and so urgent the need in the interests of the ratepayer and the taxpayer to exercise proper disciplines, that the Government have decided that action is required.

The Government therefore proposes to make provision in the forthcoming Local Government, Planning and Land Bill for a new block grant system to come into operation in 1981/82 ... This block grant will bridge the gap between a local authority's 'standard expenditure' (assessed on the same basis for all) and the product of a 'standard rate poundage' levied on that authority's rateable value.

Authorities spending in line with standard expenditure – leaving an allowance for inevitable variations in local circumstances – will get the full rate of government support. Expenditure in excess of 'standard expenditure' will also attract grant ... but if it is significantly in excess of 'standard expenditure' the rate of grant will be reduced and reduced progressively as expenditure increases still further.[70]

At first the associations were united in their opposition. Consultations with Mr Heseltine in the CCLGF did not wrest any major concessions from the government and the associations concentrated their activities on Parliament, where they felt they could substantially amend the Local Government, Planning and Land (No. 2) Bill. Their campaign focused on, and gained the support of, Conservatives in the Commons, but even so it was unlikely that the government's overall majority of 43 would be overturned. The associations concentrated their attention, therefore, on the House of Lords, where it was considered possible to defeat the government. A concerted campaign was launched to mobilize the support of the associations' vice-presidents in the Commons and Lords, and briefings sent to Parliament were joint briefings from the associations. However, after the local government elections of May 1980, the AMA became Labour-controlled. Its new chairman, Jack Smart, was soon thought by the ACC chairman to be trying to beat the government under any circumstances. This mistrust ended the joint briefings for the Lords. None the less, the threat posed to the government was substantial and defeat a serious possibility. It prompted the secretary of state to meet, informally, the ACC's political leaders – meetings which led the ACC to 'call off' their peers, allegedly following an 'accommodation' on some, relatively minor, clauses of the Bill. As a result, the government won the vote in the Lords and the Bill was enacted on 13 November 1980. The conditions prevailing in 1977 when local authorities were underspending did not exist in 1980 and the grant system was 'reformed'. (For a detailed account of the passage of the 1980 Act see: Gyford and James, 1982, ch. 8.)

The immediate consequences of the 1980 Act for the CCLGF were all too clear – in the eyes of the majority of local government participants it rendered consultation and negotiation nugatory and caused relations between the associations to degenerate to an all-time low. Thus, in the words of an AMA adviser, 'it was clear that the Government was going to do what it wanted come what may' and any consultation with the associations was seen by them as ineffective if not futile:

> The pace of development work meant that options and consequences put forward to CCLGF could not be properly regarded as emanating from a balanced consultation process between central and local government.[71]

Other critics were less circumspect:

> Consultation has ceased since 1979 ... it isn't consultation, it's a forum where they start telling you what you're going to do.[72]

Now regrettably I don't think Michael Heseltine has ever wanted to get a view from anyone except himself, and this is our great problem.[73]

The whole concept of consultation has gone out of the window because of the attitude that they know best.[74]

It isn't particularly a negotiating body, it never has been, and particularly it is not even a consultative body these days, Heseltine uses it purely as a means for announcing what he is going to do.[75]

This consultative council is not really a consultative council ... the consultative council now is a statement from the secretary of state, a statement from each of the three associations and the secretary of state says 'We make a note of your comments, next business.'[76]

As a consultative body [the consultative council] is now almost useless.[77]

It would be a mistake to believe, however, that these attitudes were shared by all on the local government side.

There's very much more consultation, genuine consultation with this government than with previous governments of either party.[78]

They do listen to us occasionally, but it depends on the forcefulness of your arguments there.[79]

The consultative council is absolutely first class ... both sides putting their views together, consulting on something before it goes through ... but at the same time one has got to admit that government has a right to rule.[80]

The division of opinion has its roots in party divisions. Thus one of the ACC leaders who supported the 1980 Act argued that:

the Party is far bigger than the man, you can't humiliate your minister by getting a defeat on a major piece of legislation.[81]

But the consequences of support for the government were far-reaching. The AMA chairman accused the ACC of selling 'local government down the river',[82] while an LBA leading member believed that 'if it hadn't been for those bastards in the ACC we wouldn't have lost'.[83] The ADC, traditionally an ally of the ACC, was also outspoken in its criticism:

We were let down by the ACC ... they won't be allowed to forget that, I'm sure of that ... they literally ratted on the other associations.[84]

Consultation, it is alleged, no longer takes place in the CCLGF. It is bypassed both in public and in private. 'They've got a club situation where they all talk in private corners ... the Tories almost go to bed with each other they're so close'.[85] Thus:

It's what goes on in the back rooms that matters ... what really matters is what is being said at Marsham Street between the chairman and Tom King, and the chairman and Heseltine.[86]

Consultation did take place, therefore, but on a very different basis from that of the preceding years. Party channels of communication now superseded the associations and CCLGF. Thus,

Michael Heseltine blatantly demonstrated the farce that is the Consultative Council on Local Government Finance this week. He allowed selected journalists to be invited to the DoE for a briefing before he met the CCLGF for what are called 'consultations'.

At this press briefing the secretary of state gave details of the penalties to be imposed on 'overspending' authorities, amounting to £450 million. After the meeting, the AMA chairman said:

We are almost at the end of local government as we have known it in this country ... We have also told the Secretary of State in no uncertain manner that, if this is the way that consultation is done, it is not consultation as far as we are concerned. (*Municipal Journal*, 5 June 1981, p. 434)

With hindsight, the early years of the CCLGF seem like halcyon days.
As far as local government's involvement in PES was concerned the change in 1979 was less dramatic, if only because it had been so limited from the start. Since 1978 local government's involvement had been minimal although there was a surprising variety of views about its extent. Noel Hepworth, for example, suggested that local government had increasing involvement but 'its success in influencing PESC decisions probably will depend to a considerable degree upon how closely local government's own spending decisions agree with PESC forecasts'.[87] An AMA adviser, however, commenting on Hepworth's views, noted:

it is said that there is an increasing involvement by local government in the PESC system. I've always considered it was pretty minimal and thought that this was the AMA's view also.[88]

Nevertheless, up to 1979 the promise of real influence was still regarded as a future goal; certainly the AMA secretary had such anticipations:

> Undoubtedly the best thing for local government to come from the Consultative Council is the opportunity afforded to influence Ministers on forward planning of public expenditure.

But he conceded that this influence has not been demonstrated because of the national economic difficulties:

> It's not easy for the local authority side to make a positive contribution in such circumstances. Our Members will expect a much stronger voice in PESC when the economic climate improves.

By 1978 it was clear that local government involvement in PES was limited to their work in the expenditure sub- and steering groups, and the discussions of their reports in the consultative council. In a letter to service advisers an AMA under secretary reported that:

> the Association is concerned that local authorities have little opportunity to comment on public expenditure plans or influencing the Public Expenditure Select Committee (PESC) (*sic*) other than through the work of the Rate Support Grant expenditure sub- and steering groups.[89]

The sub- and steering groups were important because they provided informational resources essential to PES, forward planning and the monitoring of expenditure for central government. But even this limited involvement was questioned increasingly.

As early as 1976 there were complaints about the remits of the groups. A number of the steering groups emphasized the problems involved in the expenditure cuts, but were accused by a leading AMA politician of making 'no genuine effort ... to find the savings in an acceptable manner'.[90] While noting the concern, Peter Shore replied that the views expressed by the groups did not commit either side: 'we are still, on both sides, perfectly free to reject what they say. The decision is ours.'[91] Over the following years a number of reports were similarly disregarded for exaggerating the problems and consequences of government policies. The education steering group was used as a consultative forum by the DES, but this additional function had no discernible effect on the reception accorded to its reports.[92] By the end of the second year of involvement in PES the associations were 'questioning the value of the interim reports from the Expenditure Steering Groups considered by the Consultative Council in July.'[93] A year later all the associations expressed reservations about the remits given to the groups, complaining that the forecasting procedure was based not on the position facing individual local authorities, but on the theoretical base of the figures from the last White Paper. [94]

The declining utility of the groups was accentuated by the change of government in 1979 and the further rounds of expenditure cuts. Their role had been emasculated and the associations recognized this. For some, this development was not unwelcome. For one Treasury official 'it was not local government's business to get involved in PES'; [95] and one leading DoE official believed that the steering groups never had any significant impact and their decline was not important. [96]

The demise of the consultative council was sudden and dramatic and, for some commentators, it was a result of Mr Heseltine's style − 'the most disastrous Environment Secretary' (Smith, 1981, p. 76). Opinions about Mr Heseltine were unusually vitriolic:

He doesn't know what he is talking about; he doesn't know the detail, he's learnt a certain amount but he still talks in generalizations. [96]

The Sunday Times Magazine (Tadpole, 1981) caricature of Mr Heseltine as an 'ambitious charlatan' with 'only two dimensions' to his character may have brought forth chortles of amusement in the local government world, but that assessment substantially missed the point in its eagerness to denigrate. Frustration and anger at Mr Heseltine's policy spilt over into attacks on his competence. The more important lesson is that, personalities aside, when faced with a single-minded minister local government's ability, even willingness, to resist his policy is limited. The changes in CCLGF structure, the decline of consultation, the virtual absence of negotiation, and the increasing use of party channels of communication all attest to the sharpness of the transition to the directive phase in the relationship between central and local government. The resurgence of ideology in the form of a new Conservative government committed to cutting public expenditure, coupled with the recurrent and deepening economic crisis, pushed the attempt to gain control of local expenditure by agreement to the sidelines and made the CCLGF redundant. Executive authority may be a central component of the British political tradition but its reassertion was a most unpleasant surprise for many in local government and such political processes cannot be dismissed as the idiosyncrasies of individual ministers.

For the remaining years of the Conservative government, the associations witnessed 'more of the same'. Interventions continued to take the form of direction and control; the CCLGF remained but a meeting place at which the government announced its decisions on the (reduced) level of grant; involvement in PES was non-existent; communication through party channels remained the only potentially effective way of influencing the government, and conflicts within the national community intensified. However, this uniformity did not mean that the government had attained its policy objectives. It would extend the remit of this case study far beyond the CCLGF to provide a detailed account of this period (see Rhodes, 1984) but some of its more salient features are worthy of note.

Under the 1980 Act, the secretary of state could define an 'overspending' local authority and 'penalize' it by reducing the amount of central grant it received. The government now had, for the first time, direct (rather than indirect) control over the expenditure of an individual local authority. This change in the rules of the game was dramatic. Local authorities were now given an individual expenditure target and clear guidance on the appropriate rate poundage for that level of expenditure. The contrast with the attitude of Tony Crosland, who 'had almost an obsession about not giving a [rate] figure', is particularly sharp. The 'most we got him to say ... was that the rate increase ... should be "small"' (Barnett, 1982, pp. 76–7). Michael Heseltine and his successors did not suffer from such reticence.

Statutory intent and actual practice diverged, however. The threat of reducing grant, indeed actual reductions in grant, did not deter 'overspending' local authorities. Moreover, the government's estimates of the need to spend of individual local authorities – known as GREA or grant related expenditure assessment – provided an incentive to *increase* expenditure on the part of local authorities spending below their GREAs. Virtually before the new system had been implemented, therefore, the government changed it. In fact, the annual announcement on the level of central grant to local authorities acquired an element of suspense, not about the actual level of grant but about the next round of modifications to the system for distributing it. As Stewart and Jones (1982, pp. 55–6) point out, there were seven major changes in the grant system between 1979 and 1983:

1 The rate support grant system based on needs and resources elements, inherited from the previous government.
2 The system as under 1 above, but with the 'transitional arrangements' penalties applied in 1980–81.
3 The block grant system based on grant related expenditure, introduced under the rate support grant settlement for 1981–82.
4 The block grant system with holdback penalties based on volume targets, introduced in June 1981.
5 The block grant system with holdback penalties based on volume targets, but with exemptions for authorities meeting grant related expenditures, introduced in September 1981.
6 The block grant system with holdback provision related to a composite target based on GREAs and volume targets, introduced in the rate support grant settlement for 1982–83.

7 The arrangements which ... follow[ed] the abolition of supplementary rates under the Local Government Finance Act, 1982.

And this list covers actual, not proposed, changes. For example,
because local authorities were levying supplementary rates to compensate for loss of grant – that is, they issued a second mid-year demand
for rates – the secretary of state proposed legislation requiring them
to hold a referendum before so doing. The proposal was opposed by
the associations, and crucially by Conservative backbench MPs, and
had to be dropped. Undeterred, the secretary of state introduced the
Local Government Finance Act 1982 which abolished supplementary
rates. In short, instability became as central a feature of the grant
system as direction. Central–local relations take on the aspect of
boxing match with each change in the grant system a new round in the
contest. Nor was instability the only consequence of note.

The objective of this exercise in financial reform was to reduce local
expenditure (see Table 4.4). The controls on capital expenditure were
certainly effective but current expenditure continued to increase in real
terms. If the associations were unable to regulate their members when
acting in concert with the government, then the government
discovered that it too had similar difficulties. The gap between
planned and actual expenditure widened and the former figures (or
targets) were regularly revised upwards. The definition of 'overspending' was transparently arbitrary and local authorities which
manifestly supported the government found themselves castigated as
overspenders and penalized. Assuming that the targets were
deliberately symbolic and exhortatory, they were *not* designed either
to bring about an increase in current expenditure or to penalize the
government's supporters.

All the associations were bystanders to government decisions on the
grant system but for the ACC in particular the consequences of this
new style of relationships were more marked. Its relationships with the
other associations were 'strained'. It had the ability to influence its
fellow Conservatives in the government but this ability, to be
effective, tended to require prior agreement on the policy. Perhaps
most important, the actual impact of the 'cuts' in local expenditure
led to splits in its own ranks. Not only did the 1981 county elections
substantially increase the Labour minority but differences emerged
between the 'dry' and 'wet' Conservative counties. And, irony of
ironies, these differences were fuelled by the government's imposition
of penalties on 'responsible' counties. The policy of continued
support for the Conservative government was challenged by demands
to protect the interests of local government. Not only did a number
of counties threaten to resign from the ACC but some actually did
so. The monolithic front the ACC had presented to the world for a
decade had begun to fissure. The hoped-for integration of the national

Table 4.4 Local Government Grant, Current Expenditure and Capital Expenditure, 1972–83 (Constant Money Terms Using GDP Deflator: 1972 = 100)

	1972	1973	1974	1975	1976	1977	1978	1979	1980	1981	1982	1983[a]
Central grants	100	108	123	147	161	161	152	150	152	151	142	138
Capital expenditure	100	114	141	126	109	96	80	75	75	67	59	58
Current expenditure	100	103	115	116	118	120	117	120	123	124	127	129

[a] estimate.
Source: Table supplied by Ed Page (University of Hull), who has revised and updated the figures in Page, 1983.

community had foundered on a barrier reef prosaically known as 'the 1980 Act'. There could be no clearer demonstration of a problem common to the national community and its constituent organizations – namely, the diversity of interests.

The era of direction witnessed, therefore, the demise of the CCLGF, the continued expansion of local government current expenditure, deepening fissures within the national community of local government and increasing instability in the grant system. Routine contacts and the sharing of information continued at the official level, the CCLGF and various groups (most notably OSG and GWG) continued to meet, co-operative behaviour within the national community continued but the most distinctive features of this period are unilateral action by the centre, the fall from grace of the national community and the recalcitrance of individual local authorities. The strategy of incorporation had been tried and found wanting. The strategy of direction had supplanted it and, if found wanting, had been intensified rather than abandoned. Irrespective of the actions of future governments, this case study demonstrates that there is a key institutional weakness at the heart of the system of intergovernmental relations. If incorporation is the preferred strategy, the diversity of interests within the national community, differences in political control and its inability to regulate members are insuperable constraints on its success. Faced with a government prepared to abrogate the rules of the game, however, the weaknesses of the national community are even more manifest. The diffuseness of the national community renders it a reluctant tool in the hands of both centre and locality.

SUMMARY CONCLUSIONS

The major findings of the case study of the CCLGF will be summarized briefly at this point. They will be discussed in more detail in the concluding chapter.

First, the prime objectives of *both* Labour and Conservative governments in grant negotiations have always been to control the amount, rate of growth and distribution of local expenditure in the light of the prevailing state of the national economy.

Second, the public expenditure survey sets the limits to these negotiations and local government involvement in the PES process has been minimal: the expenditure policy community is closed to 'outsiders'.

Third, the strategies of intervention adopted by government are a direct result of its views on the management of the economy. In periods of growth, local government could exercise influence as the experts 'in the field'. Economic decline reduced substantially the scope for negotiation over both the total amount and the rate of growth if not, necessarily, the distribution of grant.

Fourth, in response to economic decline, the government forsook bargaining strategies in favour of, initially, incorporation and, subsequently, direction. The CCLGF was a key institution for an effective strategy of incorporation, providing both the means for aggregating local government interests and for co-ordinating central departments.

Fifth, the government has structural power: it can unilaterally change the rules of the game and it has the capacity to choose between the available strategies and to enforce its preferred strategy of intervention.

Sixth, there were two crucial changes in the rules of the game. The Labour government 'reclassified' local expenditure, treating it as an integral part of the national public expenditure process and, therefore, as a legitimate target for Treasury influence in the management of the national economy. The Conservative government moved from control at the aggregate level to control over the expenditure decisions of individual local authorities.

Seventh, the Treasury moved to centre-stage in grant negotiations, initiating, for example, cash limits and the CCLGF; participating in consultations with local government; and supporting the continuous search for more effective means of control. Moreover, as the guardian of the purse strings, it aimed to regulate not only local government but also the spending of central service departments.

Eighth, the creation of the CCLGF served to build up the associations as *the* peak associations of local government and make them the primary (if not quite the sole) channel of communication not only for grant negotiations but also for all policies with financial implications. Equally, the adoption of directive strategies by the central government was an attack on the pre-eminence of the national community as well as such corporatist devices as the CCLGF.

Ninth, the national community has always been the 'junior' partner in grant negotiations because it accepted the centre's rules of the game (for example, the right to manage the national economy) and became incorporated into Whitehall's 'village community'; because it lacked resources to challenge, for example, the centre's assessment of the need to spend; and because of its own multiplicity of interests, particularly those arising from type of authority and political allegiance.

Tenth, professional expertise played a key role in the negotiating process with the technical paraphernalia of RSG serving to obscure, on occasion, the political decisions being made – for example, the redistribution of grant towards the cities appeared to be 'objective' because of the attention devoted to the choice of factors and regression equations. As the associations became more familiar with the new procedures, these ostensibly technical matters became bargaining counters.

Eleventh, the ability of the national community (and the CCLGF) to 'deliver' the 'cuts' desired by the government was limited by the inability of the associations to regulate their members; they had no sanctions to bring to bear on them. The success of the strategy of incorporation was threatened by the absorption of the national community into Whitehall and hinged on the 'responsibility ethic' of local government (or its acceptance of the centre's views on the appropriate level of local expenditure).

Twelfth, under the impact of economic decline and government direction, the national community began to fissure, revealing that there is a key institutional weakness at the heart of the system of intergovernmental relations.

Thirteenth, the success of the CCLGF was a conditional success which hinged on the effectiveness of the instruments of control (for example, cash limits); the mid-term swing to Conservative control at the local level; local government's 'responsibility eithic'; and a consensus on the centre's definition of, and its tools for managing, national economic problems. Such a conjunction of factors was inherently unstable and the rise and fall of the CCLGF illustrates both the transient nature of such corporatist devices and the special conjunction of circumstances necessary to their success.

Finally, the trends in intergovernmental relations observed in this case study reveal the common ground between the two major parties. Direction by the Conservatives was presaged in Labour's 'reclassification' of local expenditure. Equally, governments of both persuasions have asserted their executive authority only to find that its successful exercise depends on local compliance. The tension between the interdependence of centre and locality and authoritative decision-making by the centre has plagued governments of every political complexion.

NOTES AND REFERENCES: CHAPTER 4

1   Joint association report, *Rate Support Grant, Third Period* (January 1971), p. 7.
2   HM Treasury, *Public Expenditure White Papers. Handbook on Methodology* (London: HMSO, 1972), p. 19
3   Secretary (AMA) to Under Secretary, DoE, 7 August 1980
4   Interview with Peter Shore MP, Secretary of State for the Environment, notes.
5   Interview with principal finance officer, DoE, notes.
6   Secretary, ACC, to DoE, 28 May 1971
7   Letter from DoE to all association secretaries, 15 August 1973
8   Interview with Sir A. G. Taylor, chairman, AMA, transcript
9   Interview with Sir F. Marshall, chairman, AMC, transcript.
10 Interview with secretary, ACC, notes.
11 Interview with secretary, ACC, transcript.
12 Interview with Sir M. Whittaker, chairman, ACC, transcript.
13 Interview with secretary, ACC, transcript.
14 Letter from A. Crosland MP, Secretary of State for the Environment, to AMA chairman, 11 April 1975.

15 The private papers of the late Anthony Crosland contain no information on the CCLGF. Interview with D. Lipsey, political adviser to Mr Crosland at the DoE.

16 J. D. Stewart, 'New procedures and new institutions for expenditure control: a discussion paper', Layfield Control Group, Paper C26, 30 December 1974.

17 J. D. Stewart, 'New institutions for the review of central–local relations', Layfield Committee, Paper C36, 15 January 1975.

18 Minutes of Layfield Control Group, 29 July 1975, Paper MT4/24.

19 Interview with under secretary, Treasury, notes.

20 Interview with financial adviser, ACC, notes.

21 Interview with financial adviser, AMA, notes.

22 Interview with under secretary, Treasury, notes.

23 Interview with under secretary, Treasury, notes.

24 Interviews with under secretary, Treasury, notes; and principal finance officer, DoE, notes.

25 Letter from A. Crosland MP, Secretary of State for the Environment, to association chairmen, 11 April 1975.

26 A. Jones MP, *Hansard*, 17 April 1975, pp. 780–2; and letter to AMA, 21 April 1975.

27 Interview with secretary, ACC, transcript.

28 Quoted in *Municipal Review*, April 1975, p. 57, and *County Councils Gazette*, September 1975, p. 168, respectively.

29 AMA policy committee minutes, 20 May 1975.

30 Joel Barnett, speech to the CIPFA annual conference, April 1975, reported in *County Councils Gazette*, July 1975, p. 93.

31 Sir A. G. Taylor, chairman, AMA, quoted in *Municipal Review*, July 1979.

32 DoE, 'Membership, terms of reference and procedure', CCLGF (75) 4.

33 DoE, 'The nature of business to be discussed by the consultative council: a discussion paper', CCLGF (75) 15.

34 *Hansard*, 15 December 1975, cols 980–91.

35 Unsigned draft paper for official steering group, circulated to all the associations, 12 January 1976.

36 This description of the functions of the sub- and steering groups is paraphrased from the joint association report, *Rate Support Grant, Eighth Period* (January 1977), appendix 1.

37 Interviews with secretary, AMA, notes; and under secretary, ACC, transcript.

38 Internal AMA paper, 4 November 1975.

39 P. Shore MP, Secretary of State for the Environment, statement made at the statutory meeting, 22 November 1976.

40 Letter from secretary, AMA to all associations, 21 May 1976.

41 Notes from local authority side meeting of grants working group, 10 June 1976.

42 Letter from adviser, LBA, to chairman, LBA, 11 June 1976.

43 Letter from adviser, AMA, to secretary, AMA, 25 June 1976.

44 Deputy secretary, DoE, to association secretaries, 30 July 1976.

45 Letter from secretary, AMA, 3 August 1976.

46 Joint departmental circular, 'Local authority expenditure 1976–78', DoE 84/76, 26 August 1976.

47 Local authority side secretariat to association secretaries, 23 August 1976.

48 P. Shore MP, Secretary of State for the Environment, statement at the statutory meeting, 22 November 1976.

49 Letter from P. Shore MP, Secretary of State for the Environment, to chairman, AMA, 11 August 1976.

50 J. S. Blackburn, 'Bringing local authorities into the annual review of public expenditure', 15 November 1976.

51 Local authority side secretariat, 'Consultative council post-Layfield', discussion paper for local authority side meeting of CCLGF 25 November 1976.

52 Meeting of association negotiators and subgroup convenors, minutes, 23 October 1976.
53 DoE, introduction notes to first official level meeting with the associations to discuss expenditure steering groups' final reports, 6 October 1977.
54 Secretary, AMA, to under secretary, DoE, 7 August 1980.
55 Interview with Sir A. G. Taylor, chairman, AMA, transcript.
56 See, for example, interview with under secretary, Treasury, notes.
57 Interview with local authority side secretariat, transcript.
58 ACC, 'Comparison of needs element allocation 1974/5 to 1976/7', CCLGF (76) 11, 1 April 1976.
59 Freezing the data, as its name implies, is simply using the same data as used in the previous year; 'safety nets' specify an amount and no authority could lose more than this amount as a result of the new formula; and 'damping' refers to the technique of distributing only a certain proportion of the available grant by the new formula, the rest being distributed by previous year's formula.
60 Joint association report, *Rate Support Grant, Ninth Period* (March 1978), p. 67. See also Layfield Committee, 1976, p. 234.
61 Interview with P. Shore MP, Secretary of State for the Environment, notes.
62 Interview with under secretary, ACC, transcript.
63 Interview with Sir J. Grugeon, chairman of policy committee, ACC, transcript.
64 Local authority side secretariat, 'Consultative council post-Layfield', discussion paper for local authority side meeting of CCLGF, 25 November 1976.
65 Interview with under secretary, Treasury, notes.
66 Interview with under secretary, DoE, notes.
67 Joint association report, *Rate Support Grant 1980–81, Eleventh Period* (February 1980), p. 3.
68 Secretary, ACC, to DoE, 5 September 1979.
69 'Work of the expenditure groups in 1980's', CCLGF, (80) 5.
70 Statement by M. Heseltine MP, Secretary of State for the Environment, at statutory meeting, 16 November 1979.
71 Interview with adviser, AMA, transcript; and joint association report, *Rate Support Grant (England) 1981–82* (May 1981), p. 96, respectively.
72 Interview with J. Smart, chairman, AMA, transcript.
73 Interview with Sir A. G. Taylor, chairman, AMA, transcript.
74 Interview with J. Toft, Labour group leader, ACC, transcript.
75 Interview with under secretary, ACC, transcript.
76 Interview with assistant secretary, ADC, transcript.
77 Interview with R. Shaw, Labour group leader, LBA, transcript.
78 Interview with Sir G. Walker, chairman, ACC, transcript.
79 Interview with Sir J. Grugeon, chairman of policy committee, ACC, transcript.
80 Interview with I. McCallum, chairman, ADC, transcript.
81 Interview with Sir J. Grugeon, chairman of policy committee, ACC, transcript.
82 Interview with J. Smart, chairman, AMA, transcript.
83 Interview with R. Shaw, Labour group leader, LBA, transcript.
84 Interview with Sir D. Lock, chairman, ADC, transcript.
85 Interview with J. Toft, Labour group leader, ACC, transcript.
86 Interview with assistant secretary, ADC, transcript.
87 N. P. Hepworth, internal AMA paper, 21 November 1977.
88 Adviser, AMA, November 1977.
89 Under secretary, AMA, to service advisers, 11 April 1978.
90 Letter from Sir R. Thomas, chairman, AMA, to P. Shore MP, Secretary of State for the Environment, 12 July 1976.
91 P. Shore MP, Secretary of State for the Environment, to chairman, AMA, 21 July 1976.
92 Secretary, DoE, to CCLGF; under secretary, DES, notes. See also chapter 8, pp. 334–6 below.

93 Local authority side secretariat to AMA secretary, 17 January 1978.
94 Joint association note to official steering group, 'Expenditure forecasting', 8 March 1979.
95 Interview with under secretary, Treasury, notes.
96 Interview with under secretary, DoE, notes.
97 Interview with Sir D. Lock, former chairman, ADC, transcript.

Chapter 5

PAY NEGOTIATIONS AND THE LOCAL AUTHORITIES' CONDITIONS OF SERVICE ADVISORY BOARD

INTRODUCTION

The case study of the consultative council documented the changing strategies employed by the government in order to restrain both grant and local expenditure. Local government's pay negotiations were subject to the same variety of interventions. Indeed, given the key importance of pay settlements for local expenditure, the negotiations over grant and pay became inextricably entwined under the impact of economic decline. This chapter analyses the changing relationships between the national government environment and the national local government system in the policy area of pay and conditions of work for the period 1970–83.

As with the consultative council, the case study explores one of the central interests of the national community. However, there are important differences between the policy areas of grant and pay. First, pay negotiations are not conducted directly by the associations but indirectly through the vehicle of a joint body, the Local Authorities' Conditions of Service Advisory Board (LACSAB). The scope of this case study is broader, therefore, than that of the consultative council, exploring the role of actors other than the associations within the national community of local government. And, given the pre-eminence of the associations, it also raises the question of the relationship between them and LACSAB. Whilst this chapter will not provide the last word on the internal relationships of the national community, it begins the examination of the topic.

Second, the case study includes a broad range of actors from outside the national community of local government. Although the DoE and the Treasury remain prominent amongst central departments, this study of pay negotiations also involves the Home Office and the Department of Employment (DE). It will be possible to explore, therefore, the different styles of central departments. Additionally and unsurprisingly, the role of the trade unions is of importance. For the most part, trade unions are excluded from the national community of local government and this case study provides the first opportunity to explore their relationship with the national community.

Finally, the incorporation phase of grant negotiations saw the government relying on a specific institution to gain agreement for its policies. There has been no equivalent structure in the pay bargaining field and it is possible to explore, therefore, the other means employed by government to regulate local government.

It is important to recognize the differences between the two policy areas but there are some equally important similarities. The study covers periods of Conservative (1970–4 and 1979–83) and Labour (1974–9) governments and also changes in political control in the AMA. Once again, therefore, it will be possible to explore the impact of party politics on relationships. Nor are party differences the only cleavage within the national community. As well as the ever-present and all-pervasive influence of type of authority, joint bodies are a potential source of cleavage. LACSAB serves multiple constituencies and, through the provincial council machinery, individual local authorities can attempt to influence pay negotiations. These arrangements serve to multiply the range of interests articulated at the centre and further complicate the search for an integrated national community. The claim by the associations to be *the* channel of representation for local government can be further explored in the context of pay negotiations.

In short, this case study explores the means of regulation employed by central departments as an alternative to institutional incorporation; the relationship between the associations and one of the major joint bodies; conflicts of interest within the national community; and variations in central departmental style and their consequences for relationships with the national community. In the first instance, the context of pay negotiations is described. Subsequently, attention is focused on the several rounds of pay negotiations and the various regulatory means deployed by government.

THE CONTEXT OF PAY NEGOTIATIONS

The characteristics of the negotiating machinery
The existing local government pay negotiating machinery is concerned with one of the largest 'industries' in Britain – essentially voluntary, complex, highly centralized and based on collective bargaining. Thus, there are 2½ million local authority employees, or 10 per cent of the total national employed workforce and not far short of 20 per cent of total trade-union membership. The total current pay bill is approximately £13,000 million which constitutes 70 per cent of total local authority expenditure. Local authorities are under no obligation to belong to the system and, legally, they are free to set such conditions of service and levels of pay as they wish. By participating in the present system individual local authorities have, as Poole (1978, pp. 69–70) implies, surrendered their fundamental right – and one of the main functions of an employer – to settle levels of pay and conditions of service for their employees. In fact, not all local authorities

participate in the system. Both the GLC (in respect of white collar staff) and the City of London still retain such independence.

The present negotiating system is also voluntary, in the sense that agreements entered into by the national negotiating bodies take the form of recommendations to individual employing bodies. However, the authority of the machinery depends upon authorities standing by national level agreements. One caveat is that both teachers' and police officers' pay levels are determined by ministerial regulations on the recommendations of the pay negotiating bodies. From 1947 until 1959 the same was true for the Fire Service. In 1959 statutory regulations were replaced by a national 'scheme and conditions of service' which sets minimum terms and conditions of service. In the Police Service terms and conditions of service and pay, once accepted by the Home Secretary and approved by Parliament, are embodied in statutory instruments and obtain the force of law. Under the terms of the Education Act 1944, pay settlements arrived at in the Burnham Committee, and thereafter accepted by the secretary of state, are mandatory upon local education authorities.[1] These compulsory elements exist nowhere else in the local government service.

There are forty national negotiating bodies, which differ in size (that is, in the number of employees for which they are responsible), scope (number of occupations and functions covered), constitutions, structures and procedures. There are over 500 occupational groups – professional and non-professional, skilled, semi-skilled and unskilled – employed in 548 local authorities (in England, Wales, Scotland and Northern Ireland), which are of eight main different types. In short, the system is complex. It is also centralized.

Before the Second World War, many local authorities chose to preserve their independence in determining pay and conditions of service; some refused to pay the negotiated rates, and others paid above them:

> Wages and salaries ... were determined by random and piecemeal bargaining, and varied in different parts of the country for the same type of worker doing the same kind of work.

Not surprisingly, the result was that unions 'played one local authority off against another'. By 1939, however,

> local authorities and their associations, though still nominally adhering to the policy of local authority autonomy ... were increasingly conscious of the dangers of isolated action. (McIntosh, 1955, pp. 151–2)

The first serious erosion of local authorities' independence, and a principal foundation of the present-day negotiating machinery, was the compulsory arbitration system introduced by the government in 1940, the pressures of which

> led to a greater centralization of negotiating procedures and a greater standardization of pay and other employment conditions. (Levinson, 1971, p. 8)

By the end of the 1940s, joint councils or committees (the difference in terminology is immaterial) had been established for most local government employee groups. For example, the Fire Services Act 1947 consolidated the NJC for Local Authority Fire Brigades and the NJC for Chief Officers of Local Authority Fire Brigades.

Before the Second World War, the local authority associations played only a limited part in negotiations. However, as the number of negotiating bodies proliferated, none with provincial councils, the associations came to play a much more prominent role, being the obvious reference point for employer representatives on the negotiating bodies.

There are two exceptions to this national pattern – the NJCs for Administrative, Professional, Technical and Clerical Staffs (APT and C) and for Manual Workers. These councils are the only ones with provincial councils (or a regional tier) and, constitutionally, membership of the NJCs is appointed from the associations and the members of the provincial councils. Currently, the NJC for APT and C has thirteen provincial councils and the NJC for Manual Workers has fourteen. Each of these twenty-seven provincial councils, covering England and Wales, has the same Whitley pattern of employer and staff sides as the national councils. There are similar councils covering Scotland and Northern Ireland. All are independent bodies with their own constitutions: they are in no way answerable to the national joint councils. (For a description of their origins and functions other than pay negotiations – for example, training – see Poole, 1978, ch. 4 and p. 169.)

The employer sides of provincial councils comprise elected members from all the local authorities within the areas of the councils. Thus they have always had a preponderance of representatives from smaller local authorities. Representation on the NJCs for APT and C and for Manual Workers balances the need to give effective representation to the local authorities with the largest number of employees with the need to ensure that the national implications of settlements are taken into account. Table 5.1 shows the employers' side representation on the two largest NJCs as well as the staff side composition. This table clearly shows that the provincial council representatives on the members' sides outnumber those from the associations. It also shows that the employers' side in each council is larger than the employees' side – considerably so in the case of the NJC for Manual Workers.

Table 5.1 *Composition of the NJC for APT & C and the NJC for Manual Workers (1981)*

| | Employers' Sides | | | | | | | Employees' Sides | | | | | | | |
| | Local authority associations | | | Provincial councils | | | | Trade unions nationally | | | | | Provincial councils | | |
	ACC	ADC	AMA	ENG. and WALES (12)	GR. LON-DON	SCOT-LAND	N. IRE-LAND	NALGO	GMWU	NUPE	TGWU	COHSE	ENG. and WALES (12)	GR. LON-DON	SCOT-LAND
NJC for APT & C	6	4	6	12	4	4	—	8	3	2	1	1	12	4	4
	16			20				15					20		
	36							35							
NJC for Manual Workers	6	4	7	20	—	4	2	—	12	9	9	—	—	—	—
	17			26				30					30		
	43							30							

Source: LACSAB, Annexes to Evidence to Inquiry into Civil Service Pay, Annex II/1 and II/2 (London: LACSAB, 1981) mimeo.

The composition of employers' sides is designed to reflect the varying functions of local authorities. Thus, since non-metropolitan district councils are not education authorities, the ADC, as the representative body for this type of authority, is not on the employers' side of the Burnham Committees. Nor is the ADC represented on the two fire service NJCs; although the Convention of Scottish Local Authorities (COSLA), representing Scottish fire authorities, is part of the employers' side of each. On the other hand, because they operate a different education system, the Scottish local authorities are not represented on the Burnham Committees.

The membership of the employee sides of the national negotiating bodies and of the provincial councils comprises representatives from amongst approximately eighty trade unions and staff associations. The precise composition of the staff sides ostensibly depends upon the numbers of employees in those unions and/or staff associations. However, it has been difficult for newer unions to gain membership of the staff sides, even when they obviously represent a substantial proportion of the employees concerned. They must secure the agreement of the existing members before they can gain representation. Existing staff side members are reluctant to admit other bodies because it threatens their influence.

Each side of every negotiating body appoints its own secretary, as do the provincial councils. In the case of the latter, the employee side secretaries will usually be local full-time union officials; the employer side secretaries are shared in the case of some provincial councils. On the national negotiating bodies, the staff side secretary will be provided by the union/staff association with the most representatives on the employee side of the negotiating body. On the employers' side of the national bodies the secretary is one and the same person — the secretary of LACSAB. The joint secretaries are responsible for the conduct of negotiations between meetings of the negotiating bodies (and their committees). They act as advisers and will also generally present their respective side's case in such meetings. The postwar years have seen the emergence and consolidation of a centralized bargaining structure within which the associations have come to play a more and more prominent role. The role and position of LACSAB has similarly been strengthened. The only decentralized element in the formal bargaining machinery is the provincial council structure for the Manual Workers and APT & C and the tensions thereby generated are an important complicating factor in the relationship between LACSAB, the associations and individual local authorities.

There is no single settlement date for collective bargaining in local government. The 'pay round' begins in the autumn, and the principal settlements are spread throughout the year with the police negotiations in September, the manual workers in November, the fire service in November, the teachers in April, and APT & C in July. Although there have been calls recently from the unions for a single settlement date, the local authority employers would resist such a change, on the grounds of its impracticality alone.[2] Typically, the first stage in negotiations is for the staff side secretary formally to submit a claim to be placed on the agenda of the next meeting of the national joint council. Although the two secretaries are joint secretaries – and they jointly sign decisions taken in negotiating bodies – the employers' side by convention carry out the administrative work of the bodies. The administrative costs of the bodies are borne equally by the two sides.

At the first meetings of the national councils, union claims will merely be noted by the employers' sides and thereafter notified to individual local authorities – a process which varies depending on whether or not the negotiating bodies have provincial councils. Traditionally one of the most important functions of the provincial councils of the NJCs for APT and C and for Manual Workers is to act as sounding boards.

Thus, when a staff side claim is received at the national level, it is circulated direct to all local authorities, provincial councils and associations in England, Wales, Scotland and Northern Ireland. At the same time a commentary on the claim is distributed covering such matters as the accuracy or relevance of any information contained in the claim, relative pay movements elsewhere and indeed any information which might be helpful short of pre-empting the views of local authorities. In recent years, the views of the national employers on what they might wish to negotiate in return for an increase has also been attached – for example, productivity deals. The replies from individual local authorities are collated by the provincial councils, which also have a special meeting to determine if there is a general view on the future form of the settlement. Local authorities also send their comments to the associations, which can issue their own advice to local authorities. The associations have their own discussions within their manpower and policy committees in order to brief their representatives. Subsequently, it is the task of the national employers to reconcile the range of opinions which have emerged from the sounding-board procedures and to build a consensus prior to actual meetings with the unions. Depending upon the course of negotiations, progress reports will be issued which will attract a second or third wave of opinion from local authorities and provincial councils. Only rarely, however, will there be a full second round of the sounding-board procedure simply because of the time involved in staging it.

This consultation process was introduced in 1979 because of complaints by many local authorities that they had been inadequately consulted about negotiations – complaints which culminated in the aftermath of the manual workers' settlement during the 1978–9 winter of discontent. Prior to 1979, the NJCs for APT and C and for Manual Workers had relied on a sounding of provincial council views. The present arrangements, however, cannot remove the need for the NJC, during the height of negotiations, to take decisions without reference back to authorities. It is expected that NJC representatives (a majority of whom, of course, are provincial council appointments) will take final decisions in the light of views expressed by local authorities. There are still complaints from some authorities about inadequate consultation by national negotiators. And some dissatisfaction is inevitable: the details and circumstances of negotiations can change considerably between the time when an initial claim is considered and when, many weeks or months later, a final settlement is reached. Some authorities will consider that their initial comments on a claim were ignored or disregarded, even when they have a member as representative on the NJC. However, such representatives are not mandated delegates. In final negotiations they must exercise their own judgements on the merits of each offer and claim. None the less, they will remain conscious of the impact of any proposed settlement on the budgets of their own and other local authorities.

For those negotiating bodies without provincial councils, the employers' side secretary of the NJC (that is, the LACSAB secretary) will notify directly the local authorities concerned and invite their comments. Subsequently, after all meetings of the NJC, he will send a bulletin to local authorities informing them of the substance of negotiations. Once again, some authorities have complained about the inadequacy of these arrangements. One problem for the national employers, however – and for the LACSAB secretary – is that information to local authorities must often be couched in general or even vague terms. The confidentiality of the bulletins cannot be guaranteed amongst a large number of local authorities, some of which will have members who support union claims. To give national negotiators a bargaining position at all, therefore, information to local authorities during negotiations tends not to specify the details of the employers' negotiating stances. It ought to be added that confidentiality cannot be guaranteed in the national negotiating bodies. They are composed of members with different political affiliations, some of whom will sometimes be more sympathetic to a staff side claim than to the employers' offer.

The position and role of LACSAB

As the number of national negotiating bodies increased after the Second World War, it rapidly became apparent to the employers' sides that they urgently required a means both of servicing the various bodies and of co-ordinating them. Thus, in 1948, the existing national negotiating bodies, the four English and Welsh and the three Scottish local authority associations,[3] formed the Local Authorities' Conditions of Service Advisory Board (LACSAB). In fact, although it has always been a principal objective of LACSAB to co-ordinate the activities of the employers' sides of negotiating bodies, this has never been its sole objective. In recent years, although servicing pay nego- tiations has remained the board's central function, its work has burgeoned and it has taken on the role of advising local authorities on all aspects of local authority manpower and industrial relations. LACSAB exists to provide this comprehensive service not only to in- dividual local authorities but also to each of the negotiating bodies, to provincial councils and to the associations. Although it is the employers' umbrella organization for the negotiating bodies, it cannot direct their negotiations: it can only advise and seek to provide a framework for co-ordinating settlements. LACSAB, however, claims that this advice 'would never be lightly disregarded' (LACSAB, 1978). The composition of the board is given in Table 3.4.

The constitution, functions, financing and staffing of LACSAB have been the subject of dispute between the associations and provin- cial councils (and are discussed in detail in Chapter 7). It is sufficient to record here that individual local authorities are represented on LACSAB through two different channels: first, via their membership of the associations, which appoint members to the board; second, via NJCs, which also appoint members to the board, and which are composed (at least in the case of APT and C and Manual Workers) predominantly of provincial council representatives. The latter are in turn appointed by the individual local authorities within their areas.

One thing about which there is no contention is the complexity of the negotiating machinery itself. What has been and remains conten- tious is the relationship between successive governments and the local authority employers. Poole (1978, p. 78) has asserted that LACSAB has been 'regarded by successive governments as their agent in apply- ing incomes policies to local government'. LACSAB's role has never been so clear or explicit.

LACSAB AND RELATIONS WITH GOVERNMENT

The period of this study has witnessed marked changes in the attitudes of successive governments to incomes policies. Throughout, local government faced five broad 'problems' in its relationship with central government: inadequate consultation; inconsistent settlements elsewhere in the non-trading public sector, and in the private sector; interference in actual negotiations and the imposition of inquiries; control of manpower numbers; and cash limits. This section expands on the nature and extent of each problem.

The era of the 'Social Contract'
The general election in March 1974 had been called by the Conser- vative government to secure backing for its pay policy in the face of opposition from the unions and outright confrontation with the

miners. In its final stage 3 policy, introduced in November 1973, the Conservative government proposed to allow earnings increases of £2.25 or 7 per cent per week up to an annual limit of £350. It also introduced threshold payments of 40p per week for every 1 per cent increase in the RPI above 7 per cent. The government did not anticipate that their effect would be equivalent to automatic wage increases:

> costs rose unexpectedly because of higher world commodity prices, and then came the Middle East war, the oil crisis and the quadrupling of oil prices. The provisions of Stage 3 now fuelled inflation instead of containing it, as the RPI triggered off the threshold increases in wages. (Pliatzky 1982, p. 118)

The Labour government came to office in 1974 with a 'social contract' with the trades union: the unions would attempt to moderate pay claims in return for more involvement in formulating the government's social and economic priorities. The government duly abolished the Pay Board and all formal incomes restrictions.

Throughout the 1960s local government had been confronted by such twists and turns of incomes policy. Pay settlements generally had been reached in a sedate manner, and they were not normally accompanied by even the threat of industrial action. Local government's major problems were the unintended consequences of continuous restraint (for example, pay anomalies) and the lack of consultation. Thus, the LACSAB secretary complained that, since 1964 there had been four White Papers on pay and incomes policy:

> On each occasion it is understood that the CBI, the nationalized industries and the TUC have been brought by Government into consultation at an early and formative stage. By contrast, local government – with nearly 2 million employees and very strong interests – has been notified about the proposals virtually at the final draft stage, when there has been little or no opportunity to take into account any policy comments to be offered concerning the special position of the local authorities.[4]

Matters had improved under the Conservative government. In March 1973 the new LACSAB secretary, Brian Rusbridge, reported to the LACSAB council that he had 'been brought into the closest possible consultation by the [government] Departments ... to some good effect'.[5] Although the local authority employers were still not formally consulted about the merits of, or shape of, pay policies, there were regular discussions between civil servants and the LACSAB secretariat which enabled the national employers to be aware both of the views of ministers and of repercussions on other negotiating groups. From hereon, local government in general and LACSAB in particular were to experience a surfeit of consultation against a backcloth of threatened and actual industrial action.

The inception of the 'social contract' was followed by a massive wages explosion: between July 1974 and July 1975 earnings rose by nearly 29 per cent (Pliatzky, 1982, p. 96). Such an increase could not be contemplated with equanimity by the government and evidence of their willingness to intervene in local government pay negotiations was not long delayed – interventions which included not only a return to a prices and incomes policy but also the monitoring of local government manpower and direct government participation in negotiations.

In July 1974 a delegation from LACSAB met the new Secretary of State for the Environment, Mr Crosland, at his request, 'for an early and confidential exchange of views on guidelines for pay negotiations after the abolition of the present statutory controls which is expected some time later this month'.[6]

At the meeting, the local authority employers were asked to influence developments to the government's advantage. Mr Crosland urged the local authority employers to make settlements in their coming wage round which would embarrass neither the government in terms of its social contract nor other public sector employers. The LACSAB delegation told Mr Crosland that, in their view, the need for co-ordination lay more with central government than with local government. In subsequent meetings with ministers, LACSAB delegations were told repeatedly of the need to improve co-ordination on pay and staffing both within local government and, to avoid damaging repercussions, elsewhere in the public sector.

In a letter to Mr Crosland in February 1975, the LACSAB secretary said that the local authority employers, aware that they were pacesetters, had 'with very great difficulty' complied with government requests. It was 'with dismay', therefore, that they had seen subsequently how settlements elsewhere in the public sector had gone well beyond those made in local government; and 'that major points were conceded which local government had, despite severe pressures, succeeded in holding'.[7] For example, they had settled with the manual workers on the basis, *inter alia*, of consolidating threshold payments in three phases, effective in November 1974, January 1975 and April 1975. But Health Service ancillary workers and workers in the water, gas and electricity supply industries had consolidated their threshold payments in full from the date of settlement.

The local authority employers could, therefore, see little evidence of support for government policy by other public sector services. Mr Crosland was informed that, as a result, local authority employers were being embarrassed and under severe pressure to make supplementary awards. An urgent meeting with ministers was sought and duly held on 27 March 1975.

Three months later the LACSAB secretary was instructed to write again to Mr Crosland and to other government ministers.

to seek a greater public recognition of the responsible line held by local government and to ensure that the excessive erosion of this position arising from action elsewhere is brought to a halt.[8]

The letter reminded the ministers that they had repeatedly impressed upon local authority employers the need for restraint in wage settlements. The response of local government in holding to the national policy had, in LACSAB's view, 'been of the highest order'. Other public sector settlements had been much higher. Local government found it 'disappointing in the extreme' that ministers made frequent references to excessive settlements in the public sector without any recognition of the 'highly responsible attitude taken by local government'.

LACSAB was fully aware, however, of the potential dangers in calls for greater co-ordination of wage settlements:

The Council recognised that in pressing for a greater measure of co-ordination it increased the risk of greater control by central government on the manpower affairs of local government.[9]

Awareness of this risk had increased with the introduction of 'manpower watch'.

The origin of the manpower watch was the RSG settlement for 1975/6. One of the earliest references to a 'watch' on staff members was a paper tabled by the DoE at a meeting of civil servants and association advisers on 19 November 1974. This meeting – an early equivalent to the official steering group – preceded the 'statutory' RSG meeting a week later at which the associations agreed in principle to the setting up of a 'staff watch'. The decision was announced in the 1975/6 RSG settlement, published in December 1974.[10] The government made it quite clear that it regarded restraint in the growth of local authority staff numbers as a condition of the RSG settlement:

It is an essential feature of the Rate Support Grant settlement for 1975–76 that local authorities should provide for no expansion in present total staff numbers beyond the small increases necessary to meet inescapable commitments. In reviewing manpower budgets, authorities are asked to bear in mind the possibility of making savings in areas of lower priority to offset staff increases which are unavoidable elsewhere ... There will be no attempt by Central Government to prescribe how a local authority should change its pattern of expenditure or deploy its staff ... However, because of the need to ensure that any increases which occur are justified by inescapable commitments, the Government consider it necessary to institute a system of watching local authority staff numbers.

The DoE proposed a quarterly survey on the lines of the existing Department of Employment (DE) quarterly survey. The figures would correspond as closely as possible to the breakdown of manpower expenditure in the annual survey undertaken by local authorities for RSG purposes.

The procedures for the manpower watch were devised jointly by the central departments, the associations and LACSAB; the last assessed the practicability of the survey through extensive consultations with most authorities in England and Wales, both immediately prior to the commencement of the survey and after it had been in operation for approximately a year. The arrangements were circulated on 7 March 1975 and were intended

> to reinforce the severe restriction on the rate of growth in current expenditure by establishing the means of identifying at regular intervals fluctuations in the total numbers employed by local authorities. The aim is to establish machinery through which all parties to the RSG settlement can jointly satisfy themselves that any increases in employment are consistent with national policies and priorities. [11]

It was stressed that the government did not seek to tell individual local authorities how to deploy their staff but it did expect every authority 'to have regard to the need for the utmost economy and restraint'. The circular also emphasized that the government's interest was in total national figures and the main components of that total. For their part, LACSAB urged strongly that the survey information 'should not be used by Ministers to belabour local government either in the House or in public'. [12] The joint watch group was composed of officers from central departments and the associations, chaired by the DoE, meeting in the second month of each quarter. They would be responsible 'for reviewing the quarterly figures and assessing any changes against the needs of national policies/priorities'. [13] Any important issues of policy which emerged would be considered by ministers and leading elected members.

After Circular 30/75 was issued, the associations and LACSAB sent a joint letter to all local authorities giving additional information and clarifying the associations' own position. The associations would have responsibility for responding to government inquiries on increases in manpower, and would

> need to be prepared to give reasons and, if appropriate, to defend or justify such increases. Alternatively, the Associations, either

through or with the Advisory Board will have to take up with Authorities (or groups of Authorities) the question of increases for which justification is not apparent.[14]

No instance of the associations seeking such justification has been unearthed. From June 1975, the manpower watch surveys became part of the CCLGF infrastructure.

By June 1975, earnings for the previous twelve months had risen by 27 per cent and public expenditure during the first year of the Labour government had increased by more than 12 per cent (Pliatzky, 1982, p. 213). As a result, the government, with the co-operation of the TUC, introduced a new pay policy on 11 July 1975. The White Paper, *The Attack on Inflation* (Cmnd 6151, HMSO, 1975b), allowed, in stage 1, for a flat-rate increase of £6 per week per person for everyone earning up to £8,500 per annum. Although the TUC had influenced the form of this new pay policy, the local authority employers had not been consulted. They agreed to abide by its terms nevertheless. Apart from the general lack of consultation, they were concerned with the conflict between the government's policy of restrictions on local authority expenditure, of which manpower costs were a very significant part, and its avowed aim of maintaining levels of employment.[15] Such uncertainties to one side, it was clear that the government would exert every pressure to secure adherence to its pay policy and restraint on public expenditure.

At its council meeting on 24 March 1976, LACSAB took the view that a further pay policy was essential. A delegation from the board was to meet John Silkin, Minister for Local Government and Planning, on 4 May, and it was decided that, although they could give him advice on the basic issues, 'it was not to be expected that this would have a major influence on the policy to be adopted'.[16] At its council meeting immediately preceding the meeting with Mr Silkin, the LACSAB council accepted that the minister's offer to meet them was 'a step in the right direction' but he should be urged to consult them much earlier in future in order that they could influence the shape of any pay policy. For the present, it was merely hoped that having kept government departments informed of the board's views there was 'a distinct possibility that the Government had been able to take account of this in its discussions with the TUC'. At the meeting, Mr Silkin accepted that 'it was essential that he and his cabinet colleagues should keep in touch' (with LACSAB); he would be willing to meet regularly throughout the coming year 'and accepted that a continuing dialogue would be more constructive than a hurried consultation immediately prior to a new pay policy'.[17] The LACSAB delegation urged that the next pay policy remain voluntary, not generate a host of complex regulations and controls, and be aimed directly at controlling inflation. The delegation also stressed the importance of any pay level being within the RSG cash limits. The local authority employers recommended a 3 per cent increase with a cash maximum of £5 per week and a minimum of £2 per week. 'Productivity' should not feature in the coming pay policy; there should be a standstill on job evaluation and the twelve-month rule should remain.

Cash limits were a major innovation introduced by the Chancellor of the Exchequer, Denis Healey, in his April 1976 Budget.[18] They had been used previously, for example on construction programmes, but they were now to be used more generally to control public expenditure. Pliatzky (1982, pp. 138–9) describes cash limits as 'a 2nd-stage discipline'

> designed to ensure that the amount of cash spent on volume programmes did not exceed the approved cost. They were not designed in themselves to determine the volume or physical size of programmes.

The Treasury ministers were keen on cash limits because they saw them as 'an important back-up for incomes policy in the public sector by gearing the scale of cash provision to the target rate of wage increases'.

By the summer of 1976, the joint disciplines of incomes policy and cash limits were beginning to contain the wages spiral: the annual percentage increase in 1975/6 was 9·7 per cent compared with 27·9 per cent for the previous year (Pliatzky, 1982, p. 173 and table 5.4). But then came a new financial crisis. By July 1976 the pound had depreciated 12 per cent against the dollar. In June, the Bank of England secured credit from foreign banks, but without the desired effect. In order to restore confidence in the pound, there needed to be further cuts in public expenditure. A package of cuts totalling £952 million was agreed for 1977/8 and announced in the Commons on 22 July. At the end of that month, stage 2 of the government's pay policy was announced, effective for the twelve months from 1 August 1976. It allowed for increases of £2.50 or 5 per cent up to a maximum of £4 on basic pay. The local authority manual workers, building workers and firemen all settled within this policy in 1976.

Unfortunately, the July public expenditure cuts brought only a brief respite, and on 29 September the government applied to the IMF for assistance totalling 3,360 million SDRs (special drawing rights) or about £2,000 million. This was eventually secured in December 1976, on the basis of proposed cuts in public expenditure of £1,000 million in 1977/8 and approximately £1,500 million in 1978/9 (at 1976 survey prices). In the course of these events, LACSAB was pursuing its expressed objective of involvement in the formative stages of any stage 3 of the pay policy. At the council meeting on 18 October 1976, the secretary was instructed to write to the Secretary of State for Employment, Albert Booth, pressing this claim and indicating that 'previous pay policies created problems for local government which could well have been avoided if prior discussion had taken place'.[19] In his letter of 7 December 1976, the secretary pointed out that local government employers collectively were one of the largest single employer groups in the country but had 'hitherto been given very little opportunity to make a constructive contribution to new pay policies'. He contrasted the local authority employees' contribution, via the TUC, with that of the employers, who 'not being in membership of the TUC have no such voice'.

At its council meeting on 13 January 1977, LACSAB unanimously agreed to the need for a third phase of pay policy, but cautioned that it should allow for rectifying anomalies that had arisen in the previous two stages. A LACSAB delegation met Mr Booth and other ministers on 23 February 1977 to discuss the possibilities of a stage 3 policy. They were assured that further discussions with local authority employers would take place. At its council meeting on 27 June, however, the LACSAB secretary reported that, although he had been asked by senior DE officials to see them to discuss increments, the meeting was disappointing:

I was left with a doubt as to whether the discussion was simply a demonstration that the obligation had been met 'to engage in further discussions'.[20]

At the same meeting the secretary also warned LACSAB that the government's potential for controlling public sector pay settlements had increased greatly since the introduction of cash limits. If they were seen as setting a ceiling on increases for specific groups of workers, then local authority employers would 'become ineffective as negotiators and the Unions will deal direct with the appropriate Government department'.

On 22 June, the AMA secretary, Mr Caulcott, wrote to his chairman, Councillor Smart (Labour), similarly warning him of the crucial dangers of cash limits, and of getting 'what amounts to a pay policy for the public sector imposed on us as it were by accident'. This would happen if any coming pay policy was couched in general terms but local government had unalterable cash limits. It was essential, he continued, to secure from the government an assurance that any local government pay settlements which were consistent with national settlements elsewhere would be covered, if necessary by increases in the RSG. Councillor Smart wrote to the Secretary of State for the Environment Peter Shore, seeking such an assurance. In his reply of 29 July, Mr Shore baldly stated that:

on the assumption that settlements in the local authority field will accord with the Government's guidelines the existing cash limits should be sufficient.

Earlier in July the secretary had written to Mr Booth to express LACSAB's support for a stage 3. He reminded Mr Booth of local government's good record in adhering to stages 1 and 2 'even at the expense of a loss of good will built up over many years'. He pointed out that the record showed local authority employers acting responsibly. However, they faced a number of problems. First, if there was no generally accepted 'going rate', they had to find a point at which settlements could be made which would not be undermined by subsequent settlements elsewhere. Second, if productivity bargaining was allowed for manufacturing industry, it would need to be available in the public sector also. Third, local authority employers were operating within an overall cash limit which had an impact collectively on all negotiating groups. Negotiators were well aware of the impact of individual settlements on the overall limit, and it was, therefore, impractical for any government department 'to attempt to define or impose for any one negotiating group the exact terms and limits for a specific negotiation'. Fourth, if settlements were excessive and cash limits unalterable, the scope for balancing pay increases 'by reduction in numbers employed is not infinitely elastic'. Therefore,

> if local government in the context of pay movements throughout the economy, has no option but to come into line with higher pay settlements then ... local government inevitably will have to seek adjustments to the Cash Limits and correspondingly the levels of government financial support.

Finally, the secretary reminded Mr Booth that, when it engaged in discussion with 'employers', the government had no idea of local government employers' views if it spoke only to the CBI:

> nor does [local government] regard it as entirely satisfactory to have its views conveyed at second and third hand through Government Departments – excellent though the relationships may be.[21]

If employers were being asked to speak to the government, then LACSAB should be included in the invitation. Once again, however, the local authority employers were not party to discussions about the form and content of a future pay policy. When *The Attack on Inflation after 31st July 1977* (Cmnd 6882, HMSO, 1977b) was published in July 1977, without the TUC's support, its principal feature was a ceiling of 10 per cent on earnings. The government, however, repeatedly made it clear that they expected public sector settlements to be in single figures. They also began to seek detailed involvement in public sector settlements – interventions which were to lead to serious disputes with the local authority employers.

In a report to the LACSAB council in September, the secretary warned of local government's potential impotence in pay bargaining. He said that, during the first two stages of the government's pay policy, bargaining limits had been rigidly set and arguments had focused simply on the interpretation of, for example, increments.

> In that situation there was a certain attraction in pushing Government Departments to the fore on the basis that if they made an interpretation then the Government was morally bound to give its financial support ... [but] ... the price paid for this was to take the decision-making out of local government's hand.

In the recent police negotiations, for example, the employers' side, by

> supporting Government pay policy at every turn and by heeding the pleas of Government not to 'rock the boat' [had] been brought to the position where local government retains only a tenuous hold on Police pay affairs. If it loses this then local government's role in Police affairs as a whole will be gravely diminished.

The secretary concluded that 'from the point of view of local government any offer, at any level, at any time must *be seen to be made* by the official side and *not* by the Home Secretary'.[22] However, the next phase of pay negotiations was fluid and local authority employers could return to a positive role, making their own decisions on what were reasonable settlements. But this fluidity made close liaison between the associations and LACSAB essential. The associations were responsible for negotiating with government the resources available and LACSAB (and the national employers) were responsible for negotiating settlements consistent with the available resources. The LACSAB members agreed that it was neither possible nor appropriate to specify the level of each settlement but they recommended to the employers' side that they should try to settle within the terms of the White Paper. The members also instructed the secretary to write to all local authorities, impressing upon them the importance of not entering into local agreements or commitments, in spite of widespread anomalies, which would adversely affect subsequent national negotiations.[23]

The secretary also sent a copy of this letter to Sir Ian Bancroft, permanent secretary at the DoE. In his reply of 15 September, Sir Ian complained that LACSAB's letter to all local authorities 'did not actually spell out the need for settlements to be lower than 10% if the increase in earnings is not to exceed that figure'. He emphasized that the general level of settlements must be 'well within single figures'. He also reiterated

> the importance we place in the present stages of pay policy on being kept in very close touch with developments in local government pay; and this, of course, includes being informed in good time of any offers the employers' side proposes to make – in sufficient time, that is, for Ministers to decide whether there are any further considerations which they would wish the negotiators to have in mind before any initial offer is made.[24]

Shortly after this exchange, the secretary received a letter from the Home Office noting Bancroft's sentiments and expressing the Home Office's interest in pay negotiations in the Fire Service. They wanted to keep 'in very close touch with developments' during the forthcoming negotiations.[25]

At its meeting on 10 October 1977, the secretary told the LACSAB council of 'the need for continuous liaison between members of the Board, its officers and Government Departments'. He said that members of the LACSAB secretariat 'were talking daily with senior civil servants on aspects of pay claims and pay policy'. In fact, LACSAB officials were pressed repeatedly throughout the autumn pay negotiations to consult civil servants about the details of offers and to report on progress. In the case of the manual workers, the DoE had been urging the employers since early September to reach a settlement – despite the fact that no claim was received until 19 September. NUPE's claim for a 'substantial increase' was considered at an NJC meeting on 24 October. It was agreed that joint secretaries should enter into detailed discussions on the basis that the employers proposed to adhere to the government's pay policy. The employers put their 10 per cent offer to the employees at the NJC meeting of 8 November. The same day, the DoE was informed that the offer – which had been discussed with union officials since the beginning of October – accorded with government guidelines. On the 11 November, LACSAB officials were called to the DoE to explain the offer to DoE, DE and Treasury civil servants; they were told that the government was unhappy about the offer.

In the case of the JNC for Building and Civil Engineering Workers, the employers offered two packages, both within the 10 per cent guidelines, on 17 November. The employees accepted one of these packages subject to further discussions. The next day, the joint secretaries met to discuss exact figures. DoE civil servants phoned four times during the meeting to express their displeasure at not being consulted prior to the offer being made. On the same day, the Home Office sent a letter to the LACSAB secretary telling him that the Home Secretary 'would wish to be consulted before any specific offer was made of a further pay increase [in the Fire Service] from November, 1978'. Three days later, the LACSAB and association secretaries were summoned to the DoE and told by senior civil servants that the advanced stage of negotiations for a pay increase with building workers 'came as a surprise to us as we had not been informed that the employers were considering an offer and that you were in negotiation on it'.

The four secretaries were asked 'to hold back from committing yourselves until Ministers had taken a view of this matter'. They were told not to put the offer in writing. A letter from the DoE to the LACSAB secretary, received on 22 November, reiterated the point but phrased it as a request, not as an instruction. On 24 November, the LACSAB and association secretaries were summoned again to the DoE 'to receive criticisms on the conduct of local government negotiations in the current round' and to be warned of an imminent ministerial letter. The same day, at a meeting at the DoE, Treasury civil servants queried whether the employers' offer to building workers was within 10 per cent. Further meetings were held at the Treasury on 25 and 29 November, with LACSAB officials having to provide detailed statistical evidence demonstrating that the offer fell within the government's guidelines. The following day, after discussing figures to three decimal places, LACSAB officials were given partial clearance to proceed with the offer. The LACSAB secretary subsequently reported to the LACSAB council:

As the tortuous dialogue with Departments has continued, it now appears that new and rigid rules are being thought up as events go on.

There was, he said:

a very grave danger that sensible negotiations conducted by local government are becoming the playground for statistical and financial back-room experts from the Treasury.[26]

The consternation of the associations and LACSAB was increased by a letter from Mr Shore to the ACC chairman, Dame Elizabeth Coker, on 28 November. He said that from the start of phase 3 the government had sought, in the national interest, to reduce inflation by keeping increases in earnings to no more than 10 per cent. All public sector employers had been asked 'to keep Ministers in very close touch with developments on all major pay negotiations' and to provide information on offers 'in sufficient time for the proposals to be examined for conformity with the guidelines and possible repercussions upon other negotiations'. Mr Shore referred to Bancroft's letter of 18 September: he was, he said 'sorry to say . . . that the contact we sought has not in all respects been as close as we wished'. He was asking, therefore, 'in view of the extreme national importance of our counter-inflation policy . . . for your further help in strengthening our arrangements for ensuring that all proposed offers are cleared with the Government before any commitments are reached'. Mr Shore accepted the timetabling and other difficulties in achieving settlements, but said that:

> we need in future to have full details of proposed offers well – wherever possible at least 14 days – in advance of the date they are due to be made, together with an understanding with you that no offer will be made until it has been specifically cleared by the Government.

Mr Shore said that he was making a similar request to all other public sector employers.

The associations were horrified by this letter. Indeed, the officials who were summoned to the DoE felt that the new procedures had been 'laid out more starkly than the Minister's letter suggests'. They had been told that *detailed* offers must be submitted fourteen days in advance to the appropriate department; the department would vet the offer and seek the views of other departments; if the offer got departmental clearance, it would go to the appropriate minister; the minister would then consult his colleagues; finally, no offer could be given without formal government clearance. Not only would such procedures represent 'a fundamental change to the whole concept of negotiation in local government' but, once established, government departments would 'use every endeavour' to maintain them 'for all time'.

The associations and LACSAB were alarmed on two counts. First, the new 'rules' infringed the major constitutional principle of local government's right as employers to negotiate and settle pay and conditions of service with their employees. Second, they were almost literally amazed by the sheer ignorance amongst government departments and ministers of the conduct and complexity of local government pay negotiations. Ministers and civil servants appeared to think that the local authority employers decided upon a detailed offer some weeks in advance of the NJC meeting with employees. In reality, the employers cannot finalize a detailed offer until the last NJC negotiations with employees begins. The employers entered negotiations having decided the basis to, and the outlines of, an offer. The details only emerged after a virtually year-long series of discussions between the various constituent bodies on the employers' side and, as the settlement date approached, between employers and unions. If the government's proposals were to be adopted, there could be no negotiations at all with the employers. The unions would seek to alter the government-approved offer and the local authority employers would have to continually seek clearance for any amendments. Inevitably *'the negotiation would come to an immediate halt and unions would by-pass employers and go straight to Government'*. The secretary reported to LACSAB's council in December 1977 that the negotiating machinery was already being bypassed: there was 'an overwhelming willingness for Ministers to get into direct negotiation with unions to the detriment and discredit of local government'.[27]

Alarmed, the associations and LACSAB chairmen sought an urgent meeting with Mr Shore and other ministers. In preparation for this meeting on 8 December, the ACC, in consultation with the secretaries of the AMA, ADC and LACSAB and the Director General of the GLC, drafted a document on the relationship between central and local government in the field of pay negotiations. This document formed the basis of the local authority employers' submission to ministers on 5 December. It emphasized first that, constitutionally, the local authority employers were clearly responsible for negotiating pay settlements with their employees, subject only to certain exceptions such as the role of the Secretary of State for Education as laid down in the Remuneration of Teachers Act 1965. The associations trusted that:

central government would not wish to suggest any other arrangements which would remove or reduce this responsibility; for example, the clearance of offers as suggested in the penultimate paragraph of the letter of 25th November.

In recent years, the associations, through LACSAB, had made arrangements for co-ordinating the employers' sides of negotiating bodies 'without taking away the ultimate responsibility for negotiations from their representatives'. The associations and LACSAB had also

willingly co-operated in the long-standing arrangements for exchange of information between central and local government on matters of pay and conditions of service.

It now appeared that these arrangements had not been satisfactory to ministers. For their part, however, the associations also

have not been satisfied with Government's activities in the field of local government pay matters.

In their view existing arrangements should continue 'in the broad spirit of co-operation, with the understanding on both sides of the anxiety of the other partner'. Moreover, ministers should remember that the associations and LACSAB had openly and unwaveringly supported the government's pay guidelines, despite great difficulty. The associations were pleased that Mr Shore had acknowledged the problems in achieving settlements. The difficulties meant, however, that specified time limits were 'quite impracticable'. Finally, the associations emphasized:

> that Government interventions by submissions to both trades unions and employers at the same time, without the knowledge of employers, could be harmful and indeed undermine the whole process of negotiation.[28]

In response, Mr Shore said that he accepted the constitutional position of the local authority employers. According to the LACSAB minutes, he also:

> confirmed that there was no intention of interfering with the independence of the local government negotiators.

But the joint statement issued at the end of the meeting said merely that:

> Ministers and local government representatives reiterated their support for the Government pay guidelines and agreed to continue the existing close contacts established over the years.[29]

There followed much disagreement about what had been agreed. In their joint letter to Mr Shore the following day, the association and LACSAB chairmen claimed that:

> You did not intend your request for 14 days' notice of pay offers to be a firm rule, accepting that this would not always be practical ... You acknowledged that once joint negotiation was under way it would not always be possible to defer consideration of detailed changes to the 'package' for further consultation with Government departments ...
> You confirmed there was no intention of interfering in the independence of the local government negotiators but that the Government were requesting an input into the employers' considerations before offers were made. The final details would be left to the employers.

Mr Shore replied to the LACSAB chairman on 11 December that:

> we would still ask (and I thought this was understood by both sides on 5th December) that any limits to offers which had been agreed

between the employers and ourselves should not be exceeded even at a final meeting.

The chairmen of the three associations and LACSAB replied immediately, saying that, whilst they had every intention of maintaining close contacts,

we do not accept that any limits to offers need to be agreed between the local government negotiators and Government Departments, nor that they need to be cleared by the Government.

And, even if Mr Shore thought he knew the terms of the agreement made with the associations and LACSAB, it was evident that officials in his own and other departments did not. For instance, on 23 January, a Home Office under secretary wrote to the LACSAB secretary in connection with Fire Service pay negotiations, saying:

I cannot stress too strongly the importance which the Government attaches to its counter-inflation policy and the determination of Ministers to ensure that offers, including those in respect of all sections of the Fire Service, are cleared with them before any commitments are undertaken by the employers.

He requested information

wherever possible at least 14 days in advance so that the matter can be properly processed in Whitehall.

The letter continued:

As you know, the instructions are that no offer must be made until it has been specifically cleared by the Government.[30]

Similar exhortations were received at the same time from the DoE in respect of negotiations over municipal building workers.

In response to the above Home Office 'request', the LACSAB chairman (now Councillor Lovill) wrote to the Home Secretary, Merlyn Rees, on 30 January 1978 telling him that at its meeting on the previous day the Board had unanimously

expressed the greatest possible concern at the increased intervention by Ministers and Government Departments in the detailed pay negotiations of local government.

Councillor Lovill reminded Mr Rees of the meeting with Mr Shore on 5 December at which the associations-LACSAB delegation had told ministers that such intervention 'was undesirable in principle and unworkable in practice'. Mr Shore had accepted that it was virtually impossible to give government departments fourteen days' notice of fully costed detailed offers. But, said Councillor Lovill, what concerned LACSAB even more than the impracticability of the government's proposal was the challenge to the fundamental principle of the local authority employers' freedom to negotiate with their employees. Even worse was the fact that the employers had consistently and wholeheartedly supported the government's successive pay policies, and had done so at the cost of major disputes (for example, in the fire and police services). Despite Mr Shore's assurances, civil servants daily were attempting

> to impose a detailed vetting procedure and to insist that negotiations should not proceed until the procedure has been exhausted and 'approval' has been given.

Councillor Lovill asked Mr Rees to recognize

> that the intervention as it is currently being practised is unacceptable, unworkable and indeed inconsistent as between one Government Department and another.

Clarification was also being sought from Peter Shore. On 20 January, the ACC chairman, Mrs Coker, had written to him and sought clarification of the government's position. Mr Shore's reply two months later (21 March) repeated that 'we must ... come to an understanding in advance about the limits to offers'. He said that his understanding was:

> that the employers will let us know as soon as possible in advance of actual negotiations details of the claim and of the offer or alternative offers that they propose.

The government would then:

> have an adequate opportunity to examine the implications fully and the possible repercussive effects within the public sector and beyond before the offer is made.

Following this pronouncement, the Home Secretary replied (on 7 April) to Councillor Lovill. Merlyn Rees said, 'I fully accept that the conduct of local authority pay negotiations must rest with local government.' Referring to Mr Shore's letter, Mr Rees interpreted 'well in advance' as meaning wherever possible at least 14 days in advance. In fact Mr Shore had said: '(though not necessarily the full 14 days beforehand)'. Mr Rees claimed that it was because the procedures for forewarning had not always been followed in the fire service pay negotiations 'that difficulties have arisen'. He said he hoped that his and Mr Shore's full explanation of the governments proposed arrangements would prevent further difficulties with the conduct of these negotiations.

For their part, LACSAB regarded some of the Home Secretary's interventions during the fire service dispute as 'disastrous'.[31] At their council meeting on 20 July 1978, Councillor Lovill referred to Mr Rees's letter of 7 April and expressed resentment not only about the implied criticism of the fire brigades employers' negotiations but also about the government's continued insistence on being involved in advance of settlements. The chairman of the NJC for Local Authority Fire Brigades, Councillor Brannan, reported the employers' concern at Mr Rees's interference, without prior consultation, in the negotiations themselves.

At a meeting with ministers on 11 July, requested by the Secretary of State for Employment, Mr Booth, and attended by Mr Shore, Mrs Williams (DES) and Lord Harris (minister of state at the Home Office), the LACSAB/associations delegation had been invited to express their views on problems associated with the current pay policy and points which they would like the government to consider in any future pay policy – phase 3 was about to end. The LACSAB delegation emphasized the problems that had arisen for local government in phase 3 from a rigid application of pay policy as compared with the more flexible policy which applied in the private sector. The delegation once again protested about the government's involvement in local government pay negotiations. Mr Shore repeated that the government was disturbed at the lack of prior consultation with ministers. 'It was essential', he said, 'to have the co-operation of local government, particularly because manual workers tended to "set the tone".' In response, Councillor Lovill said that local government 'was unhappy about the extended dialogues with ministers and their staffs throughout the year on the minutiae of each offer', and the lack of adequate consultation on policy. Nor could this meeting be construed as a realistic attempt by ministers to note local government's views on any future pay policy.

In reply to Councillor Lovill, Mr Booth said that what might appear to be minutiae to local government had often, from the government's viewpoint, major implications for other groups. He said that the government did not intend to leave such interpretations to employers; ministers 'would maintain a close involvement in potential offers'. The LACSAB delegation again expressed their concern at continuing ministerial and departmental intervention and argued that in phase 3 the government 'was making the rules as it went along'. Moreover, this had led to settlements (for example, in the fire service) which were more expensive than if they had been left to the discretion of local government. (See Rhodes, Hardy and Pudney, 1983b, ch. 5) Finally, Councillor Lovill welcomed an assurance from Mr Shore that better means of co-operation would be sought:

> It was local government's intention to support the fight against inflation, but the first purpose of local government representatives was to look to the interests of local government.

The LACSAB representatives:

> indicated that local government would co-operate in endeavouring to implement pay policy, but this could not be based on rigid acceptance of the Government's terms.[32]

Indeed, relations between the associations and the government were to become more difficult because the AMA, like the ACC and ADC, was now under Conservative control. Nor was the government's decision on phase 3 likely to smooth the way forward. The White Paper *Winning the Battle Against Inflation* (Cmnd 7293, HMSO, 1978a) proposed a 5 per cent pay norm. Inflation was down to single figures for the first time since 1973 and the comparative restraint in incomes and public expenditure seemed to be bringing their just rewards. The implication for local government was that, pay norms notwithstanding, they could expect to receive massive pay claims.

The employers' side of the NJC for Manual Workers requested a special meeting of LACSAB (called on 4 October) to discuss this very eventuality. The employers were concerned about the irreconcilable gulf between the anticipated pay claims and the White Paper's 5 per cent guideline. Noting that the manual workers' claim was one of the first under phase 4, LACSAB concluded that 'local government did not wish to be in the front line'. Civil servants at the DoE, DE and Treasury had been told of the anticipated problems and LACSAB decided it needed another meeting with ministers to make clear that local government negotiators 'should be free to negotiate on their terms within cash limits or pay guidelines without interference or rigid interpretation by Government Departments'.[33]

It was not to be: the 'winter of discontent' was just beginning and government intervention in local authority pay bargaining was to become more intense than ever. One of the major problems for the government with phase 4 had been the lack of support from the TUC and in Parliament. As the autumn pay round progressed in 1978, it became clear that the government's 5 per cent guideline was being widely ignored in the private sector. In September British Oxygen reached a 9 per cent settlement with 3,000 manual workers. In October Ford's reached agreement on a 17 per cent offer with 57,000 manual workers. In November, 30,000 bakery workers accepted a 14·4 per cent offer, and 100,000 grocery workers accepted a 20 per cent offer. In each case, the agreements included productivity clauses.

In a speech in the House of Commons on 16 January 1979, the Prime Minister, Mr Callaghan, referred to the highly publicized Ford and British Oxygen settlements, which breached the pay policy. The government's policy of invoking sanctions against firms which did not observe the pay guidelines had been defeated in Parliament. Since that defeat, oil tanker drivers and road haulage drivers had gone on strike in support of claims respectively for 30–40 per cent and 20–30 per cent. Mr Callaghan referred to the 'awful warnings' of 1975 when settlements started in double figures, but by the end of the round had 'rocketed to over 30%'. Here, he said, was

> the reason why the Government do not intend, wherever they have influence, to depart from the guidelines they have laid down and which are best for the country as a whole.

And the public sector was an area where the government did have influence. The coming settlements in the public sector – for example, local authority manual workers and workers in the water, gas, electricity and steel industries – were 'crucial to the future health of our country. The Government's policy is that the country should not go through once again what it went through 4 or 5 years ago. We shall adhere as closely as possible to the pay limits that have been laid down'. Deprived of the use of the sanctions it had sought, the government must, said Mr Callaghan, 'make the best use of such instruments as are available to us'. He said that 'If local authority pay settlements are as high as 15 per cent, domestic rates will rise on average by up to 27 per cent', resulting in poorer services for the public. The government was prepared to countenance increases of more than 5 per cent for the lower paid (those on less than £44.50 per week) up to a maximum of £3.50 per week:

> As to local authorities – this development in the pay policy would have implications for next year's cash limits ... I should like to make clear to the local authorities that the Government will be ready to meet their share of the extra cost to the local authorities of these proposed increases to the lower paid.

Mr Callaghan also spoke of the need to secure fair rates of pay for the public sector and of the government's readiness 'to see ... a greater role for comparability in determining pay'. He said that ministers had begun discussions with employers and unions concerned to see whether such an investigation had a contribution to make 'in the context of their current negotiations'.[34]

Ministers had begun comparability discussions with the local authority employers on 22 December, when LACSAB members had been called to a meeting with Peter Shore and Albert Booth. The ministers confirmed that there had been discussions between the government and the TUC on 'comparability' – something that LACSAB members had previously only been warned about. At the same time, on 12 December, at a meeting of the manual workers' NJC, the employers, consistent with the government's pay policy, offered 5 per cent plus a minimum earning guarantee, increased shift allowances and a review of gradings. The unions rejected this offer. Comparability and the manual workers' settlement were now to become entwined.

The secretary of LACSAB felt that local government had been placed in an invidious position. The desultory discussion of comparability in December had placed local government 'in the position of having been consulted and having been invited to make suggestions – possibly on a joint basis with the unions'. If LACSAB did not respond, the government would certainly go ahead and formulate its own proposals. The board's initial response at the 22 December meeting was that it 'would co-operate with an Inquiry set up to examine the *methods* for arriving at pay levels in the Public Service on the understanding that it would embrace all groups'. There was no forward commitment, nor was the inquiry to be asked to define levels of pay, nor was any one group to be considered in isolation. Its task was simply to explore whether there were better methods of handling pay determination in the public sector. LACSAB's understanding:

was that the suggestions of the Inquiry would be referred to the interested parties, including local government, before any decision was taken about whether or not to set up a permanent body with a task of determining or recommending specific wage levels.

There followed a series of intense discussions between the government and TUC, interspersed with discussions between ministers and LACSAB. According to the LACSAB secretary,

Ministers were almost single-minded in seeking a form of comparability study which would produce a settlement for manual workers in Health, Universities and Local Government.

At another meeting, called at short notice by Shore and Booth on 9 January, LACSAB again stressed that the local authority manual workers' negotiations could not be seen in isolation. Ministers, however, throughout all the discussions concentrated on the manual workers.

At the LACSAB meeting on 18 January, the secretary reported that local government was 'probably the Government's last bastion for defending the 5% policy'. The government could 'choose whether or not to face a full-scale confrontation on 5% or whether to compromise in some way'. Local government 'must continue to hold the line that it will not enter into increased financial commitments unless there is a prior understanding by central government that it will be supported in cash limits/RSG terms'.

This understanding had been given by the Prime Minister but:

If the Government decides to meet the public service unions in a head-on clash on the 5% issue it embroils local government in massive industrial action. The Advisory Board needs, therefore, to be prepared with a public statement ... on whether or not it supports the Government action. Since the Government holds the financial strings, it will, in any case, call the tune, but it is a question of whether or not local government is seen to be a willing or unwilling partner.

At the 18 January meeting of LACSAB, the two senior Labour members, Councillor Smart (now leader of the opposition at the AMA) and Councillor Collins, proposed a resolution that, given the Prime Minister's statement on the possibility of establishing some form of comparability,

the local government employers would be willing to accept such an investigation for local government manual workers in an attempt to resolve the problems of their pay.

In the ensuing discussion, it was argued that the board could only support a feasibility study, without any commitment about its outcome or any subsequent pay increases. Also, the board would prefer the inquiry to be undertaken by the employers and unions together rather than by some independent body. On a vote, Councillor Smart's resolution was lost. By a narrow majority the board decided that, if there was to be an independent body, LACSAB should give it the necessary information, whilst retaining control of negotiations. And, although this decision reflected worries that settlements arising out of comparability studies were more expensive than those won at the negotiating table, it also reflected the increasingly adversarial stance of the Conservative-controlled associations towards the Labour government.

However, the settlement of the manual workers dispute was close at hand. In bare outline, the employers offered 8.8 per cent at the NJC meeting of 7 February. This offer was rejected by the unions. The following day, a LACSAB delegation met government ministers to notify them of the outcome of negotiations. They were assured that the government stood by their 8.8 per cent offer. On 10 and 11 February, ministers met the TGWU, GMWU, NUPE and COHSE (together with TUC General Secretary, Len Murray). The outcome of these meetings was the framework for a four-part settlement based on productivity agreements, guarantees on local government's financial support from government, a comparability commission, and a pay settlement back-dated to November 1978. On 12 February, a LACSAB delegation was invited, at short notice, to meet Mr Shore with no indication of the meeting's purpose. Mr Shore said that the government had decided that it had to take the initiative. The LACSAB representatives were then informed of the terms of the settlement and handed the terms of reference of a standing commission on comparability. The delegates said they would consider this at an emergency meeting of the board.

The means by which this settlement was arrived at were, however, a substantial bone of contention between LACSAB and the associations. The negotiations were extremely delicate and required careful handling. Rather too late in the day, in the eyes of the local government negotiators, ministers began to shift their ground and there were signs that they would support a settlement in the region of 8–9 per cent without any strings. The local authority negotiators and political leaders felt that it was important for any initiative to come from them. In particular, the associations felt that, before any initiative could be taken, they had to have an undertaking from ministers to support any pay increase through the RSG settlement. Given that threefold negotiations were under way with the unions and with ministers on the level of both pay and grant settlement, the 'traffic on the network' was extensive. It was normal practice for general discussions to take place, informally, on 'the state of play' in this way, it is possible to develop 'a feel' for the negotiations and anticipate the 'kind of level' at which a settlement may be possible. The following exchange illustrates the probing through which this 'feel' for the current 'state of play' is built up:

Employer: Well, what I want your advice on is this ... We have talked informally and Ministers have talked informally with you about moving possibly to somewhere between 8 and 9 per cent for lower paid, and I haven't authority to put forward on that basis yet, one would have to talk to the Employers about it first. If then we were – I ask you this informally – if we were talking in that area between 8 and 9 per cent ... what do you think is going to be the reaction of your side?...

Union: Well at this point in time I wouldn't be happy about saying we could make any sort of a settlement at all. On the other hand we have a duty, it seems to me, to indicate the position from time to time to our members and not to stand between them and any offer that has been made.

Employer: Listening to you, am I going too far if I suggested to our members that we might be on the road to a settlement?

Union: I think that would be too far. I mean, we made our position absolutely clear to you the other night there, but having said that ...

Employer: Well, what was that – can you tell me that again – what that position is ...?

Union: Well, the position is that so far as speaking from the national officers' point of view, obviously we have got to seek the going rate and in our opinion the going rate is considerably in advance of 9 per cent.

Employer: What is the going rate?

Out of circumlocution and indirectness come offers. But such conversations, whether with trade union negotiators or civil servants, presuppose a shared familiarity with the ground rules of pay negotiations and the LACSAB secretary was becoming increasingly concerned about both the party political dimension to the negotiations and, as he saw it, the inexperience of civil servants at the DoE who 'were failing entirely to appreciate the sensitivity of the position'. General discussions designed to convey the 'mood' of the meeting were being taken literally. In spite of instructions to LACSAB staff *not* to 'speculate' with civil servants, the informal opinion of a LACSAB official about the possible level of a settlement was conveyed to the secretary of state by his civil servants. Peter Shore took this 'speculation' to the Cabinet and gained support for the initiative. Thus, when Peter Shore called the meeting to announce 'his' agreement to a settlement at 8·8 per cent, the AMA and ACC leaders were furious at the news. Not only had the initiative been taken away from them but Peter Shore announced that he had been informed that LACSAB officers were reasonably confident that a pay settlement in the region of 8–9 per cent could be reached. This suggestion that a private deal had been done between LACSAB officials and civil servants behind the scenes provoked a violent reaction from the association politicians. The resultant atmosphere of suspicion did considerable damage to relations between LACSAB and the association. The secretary was to comment some six months later:

In such conditions, with Civil Servants constantly on the telephone in the middle of critical and fast moving negotiations, a chance comment or an expression of opinion can easily be given undue weight by Civil Servants and conveyed to Ministers accordingly. This, in fact, happened at a critical stage of the Manual negotiations early this year when leading members of the Local Authority

Associations were involved. It created an entirely wrong but unfortunate impression that the Employers' Secretariat was developing a line of action which was out of gear with the wishes of members.

Such a statement verges on classic English understatement, matched only by the view of Councillor Taylor (Conservative chairman, AMA) that 'Because of LACSAB officers' discussions, the Cabinet accepted the possibility of a settlement at 8·8%'.

To add injury to insult, the 8·8 per cent offer was no longer acceptable to the unions because, at the selfsame time, the government had approved a water settlement at a much higher level. Nor was ministerial self-restraint to become a central characteristic of the negotiating process. They again took the initiative and the result was the 'strange' settlement of 9 per cent with massive strings. At the emergency meeting of 14 February, LACSAB representatives expressed their 'acute concern' that after meeting ministers as recently as the 8 February, when they had agreed to stand by 8·8 per cent, ministers had

> without consultation met and made agreements with the trades unions going beyond 8·8 per cent and committing local government to an unknown amount for the future.

The board also agreed that

> the proposals were a dangerous trend towards centralism leaving very little on which local government could negotiate.[35]

In his report to the board, the secretary referred to ministers acting as 'pseudo-negotiators'; it was right, he said, for local government to refuse 'to be shanghaied by [them] into panic meetings of the NJC'. But he advised the board that it had recently simply been reacting to government initiatives; it was time, he argued, 'for local government to reassert itself − to *tell* Ministers what it proposes to do − then to give a positive lead to the unions'. LACSAB members were extremely critical of the government having gone first to the trade unions, having entered into a commitment with them which had not been agreed to by the local authority employers (and which, in the secretary's words, was 'mortgaging the future') and having thus established a *fait accompli*. The proposal to accept a standing commission on comparability was put to a vote and was carried by only 12 votes to 10 − subject to it being independent and to it studying pay in the public sector across the board.

After this emergency meeting, a LACSAB delegation again met ministers and persuaded them to make six detailed amendments to the terms of reference of the standing commission (for example, the choice of jobs to be compared). And, once again, the associations pressed for the financing of the settlement through RSG. After this meeting, Mr Shore's private secretary wrote to the LACSAB chairman, Councillor Lovill, to say:

> the Secretary of State asked me to confirm the assurance he gave you this afternoon on RSG ... That the government would think it right when considering the cash limit at Increase Order stage to ensure that an undue financial burden was not placed on local authorities.

On 21 February, at the Manual Workers' NJC meeting, the employers offered a four-part package comprising an overall 9 per cent increase with £3.50 per week on basic rates backdated to November 1978, and reference to the Standing Commission on Pay Comparability with an agreement to pay half of any recommended award from the date of the Commission Report, 1 August, and the other half from 1 April 1980. The unions decided to recommend their members to accept the offer. Speaking at a news conference after the NJC meeting, Mr Shore described it as 'a fair – even generous settlement – which recognises the legitimate claim of the low paid local authority workers'.[36] But, he added, 'it would be both foolish and wrong for other groups to claim for themselves the exceptional measure which we have thought right to introduce for the lower paid'. He said he regarded the referral to the comparability commission as perhaps the most important feature of the offer; but these arrangements were 'very exceptional', and it would need exceptional circumstances for other groups to be referred. In fact, by this stage, NHS ancillaries, ambulancemen and university manual workers had also been referred to the commission.

On 23 February, the LACSAB chairman wrote to Mr Shore to request that LACSAB be consulted about appointments to the commission and about its method of working. Mr Shore replied on 7 March, saying that 'It was decided not to consult ... on the membership', and informing Councillor Lovill that the Prime Minister was due to announce the commission's membership that day. Its chairman was Professor Clegg.

The introduction of pay comparability by the Clegg Commission was partly responsible for bringing to an end the series of public sector disputes. But for the Labour government the settlements came too late: the damage of the 'winter of discontent' had already been done.

Under the Labour government, the national community had sought ever more extensive involvement only to discover that there were little or no returns for local government. The government and the employers may have had a shared interest in reducing the level of pay settlements but the strategy of continuous intervention merely infuriated the employers and led them to doubt the wisdom of seeking incorporation into central policy-making on pay settlements. Their doubts were rendered irrelevant by the incoming government.

The era of 'cash limits as incomes policy'

In May 1979, the Conservatives came to office pledged, *inter alia*, to govern without any formal incomes policy. The new Chancellor of the Exchequer, Sir Geoffrey Howe, soon made clear the new Conservative government's attitude to public sector pay bargaining. Speaking in the House of Commons on 22 May, he said: 'We intend to avoid detailed interference with the pay bargaining process.' He continued by saying:

> We shall use cash limits vigorously ... as an effective control on public spending. No increase will be made in the published cash limits for this year – either for central or local government – to accommodate higher price increases ... It will be for the local authorities themselves to make the necessary economies.[37]

On the same day, the new Secretary of State for the Environment met the chairmen and secretaries of the associations, and afterwards issued a statement:

> Because so much of public expenditure, in both central and local government, consists of manpower costs, restraining public expenditure must mean restraining manpower. As part of this policy on public expenditure the Government has, therefore, announced a freeze on civil service recruitment. Similar action is needed for local authority manpower and the Government will approach the expenditure needs of local authorities on the assumption that a vigorous policy of manpower restraint is being pursued. The Government, therefore, expects local authorities to review urgently the manpower requirements of the respective services they administer and, meanwhile, to freeze recruitments wherever possible.[38]

Current senior members and officers of LACSAB have confirmed that the government generally has been true to its word on both counts: first, they have avoided *detailed* interference in pay bargaining; second, they have used cash limits most vigorously.[39] Indeed, the two things are directly related – the government has no need to intervene in detailed bargaining precisely because cash limits so rigidly set the limits to bargaining.

Pliatzky (1982, p. 175) recalls that, when asked at the Treasury 'what we would do about cash limits if there were no income policy', he had replied that 'in that case perhaps cash limits would be our incomes policy'. The new Conservative government maintained the cash limits already in force and in effect told the local authority employers that it did not intend to match pay settlements with RSG increase orders – even if such settlements stemmed from the Clegg Commission's recommendations. If necessary, pay increases would have to be offset by manpower cuts. The new government intended to use cash limits 'as a form of budgetary control on local government expenditure'. The LACSAB secretary warned board members in June 1979 that existing pay commitments would breach the RSG cash limit figure. He emphasized the need for more effective co-ordination between the national employers' sides of all negotiating bodies and the need to improve consultation between national employers and individual local authorities.[40]

As the 1979/80 pay round began, however, the local authority employers faced two problems. First, the cash limits for the coming year had not been specified. Second, comparability studies had accentuated the problem of staged settlements overlapping with the new pay round. At its meeting in November 1979, the LACSAB council rejected by 16 votes to 10 a proposal that there should be no more referrals to the Clegg Commission. There was, however, little enthusiasm within LACSAB for making such referrals. The commission would never tell LACSAB staff the basis upon which comparisons were made. There is also a firm conviction amongst senior LACSAB members and officers that settlements arrived at by all types of government-imposed commissions of inquiry are invariably more costly than any local-government-negotiated settlements. There is an equally firm conviction that, in LACSAB's words, local government 'has an excellent track record of moderate pay settlements'.[41]

With the present government there are far fewer discussions between ministers and LACSAB members, but resentment is less intense because at least local authority employers are treated no less favourably than the unions. In the autumn of 1980, Mr Heseltine invited LACSAB members to have a general discussion about the coming pay round. Local government members regarded the discussion as useful; they could impress upon Mr Heseltine, and the other local government ministers, the responsible approach of the local authority employers over the years. There was similar meeting with ministers at the beginning of the subsequent pay round in the autumn of 1981 but, in 1982, LACSAB decided not to initiate such a meeting because it did not wish to seem to be inviting instructions. Although meetings with ministers are now much less frequent than under the previous Labour government, there are extensive meetings between officials and civil servants and meetings with ministers took place in the latter half of 1982. Relations are much more cordial because there is no longer detailed interference in pay negotiations.

If relations are cordial, however, cash limits as incomes policy created problems for the national community, many of which had their roots in settlements approved under the previous Labour government. For example, the firemen's strike of 1977–8 had been settled employing a government-backed formula which effectively removed firemen from the annual pay debate. However, the Labour government's undertaking to meet the costs of this formula was for two years. The Conservative government abided by the previous government's commitment in 1979, even though the settlement produced a 20 per cent pay increase, but in 1980 when the government was trying to contain public sector settlements within tight cash limits, the automatic increase of 18·8 per cent created severe problems.

On 6 November, the government announced that the 1980/81 RSG settlement would assume pay rises of only 6 per cent. The next day, the employers decided by 18 votes to 12 to reject the pay formula and offer the firemen 6 per cent only. The Labour members from the AMA and COSLA had voted against ending the formula, but had been outvoted by the ACC and AMA Conservatives who adhered to the Conservative government's implicit (public sector) incomes policy and reneged on a binding agreement with the employees. The Fire Brigade Union's (FBU) executive council decided on 10 November to call a delegate conference for 21 November to plan strike action if the formula was not honoured. At this conference, delegates agreed upon a series of one-day strikes if the negotiations did not yield a satisfactory agreement. To add to the potential problem for the employers, the National Association of Fire Officers (NAFO) decided to take similar action.

At further meetings of the NJC on 27 November and 1 December, it was agreed to implement the 18·8 per cent offer in two stages: 13 per cent from 7 November 1980 and a further 5·8 per cent from 1 April 1981. The FBU and NAFO reluctantly accepted this offer. It entailed losses of approximately £150 for each fireman but the employees did not wish to take industrial action for such a small amount. And this final offer came only after a majority vote in favour of it amongst the employers' side and following a threat by the NJC chairman (Councillor Brannan) to resign if 18·8 per cent was not offered. Councillor Brannan had been the NJC chairman when the pay formula had been agreed initially and he regarded it as a binding commitment by the employers. He was urged by senior ACC members to heed the government call for lower public sector settlements but he declined to do so saying he would resign rather than go to the NJC with a lower offer. He won the vote.

Pressure to withdraw from the pay formula was mounting. The employers' intentions changed, however, with the shifting political balance of the NJC. Labour regained control of the AMA and of its Police and Fire Committee after the local elections of May 1981 and, with a Labour chairman of the NJC the employers confirmed that they would keep to the pay formula. For the time being firemen's pay remains outside the annual pay debate.

It is clear that the local authorities are heavily constrained by the government. In part, the constraint is self-imposed: the employers have been and remain willing to accept the limitations of successive government incomes policies, whether explicit or implicit. The employers argue that any other position would not be 'realistic'; government decisions on RSG determine how much the local authorities can afford to offer in the era of cash limits. But equally, as employers, the local authorities share the government's objective of containing the size of settlements: it is no part of LACSAB's brief to outbid the unions on the level of increase. In the unions' view, the employers 'have always hidden behind the Government's guidelines'.[42] Such a strategy was indeed employed and not reluctantly: the employers have strongly affirmed their positive support for government guidelines on various occasions over the past decade.

The 1979–83 Conservative government may have employed indirect controls over the level of pay settlements but it pursued a more direct approach in its efforts to restrain, and indeed to cut, local authority manpower. By 1977, meetings of the joint manpower watch had ceased: it had been agreed that, since the machinery was well established and working adequately, meetings would not normally be necessary. There were, therefore, no meetings between 21 June 1977 and 9 August 1979. Any discussion was by correspondence. However, at the end of 1979 regular meetings of the group were renewed in order to effect a major change in the objects of the joint manpower watch returns. In what was very much a personal initiative, Mr Heseltine proposed that henceforth manpower figures should be produced for individual local authorities and not just as national totals. From 9 August 1979 until 22 October 1980 there were eight meetings of the manpower watch group. Subsequently, as the procedures for collecting these figures have been agreed, the frequency of meetings has again lessened. There was only one meeting of the group in 1981.

When the joint manpower watch was introduced by the Labour government it undoubtedly reflected the government's concern about the rapid growth in local authority manpower, but it was not seen as a pretext for effecting manpower cuts in individual authorities. The present government is prepared to use the survey to expose what it regards as overmanning in individual local authorities. The associations are confronted with a problem. On the one hand, they know that many member authorities do not wish to send the necessary figures and the associations are, therefore, reluctant to ask them to do so. On the other hand, the associations are aware that if authorities do not comply with a voluntary survey the government can consider making regulations to force them to submit figures. For instance, in April 1980 Mr King wrote to the association chairmen seeking a complete coverage in survey returns. He described the publication of the previous month's figures for individual authorities as 'an important innovation'. But nineteen local authorities had refused to allow figures to be published or to take part. The minister wrote:

> Rightly or wrongly their non-participation suggests they may have
> something to hide; and while it does not undermine the survey in
> which over 90% of the authorities voluntarily take part, it devalues
> it unnecessarily. I hope you will feel able to endorse what I've said
> and to add your support to my request that they should take
> whatever steps are needed straight away to ensure that their figures
> are included.[43]

The associations' subsequent appeal to member authorities was an
'appeal to their better instincts; if we don't do it voluntarily, we'll be
forced to do it'. And, by March 1983, local authorities were so
forced.[44]

CONCLUSIONS

This chapter has focused on the government's means of regulation,
relations between the associations and LACSAB, conflicts of interest
within the national community and varieties of departmental style. In
summary form, these conclusions discuss the major findings of the
case study on each of these topics.

First, there can be little doubt that local government has always
attempted to meet successive governments' pay guidelines, even when
there has been disagreement about the form of such guidelines and
resentment about the lack of adequate consultation. There is also no
doubt that inadequate consultation coupled with detailed interference
were a problem for local government. In particular the Labour
government's attempt to seek 14 days' notice of pay settlements can be
seen as *the* low point in relations between central and local government in pay negotiations. It marked the final stage in the attempt by
central government to incorporate LACSAB into the central bargaining
process. It also marked LACSAB's and the associations determination to take a stand against the erosion of one of local government's
traditional, constitutional rights. To a substantial extent, local
government's wounds were self-inflicted. The attempts by local
government to attain equivalent status to the TUC and the CBI can
be viewed as an invitation to the government to see LACSAB as their
agent in applying incomes policies to local government. The present
government has abandoned any attempt at incorporation. It has
simply presented local government with strict financial limits within
which such bargaining can take place. There is no need for a formal
incomes policy: cash limits are, *de facto*, the incomes policy. And, if
pay increases are gained at the cost of manpower cuts, then, from the
government's viewpoint so much the better.

Second, and unfortunately for the associations, close involvement with government courted the danger that by agreeing to send the government's message they appeared to lend approval to it. The risk for the associations, as for LACSAB, is that in seeking to become involved and maintain an involvement in the determination of policies they become mere agents for implementing those policies. The same problem had arisen for the associations with their involvement in the CCLGF.

Third, the involvement of the national community with central government in pay negotiations contrasts sharply with its involvement in grant negotiations. Perhaps the most important difference lies in the goals and interest of the participants. In the CCLGF the goals and interests of central departments and local authorities can and do diverge markedly. Each association seeks to increase both total grant and the share for their type of authority whereas, for the past decade, the DoE and the Treasury have sought to restrain the expansive proclivities of spending departments and local authorities. Such clear conflicts of interest are conspicuous for their absence in pay negotiations. Both the central department and the national community have a shared interest, albeit for somewhat different reasons, in restricting the size of pay settlements. The disagreements and tensions between the two levels of government focused upon how settlements could be contained, not on whether they should be contained.

Fourth, the means for regulating pay settlements were very different from the means for deciding grant and its distribution. No new 'corporatist' institution was created. None the less, there was extensive intervention by central government and new 'rules' were invented to facilitate central control. Central government faced the problem, of course, that pay settlements were the prerogative of the employers. In sharp contrast to the CCLGF discussions, the secretary of state could not decide on the level of pay settlements. The government could, periods of statutory pay policy apart, persuade, cajole, or bully but it could not unilaterally specify the total money available. Indeed, the major sanction was the government's ability to specify the level of grant which, with cash limits, could provide a clear disincentive to 'excessive' settlements.

Fifth, if local government's major resource was the capacity to decide pay settlements for itself, and if central government sought new means of influence without seeking statutory controls, the most striking feature of the national community's behaviour was 'compliance'. Just as the CCLGF saw local authorities accept central government's views on the management of the British economy and reduce expenditure in accordance with central guidelines, so informal intervention in pay negotiations was seen as providing a set of binding constraints on the level of settlements. And in both cases the national community accepted the government's views on the economic problems of the country and actively sought more extensive and more formal involvement. The reality of local government pay negotiations was that central government could rely on the 'responsibility ethic', as well as the self-interest of the employers, to bring forth the desired conformity.

Sixth, although the government created no new institution, it did employ a broad range of strategies. Persuasion and advice apart, the 'fourteen day rule', 'cash limits' and manpower watch are examples of *regulatory* innovations. It could be argued that the creation of manpower watch, coupled with experience of cash limits, encouraged compliance because both were clear demonstrations of what would happen if local government failed to co-operate. Throughout the period, however, the response of the national community was to seek involvement at the earliest possible stage in central policy processes. At times it seems as if the national community was seeking the status of 'central department'. It is as important to stress, therefore, that the desire to create peak associations was common to *both* levels of government as it is to stress the means of influence available to the centre.

Seventh, the creation of manpower watch, its subsequent incorporation into the CCLGF, the developing role and prominence of LACSAB, and the frequency and level of access to government all attest to the emergence of the national community as *the* channel of communication with central government. In the case of manpower watch, for example, the national community agreed to share one of its key resources – information – in return for this privileged access. Under the Conservative government, however, as it has become clear both that there is no privileged access and that this information can be used to criticize the staffing policies of individual local authorities, local government has become markedly more reluctant to co-operate. Unfortunately, the national community has discovered that disengagement is more difficult than involvement.

Eighth, the relationship between the associations and LACSAB compounded the problems of the national community in its dealings with government. The major weakness of the social contract between the Labour government and the trade unions lay in the inability of the peak association (TUC) to deliver its members. The national community experienced the same problem with its participation in the CCLGF. If anything this problem was more acute in pay negotiations, primarily because of the complex relationship between LACSAB and the associations. LACSAB represents individual local authorities through the provincial councils and it is not financially dependent on the associations: potentially, it could act independently of association policy. Such conflicts within the national community are the fatal flaw in the strategy of creating an integrated national presence for local government.

Ninth, LACSAB, and the board's secretary in particular, is of central importance. As joint secretary of the NJCs, the LACSAB secretary is *the* focal point of contact between employers, between employers and employees, and between central government and local authorities. He prepares the employers' side agenda. With his various chairmen, he presents the employers' case in the NJCs. And, of key importance, he is responsible, together with the employee side secretaries, for preliminary negotiations in which the frameworks for settlements are established. And it is worth noting that the secretary of LACSAB is personally involved. Whilst his staff do conduct negotiations, all major negotiations are conducted by the secretary and deputy secretary, as are any other negotiations deemed to be 'sensitive'. LACSAB staff prepare background briefing documents at each stage of negotiations and there are regular, at times daily, meetings of senior staff to discuss not only the state of play in individual NJCs but also the relationship between pay settlements.

Tenth, the associations are in no position to challenge the preeminence of LACSAB in negotiations because they have neither the staff nor the time.

Eleventh, there is an air of inevitability about the conflict between the associations and LACSAB. As pay negotiations became entwined with grant negotiations, the sensitivity of the associations' political leaders to their outcomes was bound to increase. Equally, in an era of growing militancy by public sector unions, the complexity and unpredictability of the negotiations intensified.[45] The conflict over the manual workers' settlement illustrates neither the 'independence' of LACSAB nor the unreasonableness of the associations but the impossibility of control, no matter how urgently it may be desired or needed, when decisions have to be bargained, not imposed. However, the 'problem' of LACSAB has many other facets and the relationship between it and the associations will be explored further in Chapter 7.

Twelfth, the conflict between the associations and LACSAB was not, of course, the only source of cleavage within the national community. Once again, the political control of the associations served to complicate internal relationships – for example, the firemen's formula, the comparability study for the manual workers.

Thirteenth, for all its diversity of interests, the national community remained closed. The trade unions are not even allies in a fight against pay policy. The national community objected to inadequate consultation by central government, to inconsistent settlements elsewhere in the public sector, to the control of manpower, and to the use of cash limits. But, above all, it objected to government departments acting as if they were the employers and negotiating directly with the unions. Consultation meant consultation between the employers and government. Any and all consultation between the unions and government was looked upon with intense suspicion and, almost invariably, seen as undermining the employers' position. At no stage was a joint union–

employers approach to government contemplated, even though both 'sides' agreed on the iniquitous effects of, for example, prices and incomes policy. Obvious though the point may be, the national community is an employers' community and the associations and LACSAB continuously asserted their exclusive right to conduct negotiations.

Fourteenth, it is misleading to suggest that the relationships between the national community and central departments are uniform. Various authors have noted the distinct styles of central departments not only in their relations with local authorities (Griffith, 1966, pp. 515–28; Sharp, 1969, pp. 25–6; Regan, 1979, pp. 33–4), but also more generally. To take one relevant example, Shirley Williams suggested that the Home Office had 'profoundly conservative views of society' whereas the DHSS 'rather prided itself on being full of bright new ideas, radical proposals and so forth'. Sir Brian Cubben (permanent secretary, Home Office) did not think 'that a department can be described as negative or reactionary'. The department may possess

> a store of wisdom about what the facts are; about what the implications are of changes in procedure; what the consequences are of certain statements, or of certain policies that might be used; and I dare say that you would find a collective and uniform statement in the department of what that assessment was. Whether that leads inescapably on to a policy, I very much doubt.[46]

Roy Jenkins (1971) felt that the Home Office did not 'produce a totally self-confident outlook' and had 'a slightly defensive expectation that . . . it would . . . attract public blame'. Finally, one journalist with considerable experience of dealings with the Home Office has described it as 'a deeply obscurantist ministry', determined 'to maintain a closed system, at every level' (Leigh, 1980, pp. 252 and 95 respectively). 'Departmental philosophy' (Bridges, 1971) is one factor, therefore, explaining variations in the behaviour of central departments.

Fifteenth, there are clear differences between the DoE, the DE and the Home Office in their relationships with local government. The Home Office was directive in its dealings with local government, the DoE was consultative and the DE was the 'handmaiden', limited to proffering advice. The directive role of the Home Office is clear from its interpretation of the fourteen-day rule, even after it had been 'clarified' with the DoE; its adoption of the mantle of employer in direct negotiations with the unions; and its refusal to sanction agreements. The DoE intervened as frequently as the Home Office but it sought discussion, not decision-making prerogatives. Peter Shore's interventions were recognizable to an association leadership accustomed to the CCLGF and the protracted nature of the correspondence with the associations/LACSAB attests to his desire to consult rather than instruct. The DE, rather surprisingly, adopted a 'low profile'.

The Home Office was the 'lead' department for the fire service and the DoE was the 'lead' department for local government and, consequently, the DE invariably appeared as support for one or the other. The description 'handmaiden' was suggested by an interviewee and it captures the DE's position most aptly. It certainly never occupied the centre of the stage on any matters described.

Sixteenth, such broad characterizations of departments should not obscure variations either within departments or over time: the styles were not adopted for all parties, for all policies at all times. One other feature of the behaviour of central departments – namely, the wide range of strategies deployed – suggests that it would be a mistake to impute too high a degree of stability to these styles. Thus, the Home Office attempted to persuade and to consult as well as to regulate pay negotiations. And after his protracted correspondence with the associations/LACSAB, Peter Shore was prepared to insist on close involvement for his department in the course of his negotiations. In addition, the 'policies determine politics' aphorism suggests that the content of any negotiations (and its saliency for the government) may have the greatest influence on style (and the strategies employed).

In brief, the same trends permeated pay negotiations as were found in grant negotiations but the differences are more significant. This case study demonstrates that incorporation does *not* require the creation of specific institutions. On this occasion, incorporation involved strengthening existing institutions and, perhaps even more important, continuous involvement. The frequency of contact at official level is high and contact at the political level occurred on an unprecedented scale even if less frequently. And, given that central departments and the associations shared the goals of strengthening local government's national presence and of minimizing the level of pay settlements, the predisposition to extensive involvement and consultation had strong foundations. Marsh and Grant (1977) have suggested that the weakness of 'tripartism' lay to a significant degree in the lack of a consensus about economic policy. Paradoxically, this case study suggests that, where there is agreement on goals, the kinds of institutions associated with tripartism are simply not required.

However, one conclusion stands out: the importance of local government's 'responsibility ethic' for central control. If pay settlements conformed with government guidelines, the contribution of indirect control, or voluntary compliance, to the achievement of this outcome cannot be underestimated. The most important constraint on local government was self-imposed.

NOTES AND REFERENCES: CHAPTER 5

1 The present Burnham Committees are constituted under the terms of the Remuneration of Teachers Act 1965. Amongst other provisions, the Act requires

the secretary of state to establish one or more committee, to nominate departmental representatives and to appoint an independent chairman. For a summary description of Burnham and other negotiating bodies see LACSAB, 'Evidence to the inquiry into Civil Service pay' (London: LACSAB, 1981, mimeo).

2   Councillor Dennett (vice-chairman, LACSAB) and Deputy Secretary, LACSAB, interview notes. For a more detailed discussion see I. Kessler and D. Winchester 1982, 'Pay negotiations in local government – the 1981–82 wage round', *Local Government Studies*, vol. 8, no. 6, pp. 19–31.

3   The associations involved were: Association of Municipal Corporations, County Councils Association, Urban District Councils Association, Rural District Councils Association, Association of County Councils in Scotland, Convention of Royal Burghs and Counties of Cities in Scotland.

4   Letter from LACSAB secretary to Sir D. Barnes and Sir M. Stevenson, 28 March 1969.

5   Secretary's report to LACSAB council, March 1973, LACSAB minutes.

6   Letter from A. Crosland MP, Secretary of State for the Environment, to association chairmen, 27 June 1974.

7   Letter from secretary, LACSAB, to Secretary of State for the Environment, 12 December 1975.

8   Letter from secretary, LACSAB, to A. Crosland (DoE), A. Booth (DE), M. Rees (Home Office) and Mrs S. Williams (DPCP), 23 June 1975.

9   LACSAB minutes, 11 March 1975.

10 Joint Departmental Circular 171/74, *Rate Fund Expenditure and Rate Calls in 1975–76*, DoE, 23 February 1974.

11 DoE, Circular 30/75, *Local Government Manpower*, 7 March 1975.

12 LACSAB minutes, 7 February 1975.

13 DoE Circular 30/75, 7 March 1975.

14 Letter to the chief executives of all local authorities from the AMA, ACC, ADC and LACSAB (signed by the secretary of each), 11 March 1975.

15 LACSAB minutes, 23 September 1975.

16 LACSAB minutes, 24 March 1976,

17 All preceding quotes from LACSAB minutes, 4 May 1976

18 *Hansard*, 6 April 1976, col. 269; and *Cash Limits on Public Expenditure*, Cmnd 6440 (London: HMSO, 1976).

19 LACSAB minutes, 18 October 1976

20 LACSAB minutes, 27 June 1977. The meeting at DE took place on 26 May 1977.

21 Letter from secretary, LACSAB, to A. Booth MP, Secretary of State for Employment, dated 1 July 1977. LACSAB minutes.

22 LACSAB minutes, 9 September 1977.

23 Letter dated 12 September 1977. LACSAB minutes.

24 Letters from permanent secretary, DoE, to secretary, LACSAB, and the three association secretaries, dated 15 September 1977. LACSAB minutes.

25 Letter from Home Office to secretary, LACSAB, 15 September 1977. LACSAB minutes.

26 Preceding quotations from report to LACSAB council, 6 December 1977. LACSAB minutes. Italics in original.

27 LACSAB minutes, 6 December 1977.

28 Letter dated 2 December 1977 from secretary, ACC, to secretaries of ADC, LBA, LACSAB and Director General of the GLC, including brief for associations and LACSAB and GLC chairmen for their meeting with ministers on 5 December.

29 LACSAB minutes, 28 January 1978.

30 LACSAB minutes, 13 April 1978. My italics.

31 Report to LACSAB council, 6 December 1977. LACSAB minutes. For a detailed account of pay negotiations in the fire service which clearly illustrates the continuous intervention of the Home Office see Rhodes, Hardy and Pudney, 1983b, ch. 5.

32 LACSAB minutes, 19 October 1978.
33 LACSAB minutes, 4 October 1978.
34 *Hansard*, 16 January 1979, cols. 1551–2 and 1554. LACSAB minutes, 19 March 1979.
35 LACSAB minutes, 8 February 1979.
36 Quoted in *Local Government Manpower*, vol. 23, no. 2, March 1979, p. 3.
37 *Hansard*, 22 May 1979, col. 903.
38 LACSAB minutes, 19 June 1979.
39 Councillors Lovill (LACSAB chairman), Dennett (LACSAB vice-chairman), secretary and deputy secretary, LACSAB, interview notes. It should perhaps be noted that some respondents felt that detailed intervention was rendered unnecessary because of extensive, informal liaison between the Conservative-controlled associations and the government. The contention is plausible but I have no evidence confirming or refuting it. It is perhaps worth emphasizing that my conclusion of no detailed government intervention in local government pay negotiations refers to the period 1979–83 and only to local government.
40 Secretary's report to LACSAB board, minutes, 19 June 1979.
41 Interviews with chairman, vice-chairman, secretary and deputy secretary, LACSAB.
42 Interview with general secretary, FBU, transcript.
43 Letter from T. King MP, Minister of Local Government (DoE), to association chairman, 30 April 1980. LACSAB minutes.
44 It should be noted that there have been five meetings related to manpower watch since October 1981, covering some important issues including survey dates, seasonal adjustments of data and the exclusion of (MSC) STEP (special temporary employment programme). Most important, since August 1981 and on a voluntary basis, local authorities were recommended to publish a detailed manpower statement each quarter. The objective was to enable ratepayers and the media to assess and compare the levels of staffing with which local authorities perform their functions. However, because a number of authorities refused to publish statements or did not publish in accordance with the voluntary code, regulations were brought into operation on 1 March 1983 requiring local authorities in England to publish detailed information quarterly on a consistent basis.
45 It ought to be stressed that this account has simplified the nature of claims and offers almost to the point of distortion – my concern has been the roles of institutions and not pay bargaining itself. To this intrinsic complexity must be added the links between negotiations for all local authority groups as well as negotiations elsewhere in the public sector.
46 All preceding quotations from Young and Sloman, 1982, pp. 23–4.

Chapter 6

THE REORGANIZATION OF LOCAL GOVERNMENT

INTRODUCTION

It is impossible to explore the structure and behaviour of the national community of local government without examining the reorganization of local government: it is important for all the organizations within the national community. Although there have been few studies of the associations, there have been a number of studies of the 1972 reorganization.[1] It is not necessary to repeat that particular story. As Wood (1976, p. 15) stressed, the reform of local government had been on the political agenda for all of the postwar period. He starts his study in 1966 but recognizes that this date is arbitrary. Also his suggestion that 1974 is not an 'absolute end point' could not have been more percipient: scarcely had the new local authorities been created than there were proposals to change the distribution of functions between county councils and district councils. The reorganization of local government is not only a major issue for the national community, it is also a perennial one. This chapter describes and analyses the most recent, and only partially realized, bout of reform, known as 'organic change'.

'ORGANIC CHANGE'

Origins

The origins of organic change are not lost or obscured by the mists of time, they are simply diffuse. It makes no sense to point to a particular speech, document or problem as the source of the policy. Like Topsy, it grew inexorably until there was a fully fledged policy for redistributing functions between county councils and some of their districts. And, although the proposals never reached the statute book, the policy underwent a mutation and several elements were enacted subsequently. The story of organic change begins, however, with the reorganization of 1972.

The 'county borough problem' The distribution of functions between county and districts was one of the major bones of contention during the reorganization of local government in 1972. The AMC, RDCA and UDCA had all lobbied strongly for an increase in the functions of districts and had obtained concessions in the planning, highways, traffic management and agency clauses. Welcome though these changes may have been, they did not resolve the issue of the distribution of functions. Perhaps the most severe conflict arose over the agency clauses. Department of Environment Circular 131/72 said that:

> where the previous distribution of responsibilities has been modified by the Act, agency agreements should not be regarded simply as a means of one authority to 'claw back' from another the services which were provided by its predecessor.[2]

Such hopes were not to be realized. As the chief executive of one major city put it:

> We are a great city and we will always be so, and whatever the local government institutions, it is imperative that we should be able to talk to the county on equal terms ... If you can't do that, you might as well have parish council status.[3]

In short, agency agreements became the flashpoint for the 'county borough' problem. Former boroughs anxious to preserve their powers and status used the agency clauses to achieve that end. The origins of organic change lie, in part, in this continuing discontent of the former boroughs. Such discontent originated in the decision to adopt a two tier system of local government and were fuelled by conflicts over agency and concurrent powers. Alexander (1982, p. 66) concludes:

> It is clear that district councils, as a class, are perceived as having interests that conflict with those of the counties. This is a damning indictment of a major institutional reform that was intended to end uncertainty and to bring to a conclusion the wrangles – on autonomy, tax base and status – that had characterized the old system.

The passage of time merely exacerbated the problem.

Opposition to the division of functions in the 1972 Act crystallized as early as 6 November 1975 when the first meeting of the non-metropolitan district councils with populations over 200,000 took place. The meeting was called by Derby Council and the following resolution was passed:

> That this meeting of District Councils, representing district councils with populations over 200,000, draws the attention of the Secretary of State for the Environment to the complete dissatisfaction of these Authorities with the restricted powers available to them as a result of local government reorganisation. These powers have been found to be completely inadequate to deal with the challenges and problems in complex urban situations. It urges the Secretary of

State to take effective action now to enable these authorities to deal more effectively with the responsibilities for the government of these important cities and towns so that local government can once again become really local.[4]

The policy committee of the ADC considered this resolution on 14 January 1976. They were conscious that many of the problems also applied to other district councils and the resolution was passed to the Secretary of State for the Environment.[5] The 'big nine', as they were colloquially known, were thus assured of a sympathetic hearing at the ADC. However, it would be misleading to suggest that the lobby in favour of some change in the distribution of local government functions was limited to the 'big nine'. Individual local authority leaders, only some of whom represented the large cities, were assiduous in campaigning for some adjustment of functions. This lobbying took place within the Labour Party and it had no formal organization: it involved concerned individuals using their contacts and positions within the party. The story of the Labour Party's policy on local government after the 1972 reorganization will show the importance of such political networks. The 'big nine' can be left until the other strands supporting organic change have been described. One point is, however, very clear: the 'county borough' problem provided considerable impetus to this policy initiative.

The Labour Party – regaining lost ground   The complaints of the 'disinherited' in reorganization are perhaps predictable and may not have achieved prominence if change had not remained in the wind. Contrary to expectations, reorganization did not end the debate about the structure and functions of local government. Internally, the Labour Party was debating regional reform and the Labour government was embroiled in the issue of devolution. Neither ostensibly affected the structure and powers of local government – the two issues had been deliberately divorced by Harold Wilson – but theory and reality were reluctant to part company (see Wilson, 1974, p. 725; Keating, 1982, p. 243).

Without recounting the history of the Labour Party and regionalism, the most convenient starting point is Harold Wilson's (1973) statement to the Labour Party local government conference, in which he called for 'democratic regional authorities'.[6] At the same time, Welsh and Scottish demands for devolution were on the upsurge and the party had to respond. *Bringing Power Back to the People*, issued in September 1974, noted:

there are areas of *governmental* decision-making which are themselves subject to inadequate democratic control.

Particular attention was placed on the profusion of *ad hoc* bodies, particularly the health, water and sewerage services, and the regional offices of central departments. The 'gap' between local authorities and central departments should, it was argued, be closed. The bulk of the policy statement concerned devolution to Scotland and Wales and, of great interest given subsequent developments, said that:

> A further common feature to our proposals for both Scotland and Wales is our intention *not* to take existing powers away from local government to the Assemblies ...

> the new authorities created by recent local government reorganisation will have time to settle down in their new functions before the Assemblies take office.[7]

The focus on the periphery was quickly challenged. At the Labour Party's local government conference in February 1975 the 'feeling was strongly expressed that the English regions were being left out'.[8] Gyford and James (1982, p. 99) report that this reaction was communicated to the Regional and Local Government Sub-Committee of the NEC 'in no uncertain terms'.

Throughout 1975 and 1976 the Regional and Local Government Sub-Committee produced background papers and held a series of regional conferences. The discussion paper *Devolution and Regional Government in England* was produced in September 1975 to guide these consultations. The rationale for the proposals lay in the fact that areas of governmental decision-making were not subject to democratic control and also in 'The botched job which the Tories made of local government reorganisation'. The division of the planning function between counties and districts was said to be 'inappropriate' and the new boundaries to perpetuate the split between town and country with adverse consequences both for planning and the provision of services in urban areas. The consultation document outlined a number of options and, mindful of the recent reorganization of local government, noted that a 'stage-by-stage approach to regional government' might be the best way forward.[9]

The regional conferences produced a small majority in favour of some kind of regional reform but no agreement on its form. As a result, the commitment to regional government entered into at the 1976 annual conference was vague. It pledged the party to:

> A dozen directly elected regional authorities responsible for planning and for infrastructure development ... they should take over from the *ad hoc* authorities for water and sewerage, health and economic planning, plus certain powers devolved from central government ...[10]

Many details, not least the effects on local government, remained to be clarified. But one point had become much clearer: local government was to be reformed once again. The aim was to simplify the structure and to create multi-purpose district authorities.

The process of consultation and subcommittee meetings continued with the annual local government conference acting as an important forum for discussion. A background paper entitled *Options for Regional Authorities*, written by Derek Senior, Lord Crowther-Hunt and the party's local government officer (Ed Miller) was agreed by the Regional and Local Government Sub-Committee on 20 December 1976 and discussed by the working group on regional authorities at the local government conference in January 1977. It distinguished between a 'local government model' and a 'Welsh model'. In the former, the new regional authorities would be the top tier of local government and their main responsibilities would be strategic economic, social and physical planning; infrastructure development; the allocation of capital expenditure; the provision and management of public services of a regional character (higher education, health, fire, police); and raising revenue through, *inter alia*, supplementary income tax. The all-purpose district authorities would retain all the present district functions plus education, personal social services, district services of the National Health Service, consumer protection and non-strategic structure planning. The Welsh model involved the creation of English regional assemblies along the lines of the proposal for a Welsh assembly: that is, the devolution of central government's executive responsibilities for local government, education, health, personal social services, housing, physical planning and roads.[11] These proposals were 'enthusiastically received' and on 29 June 1977 the NEC agreed that a discussion document incorporating these proposals and entitled *Regional Authorities and Local Government Reform*, should be published for discussion within the party to be followed by an NEC statement to the 1978 conference.[12]

At the same time as the Labour Party was moving towards a further reform, the government published its consultative document *Devolution: The English Dimension*.[13] In three years, the Labour Party had moved from a discussion of devolution to Scotland and Wales to a thoroughgoing reform of the subnational structure of government which involved the abolition of the 'new' county councils and the creation of multi-purpose districts. It is no coincidence that the Labour Party's movement towards another reform involved the very councillors who were also raising their voice on behalf of the former county boroughs.

Devolution in England Devolution in England may not have materialized but the muted debate it engendered was an important catalyst to organic change. Following the report of the Royal Commission on the Constitution 1969–73 (1973), the government published *Democracy and Devolution: Proposals for Scotland and Wales* (Cmnd 5732, HMSO, 1974), which noted that any conclusions on England would be premature and announced the need for further consultation. It would be an overstatement to say that the resulting silence was deafening but it is clear that the prospect of English devolution generated little enthusiasm. Although a further document was expected before Christmas 1975,[14] it did not materialize until 9 December 1976 and it contained no concrete proposals. Rather, it summarized the proposals for Scotland and Wales and discussed their implications for England; and it 'set out the factors to be taken into account in assessing the case for and against various possible changes in England'. There was, however, a sting in the tail. The consultative document distinguished between a radical change – that is, elected regional assemblies – and a limited change. Under the latter heading, the document suggested:

> There are also options for limited change at the local government level. Wholesale reorganisation of the present structure may not be the only approach. An alternative might be to examine the present framework to identify its strengths and weaknesses, and to see what improvements could be made without tearing up local government by its roots: *to embark, in short, on a process of local government reform*.

If the spectre of more reform was insufficiently daunting to many in local government, the document also noted that:

> There has been a good deal of criticism of the distribution of functions within the present two tier system, including for example the functional relationship between districts and counties in metropolitan areas, the division of planning powers between counties and districts generally and the extent of the various powers held concurrently by both tiers. The problems which have arisen under the 1974 structure do not affect all areas in the same way. A reform approach could start with a review of the tiers at which local authority functions are performed, *desirable changes could take place selectively* and if necessary with different patterns in different parts of the country. (*Devolution*, pp. 5 and 14–15, especially paras 59 and 60(a); my italics)

These gentle phrases did not figure prominently in the initial reaction to the consultative document. The AMA commented:

> Another major reorganisation of English local government may

seem tempting, but another reform on the scale of 1974 cannot be contemplated at this time of economic crisis.[15]

Gervas Walker, chairman of the ACC policy committee, whilst rejecting any radical changes, did concede that some more limited change was a possibility. An examination of the distribution of functions between the counties and districts was 'likely to receive support' although the matter would 'require more detailed examination'.[16] Initial reactions focused on the 'radical' options and were, for the most part, hostile. In customary fashion, however, the associations consulted their members and set up the appropriate working groups/subcommittees to produce the expected, considered response for the government. Indeed, the DoE letter inviting such comments stated:

> Copies of the document have also been sent for information to all county and district councils in England and it has been suggested that they should channel any comments they may have through their association.

Some have consultation thrust upon them!

The strands coalesce   There is one essential ingredient missing before the transmutation of *Devolution: The English Dimension* into 'organic change' can be explained: Peter Shore, who became Secretary of State for the Environment in April 1976, succeeding Anthony Crosland. At the time, the department was undertaking a thorough review of housing policy and work on the Green Paper *Local Government Finance* (Cmnd 6813, HMSO, 1977b) was well advanced (Crosland, 1982, pp. 264, 283 and 294). A number of interviewees suggested that 'organic change' was Shore's initiative – the policy with which he would make his mark as a minister. Certainly the former secretary of state, Anthony Crosland, had rejected any further reorganization in spite of the pressure from individual local authority leaders. To favour reorganization was a break, therefore, with the immediate past. Speculations on these kinds of motives are invariably inconclusive. Individual local authority leaders who spoke to Peter Shore found him receptive and felt that the only argument that had a major influence on him was the argument in favour of flexibility rather than uniformity in the structure and functions of local government. Peter Shore was adamant that he conceived of organic change independently of the 'big nine' lobby, the Labour Party debate and devolution. He said that it was 'absurd' that great cities should be stripped of their powers. In fact, he had had to convince the Labour Party that there was a need for this particular reform: that organic change would facilitate rather than hinder further long-term changes. There was no doubt in his mind that the policy was his initiative and that his objective was 'to save the city'.[17]

The contradictions between these several strands are more apparent than real and they interlock in a number of ways. There can be agreement that a problem exists without there being any consensus on the appropriate solution. An issue can win a place on the political agenda before the means to resolve it are either clear or agreed upon. The achievement of the 'big nine' was to win recognition of their 'problem' not just in the obvious places, such as the Labour Party, where they were well represented, but in such unlikely places as the constitution unit of the Cabinet Office. When the *Devolution* document was being drafted the constitution unit was looking to keep as many options open as possible. The option of 'limited change' was introduced for two reasons. First, as Lord Crowther-Hunt points out, 'most civil servants were fundamentally opposed to devolution, and so, for that matter were most ministers' (Kelner and Crowther-Hunt, 1980, p. 210), a statement corroborated by our respondents. As a result, the *Devolution* document tried to make it clear that regional government was *not* the only option. Second, the pressure from the ex-county boroughs for some change in the structure of local government had been noted as had the deliberations of the Labour Party's Regional and Local Government Sub-Committee. These pressures for change dovetailed neatly with the desire to expand the range of options beyond a consideration of regional government. For whatever motives, 'limited change' had made its first appearance on the government's agenda.

The county borough problem was widely appreciated within the Labour Party. Their discontents were being fuelled by the anticipated Conservative gains in the 1977 county elections. If county–district relations had their difficulties when both were Labour-controlled, the prospects after the local elections seemed daunting. Leading members from cities such as Bristol and Norwich had good contacts within the Labour Party in general and the Labour government in particular — for example, with Jack Straw, then Peter Shore's political adviser. They were peculiarly well placed to air their concerns. Pat Hollis (Norwich) and Charles Merret (Bristol) had seen Peter Shore informally within weeks of his appointment as secretary of state in order to press their views on the need for some change in the distribution of functions. Diaries record meetings on 21 June and 12 July but at least one meeting at a social event predated these two encounters. As a result of these meetings Jack Straw 'took up' the case for organic change — the phrase was reputedly coined by him — and made Peter Shore 'available' to the local authority leaders. He also actively supported organic change in the Regional and Local Government Sub-Committee meetings. Both Hollis and Merret were regional representatives on the Regional and Local Government Sub-Committee and its meetings provided a further opportunity to raise the matter, as did the Labour Party's local government conference. In Pat Hollis's words:

> We ... at least contributed to changing the climate of opinion in which the presumption is that you go as small as possible co-terminous with efficiency, not as big as possible coterminous with local government finance. [18]

In a very real sense, therefore, the 'big nine' lobby did not influence Peter Shore. The activities of this particular group were perhaps less important than the activities of individual local authority politicians who held positions within the Labour Party organization. However, access to the minister did not mean that organic change was Labour Party policy. The support of a senior political figure was essential if the policy was to get off the ground but the way forward for the Labour Party was not the way of 'organic change' and Peter Shore did indeed have to convince the party of the merits of his proposals. None the less, change was on yet another agenda.

There is one specific sense, therefore, in which the county borough problem, the Labour Party debate and the *Devolution* consultative document can be described as the origins of 'organic change': they all articulated the problem of the division of functions between counties and districts, particularly as it affected the big cities. But, equally, Peter Shore can be seen as the originator because he determined the form and timing of the change. The timing was right and the climate was favourable. Thus, on 29 January 1977, at the Labour Party local government conference at Harrogate, he announced that:

> Whatever we decide one thing is clear — we have to seek ways of improving the existing system of local government. This may in the long run necessitate a regional tier but it may be possible to secure some significant changes in the running of local government in a shorter timescale, without pre-empting the possibility of more fundamental change involving regionalism at a later date. ....
>
> So what I want to see is whether it is possible to introduce a substantial measure of flexibility into the present structure to allow for change in functions and responsibilities where this may be desired by particular authorities or groups of authorities. I would describe this kind of change as 'organic' because its pace can be a natural one, and can take account of local circumstances. What such change would mostly involve would be the transfer of functions from one tier to another and the ending of duplication of functions. We have the situation of former large county boroughs outside the metropolitan counties — Bristol, Norwich, Leicester, Nottingham, Plymouth and Hull, to mention only a few — the great cities with their own individual characters and traditions which once

provided all local services and which on reorganisation suffered a traumatic reduction in functions and status to not more than urban district councils and whose citizens may still be wondering just how they have benefited from the reorganisation that took place.

If we agree that there is no great case for imposing the same pattern on all areas, then it is surely sensible to examine whether some functions could be returned to some of the authorities who previously ran them, while still leaving a satisfactory role for the counties with regard to the rest of their areas. [19]

All the threads discussed earlier can be discerned in this speech — the loss of status of the big cities, the genuflection to the Labour Party's concern with regionalism, the limited, now organic, change strategy of the *Devolution* document. But the 'very tentative' proposals of the White Paper were becoming a policy. It was to take two years for this general statement of intent to be translated into a series of specific proposals: a process scarcely less tortuous than the origins were diffuse. For it is a measure of Peter Shore's initiative that this announcement was totally unexpected by his Cabinet colleagues. The time may have been right but not everybody was watching.

This description of the origins of organic change identifies a number of contributors to its gestation, including initiatives from the associations. And yet it is commonplace to argue that the associations are 'reactive' and that their involvement is primarily at the implementation stages. Clearly such an assessment of the associations' role in policy making is misleading: they can and do become involved in policy formation. The nature of their involvement, however, has a number of distinctive features. First, the appellation 'association' can distract attention from the groupings *within* an association. Thus the 'big nine' were the prime movers within the ADC and, even with the qualified support of the ADC, they continued to act independently. The AMA is usually seen as the prime example of an internally divided association. Such a condition is by no means unique and further enlarges the range of interests and multiplicity of goals within the national community of local government.

Second, the associations are by no means the only channel of communication for groupings of local authorities. Labour Party channels of communication were clearly of considerable importance in placing organic change on the government's agenda. The two channels were not distinct, however, for the same local political leaders were active both within the party and the ADC. The association can influence policy formation but only when the political parties are discussing their future policy, not when a government department is drawing up its legislative timetable for the next parliamentary session. If the origins of organic change lie in the 1972 reorganization, there is at least one major difference between these two attempts to reform the structure and functions of local government: in a tangible sense an association was one of the sources of initiative for change.

From proposal to White Paper

For the associations, organic change was still entwined with devolution for the remainder of 1977. The secretary of the ACC recalled that the issue had been 'floated' early in 1977 and that his association had 'noted' Peter Shore's Harrogate speech but no more. He added, with some amusement, that you couldn't take action on every press report. Certainly the ACC's minutes bear out these recollections.[20] At this time their major concern was to react to the government's *Devolution* consultative document.

Indeed, for much of 1976 the ACC had been concerned with devolution to Wales. The Welsh Counties Committee had produced observations on the government's proposals and the ACC itself had appointed an officers' working party on regional devolution with subgroups to consider the detailed provisions of the Scotland and Wales Bill. When the *Devolution* document was published, therefore, the ACC had already created the necessary internal mechanisms for evaluating it.[21] They were able to respond quickly and on 24 February the policy committee issued its 'preliminary' reactions to the consultative document, stressing that 'the main need for local government in England and Wales at the present time is the knowledge that it faces a period of stability'.[22] Copies of this statement were circulated to the relevant central departments.[23] Concurrently, the ACC was seeking the views of its member councils and on 18 April it issued a further press release announcing that its survey revealed overwhelming support for the view that there should be no further restructuring of local government or the setting up of a regional level of executive government.[24] Armed also with a report from a members' steering group set up to consider the officers' working group observations on *Devolution*, the ACC was now in a position to send its response to the government. This memorandum was approved by the executive council on 27 April and duly circulated to selected MPs and peers as well as central departments.

The association rejected regional government and stated that there was

no reason for any of the radical changes in the machinery of government, nor do they find any reasons for the limited changes other than a clear need for democratising nominated bodies such as water and health authorities ...

It cannot be too strongly stressed that suggestions such as the transfer of education or social services to district councils are completely mistaken ...

Certainly, the suggestion that particular functions should be allocated to non-metropolitan districts which were formerly county boroughs could only be harmful to the present system.

In the same document, therefore, the ACC rejected the radical and limited change options of the *Devolution* document *and* the transfer of functions envisaged under organic change. It was prepared to concede that 'strictly limited' adjustments in the operation of some services could be considered, but by collaboration. They did not need new legislation. Above all, local government required a period of stability.[25]

The response of the AMA was scarcely less trenchant. It argued that there was no evidence that 'the people of England want devolution'. The AMA was 'united in its opposition to unnecessary upheaval'. Rather, it urged the government to give local government more powers and eliminate the complex network of central controls. The AMA's role in this issue was very much that of bystander. Thus, there were a limited number of delegations to ministers and memoranda of observations on organic change. As late as 12 March 1979, the secretary of the AMA wrote to the secretary of the ACC declining to participate in a joint working party on organic change: 'there is no point in my meeting you ... to discuss something in which we are not involved'. The AMA considered, however, that development control was a district function − its sole public pronouncement on organic change. For the most part, however, the AMA was to remain on the sidelines and not because the policy had few implications for its members. Rather, the policy of standing aside was a conscious one because the division of functions between metropolitan counties and districts was (and remains) a potentially explosive issue. It was not on the government's agenda and attempts by, for example, Birmingham Metropolitan District Council to force the issue onto the agenda were rejected within the AMA. Silence helped to keep the lid on the AMA's internal divisions.[26]

The ADC suffered from no such reticence. It issued a circular to its members on 16 December 1976 requesting their views on the *Devolution* document and a devolution subcommittee was established. The first draft of the ADC memorandum of observations was available for discussion at the initial meeting of the devolution subcommittee on 9 February 1977 and contained a phrase which was to be the cornerstone of their position:

> The Association wishes ... to see early progress to iron out some of the deficiencies in the present dual system to give the district councils a more worthwhile role and to remove the wasteful overlap and duplication of functions between the two main levels.[27]

After discussion by the policy committee, this document was then circulated to the ADC's regional councils for comment. In an accompanying circular, it was pointed out that the devolution subcommittee had now decided:

> to limit consideration at this stage to possible changes in the distribution of local government functions which might be sought on a flexible basis in the short term, and deferred consideration of the long term issues until conclusions have been reached as to the short term.[28]

A policy of reallocating functions between counties and districts was not without its dangers for the ADC. Discussions between the secretary and leading members identified some possible problems. Perhaps most important, the smaller districts might object to the larger districts receiving preferential treatment. To prevent this conflict emerging the ADC subsequently insisted in its discussions with the government that there should be no arbitrary population criterion for the reallocation of functions. It argued that a population of 100,000 would create serious anomalies and it put the case of those authorities with a population between 90,000 and 100,000 with particular force. The feasibility of this argument was a secondary matter for the association. Above all it had to be seen to be protecting the interests of *all* its members, not just a privileged few. Additionally, the ADC was concerned about the possibility that, if the larger boroughs acquired additional functions, they might leave the ADC for the AMA, and with the practical difficulties of transferring functions. Accordingly, a report on the 'Functions of non-metropolitan areas of England' was prepared for consideration by the devolution subcommittee.[29] The meeting on 23 March considered the redistribution of functions in considerable detail. These discussions were given added momentum when the policy committee was informed that, as a result of informal discussions, the DoE was prepared 'to review the working of the new functional arrangements when they had further experience of its operation' and 'the possibility of amending the 1972 Act was not ruled out'. All the ADC's standing committees were asked, therefore, to review the existing position.[30]

In the meantime, the responses of the member authorities were being collated: 53 per cent of the 132 councils which replied were in favour of limited change whilst only 22 per cent favoured any form of regional authority and 30 per cent thought that the new local authorities should be left to settle down. These various deliberations culminated in a paper entitled 'Proposals for limited short-term changes within the existing local government structure', submitted to the DoE on 19 May 1977. In the covering letter the ADC secretary pointed out that they were submitting this document because 'it is understood that the Secretary of State hopes to reach conclusions about the distribution of functions between county and district councils within the next two or three months'.[31]

The ADC's proposals for the reallocation of functions were based on the principles that:

> the provision of shared and concurrent functions is unsatisfactory and these functions should so far as is practicable be allocated to either district or county, but not both, with a bias in favour of keeping them close to the people.
>
> ... agency is not the most effective and economic method of introducing flexibility into the 1972 Act arrangements, and any changes in distribution should, wherever possible, be by direct conferment of functions as of right.[32]

These principles meant that personal social services would be returned to those districts which were 'compact urban areas'; all of the planning function, except strategic planning, would become a district function; agency agreements for highways and traffic management to be replaced by direct conferment of powers based on the distinction between principal (county) and non-principal (district) roads with large urban areas responsible for all roads; consumer protection services (including weights and measures and food and drugs) to become a district function; refuse disposal and refuse collection to be a unified service at the district level; agency agreements on sewerage to be replaced by the direct conferment of the function on districts; and all other concurrent powers to be vested in the district with certain exceptions including airports, civil emergencies, country parks, museums and tourism.[33] Such a list was unlikely to fall within the ACC's definition of 'strictly limited' adjustments.

Support for such changes was not limited to the ADC. The 'big nine' had continued to meet separately and at their second meeting on 21 January 1977 had instructed their chief executives to prepare a paper setting out their proposals for changing the present system.[34] In response to the *Devolution* document there were differences of opinion between them. Bristol City Council decided to adopt 'the principle of radical change ... as their ultimate objective' and 'to seek early organic change by urgent transfer of functions to Bristol and other major City District Councils'.[35] Southampton, however, favoured no change. They agreed in welcoming the ADC's proposals to the government and agreed to press the government for action. Individual authorities either invited or received a visit from Peter Shore, in the course of which the secretary of state was 'briefed'; and he 'listened with interest' but 'made no promises'.[36] Indeed, the ADC encouraged its members to contact both the DoE and their local MPs in support of their proposals.

The campaign was spreading. In addition to the 'big nine' there now

emerged the 'twenty-two'. Ipswich and Norwich jointly wrote to all
district councils with a population between 100,000 and 200,000
suggesting 'a gathering together of those of us who are concerned ...
in order to discuss tactics' for obtaining some 'short-term changes
within the existing structure'.[37] The letter was supported by the ADC
and the 'big nine'. But some small signs of dissent were beginning to
emerge. Norwich approached the ADC asking why, amongst others,
education and structure planning had been omitted from the new list
of district powers. The ADC replied that they had considered the
matter but

> in the event ... it was decided that, in view of the practical realities
> of the situation, there was much greater prospect of gaining support
> for limited changes in functions if education and youth employment
> were not pursued as part of the Association's case.[38]

It was also pointed out that this decision had been supported by the
'big nine', although it was conceded that these authorities 'may wish
to argue separately the case for education going to the larger districts.
The association would not wish to prejudice any submission they may
make on this issue.' The 'big nine' submitted their general proposals
covering the transfer of education to the cities to the secretary of state
in May 1977,[39] although again there were differences of opinion on
the range of functions to be transferred.

The proposals also came under fire from Conservative Central
Office, which expressed some concern over the criticisms of the
Conservative government's reorganization. Seven of the 'big nine'
were Conservative-controlled and their support for Shore's proposals
was seen as inappropriate. Michael Heseltine (opposition spokesman
on the environment) and Keith Speed (opposition spokesman on local
government) met the 'rebels' in June at St Stephen's Club in Victoria
but they did not succeed in deflecting criticism of the current distribution of functions. In the words of Michael Cufflin (Conservative
leader, Leicester), 'All we want is a few practical changes.' More
dogmatically, the Conservative leader of Nottingham, Jack Green,
said: 'We're on the side of common sense and we won't be diverted'
(*Sunday Times*, 21 August 1977). Undeterred, Keith Speed returned
to the attack, criticizing Peter Shore for persisting with his plans to
divide local government. He called for 'a more fundamental devolution of power from central to local government' and an end to
'constant checks, interference and oversight of Whitehall'. Moreover,
he pledged to 'introduce policies to achieve this objective' (*Financial
Times*, 4 August 1977).

In spite of some minor disagreements there was clearly a ground-
swell of opinion supporting the redistribution of functions between
counties and districts. The ADC was encouraged by developments and

wrote to its members that its 'Part 1 proposals are being taken seriously by the Secretary of State for the Environment, who has been in discussion with other Ministers involved'.[40] The ACC, on the other hand, was moved to

> reiterate the views of the Association that the immediate need is for a period of stability in local government and that, whilst willing to consider minor adjustments within the present framework in any area where there may be a possibility of duplication or overlapping, they are strongly opposed to any significant reallocation of functions such as personal social services, libraries and consumer protection as suggested by the ADC, which would be entirely unacceptable at the present time and for which there is no public demand.[41]

The next step for the parties was to discuss their proposals and objections with the secretary of state. Both the ADC and the 'big nine' sought separate meetings and Mr Shore's private office contacted both the ADC and the AMA, indicating that 'the Secretary of State was anxious that the ACC and the AMA should also have the opportunity to make their views on this known to him at first hand'.[42]

The ADC met the secretary of state on 2 September 1977, the 'big nine' met him on 5 September, and the ACC on 6 September. There is no record of a meeting with the AMA. In each case the secretary of state indicated that the discussion was informal and without commitment. The various deputations reiterated their positions and the secretary of state took note.[43]

There was very little else that he could do. As yet, there was no official statement of government policy and the discussions may have focused on organic change but, ostensibly, the associations were reacting to the government's consultative document on devolution. There were two difficulties facing Mr Shore. First, there was disagreement between the affected central departments (see below) and, second, the Labour Party was considering a very different form of reorganization.

In July 1977, the Labour Party issued *Regional Authorities and Local Government Reform*.[44] This document represented the Regional and Local Government Sub-Committee's latest thoughts following consultations about the respective merits of the 'local government' and 'Welsh' models of reform and Mr Shore's proposals for 'organic change'. A number of doubts had arisen within the sub-committee about the proposed reforms. First, although the principle of elected regional authorities had been accepted, concern had been expressed about the political implications of such a reform. Some of the new authorities would be under permanent Conservative control. Second, many doubted the wisdom of yet another major upheaval of local government: it was 'probably undesirable' within ten years of reorganization. Third, there were a series of problems about the size, boundaries and finance of the new local authorities/regions. Finally, it was not clear that organic change was compatible with a more thoroughgoing reform. Indeed, the conflict between an incremental approach to reform and a radical approach underlay most of the specific problems. These doubts were resolved by convincing the party that organic change was the first step towards a radical reform. Thus, the proposal for elected regional authorities and multi-purpose districts remained but it was accepted with two provisos: that 'the authorities with enhanced powers reflect "genuine local communities"'; and that the changes 'should always be presented as a step toward ... more radical reform'. The Regional and Local Government Sub-Committee was particularly concerned that:

> If the proposals of Peter Shore are not presented as an interim step to full reform of the system, the opportunity to create a new system of elected regional authorities and new district authorities may be lost for several generations. Piecemeal reform may well be the enemy of radical reform.

A number of more prosaic difficulties were identified: the administrative and practical difficulties of any transfer, the mechanisms for transfer, and the minimum size of recipient authorities. The document concluded that there was no case for the transfer of functions to be limited to former county boroughs, but it did not offer an opinion on the relative merits of specifying a minimum size over which a function would be transferred as of right as compared to case-by-case review. It also noted that the transfer of functions could 'dangerously' weaken the county council concerned and that this limited reform might only be consistent with the long-term aims if boundaries were reviewed to include the rural hinterland. In short, the document rehearsed a lot of pros and cons – manifesting little outright enthusiasm for the changes – and accepted organic change as an interim measure.

Many of the doubts and reservations were expressed again at the 1978 annual conference but the conference accepted the proposal for the 'local government model'. The only *firm* commitment, however, was to organic change at the local level.[45] By September 1977, Labour Party opinion had crystallized. Peter Shore had successfully persuaded his party colleagues[46] but organic change still existed only in principle; there were no detailed proposals to discuss or negotiate.

Even more important, Peter Shore's Cabinet colleagues had to be persuaded. They had few doubts about what had happened with his Harrogate speech: they had been 'bounced'.[47] Because the speech had been made to the Labour Party's local government conference, it did not have to be formally 'cleared', although common courtesy dictated that the speech be circulated to interested colleagues. Some last-minute amendments had been made: for example, the speech referred only to the former county boroughs and not to all district councils. But no other minister had seen the text that was actually delivered. Subsequently, discussions took the form of ministerial 'bilaterals' and there were complaints that Mr Shore employed this form to suggest to each affected secretary of state that he or she was the only one who had doubts. News of these discussions 'leaked'. Norman St John Stevas (opposition front-bench spokesman on education) reported that 'The DHSS has confirmed that reorganisation . . . was the subject of discussions' with the DoE but 'no decisions had yet been taken'. Mr Stevas wanted to know if similar discussions were taking place with Mrs Shirley Williams, Secretary of State for Education and Science.[48] 'Will Peter Shore please tell us what he is proposing?' was a plea that was widely uttered. But no answer was to be immediately forthcoming. An interdepartmental committee (referred to here as IDC 1) had been established composed of officials from the DoE, DHSS, DTp and DES, with the DoE in the chair. Its terms of reference were 'to consider the proposals put forward' but the proposals were *not* organic change. IDC 1 was considering the proposals for 'limited change' in the *Devolution* consultative document. And its report in late September 1977 was, for Peter Shore, a most unwelcome document. It was 'keenly aware' of the problems of a transfer of functions. (See also pp. 227–231 and 233–236 below.)

Clarification of detail was not forthcoming but any doubts about ministerial intentions were soon removed. On 15 November Michael Foot, Lord President of the Council, announced that there was no broad consensus of popular support for regional government:

> The Government do not propose to initiate any major constitutional change in England until there is evidence of much more extensive support for it. The consultations have, however, revealed support for limited change within the existing local government system. The Government have not yet taken a view but are giving further consideration to limited change and in due course will make a report to the house.[49]

On 23 November, Peter Shore, in the House of Commons, stated that:

> the possibility of returning some powers to the major cities which lost them on reorganisation is being examined.[50]

And to set the seal on the policy James Callaghan, Prime Minister, who was seen by his colleagues as adopting a stance of 'benign neutrality', announced on 28 January 1978 that:

> I do not think that the discussion is ripe enough yet on which

powers should be transferred, or to which authorities, or what would be the impact on the authorities of the transfer of powers, or how many authorities would be involved.

Accordingly, he had asked the Secretaries of State for Education and Science, Transport, and Health and Social Security, with Peter Shore co-ordinating, to discuss the issue with interested parties.[51] These remarks were amplified by Peter Shore at the selfsame venue:

> The Government has been considering the next step. It seems to us that the best way forward now is that my colleagues and I who have overall responsibility for the major services administered by local government should each review with the Associations and other bodies directly concerned with those services just what the problems are. We shall then give collective consideration to what emerges.

In football parlance, one year after he had floated the idea, Peter Shore and his Cabinet colleagues had fought a nil–nil draw.[52] The proposal was on the government's agenda but there was no agreement on the content of the policy which Peter Shore still had to agree with his, at best, sceptical colleagues. This 'decision' perhaps implied that assiduous lobbying might yet influence the outcome. Certainly the interested parties were not slow to exert influence.

Although unsure about the exact nature of the discussions between ministers, the ACC kept up a continuous stream of press releases and delegations. In August it issued a press statement rejecting the Labour Party's proposals for both long-term and short-term reform and in September there was a press release after each meeting of the service committees affected by the proposal. The social services committee, the education committee and the consumer services committees all issued statements condemning the proposed transfer as disruptive, inefficient and detrimental to the public.[53] Meetings were arranged with the nine counties with cities with populations of over 200,000. After the first of these meetings a joint press release recorded their unanimous opposition to any transfer of functions, whilst the second meeting was called in order to estimate the costs of any transfers.[54] 'Urgent' meetings were requested with the relevant secretaries of state because the ACC anticipated that organic change would be in the Queen's Speech. In the event, it was not mentioned but meetings took place with the Minister of State for Prices and Consumer Protection (DPCP) and Gordon Oakes (and officials) at the DES, William Rodgers at the DTp and David Ennals at the DHSS, as well as Shirley Williams at the House of Commons.[55] Written contact with the DoE was maintained. A meeting with the Society of County Public Relations Officers was called to advise the ACC on its future PR strategy.[56] This activity merely intensified after the Prime Minister's and Mr Shore's speeches at Bristol.

The most important initiative in this period was the attempt to meet the ADC to find some common ground. A letter from the secretary of the ACC on 7 November suggested such a meeting to discuss 'the practical administration of certain functions, an example being town and country planning'. The letter also suggested a three-level procedure for the discussions: a procedural meeting of the respective Secretaries, meetings with advisers to discuss specific issues, and inter-association discussions at member level.[57] The ADC secretary replied in a somewhat discouraging vein:

> You will appreciate that the burden of the ADC case was that the problems of overlap and duplication are not capable of solution within the present statutory framework, and that voluntary arrangements between county and district councils, even if they could be accomplished, could not overcome the fundamental defects and problems inherent in the new structure.
>
> I am therefore in some difficulty about the suggestion that the ADC and the ACC should discuss problems of practical administration in the planning and possibly other services. If these discussions were to be meaningful they would need to cover possible changes in the law and I shall be glad to know whether you are agreeable to an examination on this wider basis.[58]

The ensuing correspondence can be described as amiable but distant: the ADC's objective of seeking legislation was unacceptable to the ACC. The ADC did not want to 'rush into' any such meeting and it was suggested that the ADC should 'play it cool'.

For the ADC the Bristol speeches were welcome. There is, therefore, little evidence of frenzied activity. Rather the association arranged meetings with the affected ministers to put their case. But 'it was now clear that it has now become necessary to move from general statements to more detailed justification'.[59] Clear evidence of this move is provided by the informal meeting on 9 March between Peter Shore (and official) with Sir Duncan Lock (chairman of the ADC) and the ADC secretary. The meeting produced a timetable for the ADC according to which they would see all the relevant ministers by Easter, identify the areas of agreement and disagreement and clarify the details. There would then be a further informal meeting after the views of the central departments were known and the secretary of state would make a further statement before the summer recess. In the autumn, there would be service-by-service discussions involving the affected departments and associations. It was also suggested that the ADC should find out if the 'big nine' would withdraw their request for the transfer of education and that it should submit additional evidence to the Royal Commission on the National Health Service.

The secretary of state indicated that he did not want to be involved in the transfer of water and sewerage functions. There is no record of an equivalent meeting with the other associations and, at this stage, there had been no meeting between the group of ministers which the Prime Minister had announced at Bristol. In sum, the secretary of state saw the ADC as an ally which could assist him in his negotiations with colleagues. An article in the local government press under the headline 'Political knives are being sharpened' suggested that rapid progress on organic change was unlikely not because of local government opposition but because of disagreements between ministers and central departments (*Local Government Chronicle*, 10 March 1978, p. 271). The ADC duly sent delegations to the relevant central departments and submitted its supplementary evidence to the Royal Commission on the National Health Service.[60]

The 'big nine' and the 'twenty-two' were not idle. The views of the 'big nine' were not identical with those of the ADC. The group of chief executives who produced the original general statement for the cities, now decided (22 February) to produce reports on the transfer of functions in education, libraries, town and country planning and social services, as well as a report on the constitutional implications of an uneven distribution of functions. These papers were edited as a booklet which was submitted to the secretary of state on 15 June 1978 'in addition to the observations of the ADC which have the general support of the Big 9'.[61] The most important difference was the transfer of education to the cities: a proposal which did not command wholehearted support within the group — Southampton restricting its claim for functions to minor changes in the transportation and planning fields. In addition, the group sent a series of delegations in their own right to the several government departments.[62] In a similar fashion the 'twenty-two' produced papers on the transfers of social services and highways and traffic management to the districts and, in their own right, sent delegations to central departments.[63]

Whilst there had been no meeting between the relevant central departments, individually there had been a deal of activity on organic change. The DHSS and DES both issued letters (24 February and 9 March) to interested parties inviting their views. On 25 April the DoE issued a draft discussion paper, 'Development control: responsibilities of counties and districts', which explored the scope for clarifying the roles of counties and districts. There was also a further round of meetings between the DoE and the associations.[64] Although the associations were very prominent in these consultations, they were not the only participants. The DHSS had written to selected districts with populations of between 100,000 and 200,000 — a letter which incurred the public wrath of the ACC because it mentioned the ADC's proposals but not the objections of the ACC.[65] The DHSS replied that it was merely summarizing the proposals for change, not the range of opinions on those changes. The DES wrote to twenty-four interested parties, including the various professional societies, but the replies 'were not very informative' and generally unfavourable. Of greater importance was the view of the inspectorate, which felt that, with the exception of Bristol, any change would have adverse consequences for the standard of service.

To this point, it could be argued that organic change had proceeded in a fairly typical fashion: the various parties had consulted and the pros and cons of the issue had been identified. Only the ACC, which had made eighteen press statements by June 1978, was treating the issue with any urgency. Several local government professions were affected by the proposal and had prepared briefs for submission to the relevant central departments as well as, in the case of the county societies, giving advice to the ACC. [66] However, it is important to note some of the differences between organic change and the previous reorganization.

First, in 1972, the government had made a clear decision on the principles of the policy and consulted about its detailed application. For organic change such a firm decision was not taken until fairly late in the day. Consultation was not limited to the details of the policy. In both cases, central departments were dependent on the associations and the local government professions for information about the likely effects of the legislation but in the case of organic change this information influenced the substantive content of the policy; for example, the functions which would be reallocated. Second, the range of interests and goals within the national community continued to multiply. The 'big nine' had been joined by the 'twenty-two' and the specific aims of these two groupings differed not only from each other but from those of the ADC. Third, the professions were seen as a major catalyst of change in the 1972 reorganization (for example, Brand, 1974, pp. 157–8). For organic change, they were substantially opposed to any reallocation of functions and can be viewed as a major component of the institutional inertia which Peter Shore and the DoE had to overcome if there was to be any reform. Fourth, there were no established coalitions within the national community. Each of the major associations had its own distinct position and sought allies amongst central departments and the professions, not within the national community. Finally, belying the usual comments about the ability of central government unilaterally to legislate, there were clear constraints on Peter Shore's attempted intervention. It is a convenient shorthand to refer to 'the government'; in this case the expression obscures the disagreements within government. No firm decision on organic change was forthcoming because the affected central departments had not agreed a policy; the negotiations between them now began to play an increasingly prominent part in the evolution of organic change.

If the distinctive feature of organic change was that it remained a policy in principle and without substantive content for some considerable time, the speech by Peter Shore at the ADC's annual conference in Torquay did a little to clarify the position. He pointed out that the government were not considering a 'root and branch' upheaval of local government. They were mainly concerned with transferring the social service function to some districts; with an increase in district responsibilities in highways and traffic management; with improving the county–district relationship in planning; and they were considering whether some changes in education might not also be appropriate. The next stage was 'collective ministerial consideration'.[67] Such a general statement was hardly guaranteed to remove 'uncertainty' or to reassure the ACC.

The promised statement in the House of Commons before the summer recess added a little more detail. In a written reply to A. Palmer (Labour, Bristol) he announced that:

> Although opinion is understandably divided on these matters the Government believes that there is a good case for 'organic' or limited change in some of these functions. Discussion has centred on four main functions: personal social services, education, highways and planning.[68]

For the personal social services a minimum population size of 100,000 seemed appropriate whereas for education most district councils were too small and consideration would be limited to the 'big nine'. For highways and traffic management, the government proposed 'to place the sole responsibility ... for all but a narrow group of specific matters with all district councils'.

The government's policy was becoming clearer, and a further statement by Peter Shore in Bristol on 7 September 1978 added more detail:

> We have stated our view that change is needed: what remains is to settle the range of authorities and functions to which it should extend and then to introduce the legislation to give effect to all this.[69]

There would, however, be no changes in boundaries. The imminence of change was all too clear when the Queen's Speech on 1 November announced that the government would bring forward proposals to amend the Local Government Act 1972 'to secure the better functioning of local democracy in a number of large towns and cities in England'. Change there would be, even if precisely who would get what still remained unclear.

There were some notable variations on the usual reactions of the associations. At the time of Peter Shore's speech to the ADC in Torquay Sir Duncan Lock noted:

Unfortunately, it has not proved possible either at Association or political level to shift the ACC from their entrenched and defensive position, that no change is necessary.[70]

The amicable but distant relationship between the ADC and the ACC was, in the future, to be only distant. Gervas Walker replied sharply that the ACC had made a number of approaches to the ADC and that the most recent letter suggesting political level discussions[71] had never been acknowledged.[72] The ACC's reactions to Mr Shore's statements were also hardening. His Torquay speech was described as 'utterly misguided'.[73] Following the NEC's statement to the annual conference entitled 'Local Government in England',[74] a joint policy committee executive council statement was issued which urged the need for stability and noted that one of the advantages of organic change was openly admitted to be party political. Concern was expressed at the 'serious and regrettable effects on the morale of both members and staff' which arose from the continued uncertainty. The statement flatly asserted that 'the association will continue to resist any proposals for major changes or for the transfer of main functions from county government'.[75] According to *The Times* this was the ACC's 'most uncompromising stand against proposals for change'.[76] Certainly Gervas Walker in a prior press release did not mince his words:

We have always predicted that so-called 'organic change' was the first stage of a massive reorganisation of local government designed to take the real control of local services away from local authorities and place it in the hands of regional authorities with ultimate total control by central government. Now we know it to be true.[77]

Similarly Elizabeth Coker condemned Peter Shore's parliamentary statement:

The Government's preliminary views are a prescription for expensive confusion with a hotch potch of differing arrrangements.[78]

And his September speech in Bristol was described as 'the last attempt by a dying government to foist on the public and the local government service yet another costly upheaval'.[79]

Rhetoric was not the only weapon in the ACC's armoury. After informal discussions with Professor John Stewart of the Institute of Local Government Studies at the University of Birmingham (hereafter referred to as INLOGOV), it was agreed in September that he would produce an independent assessment of Peter Shore's proposals. The report was to cover the constitutional, management and financial aspects of the proposals. The 'independence' of this commissioned report became a matter of some dispute. It is worth noting, therefore, that the ACC was worried about employing an 'outsider'. The secretary remembered that:

> some of our side said this is a risk. Someone may come along and say 'This is a good thing' and we said 'Yes. There is a risk but take a chance because surely our case is so strong, so fundamentally strong' ... We knew John was not politically bound to a Conservative point ... on the other hand he was a local government man. He understood the weaknesses and the strengths in the reorganisation. He understood the need and the hope for some stability and we thought 'Oh well: let's take a chance on it.'[80]

The ACC sought outside advice in an attempt to establish 'that this was not a case of an association grinding its axe yet again' and Professor Stewart accepted the commission 'on the basis that he wasn't accepting anybody's ideas in advance'.

Meanwhile, the ACC had submitted its observations on the consequences of organic change for the individual services to the respective government departments.[81] It also wrote to various leading figures seeking their support[82] as well as a host of local government professional societies seeking their views and assistance.[83] In a number of instances they were preaching to the converted. The Association of Directors of Social Services had already submitted their views on organic change to the DHSS and had argued against any change.[84] The County Surveyors Society had prepared a report on organic change, after Peter Shore's statement in the House of Commons in July in anticipation of a request for advice from the ACC (Laffin, 1982, p. 177). The Society of Education Officers similarly made its objections known.[85] The planning profession was not unanimous. There was no agreement between the county (CPOS) and district (DPOS) planning societies on the extent of any changes.

The Royal Town Planning Institute preferred some radical changes and urged that the planning anomalies of the 1972 Act should be eliminated as soon as possible.[86] The Town and Country Planning Association, although not a professional society, published criticisms of organic change. As planning was the only function with a strong professional presence at the district level, it is scarcely surprising that such divisions existed. All of these initiatives can be seen as an attempt by the ACC to build up support for its position and to avoid the accusation of narrow self-interest. The next round of public relations was to follow receipt and publication of the Stewart/INLOGOV report.

The ADC was delighted by Peter Shore's several pronouncements. Various press releases 'warmly welcomed' his proposals, although the ADC pointed out that it had not given up the fight for libraries and consumer protection and that it considered population criteria arbitrary and undesirable.[87] The association's main concern was over the timing of the proposals. They wrote to the DoE asking when the next round of consultations would begin, stressing the need not to lose the impetus for change.[88] Peter Shore said he expected 'to get a measure before the House during this session' but he also said that 'I cannot say exactly how long the session will last'; a comment which no doubt reflected the widely expected call for a general election.[89]

Nationally, the Conservative Party was still trying to make organic change a partisan issue. Michael Heseltine warned:

The real purposes behind the proposed changes in the Labour Party document are not to improve local government or make the services more efficient. The real purposes are to give a better chance for the Labour Party to have greater control over larger sections of local government. It would be both naive and irresponsible if Conservatives did not recognise this.[90]

The districts were told to 'beware of Shore's insidious seductions'.[91] But some concessionary words were also necessary. It was now accepted that there should be some improvements to the system, but in many instances the problems could be overcome by discussions within the party. The adversary style of national politics was suffering at least a minor hiccup when applied to organic change in local government: it confronted the self-interest of the cities.

When it was clear that a general election would not be called for October, work on organic change gathered speed only to meet once again the brake of interdepartmental negotiations. A second interdepartmental committee (referred to here as IDC 2) had begun work in August and it had reported in September. Its terms of reference made it perfectly clear that there was an organic change policy and its role was to lay out the means for achieving it. The 'dispassionate analysis' which accompanied the report of IDC 1 would not be welcome. Subsequently the DoE 'did the rounds' to 'clarify positions'. Neither IDC 2 nor the 'bilaterals' involved interdepartmental negotiation. These negotiations were reserved for the Cabinet Home Affairs Committee in the first months and then for the Cabinet committee known as GEN 117.

Some evidence of the difficulties which surrounded the interdepartmental negotiations can be gleaned from the timetable. Initially, the White Paper on organic change had been scheduled for October. The Prime Minister had agreed to concurrent legislative approval and, accordingly, the policy had been accorded some priority. Some 'slippage' could be explained by the expectation of an early general election. However, the first draft was not circulated until 13 December 1978 and an agreed text was not produced until 23 January 1979. The White Paper, *Organic Change in Local Government* (Cmnd 7457, HMSO, 1979a), was published on 25 January but it was a 'White Paper with green edges' because 'its second function is to serve as a document for consultation on those more detailed matters which were not or could not be resolved in the earlier discussions'. The 'earlier discussions' had lasted some eighteen months!

The main opposition to the proposals came from the Department of Education and Science. The phrase 'limited change' contained in the *Devolution* consultative document was described as 'weasel words' and the department's position, as well as that of the affected professions, was said to be 'hostile', although great care was taken to limit the opposition to the educational aspects of organic change. The department did not oppose organic change itself. The secretary of state was seen as 'holding to the ministerial line'. To local Labour politicians she was the 'biggest single obstacle', whereas to her officials she did not seem to accept wholly their arguments. In their eyes she had to support a fellow minister whilst holding out for concessions. Ultimately they saw her as sympathetic to Peter Shore's proposal but not to its timing: it was too soon after reorganization.

The political pressures on their secretary of state did not prevent her officials making 'a considerable nuisance of themselves' and ensuring 'that the disadvantages were fully discussed'. The DoE officials were seen to be caught in a cleft stick. On the one hand the policy they had to steer through faced innumerable obstacles and problems but on the other hand their secretary of state was personally committed to the policy and 'the credibility of the Department was at stake'. The process of clarification in IDC 2 and the 'bilaterals' was not, therefore, a process for arriving at consensus but for specifying disagreements; and the DES had a formidable list.

A brief to the Secretary of State for Education and Science listed a series of problems and top of this list was the perennial one of 'size'. The DES felt that virtually all districts (including most of the 'big nine') were too small to run an effective education service. They rehearsed the effects of size in some detail, paying special attention to the impact of falling school rolls. Thus, they argued that any reallocation of education to districts would increase costs in further education. Small local authorities could not maintain the appropriate range of specialist teachers and they could not meet the needs of pupils in special categories. Parental choice of school or college would be restricted. Co-ordination of provision for the sixteen- to nineteen-year-olds would be more difficult and there would be a deleterious effect on the careers service. Finally, the problems of redeploying staff in the smaller authorities would be more acute especially as school rolls fell. Moreover, these problems were not limited to the 'new' education authorities; they would also be present in the 'rump' counties. The DES argued, as they had to the Royal Commission on Local Government in England, that the advantage of large authorities was economies of scale.

Size was only the first problem. The remainder covered the need to avoid disruption so soon after the 1972 reorganization; the suggestion of automatic transfer – the DES preferred case by case review; and the cost of a further change. Voting rights (see below) were *not* part of the brief at this stage. Most if not all of these problems could not be resolved at official level and had to be referred to ministers, usually in Cabinet committee, for decision.

With the DES to the fore, other central departments could adopt low-key postures. The DHSS was said to have adopted such a profile. There was no need consciously to co-ordinate opposition. DES were the main opponents and the DHSS 'simply fell in behind them'. The two departments fought 'a classic Whitehall defensive campaign'.

Care should be taken in interpreting these remarks. There was no need to look for problems or employ the spurious delaying tactics we have grown to love and respect in 'Yes Minister'. Organic change contained within itself innumerable practical problems. To insist, as any civil servant would, that the practical problems must be discussed provided all the ammunition anyone could desire. The policy contained the seeds of its own delay.

For the DHSS the main problems were the opposition of the affected professions; the small size of the recipient authorities; the absence of criteria for evaluating applications for social service powers; and the allocation of facilities between soical service authorities. Not only the Association of Directors of Social Services but also the Personal Social Services Council had published their (negative) views on organic change.[92] Indeed, their views were so clearly expressed that 'it was not really necessary' to consult with them formally. The British Association of Social Workers (BASW) similarly opposed any change.[93] But, on the other hand, David Ennals, their secretary of state, was the member for Norwich, a leading authority in the 'twenty-two', and he did not see himself, nor was he seen by his civil servants, as an outright opponent of organic change. Therefore, any opposition by the DHSS civil servants had to be realistic. They had to recognize that a political decision on organic change had been taken and that their secretary of state supported a measure of reallocation. Accordingly, the department focused on the practical problems of such reallocation. When asked what they wanted from the negotiations the answer was cryptic but precise: 'the relevant sections of the White Paper'. In other words, the minimum size criterion of 100,000 was to be supplemented by a range of other criteria including case-by-case review of applications by an independent advisory body; effects on the county council of reallocation; the capacity of the district council to provide services efficiently, with the compact urban districts especially the former county boroughs 'more likely to prove able to provide social services efficiently'; and links with other services, especially education and the National Health Service.

The DHSS sought for and found a definition of 'compact urban areas' that would do the least damage to the service without opposing the threshold of 100,000.

The position of the DTp differed little in form from that of the other departments. Thus William Rodgers was sceptical of another upheaval of local government and was particularly concerned that the strategic role of the county councils should not be impaired. Given the political commitment to proceed with organic change, it was necessary, however, to find a formula and discussion focused on the most appropriate way of dividing the traffic and highways function – with the ADC's distinction between principal and non-principal roads being rejected as potentially capable of generating even more conflicts between county and district – and on the definition of 'urban areas'. William Rodgers was not strongly opposed to the policy and once again the practicalities of the transfer were the predominant issue.

The DTp was well briefed on these problems by the County Surveyors Society. Although there is no record of a formal meeting or delegation, the president, vice-president and secretary had 'private' meetings with the under secretary (local transport). Three or four meetings took place each year and were said to 'involve full and frank exchange on issues of concern to both sides' (Laffin, 1982: ch. 6, n. 84). All the central departments had close contacts with the relevant professions, thereby providing themselves with an additional source of information on policy proposals.

For the DoE the discussions with the departments were 'as difficult as anything I have been associated with'. This statement does not refer to the nature of the opposition but to the number of other departments involved and the relatively low political priority afforded to organic change at Cabinet level. The department's position was complicated by 'the obvious problems of organic change'. None the less the secretary of state was 'determined to have this policy' and they had to get it for him. And in order to get it for him Peter Shore had to be continuously involved. The DoE officials had to take many matters to ministerial level in order to get them resolved. That Peter Shore was determined is not in dispute. As Joel Barnett (1982, p. 94) points out (in a different context):

he [the Prime Minister] was just not willing to push Peter, who could be so touchy and ill-tempered and ready to get passionate and thump the Cabinet table, often on quite trivial issues, that everybody was frightened to upset him ... On this basis, the moral for spending Ministers must be to behave in as prickly a manner as possible. Better still, leave the impression that if you lose, you might not only resign, but become so convulsed with the strength of your case as to push your blood pressure right up and collapse on the Cabinet table.

Others suggested that but for Shirley Williams's absence on a visit to China in August 1978 the policy would have foundered at this stage.[94] The details of bargaining may be vague but all our respondents agreed that Peter Shore pushed the policy through at ministerial level and that the negotiations were 'difficult'. None the less, it was agreed that organic change was government policy and that a White Paper would be issued.

The associations were not consulted at this stage but they were still able to influence events. On 30 November the first draft of the Stewart/INLOGOV report was received by the ACC and, in the opinion of the secretary, 'it is quite clear that it is going to be a most important weapon'. Certainly the report was highly critical of organic change. Given the date of its publication, the report had to speculate on the precise form of organic change. In attempting to predict the effect of the proposed changes, therefore, the report distinguished between certain qualifiers for the transfer of functions, probable qualifiers and possible qualifiers. It concluded that any change would have a substantial impact on the local government system:

> The majority of English counties are likely to be significantly affected in that 20 of the 39 counties, either contain one of the 'big nine' or at least two districts where transfer would take place on Assumption One (certain qualifiers) or Assumption Two (probable qualifiers). (Stewart, Leach and Skelcher, 1978, p. 13)

In short, organic change was not limited change: it would have widespread repercussions.

But the key issue raised by the report lay in the discussion of constitutional issues: in different parts of the county, the county councils would exercise different functions and problems would arise on 'voting rights'. Thus, a county councillor elected for an area in which the county did not provide the education service could none the less vote on the provision of education in the remainder of the county. But if the council was differentiated, with county councillors only able to vote on matters for which the county was responsible in their electoral division, the result would be a confusion of accountability and many disputes. Nor were the constitutional issues restricted to 'voting rights' in the council: they also extended to the composition of committees, decisions on the allocation of resources and political control. One further example of the potential complications will have to suffice. Where a council was controlled by the Labour Party, excluding councillors from the urban district would endanger Labour control of, for example, education in the rest of the county. Labour is normally strong in urban areas and conceivably their exclusion from voting on educational issues outside the urban area could vest control in the Conservatives! (For a more detailed survey of the constitutional issues, see Stewart, Leach and Skelcher, 1978: ch. 3)

These problems were not the product of fertile imaginations. The report reviewed Scottish experience with differentiated councils and concluded that:

> The problems are real and serious. This is no accident. The constitutional problem is not an abstract issue. It is concerned with the nature of local elected control and that lies at the heart of local government. It is inevitable that a division in the system of elected control ... will create basic divisions in the structure of local authorities ...
>
> It is important ... that before any change takes place the Government makes clear its attitude to these problems, the weight they attach to them and the approach they propose to adopt to them. (ibid., p. 37)

The report also discussed the financial and management problems that could arise from organic change but the kernel of its critique lay in the scope of the change and over constitutional issues.

The ACC saw the report as 'our greatest possible defence against organic change' and launched its findings with considerable publicity, although Professor Stewart declined to participate at the press conference. On 10 January the report was sent to all permanent secretaries, MPs and peers and on 12 January copies were sent to their fellow associations. At the press conference, Elizabeth Coker emphasized the 'chaos' that would ensue from organic change and John Grugeon pointed to the 'total lack of any acceptable solution of the serious constitutional problems'. In short:

> We trust that in the light of the Stewart Report, the Government will at long last be convinced that the best thing they can now do is to give their proposals the organic fate they deserve – a burial.[95]

It was presumably the analysis of the report rather than the coruscating wit of Elizabeth Coker's conclusions which stung Peter Shore into a very prompt and strongly worded press statement:

> The Government have yet to produce their detailed proposals on 'Organic Change in Local Government'. Therefore it is both

premature and unwise for the ACC to utter such intemperate views at this stage. These are not so much considered views as the predictable reflexes of those who have a vested interest in the status quo.[96]

He also opined that there was not much relationship between the ACC report and the chairman's comments on it. He recognized that there would be problems and he looked to the normal process of consultation with the associations to resolve them. The ADC response was less virile, simply commenting that the report raised 'narrow, although practical, problems and should be played down'.

When interviewed two years later Peter Shore said he had no recollection of the Stewart report and that it had had no effect on his deliberations.[97] Similarly his officials played down the importance of the report, calling it 'ill-advised' and 'partisan', commenting that 'John did himself a disservice'. Be that as it may, and memories of particular reports fade rapidly, the collective DoE assessment of the report's impact seems to be inaccurate. Indeed the ACC would have been delighted if they had known the effect 'their' report was to have.

In one sense, the DoE assessment of the report is accurate; it did have limited or no effect *within* the DoE. The issue of voting rights had been identified and discussed in IDC 2 and, given the influence of the devolution debate on organic change, it would have been very strange if they had not been aware of the 'West Lothian' problem.[98] Nor should the problems have been novel to many other participants in the lengthy consultation process. For example, the 'big nine' had produced their own paper on the constitutional implications of any changes in February 1978. The position is best summarized by the following exchange:

Q. Did the Stewart report have any effect on the other departments such as the DES?
A. It was a hobby-horse. The matter had already been considered. We didn't have the sort of detail in the Stewart report — you know, the stuff on obscure Scottish authorities — but our attitude was 'you don't raise obstacles'.
Q. At least a second time?
A. Especially then.

In short, the Stewart report reopened an issue by identifying a whole series of new detailed questions which had not been 'thoroughly reviewed'. Given the protracted nature of the negotiations with the other departments, such a development was unwelcome within the DoE, especially as officials were conscious that too many practical objections to limited change had been raised by IDC 1.

Self-evidently, the DES reaction was less critical. They had received the first draft of the White Paper on 13 December. A memo on the education chapter of the White Paper from the secretary of state to Peter Shore on 17 January stated that 'This chapter tells a one-sided story'. Indeed, the DES still saw the White Paper as a consultative document: for the officials, its status was an open question. They felt that Peter Shore was 'unscrupulous in minimising the difficulties and asserting the advantages'. The Stewart report's discussion of voting rights raised a 'consequential but insoluble problem' which contributed to 'a thorough review of all points'. And the impact of that report can be judged by the fact that voting rights had *not* been part of the DES's original brief; it was named in the above memorandum to Peter Shore, and it was discussed at the second and third meetings of GEN 117.

Yet again care has to be taken in interpreting the discussions which surrounded the White Paper. First drafts of White Papers have to be shown to the secretary of state and as a result 'you have to write the things he would like to see and not necessarily what has been agreed'. Consequently a lot of familiar ground has to be retrodden. At no stage did the DES challenge the policy of organic change. Their concern was to minimize any adverse effects on the education service and, as was the case with all other departments, they focused on the practical problems of implementing the policy – a 'traditional' stance for civil servants. In defence of their service, the DES consulted with whomsoever could help them. They had contacts with the deputy secretary of the ACC on voting rights at a time when the DoE refused to see delegations from the associations and was particularly firm about not seeing the 'big nine' or the 'twenty-two' because they did not wish to encourage splits within the ADC. However, delegations involve consultation at the political level. Informal contact between officials is not out of court. The DoE also had informal contact with officials at the ADC, AMA *and* ACC. The DES can perhaps be best described as assiduous in defence of its interests and not, as a number of officials suggested, as hostile.

The results of the discussions between central departments are clearly spelt out by the following memorandum:

> Now that the text of the White Paper has been settled, and we know it is to be published in a few days, it is perhaps worth summarising the improvements that have been made from our point of view compared with the first draft that you circulated on 13 December.
>
> *Personal Social Services*
> As with education, there is to be case review, even for the Big 9 and the rest of the former county boroughs.
>
> *Education*
> All . . . points of substance have been accepted. The 'seamless robe'

has been preserved: there is to be a separate review body, free to make recommendations; and it is recognised that there must be Parliamentary approval for any transfer of responsibilities.

Other Functions

Libraries are to stay with education (subject only to the qualification that if representations are made and convincing reasons found for the transfer of libraries independently of the education function, the position will be reviewed; and there is no specific reference to the possible ending of concurrent powers over the arts).

Finance

The White Paper now just about recognises the importance and difficulty of the RSG issue, which is no longer treated as ancillary or technical. Moreover the discussions on the subject in the Consultative Council will only begin 'when the Government are ready to put forward proposals' ...

Staffing

It is now recognised that even if there are savings in relation to some functions as a result of transfer, there are likely to be additional costs in relation to others if the level of services is to be maintained.

Voting

The efforts of Professor Stewart have persuaded ministers that this issue cannot be avoided and there will be a clear statement that 'Where these functions (education and personal social services) are transferred, the principle of accountability would have to be reflected in voting powers'.

Whether this list of changes means that the DoE 'lost' and the other departments 'won' is an unanswerable question. Changes in the White Paper were expected: it was for the DoE to present its White Paper and 'let the others chisel away at it' – concessions are not made at the outset. It is claimed that the DoE not only knew that it would have to make concessions but also which concessions it would make when the draft was initially circulated.

The opinion was expressed at the DoE that William Rodgers and the DTp 'lost', although it was not a major issue for them. They did not want any change and had to accept some but did not 'oppose strongly'. David Ennals and DHSS, it is claimed, 'lost badly'. Ennals's attitude was said to be that any change would be 'over his dead body'. It was also suggested erroneously that 'he might not want to talk to you'. Both he and his officials were perfectly willing to talk and they felt that the concession of a case-by-case review substantially met their objections. Ministerial and constituency pressures undoubtedly influenced

Mr Ennals. There was a meeting between him and officers of his constituency party on 22 July 1977, and the general management committee passed a resolution in favour of organic change on 9 December.

The local party felt that he was a less than enthusiastic supporter but by 23 September he wrote to a constituent suggesting that reports of a split between himself and Peter Shore were 'entirely incorrect' and emphasizing the need to consult the range of affected interests. If David Ennals was an outright opponent of organic change — and he denies that he was — he had ceased to be so at an early stage in the development of the policy. Given the contradictory pressures from constituency, ministerial colleagues, departmental civil servants and social service professionals, he argues that his major concern was to establish sensible criteria for the reallocation of functions. No evidence contradicts his assessment, and his public utterances give added credence to it. Thus, in a speech to the ADSS annual conference, he spoke of the need for 'evolution not revolution': three words which seem adequately to capture his cautious acceptance of some change. [99]

The DoE's assessment of their own situation is more reliable. Organic change was seen as a 'solo run' by Peter Shore and the eventual publication of the White Paper was 'a case of a strong minister winning through' (see also Barnett, 1982, pp. 18 and 126). Undoubtedly this view is correct. But, and it is a very important but, some important concessions had to be made en route and the DoE tends to minimize both the extent of the pressure placed upon them and the importance of the concessions they had to make. It could plausibly be argued that case-by-case review for education and social services would have the effect of delaying considerably any reallocation of functions. The length of the list of relevant criteria, especially for education, was such that there were a great many grounds for such opposition. And informally the DES is prepared to admit that they hoped for this outcome — after all, they had always argued that Bristol was the only authority capable of providing an effective service at the district level. In short, a strong minister had got his policy where lesser men would have given up months before but the concessions the DoE had made contained, at the very least, the potential seeds of the policy's destruction.

But, to the associations, little of this process of ministerial and departmental debate was visible. They knew that agreement between the affected departments was proving difficult but the 'traffic on the network' was confined to the central departments. With the publication of the White Paper on 25 January, they could once again consult and attempt to influence the government's thinking. [100]

Contrary to the experience of 1972, it is clear that the associations were able to influence the policy initiation stage. It is equally clear that they were only able to do so because of the divisions within central government. It is ironic that the national community, which has been frequently criticized for its failure to present a united front, should exert influence because its traditional opponents were divided. However, some care has to be exercised in discussing the influence of the ACC and the ADC. In both cases the information they supplied to central departments had an effect not because it was backed by the authority of the ACC or the ADC but because it was used by a central department. The influence of the associations was indirect and they were junior partners in the negotiations between central departments. In no sense were either the ADC or the ACC able to impose binding constraints on the government. Rather the information the ACC supplied enabled the DES and the DHSS to make the DoE's life unpleasant whilst the information supplied by the ADC enabled the DoE to counter its critics. Moreover, it is slightly misleading to stress the importance of the information controlled by the associations. An equally important reason for their indirect influence was the ability to identify the appropriate allies and support them with the appropriate strategy. Thus, the ADC maintained a 'low profile' and provided Peter Shore with the information and advice which was requested. The ACC, on the other hand, publicly campaigned and cultivated fellow opponents of the policy whenever possible, whether amongst the professions or amongst central departments.

The strategy of the DoE during the 1972 reorganization has been characterized as 'consultative' (Wood 1976). The same description remains appropriate for its relationships with the major associations during the evolution of the policy of organic change. However, there are some important qualifications to this conclusion. The DoE did not simply consult with other central departments, it had to bargain with them. In the early stages of organic change, the DoE was prepared to consult widely but, in the later stages, it insisted on restricting con-sultation to the major associations – that is, it excluded the 'big nine' and the 'twenty-two' – doubtless to minimize conflict. The form of consultation also varied. The major associations readily obtained access for both formal delegations and informal discussions whereas other groups were only able to obtain a formal hearing. Similarly, for other central departments, some professions did not request formal meetings purely and simply because it was irrelevant: their informal contacts were more than adequate to making their views known. In short, the strategies of central departments varied between informal consultation, formal consultation and bargaining, depending on the extent of conflict, the stage of the policy process and the status of the participants.

Finally, the professional societies' role was one of sustaining opposition to organic change. In contrast to 1972, they did not play any role in facilitating change. Rather they defended the 1972 reorganization against any alteration in the distribution of functions.

There is limited evidence of overt lobbying, although it was admittedly somewhat premature to approach parliament, but, as in the past, the professions articulated the 'functionalist' ideology on the benefits of scale for the delivery of services. These arguments figure prominently in the statements of the opponents of organic change.

From White Paper to dissolution

It was somewhat unusual for the Queen's Speech of November 1978 to include an announcement of legislation on organic change *before* a White Paper had been agreed, let alone published. It does, however, indicate the urgency with which the policy was being pursued. The publication of the White Paper with green edges now placed considerable pressure on the associations because their reactions were required by the end of March. With the dissolution of Parliament imminent, any legislation would have to be rushed through. The ACC wished to have consultations because it had many criticisms of the White Paper.

Many of the points in the White Paper have already been summarized in the account of its drafting. Education and the personal social services would be transferred on a case-by-case basis and subject to the district satisfying a long list of criteria. On highways and traffic management the government decided that it was not possible to separate strategic planning and resource allocation from the provision and maintenance of highways. It decided that traffic management could be transferred to selected districts, that is, those with a population greater then 100,000 and an urban nucleus of more than 50,000. Development control was to be a district function with only certain, quite specific, categories (for example, mineral workings) being county matters. The government also indicated that it would be willing to listen to views on concurrent powers but was not proposing to act at this time. The White Paper also specified the procedures and machinery for the transfer of functions and indicated that there was a problem about voting on county councils without suggesting how the problem could be overcome. Similarly on finance it indicated that there were problems which would have to be discussed in the Consultative Council on Local Government Finance. Finally it discussed the transfer of staff and property.

The ADC welcomed the White Paper. They regretted that the government's proposals 'did not go as far as the ADC had sought' and indicated that they would 'continue to press for early legislation'. Without quite realizing the full import of their remarks, the ADC did spot some of the major weaknesses in the White Paper. On personal social services they noted that the proposed criteria were 'considerably more restrictive'; on education they commented that the criteria place 'an unreasonable burden of proof' on the applicant authority and that only the 'big nine' are to be considered. They did not consider it necessary to appoint an independent review body especially when the secretary of state would take the final decision. They expressed disappointment at the decisions not to transfer highways and libraries or to reallocate concurrent powers. [101] In short, the White Paper omitted many of the functions which were originally candidates for transfer and hedged the education and personal social services transfers about with a series of restrictive criteria and a two-step review process. None the less quiet satisfaction emanated from the ADC. In a circular to member authorities, the association noted that the Bill should not be a long one and that 'legislation should be completed by the summer recess'. [102] It also urged member councils to combat the ACC's public relations campaign by explaining the merits of organic change locally.

Perhaps the ACC should not have been so disappointed with its efforts to persuade the Secretary of State for the Environment of the error of his ways – the scale of the proposed changes had shrunk. But there was little satisfaction at the ACC. The association complained to the DoE that the government's timetable was very tight, and 'of course' they wanted to speak to the minister. [103] The ACC received a letter from the permanent secretary of the DES confirming that the Stewart report had been considered 'during the final discussions of the text of the White Paper' and that a number of the issues raised by that report were to be the subject of consultation now that the White Paper had been published. [104] A circular letter to all county councils spelt out the ACC's proposed course of action. There was to be a series of meetings of the working party of officers on devolution and the organic change subcommittee (members) to prepare the ACC's memorandum of views. The public relations officers of the nine counties were to meet to plan a publicity campaign; a public relations consultant – Butler Miller Associates Ltd – was appointed; and they were preparing a brief to circulate to MPs and peers. Member counties were requested to provide any information which would assist in making the ACC's case. [105] On 9 March, the secretary wrote to the relevant central departments requesting further consultations before any final decision was taken and indeed the DES had written to its twenty-four 'interested parties' once again seeking their views on organic change. The ACC also publicized the views of the professional societies. The criticisms of the Society of Education Officers, ADSS, PSCC and the Libraries Association were all aired in the *County Councils Gazette*. [106]

The pros and cons of the policy were well known to all sides at this stage. Thus the ADC stressed the duplication and overlap of functions and the attendant waste and reiterated its faith in the principle that as many functions as possible should be located at the lowest level of government in the interests of democracy. It expressed disappointment at the exclusion of highways, libraries and concurrent powers from the government's proposals and again criticized the population criterion as arbitrary, predicting that it would generate serious anomalies. [107] The ACC pointed to the inefficiency of breaking up existing services, the lowering of staff morale, the constitutional problems, confusion for the users of services, further complications in the system of financing, renewal of the old separation of town and country and the damage to services in the 'rump' counties. [108] By now even the arguments had a care-worn air to them. But the vicissitudes of political life were now to exercise a decisive influence: on 28 March 1979 the government lost a vote of confidence in the House and a general election was called for 3 May. Three days before the associations were due to submit their observations to the government there was no longer any point. Legislation would not now be forthcoming by the summer recess, even though the DoE had begun to draw up its brief for parliamentary counsel.

It is in the nature of organizational routines, however, that the participants should continue to go through the motions: the memoranda of observations were duly compiled and, on 3 April, the ADC had a meeting with both DoE officials and Peter Shore and Shirley Williams. At a press conference on 5 April to launch its memorandum, the ACC returned to the attack:

> As the last hours of the present Government tick past, the ACC today tells the outgoing administration once and for all that their suggestions for tampering with local government reorganisation disguised as so-called 'organic change' should be abandoned. [109]

They issued figures suggesting that the total cost of organic change would be between £15 and £20 million. The publication of their memorandum and the press conference were seen as highly provocative by the ADC. Although not in itself a matter of concern to the ACC, this was of some importance because the Conservative Party had re-entered the fray.

At the Conservative local government conference on 3 March 1979, Michael Heseltine ruled out another major reorganization of local government and the transfer of education and social services but he did propose a joint working party of Conservatives on the ACC, ADC and AMA to examine the working of the Local Government Act 1972 in planning, highways and transportation. This working party would function under the auspices of Conservative Central Office. Mr Heseltine was concerned that the current arrangements might be creating delay and increasing costs. [110] At first there was some confusion in the associations about this proposal. The ACC secretary thought the proposal was for a joint association working party but his fellow secretaries felt that it was a Conservative Party initiative. [111] Subsequent developments were to make the matter academic. Mr Heseltine had proposed an examination of unnecessary duplication and overlapping of services between counties and districts and it was clear that at least some facets of organic change were not to disappear should the Conservatives be returned to office.

It was now in the interests of the ADC to meet the ACC to see if any reallocation of functions could be agreed. Such an initiative had already been launched when the ACC made its final attack on the outgoing Labour government. The ADC was furious. In a letter to Lord Thorneycroft at Conservative Central Office, Sir Duncan Lock explained why the ADC was to mount an attack on the ACC, complaining that they had withheld publication of their own observations on the White Paper in the interests of preserving calm.[112] On 6 April Sir Duncan described the ACC's reaction as 'Hysterical, emotive nonsense' and their cost figures as 'scaremongering propaganda'.[113] The circumstances were scarcely propitious for inter-association negotiations.

Peter Shore was similarly unimpressed by the ACC's pronouncements. Their cost figures were described as 'flights of arithmetic fantasy'.[114] In a speech a few days earlier he had once again restated the case for some change in the local government system, claiming that democracy could only be served by returning powers to the larger towns and cities. 'Yet Mr Heseltine is having second thoughts,' he noted, and many of the supporters of organic change were Conservative controlled authorities.[115] Even if organic change was not to reach the statute book some change seemed inevitable.

The first moves towards that end were already under way. Mr Heseltine had stressed in his March speech that 'I hope my colleagues in county and district authorities recognise that the interests of our party transcend any local interests we have.' His announcement of a joint working party followed a meeting with John Grugeon (ACC), Ian McCallum (ADC) and 'Tag' Taylor (AMA); it was not, therefore, a suggestion but a decision. In spite of the heated exchanges between the ACC and the ADC, therefore, a joint working party to consider the planning, highways and transportation functions was established on 11 April. Following the Conservative victory in the general election, discussions were given added impetus on 24 May when Tom King, the Minister for Local Government and Environmental Services, wrote to the associations announcing a review of the workings of the 1972 Act to identify and eliminate overlap and waste. He continued:

> In undertaking this review I want to stress at once that we do not seek another major reorganisation of local government and in particular we do not believe there is a case for changes in the field of education and social services.[116]

Organic change was officially dead. But before the election Michael Heseltine had:

> encouraged the setting up of a joint working party of the local

authority associations so that local government's own agreed recommendations on these issues could be made available to us at an early stage.

As the new secretary of state he was:

... now very keen to get ahead with this review as quickly as possible and I am anxious to involve the Associations at the earliest practical stage, for I would not want the Government to set anything in motion without first having the opportunity to hear your own joint proposals.

The proposals were to be submitted to the minister by June 18. In an attenuated form, therefore, organic change still lived.

The origins of organic change were diffuse and its ending was indeterminate. The next round of discussions on the allocation of functions between county and districts was beginning – a round which was to have a finite outcome. For this time the government did legislate and development control became a district function (with a few specific exceptions) under the Local Government, Planning and Land Act 1980. In addition, the associations agreed a code of practice covering agency in the field of highways and traffic management. [117] These developments are a separate story (Laffin, 1982, pp. 175–206) in so far as the reorganization of local government can ever be seen as a series of discrete events. For just as organic change had its roots in the 1972 reorganization so more recent changes grew out of the discussions about organic change. The reform of local government has been debated throughout the postwar period. It has shown little or no sign of being removed from the political agenda since 1972. Indeed, following the adjustment of functions of the Conservative government, the 'twenty-two' re-emerged with yet another plea for the return of functions to the larger towns and cities and in 1983 the government proposed the abolition of the GLC and the metropolitan counties, returning some functions to the boroughs and districts and creating joint boards for others. [118]

CONCLUSIONS

To what extent can organic change be described as a typical issue for the national community of local government? It is certainly a general issue, like grant negotiations or pay bargaining, in which the national community in general, and the associations in particular, invariably play a prominent role: organic change was central to the interests of the national community. It is not typical in one obvious way: there was no legislation and the proposals were not implemented. Of necessity, the analysis of the roles of the associations omits the very stage of the policy process at which they are said to exercise the greatest influence.

Perhaps more important, however, is the simple fact that organic change is a case study of policy being formulated and that the decision on the principle was a protracted affair upon which the associations were able to exercise some (admittedly indirect) influence. Allied to this point is the conflict between government departments. The lack of an agreed policy created the opportunity for the associations to influence policy formulation and it illustrates the dangers of simple generalizations about 'government policy'. Just as coalitions are a feature of the behaviour of the national community, so they are the key to understanding the centre's policy of organic change.

Organic change does not admit of any easy characterization of central–local relations. Ashford (1982, p. 224) argues that it illustrates the 'dogmatism' of British policy making:

Shore's plans for 'organic change' ... reveal how easily national politicians can intervene in issues of immense complexity at the local level with little regard for the consequences. Perhaps even more lamentable, the structural division of national and local administration means that even if a minister were prepared to take local advice it would be most difficult to assemble advice in usable form and within narrowly conceived partisan objectives.

In fact, organic change illustrates the interdependence of centre and locality. The parallel with the debate about the reorganization of local government in the 1950s and early 1960s is striking. Brand (1974, pp. 91–6) argues that the associations' resources made them effective agents of delay. Similarly, Duncan Sandys opined that it was impossible to reform local government without the support of the major associations. The failure to reorganize local government before 1972 is not, however, an example of obstructionism or veto by the associations but of 'banana time' (Goodin, 1982): that is, for all of the 1940s and 1950s and much of the 1960s 'the time was not ripe' for any change. As Isaac-Henry (1975, p. 8) shows:

When in the early 1940s the Associations pressed for some measure of reform, the government of the day declared that the time was not ripe. This was a line which was followed by the various governments up to the 1960s ... all the governments skirted round the problem by making consensus of views by the Associations a pre-requisite of reform. There was, of course, as well they knew, no likelihood of any such agreement on any radical reform.

He also suggests that:

The 1940s and 1950s were periods of great social reforms in the fields of education, housing and social services. Whilst this was going on it might have been thought inappropriate to embark on extensive reform since the resulting upheaval could have caused delay and might have affected the quality of these services. Furthermore in order to carry out these new measures successfully the enthusiasm and goodwill of local authorities would be essential.

The time was ripe, therefore, after the extension of social welfare programmes when the disruption of existing political routines would be minimized. Reorganization consolidated change; it was not the precursor of it. And, following the 1972 reorganization, the time was no longer ripe for change. There was predictably no agreement amongst local authorities but, equally, central departments disliked the proposal, seeing it as an unwarranted disruption of newly established political routines. The resultant complex alliances between centre and locality represents a return to the pattern of policy-making predominant in the 1950s. In many ways organic change is a typical policy. The 1972 reorganization and the 1984 proposals to abolish the GLC and the metropolitan counties, both characterized by the unilateral exercise of executive authority, are distinctive. Whilst it is important to note the distinguishing features of organic change, no policy can ever be described as typical: all have their idiosyncratic features. It is best viewed as one episode in a continuing saga – an episode which illuminates many facets of central–local relationships.

First, there are multiple lines of cleavage within the national community and the patterns of coalitions are many and varied. And the obvious difference of interest *between* types of authority (and associations) can also be found *within* particular associations – for example, the AMA's 'silence', the 'big nine' and the 'twenty-two' in the ADC.

Second, in spite of the national community's multiplicity of goals, all the associations could point to gains. After two years of negotiations, the transfer of functions remained to be negotiated on a case-by-case basis with a review body – a classic instance of 'muddling through' (Lindblom, 1959). The ADC would have gained, and indeed did gain, functions for its members; the AMA remained united; and the ACC effected a marked reduction in the scale of the proposed changes. The 'losers', if losers there were, were the DoE, which saw its policy eroded, and the 'big nine' and the 'twenty-two', neither of which regained functions to the desired degree.

Third, the major resources controlled by the associations were information and organization but, if they had ammunition, the associations had no way of firing it. They relied on central departments to provide the gun. To a significant degree, therefore, the ACC were a resource for the DES and the former's 'indirect' influence hinged on conflicts within central government and especially on the opposition of the education policy community to any change – hence the favourable reception of the Stewart report which, in a happy conjunction of inclinations, supported the DES position. However, this conclusion applies to the associations' attempts to influence the principle of the policy. In the 1972 reorganization, the organizational resources of local government enabled them to exert considerable influence over the implementation of the policy.

Fourth, the government controlled the agenda of, access to and the timing and content of consultation. In the 1972 reorganization the government took a firm decision in favour of a two tier system and then allowed extensive consultation, beginning with the drafting of the Bill. Organic change was a more fluid policy but once the government had alighted on the principle of the flexible allocation of functions the same conditions surrounded consultation.

Fifth, the political resources of the associations were important. Local political leaders within the ADC commanded access to government at the highest level through the Labour Party and, at the very least, were able to get their views on the agenda for discussion if not necessarily for decision.

Sixth, the strategies of the associations varied not only with the different stages of the policy process but also with their stance on organic change. Thus, the ADC was a staunch ally of Peter Shore, concentrating on the normal channels of consultation, whereas the ACC, although not forsaking consultation, pursued an adverserial strategy, including a public relations campaign and the use of outside consultants.

Seventh, all the associations seemed to have virtually unlimited access. Initially a wide range of views were sought by government but, in the later stages, the DoE insisted on channelling communication through the associations. No professional society or individual local authority commanded equal access.

Eighth, no matter how extensive the consultation, the associations were not the major influence on the policy. The policy of organic change emerged from the essentially private negotiations between ministers and civil servants. The strategies of central departments varied with the extent of conflict, stage of the policy process and status of the participants. Thus the DoE bargained with other central departments because it had to have their agreement but consulted the associations and 'noted' their objections.

Ninth, confrontation between the major political parties played a limited part in organic change. The Conservative-controlled ADC and cities supported a Labour secretary of state. Indeed, the Conservative Party was only able to mount a united front against the policy on the eve of the general election. Moreover, the difference between the national party and local political leaders demonstrated that the nationalization of local politics is nationalization in name only, at least on this issue.

Tenth, professionals enjoyed extensive access to both government and the associations, but did not exercise the same degree of influence over organic change as over the 1972 reorganization. Rather they defended the functionalist ideology – or the belief in the effectiveness of large local government units – and in so doing fuelled the objections of central departments.

Eleventh, the institutionalization of the professions in policy communities ensured that the objections to organic change were ventilated frequently and to the appropriate people. They were the bedrock of the institutional inertia that this policy initiative had to overcome.

Twelfth, the exercise of executive authority by the centre was constrained by the interpenetration of centre and locality in the policy communities (including the national community); by the heterogeneity of interests at the centre; by the relatively low political saliency of the issue for the government; and by the increasingly transparent problems that the policy would create. Government may have structural power, relations may be asymmetric but the junior partner can exact penalties for unilateral action and win concessions.

Thirteenth, given that so many central initiatives of recent years have had their roots in economic decline, it is important to note that not all policies raise issues of national economic management. In the case of organic change, a more 'economical'explanation of the policy's roots and gestation would stress the actions of central departments (and their policy communities) in defending their interests. Institutional interests and inertia, not economic processes, are more powerful explanatory levers.

Finally, the case study illustrates the problems of defining the general interests of local government. Each association acted either to promote or to defend the known interests of its particular type of authority. Such interests are easily identified. The long-term interests of local government are rarely self-evident and no academic, class of authority, or political party can define these interests with certainty or precision. Until there is a consensus, it is perhaps better that the associations disagree publicly – at least the problem is aired and the merits of the respective arguments can be evaluated.

NOTES AND REFERENCES: CHAPTER 6

1 The main sources are Ashford, 1982; Brand, 1974; Dearlove, 1979; Isaac-Henry, 1975 and 1980a; Keith-Lucas and Richards, 1978; Morton, 1970; Pearce, 1980; Richards, 1975; Robson, 1966; and Wood, 1976. See also Rhodes, Hardy and Pudney, 1983a, ch. 2, for a critical review.
2 Department of the Environment, *Arrangements for the Discharge of Functions*, Circular 131/73 (London: HMSO, 1972).
3 Quoted in Alexander, 1982, p. 62. The same point was made to us by officers and members of former county boroughs interviewed in 1982.
4 Report of the secretary, ADC, undated.

5   Minutes of ADC policy committee, 14 January 1976.

6   I would like to thank John Gyford and Marie James for obtaining copies of the several Labour Party publications referred to below.

7   The Labour Party, *Bringing Power Back to the People: a statement of Labour Party Policy*, PS 84/87 (London: Labour Party Information Department, 5 September 1974), pp. 1 and 9.

8   'Programme of work', Research Department memorandum to the Regional and Local Government Sub-Committee, February 1975.

9   The Labour Party, *Devolution and Regional Government in England: a discussion document for the Labour Party* (London: Labour Party, September 1975), pp. 8–10, 20.

10   The Labour Party, *Labour's Programme 1976* (London: Labour Party, 1976).

11   The Labour Party, twenty-first local government conference, 'Options for regional authorities' (a background paper for the working group), Harrogate, 29 and 30 January 1977. On the 'local government model' see pp. 3–4; and on the 'Welsh model' see pp. 4–5.

12   The Labour Party, *Regional Authorities and Local Government Reform. A Consultation Document for the Labour Party* (London: Labour Party, July 1977).

13   Office of the Lord President of the Council, *Devolution: The English Dimension. A Consultative Document* (London: HMSO, 1976). Hereafter referred to as *Devolution*.

14   See, for example, *The Times*, 1 June 1976 and 27 July 1976.

15   'AMA News', press release, 9 December 1976.

16   'ACC views on devolution in England', press release, 9 December 1976.

17   Interview with Peter Shore MP, Secretary of State for the Environment, notes, 23 July 1981.

18   Interview with P. Hollis (Norwich), transcript.

19   Labour Party Information Department, news release, 29 January 1977 (521/77).

20   Interview with secretary, ACC, transcript. See also proceedings of policy committee, 23 February 1977, and minutes of executive council, April 1977.

21   For much of the period described here, the ACC was also opposing aspects of the government's proposals for devolution to Wales. Both the Welsh Labour Party and the Council for the Principality favoured a further reorganization of local government. The Welsh Counties Committee opposed this suggestion. The government decided, however, to give the assembly power to review the structure of local government. The arguments and the protagonists in this debate are strikingly similar to those in organic change. The proposals for an assembly (and a further reorganization) were lost following the referendum vote. Up to the publication of the White Paper on *Organic Change* (Cmnd 7457, HMSO, 1979a) in January 1979, however, all ACC documents refer to the policy under the heading 'Devolution and local government organisation'.

22   Minutes of executive council, April 1977, appendix, 'Devolution and local government organisation', pp. 54 and 58.

23   The departments circulated were the Cabinet Office, DoE, Department of Employment (DE), DES, DHSS, Home Office, Ministry of Agriculture, Fisheries and Food (MAFF), Department of Prices and Consumer Protection (DPCP) and the Welsh Office.

24   'Overwhelming No to "Devolution – The English Dimension"', ACC press release, 18 April 1977.

25   ACC, memorandum of observations, 'Consultative Document – "Devolution: The English Dimension"', 28 April 1977.

26   AMA, '"Devolution – The English Dimension": comments on the consultative document', 28 April 1977. On development control, see *Municipal Review* March 1979, pp. 265–6. On the conflict between metropolitan counties and districts see Laffin, 1982, p. 190. On 22 November 1979, the Conservative leader of Birm-

ingham MDC moved that the AMA request the government to make statutory provision for metropolitan districts to claim highway agencies as of right. The motion was defeated 39 to 8 (AMA Minutes 79/6).

27 ADC, 'Consultative Document – "Devolution: The English Dimension": memorandum of observations', 9 February 1977.
28 ADC circular 1977/24, 2 March 1977.
29 Dated 16 March 1977.
30 Minutes of policy committee, 31 March 1977.
31 Letter from secretary, ADC, to Sir Ian Bancroft, permanent secretary, DoE, 19 May 1977.
32 ADC, 'Consultative Document – "Devolution ..."', p. 3. The council of the ADC approved a second version of this document on 20 July 1977 which contained not only the proposals for short-term changes but also proposals for *limited* changes in regional bodies. It also submitted 'further observations' on 27 October 1977, following a meeting with Peter Shore on 2 September 1977. See below, p. 217.
33 ADC, 'Consultative Document – "Devolution ..."', appendix A, pp. 7–8.
34 Although widely known as the 'big nine', there were in fact ten members at this time: Bristol, Cardiff, Derby, Hull, Leicester, Nottingham, Plymouth, Portsmouth, Southampton, Stoke-on-Trent. Because separate legislation was envisaged for Wales, Cardiff's participation was intermittent. To further confuse matters, there are, in fact, eleven districts with a population of more than 200,000: Swansea did not participate.
35 Bristol City Council, press statement, 19 April 1977.
36 Peter Shore visited Plymouth on 15 April and Leicester on 27 June.
37 Letter dated 5 August 1977. As with the 'big nine' the 'twenty-two' is a slight misnomer in that the number of local authorities involved varied. At the outset there were fourteen members and in May 1982 there were twenty-five. They designated themselves collectively as the 'Boroughs and Cities of Medium Size'. The short description the 'twenty-two' is derived from the fact that twenty-two local authorities were invited to the first formal meeting of the group on 21 January 1978.
38 Letter to secretary, ADC, from chief executive, Norwich, dated 24 June 1977. Reply from deputy secretary, ADC, dated 5 July 1977.
39 Based on a 'general issues' paper prepared by the chief executives of the 'big nine' following the meeting of 21 January 1977 and approved at the meeting of 9 May 1977.
40 ADC Circular 1977/91, dated 28 July 1977.
41 Letter from secretary, ACC, to assistant secretary, DoE, dated 18 August 1977.
42 Letter to secretary, ACC, dated 9 August 1977.
43 'Organic change in local government', note of a meeting between the Secretary of State for the Environment and the Association of County Councils, 6 September 1977, DoE LG2 Division, 14 September 1977.
44 The Labour Party, *Regional Authorities and Local Government Reform: a consultation document for the Labour movement* (London: Labour Party, July 1977). Jack Straw had prepared a paper entitled 'Short term opportunities for change in local government' (RE/LG 1163, dated May 1977) which had some considerable influence on the Regional and Local Government Sub-Committee's views on organic change. The various quotes are from pp. 4, 20 and 20–23.
45 The NEC statement of 28 June 1978 deferred regional reform for lack of support. See 'Local government reform in England' (B/025/07/78); and Labour Party, *77th Annual Conference Report, 1975*, pp. 333–7. The 1977 annual conference also passed a composite motion calling on the government to increase the responsibilities of the largest non-metropolitan districts by transferring education and social services. See Labour Party, *Report of the 76th Annual Conference, 1977*, pp. 341–6.

46 Interview with Peter Shore, Secretary of State for the Environment, notes. Interview with Pat Hollis (Norwich), transcript. Parenthetically, divisions within the Labour Party parallel the splits between central departments and considerable time had to be spent persuading the NEC's service committees to accept organic change.

47 Ministerial accounts conflict on this point, suggesting that the speech had only limited circulation.

48 Conservative Party Central Office, press statement, 4 August 1977.

49 *Hansard*, 15 November 1977, written answer, cols 108–9.

50 *Hansard*, 23 November 1977, written answer, cols 784–5.

51 Speech to the Labour Party local government conference, Bristol, 28 January 1978.

52 Two respondents indicated that the Lord President of the Council, Michael Foot, strongly supported Peter Shore and was instrumental in persuading James Callaghan to make the Bristol announcement. One respondent disagreed. It was not possible to determine what role Michael Foot played in the matter, although given his responsibility for devolution it seems probable that he would have supported the 'limited change' option.

53 The county societies, in the usual fashion, advised the ACC committees in the preparation of these reports. See ACC, 'Local government organisation: distribution of functions between counties and districts', appendices B–H for the statements of the ACC on the individual services.

54 ACC, 'Local government organisation', notes of a meeting, 10 October 1977, ACC press release 13 October 1977. The second meeting took place on 9 November 1977.

55 Meetings took place with the DPCP on 22 November 1977; an informal meeting with Shirley Williams at House of Commons on 15 November 1977; and with DES (Gordon Oakes) on 18 January 1978. For further information, see ACC, 'Brief outline of activities of the committees of the association, 1977/78', Policy Committee, para. 2, p. 3.

56 On 26 September 1977 the secretary of the ACC also wrote to the professional societies asking for information and support. He contacted ACCE, CPOS, SCS, ADSS, SCT, County Surveyors Society, Society of County Librarians, Society of County Trading Standards Officers and County Education Officers Society.

57 Letter from secretary, ACC, to secretary, ADC, dated 7 November 1977.

58 Letter from secretary, ADC, to secretary, ACC, dated 15 November 1977.

59 Letter from the chief executive, Nottingham, to secretary, ADC, dated 3 February 1978 reporting on a meeting with R. Moyle (minister of state, DHSS).

60 DTp (officials) 20 February 1978; DTp. (William Rodgers) 15 March 1978; DTp (officials) 17 May 1978; DHSS (David Ennals) 21 March 1978; DES (Gordon Oakes) 23 May 1978; and DPCP (John Fraser) 20 April 1978. See also ADC, 'Royal Commission on the National Health Service – memorandum of supplementary evidence', Policy Committee, 10 May 1978. Appendix A approved by council 19 July 1978.

61 *Organic Change: The Future Allocation of Local Government Functions* (a big-nine publication dated June 1978).

62 E.g. DoE (Peter Shore) 5 September 1977; DHSS (David Ennals) 14 March 1978; and DHSS (R. Moyle) 2 February 1978.

63 The papers included 'Organic change in local government, social services, statement of the views of the boroughs and cities of medium size', 23 March 1978; and 'Organic change in local government, highways and traffic management', 11 April 1978. Meetings included DHSS (David Ennals), 14 March 1978, and DTp (William Rodgers), 15 March 1978, as well as the DoE. The delegations included such prominent supporters of organic change as Pat Hollis (Norwich).

64 On 18 May (ACC), 24 May (AMA) and 25 May (ADC).

65 ACC press release, 6 April 1978.

66 The briefs and comments sent to the central departments by the professions are noted in the descriptions of the activities of the departments. See pages 226, 229, 230 and 237–8 below. On the role of the county societies as advisers to the ACC see page 220–1 above and pages 226 and 239.

67 Peter Shore, speech at the ADC annual conference, Torquay, 9 June 1978.

68 *Hansard*, 3 August 1978, cols 752–4.

69 DoE press notice, 7 September 1978.

70 Speech to the ADC annual meeting, 7 June 1978.

71 Secretary, ACC, to Secretary, ADC, dated 6 April 1978.

72 ACC press release, 7 June 1978.

73 ACC press release, 9 June 1978.

74 Issued on 28 June 1978. See, above, pages 33–34, 217–8 and note 45.

75 ACC policy statement, minutes of executive council, July 1978, appendix E, p. 177. See also *County Councils Gazette*, August 1978, p. 116.

76 'County councils fight change', *The Times*, 27 July 1978.

77 ACC press release, 6 July 1978.

78 ACC press release, 3 August 1978.

79 Gervas Walker, chairman, ACC, press release, 7 September 1978.

80 Interview with secretary, ACC, transcript.

81 See, for example, the submission on personal social services reproduced in *County Councils Gazette*, July 1978, pp. 56–9.

82 For example, Dame Evelyn Sharp, former permanent secretary at the Ministry of Housing and Local Government.

83 Letter sent 12 October 1978. The ACC was aware that such a move would generate support. For example the ACC's education committee reported that it was 'gravely concerned' about the effects of organic change on the service. This opinion would not have been produced without professional advice. See executive council minutes, November 1978, report of the education committee, p. 200. The other affected service committees also expressed their opposition to the government's proposals.

84 See *Social Work Today* vol. 9, no. 41 1978, p. 5; and vol. 10, no. 15 (1978), p. 4.

85 See *The Times Educational Supplement*, 2 July 1978.

86 For example, *Town and Country Planning* 46 (1978), pp. 517–18; and RTPI press release, 4 October 1977.

87 'More power for district councils', *ADC News* (press release), 4 August 1978.

88 The DoE replied to the secretary of the ADC in a letter dated 24 October 1978 that consultation would take place 'as soon as practicable'.

89 *Hansard*, 8 November 1978, written answer, col. 222.

90 Speech to the Conservative Party local government conference, Caxton Hall, London, February 1978, reported in *County Councils Gazette* April 1978, p. 19; and *Municipal Review*, March 1978, p. 349.

91 Remark attributed to Hugh Rossi MP, spokesman on housing, *Municipal Review*, March 1978, p. 349.

92 Paper from R. T. Clarke (secretary, PSSC) entitled 'Organic change in local government' to T. Luce (DHSS) dated 14 April 1978. This was followed by a statement from the PSSC Executive Council, June 1978. See also R. T. Clarke (1981, p. 45). On the ADSS, see *Social Work Today* vol. 9, no. 41 (1978), p. 5; and vol. 10, no. 15 (1978), p. 4.

93 BASW published a critical paper entitled 'The principles of organic change' as well as critical leading articles. See *Social Work Today*, vol. 9, no. 48 (1978), p. 6; vol. 10, no. 23 (1978), p. 5; vol. 10, no. 33 (1978), p. 1; and vol. 10, no. 34 (1978), p. 3.

94 *The Times Educational Supplement*, 11 August 1978.

95 ACC press release, 11 January 1979; *County Councils Gazette*, February 1979, pp. 331–2.

96 DoE press statement, 11 January 1979.

97 Interview with Peter Shore MP, Secretary of State for the Environment.

98 The issue of voting rights was also known as the 'West Lothian' problem because the same problem had arisen in the debate about devolution to Scotland when objections had been raised to the right of Scottish MPs to vote on legislation specific to England and Wales as well as legislation reserved for the Scottish assembly. It was labelled the 'West Lothian' problem because the matter was raised initially by T. Dalyell, MP for West Lothian.

99 Speech to the conference of the Association of Directors of Social Services, Bristol, November 1978, reported in *Municipal Review*, January 1979, p. 218.

100 It is alleged that changes were made in the White Paper up to the time it was published. Certainly the phrase on voting rights cited above, page 235, does not occur in the White Paper. The nearest phrase reads: 'The question of accountability is at issue' (para. 66, p. 21). This version is much weaker because it contains no commitment to preserve the principle of accountability: that is, the White Paper retains the option of ignoring voting rights. It was further alleged that this change was a result of prime ministerial intervention but it was not possible to substantiate (or refute) this statement.

101 *ADC News* (press release), 25 January 1979; and minutes of the policy committee, 28 February 1979.

102 ADC Circular 1979/15, 26 January 1979.

103 Secretary, ACC, to DoE, 1 February 1979.

104 Permanent secretary, DES, to secretary, ACC, letter dated 25 January 1979.

105 Circular letter from Secretary (ACC) to all chief executives dated 2 February 1979. Incidentally, organic change is referred to as such — rather than devolution — for the first time in Policy Committee/Executive Council minutes for April 1979 although a Special Sub-committee of the Policy Committee, the 'Organic Change' Sub-Committee, had been set up in February 1978 to consider the provision of information to the public on the costs of further changes.

106 See, for example, *County Councils Gazette*, April 1979, pp. 13–14; and May 1979, p. 48.

107 ADC, 'Organic change in local government, memorandum of observations', minutes of policy committee, 28 February 1979, Appendix B, pp. 148–60.

108 ACC, 'White Paper: "Organic Change in Local Government (Cmnd 7457)", memorandum of views', 28 March 1979.

109 ACC press release, 4 April 1979 and *County Councils Gazette*, May 1979, pp. 44–5.

110 Speech at Conservative local government conference, 3 March 1979, reported in *County Councils Gazette*, April 1979, pp. 6–7.

111 For example, letter from secretary, AMA, dated 12 March 1979.

112 Letter from Sir Duncan Lock, chairman, ADC, to Lord Thorneycroft, dated 5 April 1979.

113 *ADC News* (press release), 6 April 1979.

114 DoE press statement, 5 April 1979.

115 Speech by Peter Shore, 27 March 1979, reproduced in full in *County Councils Gazette*, May 1979, pp. 46–8.

116 Letter to Sir Duncan Lock, chairman, ADC, from Tom King, Minister for Local Government, DoE, dated 24 May 1979.

117 ACC, ADC and AMA, *Highway and Traffic Management Agency Agreements: Code of Practice* (April 1980).

118 See *Local Government Responsibilities, A Proposal for Reform* (paper by the Boroughs and Cities of Medium Size, May 1982); and Department of the Environment, *Streamlining the Cities*, Cmnd 9063 (London: HMSO, 1983).

PART THREE

OTHER RELATIONSHIPS

Chapter 7

RELATIONSHIPS WITHIN THE NATIONAL COMMUNITY

INTRODUCTION

The strategy of incorporation required not only the accreditation of the associations as the spokesmen for local government but also the creation of an integrated national community. However, there are a number of conflicts within the national community. The disagreements over the distribution of grant in the CCLGF revealed the importance of the different interests of each association. Pay negotiations were complicated by party-based disputes between the associations. Additionally, co-operation between the member organizations of the national community can falter on the relationship of the associations to 'their' joint bodies. This chapter explores in more detail such relationships within the national community.

It has been shown that the relationship between the major associations fluctuates greatly. But the ACC, ADC and AMA have links with other associations with which they share common memberships – respectively, the Welsh Counties Committee (WCC), the Council for the Principality (CP) and the London Boroughs Association (LBA). Similarly, LGTB and LAMSAC as well as LACSAB are pre-eminent joint bodies, and their activities have to be controlled and co-ordinated. The first step in exploring the degree of integration within the national community is, therefore, to describe the range of relationships and not just the conflict between the major associations.

The relationships between the major and minor associations are explored both formally (or in constitutional terms) and through case studies of their involvement in the procedures for distributing grant. If the centres' preferred strategy for English local authorities has been to aggregate their interests, it has developed separate institutions and networks for all the major local government subsystems. The brief case studies of the Welsh and London associations will demonstrate that aggregation and 'factorizing' (Simon, 1970, p. 73) are opposite sides of the same coin: both serve to simplify the problem of management by consent and hence facilitate control. The consequences of this development for the national community have been to constrain its ability to speak for local government as a whole: it speaks for English local authorities alone. The national community has been criticized frequently for its internal conflicts and failure to present a united front. This failure is not wholly a product of the diversity of interests within local government; fragmentation is also a result of central government institutionalizing this diversity of interests.

The relationship between the associations and the joint bodies is also explored formally and through a case study. In the first instance, the constitutional provisions regulating their relationship are surveyed. The relationship is then explored in more detail in a case study of the several attempts to revise LACSAB's constitution. The crucial importance of LACSAB's activities should now be obvious. That its relationship with the associations has been strained will also be clear. But the extent of the disagreements, and indeed confusions, over the role of LACSAB will not be fully appreciated. The case study of the revision of LACSAB's constitution will reveal that the simple appellation '"their" joint body' conceals the complexity of the relationship, for LACSAB has many constituents (not just the associations) and precisely who 'owns' LACSAB was a highly contentious issue. If cleavages arising out of the interests of the various types of authority and party political allegiances seem to render the search for an integrated national community nugatory, the ownership conflicts surrounding the joint bodies will suggest that the goal of integration was not a dream but a nightmare: that LACSAB was the associations' 'Damien'. And, again, the national government environment conditioned the relationship. The associations sought greater control of LACSAB to further their ambition of becoming the peak associations of local government – an objective actively supported by the government.

In sum, the objectives of this chapter are to demonstrate that the relationship between the major and minor associations compounded the diversity of interests within local government; that the relationship between the associations and the joint bodies were strained by conflicts over the ownership of the joint bodies; and that the stresses and strains within the national community were exacerbated by the actions of central government. The focus is no longer the relationship between the national government environment and the national community of local government but relationships *within* the national community (see Figure 2.3).

THE RELATIONSHIP BETWEEN THE ASSOCIATIONS

Earlier chapters have demonstrated not only the conflicts of interest between the major associations but also that the associations contain other groupings. Thus, the ADC contains the 'big nine' and the 'twenty-two' within its ranks. Similarly, the AMA has distinct types of authority in membership and regular but informal meetings take place, for example, between the chief executives and majority party leaders of the metropolitan county councils. However, the main concern of this section is to explore the ACC's, ADC's and AMA's constitutional provisions for representing the interests of members from particular geographical areas: namely, Wales and London.

The Welsh Associations

The CP's constitution states that membership is open 'to such of the District Councils in Wales as are members of the Association', the latter being the ADC. The ADC's constitution states that 'District Councils may join regional councils or, for Wales, a Council for the Principality, and county branches as they deem fit, but the constitution of such bodies shall not be inconsistent with these (the ADC's) rules'. The ADC's constitution also states that there shall be a Committee for Wales comprising the Welsh representatives, the chairman and vice-chairman of the CP, and the chairman and vice-chairman of the ADC policy committee. The same rule allows that, where matters are exclusively or mainly of Welsh interest, the Welsh districts can deal directly with the government or other bodies 'through the CP and the (Welsh) Committee'. In addition, the ADC and the CP are required to maintain close consultations at all times and the ADC undertakes to provide secretarial and other assistance as requested by the CP and the committee. The CP's constitution acknowledges this relationship by containing a proviso to its general objects that it 'will act with the Committee for Wales set up under Rule 10 [of the ADC] on any matters within the scope of the Committee'.

The ADC and CP appear to have, therefore, an extremely close relationship. Indeed, the CP's constitution requires that members of Welsh districts who are elected to the ADC council shall, as of right, be the representatives of their districts on the Council for the Principality. Districts commonly fail to meet this requirement, however, in order to strengthen the separate identity of the CP. The council has sought to emphasize its distinctiveness not simply as an assertion of national pride but because of the real party political differences between the CP and the ADC. ADC member authorities are overwhelmingly Conservative-controlled, as the association itself has been since its formation. The majority of Welsh districts, however, are Labour-controlled, as the CP has been since its formation. The relationship between the ADC and CP has been described by officers and members of both bodies as delicate and uneasy.[1] The ADC provides services for the thirty-seven Welsh districts just as it does for its English member authorities. The ADC also gives the CP a small grant (£2,000 in 1978/9) towards secretarial and office expenses.

At its inaugural meeting in 1974 the CP received a letter from the then Secretary of State for Wales welcoming the establishment of the council and looking forward to a close and cordial relationship between it and the Welsh Office. The status of the CP as *the* representative body for Welsh districts has been recognized by successive secretaries of state and is manifest in the number of appointments which the council is asked to make to external bodies – for example, the Land Authority for Wales – and for which it is the statutory nominating body. The separate rate support grant procedures for Wales accentuated calls for a strengthening of the CP's independence from the ADC.[2] Thus, the CP requested substantial financial support from the ADC – in effect a clawing back of Welsh districts' subscriptions – for a separate secretariat (see below).

However the relationship is formally described in the two constitutions and whether or not the CP is described as the Welsh arm of the ADC, it is clear that the CP enjoys a significant measure of autonomy – sufficient for it to be regarded as a separate and independent association. Despite receiving both a grant and secretarial assistance from the ADC, the CP is not supervised by the ADC; it does not act at the ADC's behest. The CP is not required to report to the ADC council – in sharp contrast to the Committee for Wales; the CP has an independent source of revenue, it has its own officers and advisers; and, moreover, in being recognized by the Welsh Office (and other government departments) as *the* representative body for Welsh districts, the access of the CP to the departments is vastly superior to that of the ADC. Indeed, according to an ADC deputy secretary, the CP

> has developed as a fairly separate body predominantly because the Welsh Office have recognized them for exclusively Welsh matters and not the ADC.[3]

The precise relationship between the WCC and ACC is ambiguous. The previous honorary secretary of the WCC said that 'the WCC is a sub-committee of the ACC'[4] whereas the current honorary secretary emphatically rebutted this description.[5] Unlike the CP, the WCC's constitution does not have as an explicit objective the promotion and protection of the interests of its Welsh members. Like the CP, the WCC's constitution, and that of the ACC, does specify the right to deal directly with government departments on matters exclusively or mainly the particular interest of Wales. The WCC's constitution also states that the committee will represent the views of Welsh county councils at meetings of the ACC and, if necessary, record and present dissenting views. The WCC is, however, neither required nor requested to submit to the ACC for approval or comment either its minutes or its reports (and submissions) to government departments.

Unlike the relationship between the CP and ADC, the relationship between the ACC and WCC is described as very cordial. As with the CP and ADC, the members of the WCC are those members of the eight Welsh counties nominated to be representatives to the ACC; unlike the CP, the WCC does adhere to this rule. These members are invariably senior and long-standing members of other ACC committees and, therefore, have developed broad allegiances. Nevertheless, on Welsh matters their first loyalty would undoubtedly be to the WCC if there were any conflict of interests. These members play, therefore, a much more active part in the work of the ACC than the members of the CP in the ADC and not simply because the size of the ADC membership restricts the opportunities for participation. (For an example see Chapter 6, pages 212 and 247, above.)

The WCC receives a small grant from the ACC to provide secretarial support and is also funded by subscriptions from its own member authorities. The WCC regards the money it receives from the ACC as inadequate and it recognizes the importance of having its own full-time secretariat, especially since the introduction of separate rate support grant procedure for Wales. However, by 1983, there had been no call for weakening or severing links with the ACC. The WCC can be correctly described as the Welsh arm of the ACC.

This description of the relationship between the Welsh associations and their 'parent' bodies demonstrates the diversity of interests within local government but it does not demonstrate the influence of the national government environment on the relationships. It has been noted that instituting separate grant procedures for Wales affected them and a brief examination of the origins of the Welsh Consultative Council on Local Government Finance will clarify both the relationship between the associations and the role of central government.

The Welsh Consultative Council on Local Government Finance[6]

In rudimentary form, the Welsh Consultative Council on Local Government Finance was established in 1975 after local government reorganization at the same time as the English Consultative Council on Local Government Finance, although the latter remained responsible for both England and Wales. Despite its name, it bore little resemblance in its nature or responsibility to its 'parent' body. It was primarily a meeting place for local government division officials in the Welsh Office and financial officials from local authorities to discuss the financial responsibilities of Welsh local authorities. Any consideration of the allocation and distribution of the rate support grant in Wales, except as a matter of information, was strictly out of bounds.

During 1975–6 Welsh officials from the finance and local government divisions were entitled to attend the England and Wales consultative council. Some of them did so and were concerned that Welsh interests were not receiving their due attention in the RSG negotiations. Their concern grew because there was rarely a representative from the Welsh authorities on the local government side of the council. If the Welsh officials promoted Welsh interests, they courted the danger of demonstrating a lack of unity on the government side with little prospect of support from the (English) local government side. Welsh officials urged the Welsh local authorities to take part in the London-based consultative council but any such participation faced the problem that a Welsh representative from one of the associations would mean one less English representative.[7]

The period 1975–6 can be described as the 'prehistory' of the Welsh CCLGF. There was little internal Welsh demand for the existence of a consultative council on local government finance. It had no real function beyond that of a talking shop and the only reason it had been established was that an English body had been created and there was no compelling reason why a Welsh equivalent should *not* be set up. As for the Welsh local authorities, no one refuses a consultative body when it is offered; although it may seem empty at first, it may, as in this case, develop into a more worthwhile body. The debate on Welsh devolution was to provide the impetus for growth.

On 16 November 1976 the Welsh CCLGF set up a joint working party to consider the design and operation of a separate Welsh rate support grant. Its terms of reference were:

> To consider, in the context of the Scotland and Wales Bill, the design and operation of a Welsh Rate Support Grant system; and to report to the Welsh Consultative Council on Local Government Finance.[8]

The working party consisted of six representatives from the Welsh Office, four from the WCC and four from the CP. In addition, various meetings of the working party were attended by two other representatives from the Welsh Office, two from the DoE, one from the WCC and three finance officers from the district councils. The working party set up four subgroups – on education, personal social services, transport and highways, and other services. Altogether a total of eighty people were involved in the work of the subgroups; thirty-five from the Welsh Office, twenty from the Welsh Counties, thirteen from the Welsh Districts, ten from the Civil Service Department and two from the DoE. The working party produced two reports, including an 'exemplification' of a Welsh rate support grant. For present purposes, the most interesting part of their work was the recommendations on the organization of the consultative machinery for local authorities and the Welsh Office. These recommendations are summarized in Figure 7.1.

The main differences between these proposals and the current machinery lie in the allocation of responsibility and the functions of the subgroups. The joint working party envisaged that the CCLGF would be responsible to the Welsh assembly. The council would include 'representative members of the assembly' rather than representatives of the Welsh Office as at present. Similarly, the subgroups were to be composed of representatives of the two tiers of

Welsh Consultative Council on
Local Government Finance
(representative members of the local authority
associations and the assembly)

|

Official Committee of the
Welsh Consultative Council

|

subgroup on	subgroup on	grant distribution
relevant expenditure	relevant expenditure	subgroup
of county authorities	of district authorities	

Figure 7.1 *Proposed organization of the Welsh Consultative Council on Local Government Finance.*

local government rather than officials. In fact, all three subgroups are exclusively concerned with technical aspects of grant. The proposed political input is now confined to the council itself.[9]

The 'devolution' stage of the CCLGF lasted until March 1979, when the Welsh people 'vetoed' the assembly in the referendum. Characteristically, the devolution era was one of expectation rather than fulfilment and the consultative council was no exception. However, through the work of its joint working party, the CCLGF served a more constructive purpose than during the first two years of its life. It had made a contribution not so much to the making of policy in Wales as to the implementation of policy. The guidelines had been laid down in London but they were filled in by practitioners in Wales. It was the first time that so many people from different parts of Welsh government had taken part in a process of developing the Welsh institutions of government. To the extent that it involved people from Welsh government with a specifically Welsh remit, this stage illustrates the Welsh consultative network in operation.[10] However, the policy initiative came from Westminster; it was in the interests of the centre to introduce a measure of devolution for Wales and a Welsh RSG with its concomitant machinery was simply a small part of this broader goal. There was still no internal Welsh demand for any such development in Welsh central–local relations. It accorded with the interests of the centre and it was to be 'allowed'. The vote on 1 March 1979 relegated the Welsh rate support grant and its machinery to the shelves to await the next time when the interests of the centre required reform in the periphery.

Two months after the devolution referendum, a Conservative government was elected and the Local Government, Planning and Land Act was introduced. This centralizing measure was opposed by Welsh local authorities. However, the Government felt that the new system would be more effective if the Welsh Office rather than the

DoE was responsible for implementing and 'fine-tuning' the system in Wales. Ironically, a separate Welsh rate support grant that was originally envisaged as part of a policy of decentralization was now included as part of a centralization package.

The proposal to introduce a separate Welsh RSG was not an issue in the passage of the 1980 Act. Welsh MPs were not members of the House of Commons standing committees on the Bill and there was virtually no comment in the main chamber on the relevant clause (see Gyford and James, 1983, ch. 8). Even when the WCC and the CP held a special conference in November 1981 during the first year of operation of the Welsh RSG, the centralist overtones of the new block grant were considered more important than the new arrangements for a *Welsh* block grant.

The Welsh local authorities were first informed of the intention to establish a Welsh RSG on 15 November 1979 when the secretary of state held a meeting with the chairmen and secretaries of the WCC and the CP in the Welsh Office building in London. There was no attempt to call a meeting of the Welsh Consultative Council to inform them because block grant is very definitely DoE policy and so the Welsh Office could only inform the Welsh authorities rather than consult them. Indeed, this simple fact was made clear at a meeting of the CP on 18 January 1980 when, in discussion of a report of a recent consultative council meeting, the minutes record:

The meeting discussed in particular the Government's decision to introduce from 1981/82 a new RSG system and the Government's Block Grant proposals. Whilst the Council for the Principality and the Welsh Counties Committee had again indicated their total opposition to the introduction of the proposed Block Grant, the Minister had indicated that it was not open to negotiation, it being a decision of the Government ... The Minister had made it clear that the following provisions were 'not negotiable':

1) the introduction of a Block Grant System
2) the introduction of a separate Welsh RSG
3) the operative date of 1st April 1981 in both cases.

The secretary of state had unilaterally ruled any discussion of the substantive policy out of bounds for the Welsh Consultative Council. The Welsh local authorities understood and obeyed these rules of the game and resolved to continue opposing the legislation while cooperating with the secretary of state on the implementation of the legislation. Thus the contradiction emerged of Labour-dominated local authorities opposing the Conservative government in London while co-operating with and supporting its representative in Wales.

It was resolved:

1) To support the ADC in its opposition to the Block Grant and to the proposed new systems of capital control and to ask all District Councils to write to their respective MPs seeking their support for the ADC's objections.
2) To request that the Chairman of the Council [for the Principality] attend the meeting with the Secretary of State for the Environment, the Rt. Hon. Michael Heseltine ...
3) That if the above mentioned government's proposals in the Local Government, Planning and Land Bill are approved by the House of Commons, to agree with the proposals for a separate Welsh R.S.G. [11]

It was not new for the Welsh districts to follow ADC advice nor to make representations to the Environment Secretary. However, it was a new experience for them to participate in the RSG process.

For the first time the Welsh Consultative Council had powers and responsibilities commensurate with those of its 'parent' body: it could now be plausibly compared with its 'parent' body. It has become the main forum for consultations between the Welsh Office and local government in Wales on all matters which are devolved to the Welsh Office and have direct or indirect implications for local government finance. There are some services, for example, rating policy and the 'protection' services of the Home Office (fire, police), which remain under the auspices of the England and Wales Consultative Council (see Figure 7.2). The major difference between the Welsh Consultative Council and its 'parent' body, however, lies in its relationship with the secretary of state. The Welsh local authorities and the Welsh Secretary have shared interests. It can be argued that there is a client relationship between the two, but it is not a straightforward one:

... the Welsh Office, in common with all other central departments, attempts to increase the resources directed towards its 'clients', in the present discussion this means the Welsh local authorities. To counter this, however, is the pressure to control such clients, as it has, particularly when a major objective of the centre is to control expenditure. Thus while increasing the grant given to the Welsh local authorities (or at least maintaining the amount they already receive) would be considered as a victory for local government it would be something of an own-goal when viewed from the DoE or the Treasury. (Gray, 1981, p. 71)

The consultative council provides an opportunity to see this unity of interest at work. The Welsh Counties Committee in July 1980

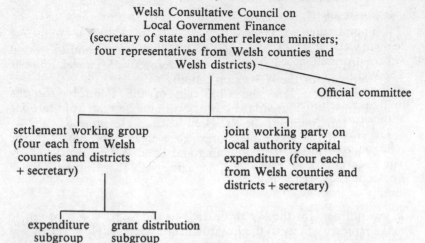

Figure 7.2   *Structure of the Welsh Consultative Council on Local Government Finance.*

recorded that:

> The chairman of the Committee stressed that the Secretary of State had listened with great attention to the Local Authorities' position ... He had requested certain supplementary information from the Committee, particularly in relation to employment levels, which would enable him to argue the Principality's case more effectively in Cabinet discussion ... The Welsh Counties Committee had a duty to give the Secretary of State as much information as possible to ensure that the particular problems of Wales receive proper regard.

At the end of this discussion a resolution was passed which included the assurance that

> the Committee's representatives on the Council be authorised to provide such additional information to the Secretary of State as might be required.

The local authorities here are acting virtually as a secretariat for the secretary of state. Any enmity between central and local government at the periphery is buried as the two join forces in order that 'the Principality's case can be argued more effectively in Cabinet' and 'to ensure that the particular interests of Wales receive proper regard'. The resources of information and access to the centre are not so much exchanged between the participants in this power-dependent relationship as shared between the two. If the Welsh Office were to deny local authorities access, it would undermine its own *raison d'être* because, if it is not arguing for 'Wales to receive proper regard', it has no job to do in Cabinet. Similarly for local authorities, if they deny the Welsh Office information they could reduce their own financial resources. The Welsh Office and the secretary of state are clearly playing the role of the voice of Wales in London rather than vice versa. Their success in that role is dependent on the active co-operation of the local authorities in Wales.

The closeness of the Welsh Office and the local authorities is also reflected in the organization of the central–local machinery in Wales. The associations do not form a separate tier in Wales as they do in England. The other public interest groups that form the national community of local government in England (for example, LACSAB) do not exist in Wales: these 'English' bodies cover both England and Wales. The Welsh associations do not have full-time secretariats but a series of advisers who are all full-time local authority officials. Even the secretaries are full-time local government officers. Similarly, every local authority, including the districts, is represented at the meetings of the associations. Thus the problem of remoteness from member authorities which can arise for English associations has no direct equivalent in Wales. In Wales there is no equivalent intervening tier of representation and consequently the Welsh Office and its 'client' authorities can be said to have a close relationship. And this closeness is facilitated by the small number of authorities involved. Welsh Office ministers are on first-name terms with many local authority leaders in Wales. The integration of the Welsh network of central–local relations is paradoxically increased by the complexity of the government machine. Because there are more positions to be filled than there are people qualified or interested in filling them, one person may hold several positions, thereby reducing the formality of the network and bringing the participants closer.

The potential for a close working relationship between the Welsh Office and Welsh local authorities is considerable, but not without its stresses and strains. Not only can the two sides differ on the definition of 'Welsh interests' but the two associations are of contrasting political complexions. The CP has an inbuilt Labour Party majority whereas the WCC has a slightly less secure majority of Independents. Thus, any Conservative secretary of state in Wales must face the prospect of one local authority association that objects to politics in local government in general and the other that objects to his politics in particular.

The development of the Welsh Consultative Council can be described as progressive because at each of the three stages the CCLGF has acquired more responsibilities. However, the progression was neither logical nor inevitable. Each stage increased the powers of Welsh local government and gave it greater independence from the

Whitehall network. Yet each stage was initiated by the centre acting in its own, not Welsh, interests. Throughout the period, Welsh local authorities have played a receptive and reactive role rather than a positive one of initiating or even pressing for changes.

In Wales all the authorities belong to local authority associations and they are also members of the 'English' national community of local government. The local government network in Wales is much smaller than in England and the associations do not form a distinct tier. There is more direct access for local authorities to their 'central government'. Before the consolidation of the Welsh CCLGF, Madgwick and James (1980, p. 105) described central–local relations in Wales as

> a complex network of consultation between the Welsh Office and local government ... The term 'network' implies a multiplicity of linkages, uneven in pattern and density, but with a significant nodal point in the Welsh Office. The quality of the flow is also uneven, ranging from regulation through information to consultation and negotiation. Command is generally too strong as a description. The characteristic mode is consultation rather than negotiation, with regulation or control as the objective.

The creation of the CCLGF can be seen as an attempt to systematize this network and, given that it was the centre's initiative, to institutionalize the 'Welsh interests'. Just as the incorporation of English local authorities facilitated their regulation and control, so institutionalizing the periphery (or factorizing) fosters the same objective. And the consequences for the national community of local government were extensive. Not only was a section of the membership divided from the rest for one of the national community's key functions, thereby limiting the constituency of the associations and their claims to speak for local government as a whole, but this separation created conflict. Both the WCC and the CP reviewed the terms and conditions of their membership of the 'English' associations.[12] Both developed their own permanent secretariats and the CP, after threatening to withdraw from the ADC, agreed to a joint working party to review the relationship. The ADC's annual conference in 1982 agreed to abolish both the CP and the Committee for Wales. They have been replaced with the Committee of Welsh District Councils, which deals directly with the secretary of state on matters primarily of Welsh concern. They have also opened a new four-person branch office in Wales to service this new committee, thereby meeting the Welsh demands for greater financial and staffing resources. The Welsh CCLGF has generated an imperative for the separate development of the Welsh associations. There is an extensive range of interests to be reconciled within the national community, and the actions of central government have sustained, even reinforced, that diversity. Incorporation and factorizing are complementary strategies of regulation and control.

The London associations

The relationship of the LBA to the AMA is different from that of both the CP to the ADC and the WCC to the ACC. The LBA's separate and independent identity is undisputed: not only does it have its own officers, advisers and constitution, but its origins predate the AMA. Although the members of the LBA are also members of the AMA, in sharp contrast to the CP and WCC membership of the LBA is not conditional upon membership of the AMA.

As with WCC members in the ACC, representation of LBA members on AMA committees is extensive. Indeed, they are constitutionally guaranteed and arranged by the LBA. In no sense does the AMA formally supervise the LBA. The LBA is not required to submit reports or minutes and it cannot be instructed by the AMA to undertake particular tasks. The LBA 'always try to make very clear that we are in no way a sub committee or subsidiary of the AMA and indeed we do not carry out the work of the AMA'. However, there is always a 'tremendous desire by the LBA to try and reconcile its views with those of the AMA'.[13]

Up to 1983 it had also been possible to reconcile the conflicting party political views within the LBA itself. However, the commitment of the majority Conservative group on the LBA to the abolition of the GLC provoked Labour members to establish the Association of Labour Authorities (ALA). Formally established in July 1983, all but two of the Labour-controlled London boroughs along with the GLC and ILEA became members and it has been recognized by the DoE for membership of the CCLGF. Initially, its future was uncertain. Bromley LB instituted legal action claiming that funding ALA through the rates was unlawful. And, given its original constitution requiring members to accept policy objectives as a condition of membership, it was clear that an authority could not remain a member if it were to become Conservative-controlled. However, the constitution was revised to remove the policy objectives and the courts declared that funding through the rates was now lawful. None the less, the future of both the LBA and ALA remains uncertain, pending the abolition of the GLC. Whatever the final outcome, it is clear that the directive strategies of the 1979–83 Conservative government intensified partisanship within the association, which simply multiplied the interests within the national community and made the search for integration even more elusive.

Strictly speaking the GLC is not an association but it is treated as such not only by the AMA, which makes special provision for representing its interests, but also by central government. The DoE may wish to limit consultation to the associations but:

> The organisation of local government within Greater London differs from that outside and in many cases separate legislation applies. It is therefore important that the GLC and the LBA should be consulted ...
>
> All consultation documents sent to the Associations should also be sent to the Director General of the GLC and the LBA, who will consider whether to respond separately. [14]

Similarly the GLC and the LBA should be invited to consultative meetings if they so wish and both have representatives on the CCLGF. The special provisions for grant negotiations extend beyond membership of the CCLGF. The London working party exists to consider the role of London within the national grant system and the distribution of grant within London. It plays a technical role in the manner of the grants working group of the CCLGF. For example, because London has high rateable values, it can maintain a given level of expenditure at a lower rate poundage than local authorities elsewhere in the country. Accordingly, up to 1980, London's needs element was reduced – a procedure known as 'clawback' – to compensate for the excess rateable value. Indeed, the labyrinthine complexities of the grant system as applied to London are awesome to behold and special procedural and consultative arrangements are essential. Finally, the political access of London may not extend to having their own secretary of state in the Cabinet, but it is extensive. All interviewees felt that it was superior to that of the AMA and the former leader of the GLC, Sir Horace Cutler (Conservative), had direct access to the Prime Minister. [15] Richard Crossman (1975, pp. 60–1 and 129) was moved to complain about the ease and frequency with which he was approached and the current leader, Ken Livingstone (Labour), had direct and immediate access to ministers, even though the gulf between his council and the Conservative government (on, for example, transport policy) could not be greater. [16]

In short, distinct networks of consultation in central–local relations are not the prerogative of the peripheral regions. The national community of local government represents English local authorities outside Greater London – a more limited constituency than is commonly appreciated. Moreover, the diverse arrangements for grant negotiations have not been extracted from a reluctant government. The case study of the Welsh CCLGF shows that institutionalizing the distinct interests of the peripheral regions serves the interests of the centre, permitting the use of a variety of regulative strategies. [17] As Budge *et al.* (1983, p. 132) have argued:

> If the mace has been the central political metaphor of the British

system of government for most of the twentieth century, then the 'maze' seems the more appropriate metaphor for the remaining years. The mace, or the myth of parliamentary sovereignty, fosters a distorted picture of the reality. The maze, or the complex inter-dependencies of public sector organisations, presents a simplified but nonetheless more realistic picture of events.

To manage this complexity, aggregation has been the centre's preferred strategy for the English local government system but, for London and the peripheral systems, the complementary strategy has been factorizing or decomposing central–local relations into semi-independent components. The separate grant systems clearly demonstrate that, even within unitary states, there can be considerable recognition of areal interests. Such diversity can serve, of course, a number of functions. For example, it could be valued for its symbolic, legitimation function. In this case, areal interests have been recognized in order to facilitate central control of local expenditure. But, if factorizing facilitates central control, it compounds the problem of integration within the national community. The 'minor' associations add to the diversity of interests. The CP, the WCC and the LBA are not formally supervised by their 'parent' associations; they vary in the degrees to which they are constitutionally autonomous and in the extent to which in practice they seek to exert their independence. The description 'parent' association appears apt only in the case of the ACC. Both the CP and the LBA are more accurately described as associations in their own right with the predictable conflicts of interest arising out of the interests of their geographically distinct members.

THE RELATIONSHIP BETWEEN THE ASSOCIATIONS AND THE JOINT BODIES

The formal pattern of relationships

Whether or not the joint bodies can be properly described as 'owned' by the associations – and seen as (collectively) an extended resource for them – depends upon whether the associations created them; whether they supervise them; and whether that supervision is effective. The associations were instrumental in creating all nine joint bodies and their potential for control is considerable if attention is focused on terms of reference and on constitutional arrangements for representation on governing and sovereign bodies. Actual control, however, depends on the degree of supervision exercised over annual reports and budgets and the imposition of requirements to submit reports or instructions to perform particular tasks.[18]

In the case of LACSAB, LAMSAC and the LGTB the associations have sought to increase their control and supervision. In the case of LAMSAC, the associations formally appointed their secretaries (in rotation) as secretary of the committee, in addition to appointing a director. In the case of LACSAB and the LGTB, which are separate legal entities, the associations' secretaries, also in rotation, informally liaise with the directors. And, in sharp contrast to the smallest joint bodies, these appointments are not nominal. There are also important differences between the relationships of the associations' secretaries to the directors of the largest joint bodies.

LAMSAC's director has described the association secretaries as having:

> the duties of a liaison link, which is the main strength of the secretaryship ... I run and direct the organization: hire, fire – apart from my own job – and generally keep the organization going ... But the secretarial link ... keeps me informed of the associations' trends, thoughts, processes and all the rest of it.[19]

The meetings, in LAMSAC's case, are held informally approximately once a month. Meetings between the Director of the LGTB and the associations' secretaries are less frequent. 'I don't suppose it happens on more than three or four occasions a year.'[20] The associations' secretary responsible for the board liaises with the other association secretaries on the directors' behalf. The association secretaries are not regarded by the directors and secretary of LAMSAC, LGTB and LACSAB as their senior officers, nor do the association secretaries treat them as such, in the sense of issuing instructions. The association secretaries are not consulted about such internal decisions as hiring staff; as with LAMSAC these are solely the business of the LACSAB secretary and the LGTB's director.

Although not subject to detailed supervision, both the LGTB and LAMSAC are subject to general control by the associations. LAMSAC's director has admitted to being baffled by the AMA's expressed wish to strengthen the associations' control of his organization because:

> They've always had close control ... they agree the work programme, they agree the resource allocation ... every year I present my budget for our allocation of resources ... that has to be approved by the Associations ... so that is the ultimate control.

And at this level it is a very detailed control: approval of the budget is not a formality. By the time the budget is submitted to the special joint meeting of the associations 'there has been a very careful screening process [at] various informal meetings and formal meetings with the Secretaries of the Associations'. Moreover, at the Section 2(7) joint meeting 'we go through the budget line by line'.[21]

There is no doubt about the extent of the associations' control of the actual amount received by the relevant bodies from Section 2(7) funds, although the degree of policy control thus bestowed on the associations varies. LAMSAC derives 50 per cent of its income from Section 2(7) monies (excluding the separate and self-financing consultancy service), and this amount determined the rest of its income because, up to 1981, the DoE matched the amount provided by the associations. Subsequently, the associations have become responsible for LAMSAC's funding – a transition which led to a review of its structure and functions. The review provided an opportunity for the associations to assess the effectiveness of their control of LAMSAC and it proved to be a tortuous process which had had no determinate outcome by mid-1983.

In the case of the LGTB the switch to Section 2(7) funding represented the loss of 'a degree of autonomy from the associations' which the board had enjoyed prior to 1978. From its establishment in 1967 the board was financed by a grant and levy system whereby the associations decided annually the maximum levy 'and gave the board moral support to collect that amount from individual local authorities'. However, the costs to the board of this direct financial relationship with individual authorities were an unpredictable and unreliable source of income which arrived only after its services had been provided. Now the board

is in direct negotiation with the individual local authority associations, not the local authorities about a specific sum of money: and it is entirely up to them to decide what that sum of money is.

The advantage for the board is that 'once they've decided what it is, we actually get it'.

In spite of this financial control, the associations have remained unhappy about their relationship with the major joint bodies. The LGTB's director claims that the AMA wrongly sees the relationship between the associations and the joint bodies as a hierarchical one. The AMA's call for greater control of the joint bodies he regards as confusing management control and policy determination: the latter can be exercised not only at the time of budget approval but on the committees of the board itself. In terms of representatives, the associations have the dominant position: both on the board and on every committee the associations outnumber the trade-union representatives. Moreover, and most important, the trade unions 'cannot vote on major financial matters at board level ... if there's a vote on the size of the levy then they are not entitled to vote against the associations'.

The board's director has stressed that when submitting its budget to the associations it has to be seen as a submission of the whole board – that is, including the trade unions – not just one set of association members speaking to another set:

> I've got to have close relations with the secretaries of the associ-
> ations, but my responsibility is to the board as a whole. I'm always
> open to criticism in everything I do by the trade unions that I am
> a puppet in the pocket of the associations.

Because of their dominant representation on the board and its committees, and because the board receives substantial funding through
Section 2(7), the control of the board by the associations would seem
self-evident. However, some of the association representatives
'become very much involved [and] develop an allegiance to the
board'; and many committee chairmen 'do see themselves as chairmen
of the board or the committee that is there to try and see that every
interest is undertaken and not just the associations' interest'. The
board's director emphasizes that 'decisions about the allocation of
funds between the programmes are not guided by the associations'.[22]
This 'independence' could be antithetical to the associations' interests
if allocations were determined by the board's officers, but there is little
or no evidence for this conclusion. Alternatively, the allocations could
be determined by the associations' representative on the board but
these representatives could see themselves as distinct from the associations and there is some evidence for this interpretation. Association
representatives, chameleon-like, take on the colouring of their immediate environment (see below, pages 286–7 and 291 *passim*).

The 'independence' of the LGTB is reinforced by the functions it
carries out – most notably the schemes it operates for the Manpower
Services Commission. In 1972 the government made proposals for a
national training agency designed, *inter alia*, to co-ordinate the work
of the various industrial training boards. The LGTB's view, strongly
supported by the associations, was that everything possible should be
done to ensure that local government retained the LGTB under its
own control. This pressure was successful but, under the Employment
and Training Act 1973, the Manpower Services Commission (which
was created by the Act) was given a statutory responsibility to ensure
adequate training in all sectors of employment. Local government
asserted that its own voluntary LGTB made the imposition of a
statutory board unnecessary; in future, however, the LGTB would
be obliged to fulfil the role that the new Training Services Agency,
acting through the statutory boards, was fulfilling in other employment sectors.

The LGTB has a necessarily close relationship with the Manpower
Services Commission and has a policy 'of seeking funding from
central services to benefit local government'. The major part of the
board's financial transactions are undertaken on behalf of the Training Services Agency: in 1978/9 the board operated seven schemes

(totalling £3·6 million) for the Manpower Services Commission. In formulating policies the board 'takes into account the national needs identified with and by the MSC'.[23] As an agent for the MSC (and DE) in attempting to implement their policies of reducing unemployment, facilitating redeployment and retraining, the LGTB serves both the particular interests of local government and performs an important function free from control by the associations.

The question of whether the associations control the joint bodies is most contentious and most uncertain in the case of LACSAB. There is dispute about whether the associations should control the board, whether they are able to control the board, and whether they actually do control the board. From their domination of the board's membership — seventeen out of twenty-eight — it seems beyond doubt that the associations are in a controlling position. However, the associations provide only 41 per cent of the board's income and it is for this reason that a past chairman of the AMA has said:

The associations don't control LACSAB ... they produce a budget for us to approve but we don't get all the figures that we ask for and any shortfall that they have ... they go to the provincial councils and raise it through them. So they are not subservient, they [LACSAB] are not creatures of the associations.[24]

A LACSAB deputy secretary, like the director of the LGTB, has argued that the associations (and particularly the AMA) wrongly see the relationship between the associations and LACSAB as a hierarchical one. Rather, the Board is not the creature of the associations and it was never intended to be so.[25] Both the AMA and the ACC argue that the associations do not but should control LACSAB. The ADC's view is that the associations can and do control LACSAB and that this control is quite properly shared with the provincial councils.[26]

The ACC's and AMA's complaints about LACSAB are twofold. First, they are critical of their lack of managerial control — that is, of their inability to regulate either the involvement of the LACSAB secretariat in detailed negotiations or the role of their own representatives in these negotiations. Second, they are critical of their lack of 'policy' control.

The dispute about the control of LACSAB will provide, therefore, a good illustration of the problems which can surround the relations between the associations and joint bodies. However, it is important to remember that the study of a crisis does not necessarily provide any insights into 'normal' relations. The problem of ownership simply does not exist for the majority of joint bodies. The case study of LACSAB's constitutional crisis is not typical, therefore, of relations between the associations and the joint bodies. Indeed, many would now argue that it is no longer typical of association–LACSAB relations and, in one sense, this comment is accurate. The period of the crisis, 1975–80, was also the heyday of self-assertion by the associations. Just as they sought involvement with central government, they also sought control within the national community. Integration was based on the pre-eminence of the associations. If the crisis over LACSAB is not typical of normal relations with joint bodies (including LACSAB), at one and the same time it is a highly typical example of the goals and strategies of the associations at this time.

LACSAB's 'constitutional crisis'

Rising doubts   In December 1972, before he had assumed his post, LACSAB's new secretary reviewed its position after reorganization, concluding that it was imperative to maintain LACSAB's special relationship with ministers and civil servants; to continue LACSAB's direct links with the individual employers; and, significantly in the light of future developments, to preserve LACSAB's status and autonomy because the secretary was often required 'to assume temporarily in negotiations an almost independent role' (see below p. 279). It was to be expected, therefore, that in one of his first reports to the board, on 21 March 1973, the new LACSAB secretary should discuss LACSAB's evolving role.

He said that in future there would need to be 'a continuing dialogue' throughout the year on problems and trends rather than the annual set-piece confrontation between employers and unions. He described LACSAB's role as:

(i)   traditional role of advice on pay and conditions of service;
(ii) overall knowledge and advice across the whole field of personnel management;
(iii) a forum for identification of manpower problems and emerging needs for manpower policies;
(iv) the collation and presentation of developments on every aspect of manpower which needs to be introduced into the negotiating and consultative machinery of local government.

Both statements were prompted by the imminent revision of LACSAB's constitution. As a private company, LACSAB could not legally exist without a correctly defined constitution. Not only had the associations changed, but LACSAB, on 1 January 1974, had taken over responsibility for servicing the Burnham and allied committees. There was no provision in LACSAB's constitution for their representation.

In November 1973 the LACSAB secretary wrote to the association secretaries informing them of the need to reallocate seats held by the old associations to the new ones. [27] The following month the AMC secretary wrote to the other associations proposing the following composition for LACSAB: ACC – 5; AMA – 3; GLC – 2; ADC – 3. The CCA replied that representation should be based on population because it 'is reasonably representative of activity, staff and expenditure' and proposed a different composition: ACC – 5; AMA – 4 (including the GLC); and ADC – 1. [28] The ADC did not yet exist but it could not be expected to accept either of these proposals.

There was a recognition within the associations (and within LACSAB) that LACSAB could not be the same body as before reorganization. The increased workload from Burnham was only one of a number of developments which had drastically increased the board's workload. The board's role was radically changing because of the increased incidence of strikes and other industrial action, and the volume of detailed work created by the intervention of the Pay Board at all levels and on all aspects of pay. The association acknowledged the need for additional resources; there was no agreement over how these should be provided.

In its estimates for 1974/5, which were approved by the LACSAB board on 18 March 1974, it was agreed that the associations' contributions should total £63,597 or 18·9 per cent of LACSAB's total income. The amounts which LACSAB sought from the ACC and the AMA were respectively £37,452.80 and £26,114.80, to cover both general secretariat charges (£8,597) and £55,000 as direct charges to a number of negotiating bodies (including for the first time the Burnham Committees). This caused some concern within both associations. The ACC secretary wrote to the LACSAB secretary complaining that this levy far exceeded the association's expectations. When the ACC budget had been prepared, the association relied on the LACSAB's statement of November 1973 that the total estimated expenditure for 1974 would be £250,000 and not the £336,430 now called for. The AMA policy committee accepted that LACSAB had faced 'a most difficult period of crisis activity'. However, the associations depended for their income on voluntary subscriptions: it was 'exceedingly worrying', therefore, to be presented with a levy substantially higher than expected when the associations' own estimates and subscriptions had been fixed. In January 1974, it certainly had not been anticipated that LACSAB's running costs would rise by 50 per cent in 1974/5. The AMA secretary recommended to the association's representatives on LACSAB that consideration be given to financing the board in future via the Section 2(7) procedure.

The LACSAB secretary undertook to look again at those association levies but was forced to conclude 'that £63,500 does not seem extravagant', [29] although it could be reduced to £40,580, if absolutely necessary. However, costs could only be cut if the workload was reduced. The board must decide what he should cease to do 'if it is considered that the costs are too heavy for servicing 2½ million employees with a comprehensive industrial relations service'. The secretary also argued that the total cost of the board's services was small compared with the total expenditure of local authorities, and in view not only of the range of services it provided but also the effect which pay settlements had on local authorities' overall financial position. (In fact, the LACSAB budget for the following year, 1975/6, of £580,000 worked out at approximately £1,000 per local authority in England and Wales.)

The new associations were not only concerned about their share of the total cost of LACSAB but also about the small proportion of the board's total income they contributed. The board's constitution provided for LACSAB's income to come *not* from levies on the association but from levies upon provincial councils, although small sums were received from other sources – for example, the Home Office for the Police Council work. The paradoxical situation had arisen, therefore, of the associations resenting the amount of money derived from provincial councils whilst at the same time objecting to increased levies on themselves. Henceforth, the associations were to argue that LACSAB be funded wholly from Section 2(7) monies: that is, not only the associations' contribution but also the levies upon provincial councils were to be replaced by Section 2(7) funding.

The change in attitude on the part of the associations was marked. In 1970, the AMC secretary had denied that the source of funding was a relevant consideration. The key point was that the money came 'from the local authorities on whose behalf the national machinery operates'. He also opined that the LACSAB staff

> fulfil everything that could ever be required of you in regard to the co-ordination of negotiations, but what we have heard, justified or unjustified, has been criticism arising out of the lack of identity between the individual authorities affected by the outcome of negotiations and those who have represented them in the negotiations.[30]

Such halcyon days were not to return for some considerable time. Indeed, the issues of representation, finance and constitutional change were, in essence, facets of a more fundamental and intractable problem: the autonomy of LACSAB and the negotiating bodies and the rights of the associations to control these bodies. This problem was to move to the centre of the stage at the seminal meeting of the LACSAB board on 7 February 1975, at which the associations took the decision, in the ADC secretary's words, 'to play a controlling part in LACSAB as representatives of local government as a whole'. At this meeting, the LACSAB secretary sought to focus the attention of

the associations on the changed manpower climate of local government, on the need for a strong and effective central body (that is, an
adequately funded and staffed LACSAB), and on the range and variety of authorities which had to be served. He argued for the prompt
resolution of the related problems of representation and funding and
a redrafting of the board's constitution. He described 'manpower' as
'the most complex, dynamic, expensive and critical area of this country's resources'.

It was imperative that the constituent organizations of LACSAB
should have a forum in which members could 'review the broad sweep
of manpower affairs'. This forum should be serviced by a secretariat
of the highest quality, able to provide advice and information on
emerging and existing legislation, to provide a negotiating service
which reflected grass-roots requirements, to command confidence and
respect of all participants, and to bring 'matters to a conclusion within
the negotiating body involved'. The secretariat should also be 'seen to
be sufficiently detached and impartial to conduct conciliation and
arbitration in all types of critical industrial disputes'. LACSAB should
be seen 'to have the standing and integrity to assemble reliable
manpower data acceptable alike to Government, Associations and
authorities – an essential defence against the increasing intrusion by
Government agencies'.

The secretary stressed the continuous burden on his staff created by
two years of 'almost constant industrial relations crisis'. They were,
he said, 'hampered by the continuing background of uncertainty'.
LACSAB's relationship with the associations were very good at officer
level but, at member level, the board was 'far from realising its full
potential . . . uncertainties in representation, constitution and finance
have hampered progress'. Three things were needed: 'a clear sense
of direction; stability for a period of years; and the support and full
confidence of all those associated with the work of the board'. He
described the reforms as urgent and also called for regular meetings
of the board.[31] LACSAB's council agreed that, because of the importance of the board's work and the effect upon local government
finance:

> means should be found for members of the Council to be more
> closely involved in future developments . . . and . . . that the
> Associations and the Advisory Board should be seen to be working
> in close harmony for the same objectives.

Accordingly, the council resolved to form an *ad hoc* committee.

Constitutional reform The composition of the special committee
reflected the importance of the constitutional reform of LACSAB. Its

membership comprised the chairmen and secretaries of the associations (including the GLC) and LACSAB and it was to review the board's objectives, policy and financing:

> in order that its Constitution shall recognise the responsibility of the local authority Associations in relation to local government as a whole.

A suggestion was made at the meeting that this special committee should include representatives from bodies other than the associations. There was no formal resolution because an assurance was given that all the constituents' interests would be consulted, and because the special committee would eventually have to report to the full board.

The respective positions of the associations and LACSAB on the form of their future relationship were becoming clear. In a context of increasing costs and calls for Section 2(7) funding, the secretary of LACSAB felt it imperative to remind council members that the board must have 'a sufficient degree of independent standing effectively to carry out its task'. He posed the following question to the council:

> If all money comes from one source closely under the purview of a single Government department will it still be possible to maintain the essential facility to resist advice from departments on how negotiations should be handled?

He asked if it was wise to prejudice the feeling of individual local authorities that they had close and personal links with LACSAB not only because they contributed financially but also because of their participation in provincial councils. He concluded that:

> On balance it would seem sensible (and safer) for the Board to continue to make levies roughly on the same basis as it is today.

The secretary's view that section 2(7) funding 'could be seen as a further step away from the independence of action insisted upon by the negotiating bodies' did not please the associations. In a note to AMA representatives on LACSAB, the association's secretary said that LACSAB 'had tended to become increasingly independent' and the secretary 'makes considerable use of this argument'. Although the negotiating bodies were independent, the AMA secretary insisted that the LACSAB secretariat was 'a total employers' secretariat and it seems a mistake to assume that it is independent'. Subsequently, the ACC chairman, Sir Meredith Whittaker, referred to LACSAB's proposals at this time as an attempt 'to do a UDI' – a charge which has been strongly rejected. Certainly much confusion has surrounded the phrase 'LACSAB's independence'. It is doubtful that it ever had the limited meaning of 'a trustworthy body which could produce unbiased, undoctored manpower data and information (e.g., for Manpower Watch)'. Indeed, the need for LACSAB to be independent had been mentioned when a federation of local authority associations was being discussed. In October 1972, the secretary had argued that he was

> often required to assume temporarily in negotiations an almost independent role – i.e. when he is called upon to give professional advice which needs to be equally acceptable to both sides ... He could never achieve this if it became apparent that he was subservient in any way to a form of Federation secretariat.[32]

This earlier definition of 'independence' accords most closely with the usage of *both* the secretary and the critics. However, times had changed. The secretary's views may have been approved by LACSAB on 18 December 1972 but the post-reorganization associations had no sympathy for them. They took exception to any expressions of independence. As the employers' side secretary, he was not required to give advice to the staff side at all, let alone make that advice acceptable to them.

With hindsight, it is perhaps unfortunate that the secretary had elaborated his remarks on 'independence' to include more than flexibility during negotiations. He had also noted that it was a 'cardinal principle' for trade unions that they were to be seen to be dealing with the top body. Any inference that the employers' side (including, of course LACSAB) 'might be under the direction of another body, e.g. a Federation ... would immediately diminish its authority'. Moreover, he described 'the special relationship [that] has been built up over the years between the Employers' Secretary and Ministers and Civil Servants', which was a very convenient avenue for probing 'what might be acceptable in the field of negotiations in many fields'. In addition, the virtues of a single building for all associations and joint bodies was disputed. The secretary suggested that LACSAB's geographical distinctiveness was psychologically important, enabling it to act as a neutral 'court of last resort'. This argument merely added to the growing suspicions about LACSAB's accountability to the associations.

Even if the LACSAB secretary had been able to allay the associations' fears about his use of the term 'independent', there remained the problem of the financing of LACSAB. The estimates for 1975/6, totalling some £580,000, were sent to the associations in February 1975, prior to their consideration by LACSAB later that month. The AMA secretary replied immediately expressing his extreme concern at the size of the levy: once again, subscriptions for the coming year had been fixed and 'did not allow for increases in demands on our resources at the rate shown in LACSAB's estimates'.[33] These complaints prompted the LACSAB secretary to repeat his doubts about the Section 2(7) funding and to suggest that 'it requires very careful thought before we give any further lever for Civil Servants to instruct members how they might conduct negotiations'.[34]

The LACSAB special committee first met on 10 April 1975 and approved a revised LACSAB budget for 1975/6 'which took very substantial account' of the associations' secretaries' 'suggestions'. Under this pressure, the budget was pruned to £519,520, with the savings equally shared by the associations. It was acknowledged that the board's role was now restricted, allowing no room for expansion. Indeed, LACSAB's secretary had reported an enormous increase in the workload of his secretariat: it was 'already over-extended' and yet there was a 'monumental amount of work generated by Houghton and other Government actions'.[35]

The LACSAB special committee met again, on 12 May 1975, and agreed that a renewed constitution should enable LACSAB to use Section 2(7) monies, if necessary. The clause was extremely general. It was proposed in this form by Councillor Dennett (vice-chairman, LACSAB) on behalf of provincial councils to acknowledge their concern at this method of funding. As a provincial council chairman he was only too well aware (as indeed was the LACSAB chairman, Councillor Sir Leo Schultz) that the provincial councils were concerned about the special committee.

A consultative meeting of all English and Welsh provincial councils' chairmen and secretaries was held on 15 April 1975. In their view, the associations now saw themselves as 'the central "voice" of local authorities and must, therefore, have overall control of the Advisory Board and the machinery of negotiations'.[36] They were also concerned about the associations' proposal to fund LACSAB from Section 2(7) and requested the LACSAB special committee to make no recommendations or final decisions about LACSAB until provincial employers had met and been given the opportunity to express their views.

This meeting took place on 14 May. The provincial councils' representatives rejected the associations' approach, and asserted that provincial councils were 'the essential link in communications between the national negotiators and grass-roots opinions in authorities'. If there was a lack of co-ordination the answer was more representation of local authority members on negotiating bodies, not 'decreasing representation of grass-roots interests'.[37] The system of local authority representation on provincial councils, and the latter's representation on the APT and C and Manual Workers NJCs, was 'in accordance with traditional democratic principles'. There could even be advantages in extending the system to other negotiating bodies (for example, police, fire and teachers). This principle should not be overturned without the representatives of local authorities and provincial councils being able to express their views. The existing system for financing LACSAB gave individual councils a voice and a direct interest in the negotiations. Funding LACSAB via Section 2(7)

> would not only give overall control to the local authority associations – it would seriously increase the risk of increased central government intervention in the system of free collective bargaining in local government.

The provincial councils maintained that local authorities had not had the opportunity to make their views known – indeed they were unaware of current developments. They should be informed of the views of the provincial councils and invited to oppose the funding of LACSAB and the negotiating machinery centrally through Section 2(7). The provincial council representatives also agreed to resist any alterations to LACSAB's constitution which diminished the provincial councils' role in negotiations. On the contrary, provincial employers' representation on the Board and on other negotiating bodies should be increased:

> to strengthen the role of the Advisory Board in co-ordinating the work of all national negotiating bodies in local government and to avoid overlapping the functions of the other local authority organisations involved in manpower.

The associations regarded the views expressed by the provincial councils as erroneous and 'grossly misleading'.[38] On behalf of all the provincial council chairmen, Councillors Schultz and Dennett wrote to all three association secretaries restating and amplifying the provincial councils' belief that:

> through the medium of direct representation of local authorities in the person of the Chairmen of Personnel Committees they are representative of 'grass-roots' opinion in authorities on personnel and manpower matters. Though the financial links, and the consultative opportunities of the Sounding Board procedures, authorities can feel they are participating in decision-making procedures with regard to pay and conditions of at least 60% of local government employees.
>
> Accepting the need to ensure that local authority machinery is responsible to current needs, the provincial employers feel strongly that this machinery must maintain the links with 'grass-roots' opinion, and possibly extend them into negotiations in respect of other employee groups.[39]

It now emerged that the associations did not agree amongst themselves about the proposals for representation and finance. The ADC secretary wrote to the secretaries of the ACC, AMA and LACSAB to say that the ADC was no longer prepared to accept the proportions of 6:6:4.[40] The ADC had agreed to this split in May 1974 but had reserved the right to raise the matter again. The secretary also said that the ADC favoured allowing the provincial councils to finance the employers' sides of the NJCs for APT and C and for Manual Workers. The ADC was willing to consider with the other associations whether the remainder should be financed directly by the associations or via Section 2(7).

Both the AMA and ACC immediately rejected the ADC's call for parity of representation, principally on the grounds that the number of staff employed by local authorities in each association differed so widely. On financing LACSAB, the AMA secretary remarked that 'the confusion is almost complete'. Conceding that there might be a case for the funding arrangements for the two NJCs with provincial councils, he repeated the AMA's view that LACSAB should be funded wholly via Section 2(7). It was, he claimed, 'extremely difficult to see the advantage of establishing numerous different schemes for collecting expenditure if we can carry out the exercise in one central settlement'.[41]

The chairmen and secretaries of the ACC, ADC and AMA agreed to meet in September 1975 to try and reach agreement over LACSAB representation and finance. At this meeting the ADC said that, in order to reach an early agreement, it was prepared to accept that the GLC should be accorded special treatment; it would accept, therefore, association representation of AMA – 6; ACC – 5; and ADC – 5. The ADC also conceded that part of LACSAB could be funded via Section 2(7) deductions and by the associations but insisted that the existing funding by the NJCs for APT and C and for Manual Workers through the provincial councils should continue. The ACC and AMA accepted these proposals reluctantly. Some concessions were inevitable because LACSAB's constitution (paragraph 2) requires any resolution altering the balance of voting power to be unanimous. Given the ADC's firm rejection of a 6:6:4 division, the other associations had to give way or totally frustrate all their efforts at reform.

One cause of confusion, whether intentional or not, was the provincial councils' assertion that Section 2(7) funding ran the risk of central government interference and control of local government pay negotiations, which could 'potentially undermine our present system of free collective bargaining'. It was not made clear, however, how this would arise; as the AMA secretary pointed out:

there is no evidence that [Section 2(7)] involves a greater degree of central government control ... or that ... it will affect the negotiating system of collective bargaining under LACSAB in any way.

Similarly, in the ACC secretary's view: 'The use of S2(7) is entirely within the control of local government – in short it is purely a procedural arrangement available to the associations on their initiative.'

To try and resolve the difficulties, the three associations (and the GLC) met a delegation of provincial employers (led by Councillors Schultz and Dennett) on 28 October 1975. Sir Leo Schultz repeated the provincial employers' view that funding via Section 2(7) opened up the possibility of central government interference in pay negotiations. He defended the existing system, arguing that the direct financial link helped to ensure 'local authorities' interest and sense of involvement in the negotiating processes' and 'a degree of responsiveness on the part of the representative employers' organisations to the needs and wishes of their constituents'. The provincial employers' represent-atives invited the associations to justify their call for changes to this system, adding that the meeting itself was necessary only because so many local authorities, when consulted by the provincial councils, had expressed their opposition to the proposed changes. Sir Meredith Whittaker and the ACC secretary argued that the proposed reforms were justified on grounds of convenience and uniformity – LACSAB should be funded on the same basis as all other joint bodies. They also argued that the real value of provincial councils to local authorities lay not in the financial link but in the appeals and disputes procedures and various advisory services, in particular, training. Neither side was con-vinced and, most significantly, the issue central to the discussions – control of LACSAB – was never explicitly raised.

Members of the LACSAB special committee had attended the meeting with the provincial employers and they held their own meeting later the same day. The special committee accepted the provincial employers' argument for provincial council funding of APT and C and Manual Workers whilst the remaining negotiating bodies – except the Police Council – would be funded under Section 2(7). The special committee also acccepted the revised association representation on LACSAB but it did not consider the representation of the negotiating bodies on LACSAB. This issue had been raised by the provincial employers at the meeting earlier in the day, but there had been no time to discuss it. The provincial employers merely stated that the NJCs were underrepresented on the Board:

> having in mind their admitted predominance in the totality of local authority negotiations and, in the existing system, the proportion of the Advisory Board's funds which they supplied.

The provincial employers requested a further meeting to discuss this issue and, although it was acceded to, the meeting never took place. Further requests from the provincial employers in November 1975 and April 1976 did not expedite matters because the associations' and LACSAB secretaries had agreed to stall for time and put off such a meeting.[42]

By the end of 1975, agreement had been reached on the main areas of contention – representation, method of financing and constitutional changes. Substantial clarification and revision had not occurred but, as the LACSAB secretary noted, it was not the wording of the constitution that was important, 'but the spirit and intentions of the people involved to make it work'. In his view, it would be better, therefore, to leave well alone, and simply make only such modifications as are specifically necessary for the sake of legal consistency.[43]

Unfortunately, the final drafting of the constitution to incorporate the agreed changes could not be completed until the GLC had accepted their changed position of one seat and one officer adviser. The GLC accepted the changes in April 1976, by which date the budget for 1976/7 had been prepared and approved. It was now hoped and expected by LACSAB that the constitution could be finally amended and the final version was duly signed on 18 October 1976.[44] On the same day, the LACSAB secretary wrote to the associations' secretaries expressing the hope that these changes would mark a new spirit of co-operation between the board and the associations. Recently he had been 'immensely encouraged by the extent to which Belgrave Square has been able to be of assistance to the Associations during the formative stages of new or changing policies'.

It was essential that the associations

> should be able to involve Belgrave Square with the confidence that it will in no way disturb the internal relationships of the Associations or the relationships which the Associations have with central government. This in turn enables Belgrave Square, with equal confidence, to bring to the attention of the Associations the possible manpower or industrial relations implications of emerging policies without it being thought that it is an unwelcome intrusion.[45]

The crisis   There was not to be a period of amicable agreement and co-operation. Yet again, the associations were worried about the board's expenditure and the 1976/7 budget did nothing to allay those fears.

Although the size of the budgetary increases was unwelcome to the associations, their concern extended to LACSAB's staffing policy. Between May 1974 and February 1975 staff numbers had risen by thirteen to total sixty-eight, despite the fact that the board had been authorized to employ only five new staff. Even worse, from the associations' point of view, the board was seeking an additional six staff by April 1975 and an establishment at the end of 1975/6 of seventy-four. Between 1971 and 1976 total staff had risen from twenty-three to sixty-nine and it had not risen to the projected seventy-four because the associations refused to pay the increased levy. At the same time as the new constitution was being finalized, therefore, the worries about LACSAB's expenditure and staffing were coming to a head. The AMA's new secretary wrote to the LACSAB secretary seeking clarification of the 1976/7 LACSAB budget and an explanation of the procedure for appointing staff within LACSAB.[46] He received no such explanation. In May 1977 LACSAB again advertised for staff without first consulting the associations – something which it was not required to do, but which the associations thought it ought to do. At a meeting of associations' secretaries, on 27 May 1977, they all agreed 'that we really need to have some system of bringing LACSAB staff under control if it is a question of expansion of staff there'. However, LACSAB agreed to advertise staff vacancies internally – that is, within the associations – in the first instance and it seemed that the issue would be defused.

The concern about staff numbers and the manner of appointment was only symptomatic of a more general unease. Since reorganization the objective of the ACC and AMA had been to secure control of LACSAB, at first by revising its representation and funding. Domination of the board's membership – seventeen out of twenty-eight – did not convince the associations that they controlled the board. They still provided less than half the board's income and they had been unable to weaken the provincial councils' position because of ADC opposition. Moreover, the provincial councils' representatives outnumbered the association representatives on the two largest negotiating bodies – the NJCs for APT and C and for Manual Workers. In 1976, the ACC began to question the provincial council representation on these NJCs, and, although the matter was raised with the AMA and ADC, neither showed any willingness to undertake a review. As far as the AMA was concerned, 'there are no proposals ... to reduce the functions or to change the status of provincial councils [or] for altering the methods of negotiating with JNCs'.[47]

By 1979, however, the position of the AMA had changed. It produced proposals aimed at, *inter alia*, weakening the provincial councils' role in the pay negotiating machinery. The proposals were first aired in a paper by the AMA secretary in March 1979 and were, in part, a reaction to the manual workers' dispute and settlement during the 'winter of discontent'. The AMA's chairman, Councillor Taylor (Conservative), roundly criticized LACSAB's role in handling this and other settlements. He said:

I am bound to say that a situation where local government as a whole can find itself committed to large increases on expenditure by members not appointed by the Associations, and advised by a secretariat over which there is little direct control, is one which I am not prepared to continue to accept.[48]

The AMA secretary's paper gave full expression to these complaints – complaints which were shared by the minority group within the AMA.

At the heart of the criticisms was the belief that decisions about pay – 'the most important decisions taken by local government on the national scene'[49] – were inadequately related to decisions about grant. The level of pay settlements crucially affected local government's cash requirements and at a time of increasingly stringent cash limits it was imperative for decisions on pay and grant to be brought together. This co-ordination would be impossible, however, as long as the negotiating bodies themselves were 'not under the political control of the Associations'. Immediately after reorganization, the AMA had argued that the negotiating machinery should remain independent; its aim then had been to secure greater control of LACSAB. In 1979, despite the changes in the composition and funding of LACSAB, it was evident, in the associations' view, that it had not achieved such control. Its secretariat was described as

> too independent. It can raise money by separate levies as well as the funds it gets from Section 2(7). As a result even its internal expenditure, let alone its policies, are not under the control of the Associations. It is, therefore, neither answerable nor accountable to the Associations nor to member control in any true sense.

This assertion is odd, in view of the fact that LACSAB's internal expenditure – referring here in particular to the appointment of staff – was and is controlled by the board members, a majority of whom are association representatives. In the AMA's view, however, association members on the negotiating bodies become identified with that body and

> Somehow the identification of this group of elected members, who are not involved on the national scene for major issues and what they regard as their staff in the LACSAB secretariat, has to be broken.

Once again the need to involve leading members in the work of LACSAB had been raised but this time it had been raised by the associations. The members representing the AMA (and each of the other associations) on the board itself undoubtedly were leading members. But the members of individual negotiating bodies were not leading members; and, it was claimed, at this point the link between pay and grant was being broken. Such an outcome is scarcely surprising. The 'junior' councillors are part-time and many will have onerous duties in their local authority as well as the travelling and committee work for LACSAB. Some degree of dependence on LACSAB advice seems inevitable. Moreover, these 'second class citizens' develop an affinity for 'their' NJC for that most human of reasons: their contribution is valued and they feel important. It is difficult to resist the conclusion that, if the link between pay and grant was being broken, association policy was a major contributory factor.

But at the heart of the AMA and ACC complaint was the over-representation on provincial councils of non-metropolitan districts, which had fewer employees in total than either the AMA's or the ACC's member authorities.[50] The sheer number of ADC member authorities (333 district councils in England and Wales) enables them to dominate the membership of the provincial councils. The previous ADC chairman defended their part in the negotiating machinery: 'They represent the feeling of local authorities, every single local authority in a provincial council is represented on that council.' There was no way that the ADC would 'agree to doing away with the provincial councils ... we want to get [them] doing more than they are at the moment'.[51]

However, the AMA secretary had proposed that provincial councils 'should lose their rights to nominate members on to main negotiating committees' and that their independent staffing should cease. The other main proposals were:

1 a reduction in the number of employers on negotiating bodies to two-thirds from each association;
2 a reduction in the size of LACSAB and its reconstitution as a joint committee of the associations;
3 the allocation of the chairmanship and secretary of LACSAB to the AMA and ACC on an alternating basis;
4 the abolition of the post of secretary of LACSAB and his reconstitution as a chief negotiator subservient to the association-appointed secretary;
5 the integration of the provincial councils' staffs with LACSAB;
6 the funding of all secretarial expenses from Section 2(7).

In this way it was intended that LACSAB would become 'a true governing body which sets the main policy lines on pay for local government staff and appoints the other negotiating committees'. It was not proposed to abolish provincial councils altogether, merely to downgrade them to undertake only their proper job on local negotiations and disputes.

The AMA chairman, Councillor Taylor, described the negotiating machinery as outdated. It had been devised, he wrote, during the 1940s and 1950s, in an age

> when only a limited range of topics was subject to joint discussion at national level; an age before the arrival of annual increases and when it was possible to reach settlements of 2 or 2½ per cent; an age when a settlement for one group would have very little impact on another; when trade union claims were simple and unsophisticated affairs; when strikes and industrial action were unknown in local government; and, above all, an age before cash limits.

Furthermore, the system enshrined the independence of each negotiating body. He contrasted the fragmentation and disunity of the local authority employers' side with the increasingly 'united, solid and professional front' of the trade unions. The employers' side was 'an uneasy alliance between four quite separate groups of independent interests – the associations, the provincial councils, various government departments, and LACSAB.

He said he had been 'appalled' at the way the previous year's manual workers' negotiations had gone. 'We just cannot continue', he said, 'with little or no correlation between leading local authority members who are involved in the RSG negotiations and the members who determine how large a proportion of that money should be spent on wages.' Instead,

> we, the local authority members, have to rise above the parochial level. We must orientate ourselves towards the national scene. The only way out of this quagmire is to integrate the decision-taking process on the major national issues on pay negotiation with a decision-taking process in the local authority associations.

The AMA chairman concluded that both the LACSAB secretariat and the system of members on negotiating bodies had to be reformed simultaneously.[52]

The AMA's proposals were discussed at a series of regional conferences of AMA member authorities in June and July. The reaction was one of support 'from the policy and finance side', but 'a lot of resentment from personnel people whose power base was provincial councils'.[53]

The criticism of provincial councillors, merely implied in the AMA chairman's speech, was trenchantly spelt out by the association's Secretary. They are, he said:

> Essentially groups of personnel chairmen and the lack of getting through the finance concept is at its worst ... in the provincial councils.[54]

The AMA's proposals did not meet with the wholehearted and immediate approval of the other associations, still less of the provincial councils. After a number of informal meetings to discuss whether there was any measure of agreement, the political leaders and senior officers of the three associations met during the associations' joint national conference in Scarborough in September 1979. In an address to this conference the LACSAB secretary had told the delegates:

> what you have in LACSAB's small central body is expertise. Your job as local authorities is to come to the centre and decide what tune you want to play. But if you cannot decide what you want to play it is no good trying to shoot the pianist.[55]

Unfortunately, the associations could not agree on what tune should be played, nor could they agree who should be the pianist – let alone whether they should shoot him. At their joint meeting, the associations' secretaries were asked to identify any common ground that might exist and provide a discussion paper for future consideration.

As was to be expected, the ADC totally rejected the AMA's proposals for affording the ACC and AMA pre-eminence over the ADC. In the ADC's view, there was a case for examining the existing arrangements, but the successful operation of the machinery 'depended upon a much wider range of considerations than those of finance and control'.[56] The essence of the system was that it was voluntary. It needed, therefore, the closest possible involvement of the grass roots. It was also a joint system which needed, therefore, the co-operation of all sides. On the employers side alone this co-operation would not be forthcoming if there was an attempt, like the AMA's, 'to exclude certain parts of the machinery from national negotiations' or 'to secure the dominance of particular sectional groups within it'. The ADC reiterated its view that the criteria for representation on LACSAB and the negotiation bodies should not, as both the AMA and ACC argued, be numbers of staff employed:

> It is obviously a nonsense to attempt to reduce the representatives of almost three-quarters of the total number of employers to the level of a junior partner in an organisation which negotiates on their behalf.

The ADC did not argue that its large total number of authorities entitled it to more seats than either of the other associations, but it wanted parity of representation.[57] The ACC agreed with the AMA's proposals that LACSAB be funded solely via Section 2(7). The ADC disagreed. Whilst accepting that it would be administratively convenient, the ADC did not think it outweighed the advantages of direct accountability to individual local authorities. The ADC would agree only that 'present arrangements for the presentation and control of LACSAB's finances should be reviewed to see what improvements can be made'.[58]

There was a further meeting of association representatives in December 1979, but the associations could not reach agreement on either funding or representation. The outlook was not wholly bleak. The associations did agree on the general aim that they should control LACSAB. They also agreed that LACSAB should have a common advisory role for all negotiating bodies and that, in the long term, there should be far fewer negotiating bodies.

The debit side of the balance sheet was distinctly longer. The AMA had dropped its proposal that the secretaries of the AMA and ACC should alternate the secretaryship of LACSAB. Following discussions with the ACC, the AMA had also dropped its equally controversial proposal – from the ADC's viewpoint – that the LACSAB chairmanship should also alternate between the AMA and ACC. The ADC also rejected the other associations' proposals on future representation and on funding solely via Section 2(7).

At its policy committee meeting on 9 January 1980, the ADC formally proposed:

(a) that LACSAB should continue to be funded as at present and
(b) that no alteration should be made to the present membership and voting strengths of the constituent members of LACSAB.[59]

It was resolved that the AMA and ACC be informed accordingly. In such circumstances, the AMA policy committee meeting on 9 February 1980 could do little but decide that, if agreement could not be reached with the other associations on its latest modified proposals, then the proposed changes should be dropped altogether.

Aftermath The ADC's position on representation and funding was unequivocal; and, even if there had been a chance of persuading it to accept these proposed changes, it was certainly lost by the provocative proposals to deprive it of the chairmanship and secretaryship. Although the ACC agreed with the majority of the AMA's proposals, it recognized their implausibility. In the view of the AMA secretary, the reforms

foundered fundamentally on the irreconcilability of getting an AMA and ACC view together on where control would be ... although it appeared that the ADC were blocking it, as indeed they were, the real truth of the matter was that even if we had got the ADC to agree on some of those changes we would never have resolved ... the fundamental integration of a command structure for the secretariat which was ... the essence of our plan.[60]

And here the secretary is referring to the change in political control at the AMA. During the crisis both the ACC and the AMA had been under Conservative control. After the local elections in 1980, the AMA became Labour-controlled and the prospect of an integrated 'command structure' becoming a reality receded even further.

The proposals for the reform of LACSAB ultimately foundered, therefore, and it might be expected that future relations between LACSAB and the associations would be subject to periodic stresses and strains. In fact, the 'constitutional crisis' had a therapeutic effect. Relations between the two have improved considerably – a view firmly endorsed by the AMA secretary. This, rather surprising, outcome poses the question of what were the root causes of the crisis. For the AMA secretary, the associations needed to control the LACSAB machine: the staff who advised the LACSAB board and the negotiating bodies – the people 'doing the real negotiating behind the scenes'. There were two major criticisms of the LACSAB secretariat. First, it acted independently in the course of the actual negotiations with the staff side. Second, their presence at meetings (both formal and informal) with government ministers and civil servants pre-empted the associations' views and decisions. But, if these criticisms were valid before 1979, they apply with equal force since that date because ostensibly nothing has changed.

LACSAB officers respond to these criticisms by pointing out that they do not take decisions: they make recommendations to members, whether of the LACSAB board or of negotiating bodies. It is up to these same members to take the decisions. Formally, this description is accurate and it is also true that no strong member would ever accept a settlement that he did not believe to be the right one. LACSAB staff would reject any charge that they determine pay settlements, presenting their members with a *fait accompli*.[61] This view is shared by members of the negotiating bodies. One former JNC chairman has testified to the unstinting efforts of LACSAB staff to service the employers' side of his particular negotiating body. He was only one of many amongst employers' side representatives – that is, association-appointed representatives – who voiced irritation with leading policy-makers in the associations. Sarcastically, it was noted that these leaders see the links between grant and pay which mere manpower/personnel people are unable to see or grasp. Interviewees were quite frank: those involved in the personnel function – national negotiators, provincial council members, LACSAB staff – generally regarded 'the great policy-makers' as simply ignorant of the manpower function and of the complexity of pay negotiations. The pros and cons of these several assertions are of less importance than the gulf they reveal in the appreciative systems of the two sides. And it is this gulf in appreciative systems that lies at the heart of the conflict.

The associations had not grasped the appreciative system of

LACSAB and the negotiating bodies. They did not understand the complex, unpredictable nature of the negotiating process and the inappropriateness of mandates in this context. Conversely, LACSAB had failed to grasp the extent to which its concern with the dynamics of the pay bargaining process exacerbated the associations' fears on the financial front. For LACSAB, there were two key actors in negotiations – ministers and unions. They determined the course of pay settlements and LACSAB's task was to find a formula acceptable to both. To be blunt, local government had to accept the formula which emerged. This appraisal of the situation by LACSAB is wholly realistic but neither flattering nor satisfactory to local government. It became downright irritating as LACSAB's importance grew with its enhanced responsibilities, as the demands for income escalated with the associations' contribution rising from 7·7 per cent in 1973/4 to 41 per cent in 1978/9, and as the financial saliency of pay negotiations changed beyond all recognition. But LACSAB viewed the associations' concern with the implications for RSG of pay settlements as but one constraint, albeit an important one, amongst many. The associations' political leaders simply could not agree with this 'demotion' of their key concern. And yet LACSAB did not accept that financial considerations were being 'demoted': rather they were accorded a deal of significance – hence the gulf in understanding. In the words of one respondent, 'The flag flying over Belgrave Square was settlement at any price.' Indeed, it would be a strange negotiating body which did not seek settlements. However, in this search, the associations and LACSAB could not agree on the currency to be used let alone the price to be paid.

The view that LACSAB measures success in terms of achieving settlements was expressed by senior association officers and members. The response of the LACSAB staff to this allegation is simple scorn: it perfectly demonstrates the gulf between the policy-makers and the personnel function. The negotiators themselves claim to drive very hard bargains with the unions – 'we're in the game to win: we try to negotiate the best possible deal'.[62] However, the point is not that LACSAB negotiated poor or expensive settlements but that their major preoccupation was to negotiate a settlement.

Such a criticism of LACSAB is seen by members of negotiating bodies as singularly unfair because, when the associations were approached about the limits to negotiations, they proffered little or no guidance. Too often the associations' leaders have asked 'what are settlements likely to be in the next eighteen months: we need to know in order to make representations over RSG cash limits'. When the reply has been 'we don't know: you tell us how much we've got to negotiate with', the reply has been 'well just negotiate the best possible deal'. Criticisms of an 'unreasonable' settlement jar when no one ever defined 'reasonable'.

LACSAB staff would further argue that they were impressing upon the associations the importance of the link between grant and pay long before the associations became aware of it.[63] One indicator of the associations' failure to appreciate the importance of the link is the delay in reorganizing their own committee structures and procedures. As one association under secretary remarked, 'it was apparent, post-reorganization, that the control of the manpower resource ... was conspicuous by its absence in all the associations'.[64]

The ACC was the first of the associations to act. In 1976 it formed a manpower subcommittee of the policy committee. Initially a sub-committee to avoid any suggestion that it would erode the manpower work of the service committees, it was not until 1982 that the ACC's executive council decided that all representatives on negotiating bodies should be appointed by the policy committee and not by the service committees. From 1976, co-ordination was achieved by appointing the chairmen of service committees to the manpower subcommittee. Both the secretariat and the controlling Conservative group also played a co-ordinating role.

The AMA and ADC did not appoint manpower subcommittees until the 1980s. Both associations sought co-ordination through their respective controlling party groups and policy committees, and by appointing an under secretary responsible for manpower – in 1977 in the AMA and 1978 in the ADC. The AMA appointed its manpower subcommittee in 1980, in recognition of the increasing importance of manpower policies and

> to give the Association's leading representatives who serve on LACSAB, the various NJCs and other manpower bodies a chance to get together to discuss common problems and to aid communications between the Association and its member authorities.[65]

The subcommittee consists of the most senior members of the association's policy committee and is usually chaired by the association's chairman or vice-chairman. As in the ACC and ADC, the subcommittee is not devalued by its close association with the respective policy committee: it 'is too important to be distanced too far from policy'. The objective of this co-ordination, however, is not 'to try to whip everybody into a political line [but] sometimes there is a necessity to agree a political one for those who choose to follow the political line'. And also in the AMA:

> they try to make [the majority party's line] one which gives discretion and judgement to the individual. That is partly a response to the realization ... that on the day, being mandated to a line that was decided three weeks before by people who were miles away from the unions is not the right way to carry on business ... you just don't get results.[66]

There is now a far greater acceptance by the associations' leaderships that individual members of negotiating bodies are aware of the ramifications of pay settlements for RSG cash limits if only from experience in their own local authorities and from personal involvement in the CCLGF. Moreover, the associations' leadership now has first-hand experience of pay negotiations and, with the exchange of personnel between the associations and LACSAB, the gulf in understanding has been substantially reduced. Indeed, there is now a greater appreciation of the *range* of LACSAB's activities. Pay negotiations are, of course, the key task but LACSAB also operates as an industrial relations consultancy service for individual local authorities, advising on all aspects of local government manpower, either at the request of local authorities or on its own initiative, and covering such matters as detailed interpretations of statutes and national agreements for individual local authorities as well as more general guides to new legislation, and digests of tribunals and appeals. LACSAB is regarded as *the* source of such expertise. The associations simply do not and cannot provide the same service. Many respondents, including the associations, value LACSAB's services highly.

Many of the major issues remain unresolved: the ADC retains parity of representation and district councils, via the provincial councils, still dominate representation on the two largest NJCs. However, these issues no longer have the same high saliency for the associations. When they are raised today, the response takes the following form:

> while that degree of commonsense obtains then there is no practical disadvantage in having the wrong proportions of representation. [67]

Both sides have a greater understanding of the other's problems and are seeking to work together.

This emphasis on the appreciative systems of the participants differs sharply from their accounts of events. Repeatedly, the importance of personality conflicts was stressed in interviews. Thus, it was argued that the 'crisis' was the result of the clash between the secretary of LACSAB and the secretary and chairman of the AMA. It was said that the secretary of LACSAB was dominant in pay negotiations and that his dominance was challenged, at times in a highly personalized manner, by an AMA leadership keen to assert its pre-eminence. Without denying that the crisis may have acquired its peculiar flavour from such clashes, 'personality' is an inadequate explanation. Conflict was not limited to the AMA and LACSAB and the same individuals worked together amicably after 1979. The root cause lies in the different interests, expectations and values of the participants and not in the way in which they voiced their differences.

The lesson of the LACSAB dispute in 19878/9 is that the national community at any one time comprises a heterogeneity of interests and relationships. The attempt by the ACC and AMA – both avowedly centralists – to tighten their control of LACSAB was resented by LACSAB staff. LACSAB has repeatedly rejected any such hierarchical relationship with the associations and stressed that it exists to serve equally local authorities, provincial councils, sovereign negotiating bodies and the associations. The proposals were similarly resented by many local authorities (and more specifically by many councillors responsible for personnel and pay negotiations), by the provincial councils and by association-appointed members of national negotiating bodies.

> In the end the settlements, the negotiations in local government . . .
> it isn't the associations negotiating, it is local authorities
> negotiating. The associations have a crucial representational role
> to play for their authorities, but we are no stronger than our
> authorities allow us to be . . . and any politician in local government
> who thinks that he is really playing a centralist role . . . is, I think,
> misunderstanding the way this pyramid is worked. It isn't
> monolithic at all.

At the end of the day:

> Individual negotiators are first and foremost individual politicians
> from individual local authorities.

Irrespective of what association political leaders may want:

> the people who are at the negotiating table have a stronger assess-
> ment of what is liveable with back at the authority . . . they are the
> people who are close enough to the consequences of problems at the
> local end to modify their judgement.[68]

In short, conflict arose between associations, between associations and one of the most important joint bodies, and between associations and individual authorities. The associations wrongly regarded LACSAB as 'their' joint body: their proprietorial claims were disputed not only by LACSAB itself but also by LACSAB's other constituents. And these constituents are also the associations' constituents – individual local authorities. It is they, and not solely the personnel function within them, which have disputed their own associations' representational role in this area. If the years after reorganization saw the associations attempting to expand their empire, 1979 saw the culmination of a dispute in which eventually parts of the empire struck back.

If the associations are the pre-eminent organizations within the national community, why were they unable to gain the desired changes? In part, of course, reform was frustrated because there was no agreement on goals. Whilst the associations agreed on the need for change, this agreement did not extend to specific changes and, accordingly, opposition from LACSAB and the provincial councils was more difficult to surmount. Just as heterogeneity of goals and interests is said to impede the national community in its dealings with central government, so it impeded the associations in their dealings within the national community. However, heterogeneity is not a complete explanation.

It could be argued that the reform effort failed because of the maladroit strategies of various participants. Thus, the AMA's proposals to exclude the ADC from the control of LACSAB doomed the initiative to failure. A key requirement of any negotiations within the national community is unanimity. Joint action is virtually inconceivable if any one association objects and the AMA initiative disregarded this fundamental rule. In reply, it has to be noted that negotiations to this point had achieved nothing of substance and that a truly radical set of proposals, even if rejected, could none the less enlarge the options considered. The AMA strategy could be seen as an attempt to surmount the conflict of objectives.

The key factor in LACSAB's ability to resist reform lay, however, in the resources at its command. LACSAB has three resources, which make it a formidable opponent for the associations. First, it is constitutionally required to act for several constituencies. In a strict, legalistic sense, LACSAB is required to resist claims to pre-eminence by any one constituency. Second, reflecting its several constituencies, LACSAB is dependent on no one source of income. It is not vulnerable, therefore, the rule that 'he who pays the piper calls the tune'. Finally, LACSAB has political legitimacy. Its members are directly elected local authorities – the selfsame authorities who are members of the associations. Provided LACSAB retained their support, the associations were not criticizing 'a bunch of officials' but (at least implicitly) their own members. LACSAB could appeal to the elective principle to justify its actions in the same way as the associations. Even if the associations had agreed on goals it is a moot point whether they could have surmounted LACSAB's political resources. Whilst the associations may be the leading organizations within the national community, they are not the only ones which command a range of resources.

This claim to political legitimacy is rejected by the associations. They argue that, if local government is to speak coherently in the pay field, it must hammer out a set of policies which unify the approach of the finance, personnel and service interests. It really does not help if the policy and finance interests are channelling their case through the associations whilst manpower and personnel is pleading separately and directly through LACSAB. LACSAB is the authorized voice of the authorities through the associations and if such an agent body were to 'purport' to speak for local government on the grounds of its 'independence' it would mean that the legitimate representation of local government at the national level would have rather badly foundered. From the associations' standpoint it may be eminently undesirable but the reality of pay bargaining in the 1970s did include an independent voice speaking for local government and the representation of local government at the national level did founder rather badly.

The conflict between the associations and LACSAB also reflects another tension which beset the national community throughout the 1970s – the regulation of members. If the 1970s saw both central departments encouraging the development of peak associations for local government and the associations actively seeking such status, it also witnessed growing misgivings about such involvement. Local authorities wanted to influence central government, wanted involvement in central decision-making, but not at the expense of emasculation. Unease about the CCLGF was paralleled by distrust of the centralizing thrust of association policies on pay negotiations. The failure to reform LACSAB is not just an illustration of the heterogeneity of the national community nor of the resources at LACSAB's command but also of the reassertion of control by members. The associations have never had an effective means of regulating members in spite of the fact that their incorporation to central government implied they could 'deliver' members. Rejection of the associations' centralizing policies is at one and the same time a critical comment on the extent of this incorporation. The ensuing years were to see such distrust intensify to the extent that disengagement from the centre is being openly canvassed and, to a limited extent, practised. And the origins of this trend lie in the reactions of individual local authorities to the policy of their own representative organizations, not in the disillusionment of the national community with its central involvement.

There is one important caveat to this last assessment. It presupposes that 'members' had a coherent view when in fact one of the problems for both LACSAB and the associations is to obtain a co-ordinated view from local authorities:

The frightening fact is that within an individual local authority it is remarkably difficult to get the view of the policy/finance leaders ... to deal with personnel matters which are regularly dealt with by separate personnel committees. I can assure you it is just as much agony now as it always was.[69]

Provincial council members may have objected to association proposals but the bulk of members did not express and may not have had
an opinion on the subject. The reaction against central involvement
is compounded of both member criticism of such involvement and the
distance between members and their representative organizations (see
Chapter 9, below).

CONCLUSIONS

The major conclusions of the case studies in this chapter can be briefly
summarized.

First, the diversity of interests within the national community is
multiplied by the provisions for representing the distinct interests of
geographical subsystems.

Second, each subsystem contains the conflicts or cleavages found in
the larger national community, especially party political conflicts (for
example CP/WCC and LBA/ALA).

Third, the actions of central government have institutionalized such
diversity of interests and exacerbated relations between associations.

Fourth, if the strategy of factorizing facilitates central control, it
also limits the constituency for which the national community can
speak: it represents English local authorities outside London.

Fifth, the national community is neither a monolithic nor a
homogeneous entity. The dispute about LACSAB was as much a
dispute between the associations as a dispute between the associations
and a joint body.

Sixth, LACSAB is not the creature of the associations alone: it is
not 'their' joint body. To the divisions between types of local authority and between political parties within the national community, it is
necessary to add the multiple constituents of LACSAB.

Seventh, LACSAB was able to resist the associations' proposed
reforms because of the range of resources at its disposal. It was and
is constitutionally required to represent a number of constituents; it
had and has multiple sources of income; it remains the source of information and expertise on industrial relations and manpower issues in
local government for the rest of the national community, individual
local authorities and central departments; and its members are individual local authorities, which provide political legitimacy for
LACSAB's actions just as they do for the associations.

Eighth, NJC/JNC representatives are part-time and, until recently,
relatively 'junior' members within the associations. Undoubtedly,
they have relied on the advice of the LACSAB secretariat and
developed 'dual loyalties' or a disposition to argue the case of the
negotiating bodies before that of the association. In so far as this is
a criticism of association representatives, it is also a criticism of
association political leaders, who failed to give local government pay
negotiations sufficient priority.

Ninth, much of the conflict between LACSAB and the associations was not wholly a function of 'personalities' – as many interviewees claimed – but of divergent 'appreciative systems'.

Tenth, the policy of building 'peak associations' for pay bargaining revealed the flaw of such a centralist strategy: that the associations could not regulate their members. Whilst local authorities favour national pay bargaining (with latitude for local settlements) to counter the threat of being 'picked off' by the trade unions, they also want diversity of inputs to the bargaining process, including both the fine filter of the associations as well as the coarse filter of the provincial councils.

The conflicts and cleavages within the national community are awesome to behold. They reside not just in the interests of the different types of local authority or in party political allegiance but also in the organizaion of the national community (for example, ownership of the joint bodies) and (yet again) the national government environment. And all the issues considered to this point have been ones for which the national community is pre-eminent. Turning to examine its relationship with single-function policy communities, the national community becomes but one amongst a set of actors. Functional diversity comes to prominence as a constraint on its effectiveness.

NOTES AND REFERENCES: CHAPTER 7

1 Interviews with secretary, CP; Sir D. Lock, chairman, ADC; and I. McCallum, chairman, ADC, transcripts.
2 Interviews with Sir D. Lock, chairman, ADC, and under secretary, ADC, transcripts.
3 Interview with deputy secretary, ADC, transcript.
4 Correspondence with honorary secretary, WCC.
5 Interview with honorary secretary, WCC.
6 I would like to thank Mari James for collecting the data on the Welsh CCLGF which forms the basis of this section.
7 See oral evidence of Ian Dewar (principal finance officer, Welsh Office) in Layfield Committee, 1976, appendix 10 (microfiche) (London: HMSO).
8 Welsh Office, *First Report of the Joint Working Party on a Welsh Rate Support Grant System* (Cardiff: Welsh Office, 1977), p. 3.
9 The preceding paragraphs draw upon Welsh Office, *Second Report of the Joint Working Party on a Welsh Rate Support Grant System* (Cardiff: Welsh Office, 1978), section 1.5, pp. 15–20 and 45–50, and annex A, pp. 51–5
10 At the same time the WCC was producing reports for the ACC on the implications of devolution for local government. See, for example, 'Draft discussion paper on proposals for further local government reorganisation' (September 1977). Both WCC and ACC opposed any further reorganization. See Chapter 6, pages 212 and 247.
11 Both quotations from Council for the Principality, minutes, 18 January 1980.
12 See *Municipal Journal*, 4 January 1980, p. 7; 6 June 1980, p. 690.
13 Interview with deputy secretary, LBA, transcript.
14 Department of the Environment, Heads of Division Circular 40/80, 'Consultations with local government in England and Wales', 3 November 1980.
15 Interview with Sir H. Cutler, leader of Conservative group, GLC, notes. See also Cutler, 1982.

16 Interview with K. Livingstone, leader of Labour group, GLC, notes.
17 The same point applies to the grant arrangements for Scotland and Northern Ireland. See Keating, Midwinter and Taylor, 1982; Heald, 1980; Connolly, 1982; and Rhodes, Hardy and Pudney, 1983c.
18 As in Chapter 3, attention is focused on the three major joint bodies. On CLEA, see Chapter 8, pages 328–33. JACOLA, LAOSC and SACLAT experience little or no supervision because of their limited importance. The associations exercise no control over LAMIT because investment management is seen as a technical function best left to the trust's officers and members. LACOTS is funded wholly through Section 2(7) monies and control of its financial and other policies has not created any problems for the associations.
19 Interview with director, LAMSAC, transcript.
20 Interview with director, LGTB, transcript.
21 All preceding quotations from interview with director, LAMSAC, transcript.
22 All preceding quotations from interview with director, LGTB, transcript.
23 LGTB, *Report and Accounts*, 1978–9, p. 4 and p. 3 respectively.
24 Interview with Sir A. G. Taylor, chairman, AMA, transcript.
25 Interview with deputy secretary, LACSAB, notes.
26 Interviews with Sir D. Lock, chairman, and I. McCallum, chairman, ADC, transcripts.
27 Letter from secretary, LACSAB, to the association secretaries, 20 December 1973.
28 Letter from secretary, CCA, to secretary, LACSAB, 31 December 1973.
29 Letter from secretary, LACSAB, to secretary, AMC, 19 June 1974.
30 Letter from secretary, AMC, to secretary, LACSAB, 21 January 1970.
31 LACSAB minutes, 7 February 1975.
32 LACSAB minutes, 31 October 1972.
33 Letter from secretary, AMA, to secretary, LACSAB, 5 February 1975.
34 Letter from secretary, LACSAB, to secretary, AMA, 6 February 1975.
35 Letter from secretary, LACSAB, to members of the LACSAB special committee, 9 April 1975.
36 Minutes of meeting, 14 May 1975. See also letter from A. Hoskins and D. Parker, Yorkshire and Humberside provincial council secretaries, on behalf of all provincial councils, to LACSAB secretary, 16 April 1975.
37 Letter from LACSAB secretary to members of the LACSAB special committee, 9 April 1975.
38 Correspondence between the three association secretaries, 24 June 1975.
39 Letter from Councillors Schultz and Dennett to the three association secretaries, 3 July 1975. This letter incorporated the views expressed at a second conference of provincial council chairmen and secretaries held on 6 June 1975.
40 Letter dated 21 July 1975.
41 Letter from secretary, AMA, to secretary, ADC, 28 July 1975.
42 Correspondence between association secretaries, 17 June 1976.
43 Letter from secretary, LACSAB, to the three association secretaries, 28 April 1975.
44 The new composition of the board was:

ACC	5
ADC	5
AMA	6
NJC for APT and C	3
NJC for Manual Workers	3
NJC for LA Fire Brigades	1
Police Council	1
Scottish Councils	1
COSLA	1
Burnham Committees	2
	28

The other major substantive amendment allowed for funding, if the Board chose, via Section 2(7), amongst other sources and the provision of a conciliation service and pay reviews. There were, in addition, a number of small procedural and legal changes.

45 Letter from secretary, LACSAB, to secretaries of the ACC and AMA, 18 October 1976.
46 Letter dated 9 September 1976.
47 AMA, *Annual Report* 1975, p. 7.
48 Report of policy committee to AMA meeting, 22 February 1979. See also Chapter 5, pp. 186–8 above.
49 Interview with secretary, AMA, transcript.
50 ACC member authority employees 1,132,764 (46·5%)
   AMA member authority employees 1,002,326 (41·5%)
   ADC member authority employees   293,202 (12·0%)
   Source: AMA, *The Future of LACSAB*, March 1979.
51 Interview with Sir D. Lock, chairman, ADC, transcript.
52 *Municipal Review*, July 1979, pp. 75–6.
53 Interview with secretary, AMA, transcript.
54 Interview with secretary, AMA, transcript.
55 See *Municipal Review*, November 1979, p. 169.
56 ADC, 'Memorandum of views on the pay negotiating machinery in local government', report to ADC policy committee, 9 January 1980.
57 *ibid.*
58 *ibid.*
59 Report of the ADC policy committee, 9 January 1980; minutes of the ADC council Meeting, 13 February 1980, p. 109.
60 Interview with secretary, AMA, transcript.
61 Interview with secretary, LACSAB, notes.
62 Interview with secretary, LACSAB, notes.
63 Interview with deputy secretary, LACSAB, notes.
64 Interview with under secretary, ACC, transcript.
65 AMA, *Annual Report*, 1981, p. 5.
66 Preceding quotations from interview with under secretary, AMA, transcript.
67 Interview with under secretary, ACC, transcript.
68 All preceding quotations from interview with under secretary, ACC, transcript.
69 Secretary, AMA, personal correspondence, 2 August 1983.

Chapter 8

RELATIONSHIPS BETWEEN THE NATIONAL COMMUNITY AND POLICY COMMUNITIES

INTRODUCTION

A key feature of central–local relations in Britain is the functional pattern of links between equivalent departments at the two levels of government. It could be argued, for example, that the links between the DES and local education departments are as strong as the links between either the DES and other central departments or the education department and other local departments. In Chapter 2 it was argued that the existence of such 'policy communities' may limit the involvement of the national community in any particular policy and that the key actors within the policy communities are the various professions and not the associations. The questions of relative influence of, and the extent of conflict between, the national community and policy communities is intimately linked, therefore, with a discussion of the role of the professions. This chapter explores relationships within the national local government system between the national community and the policy communities with the various professions (see Figure 2.3).

Earlier chapters have already provided some data on these relationships. First, it is possible to distinguish two broad types of professional: those concerned with a specific service – the 'technocrats' – and those who advise on the range of local government functions – the 'topocrats'.

For the technocrat, the national community of local government is only one point at which pressure can be exerted. Of equal if not greater relevance is the policy community, be it education, fire, police, or social work. For him, the national community can be peripheral to his service interests. Thus the professions affected by organic change did not lobby the DoE but 'their' central service department. For the topocrat, the national community of local government is the natural focus of pressure. For example, the links between the accountancy profession, SOLACE and the associations are far more extensive than links between any one service profession and the associations. The contribution of the topocrats parallels rather than complements the work of the secretariat. However, advisers remain full-time officials in their local authority with consequent limitations on the time and energy available for association work. Only infrequently are officers seconded to the associations for short periods of time. Once again, the issue of the ownership of resources raises its head.

But the analysis of policy communities and their associated professions has not been the prime concern of earlier case studies. Although it has been possible to describe the different patterns of contact of technocratic and topocratic professions, the relationship between the national community and policy communities has not been systematically analysed. This chapter *begins* such an analysis. It presents brief analyses of the relationship between the national community and the fire and education policy communities. In each case, the *formal* structure of relationships is described which, although a limited perspective, illustrates a number of important differences between the two types of community, most notably in the range of participants and in the scope of the policy agenda. The basic proposition is that the differing interests of the two communities will generate a conflictual relationship and limit the issue scope of the national community, thereby constraining (again) the ability of the national community to represent local government.

It would be foolish to expect that the relationship remained constant throughout the 1970s. Just as the relationship between the national community of local government and the national government environment changed dramatically, so the relationship with the policy communities fluctuated. Initially, the relationship can be characterized as distant but, as the associations sought the status of peak associations, they also sought to increase their involvement in the policy communities. Decisions on grant could not be divorced from service policy and the associations, recognizing this fact, attempted to increase their influence. But, with the onset of retrenchment and direction, this enthusiasm has waned and the relationship can be best characterized as one of disengagement. The relationship between the policy communities and the national government environment is *not* explored in this chapter although, from the limited amount of data available, the changes in this relationship appear to be directly analogous to the changes experienced by the national community.

The basic objectives of this chapter are, therefore, to demonstrate the existence of distinct, single-function, policy networks; to determine the extent and the changing nature of the national community's involvement in these networks; and to assess the extent to which the policy communities constrain the issue scope of the national community. There is a subsidiary objective: to compare and contrast the policy communities with each other and with the national community. It was argued in Chapter 2 that policy communities were networks with a high degree of interdependence and markedly different characteristics from the national community – for example, they were characterized by vertical interdependence and a compartmentalized horizontal structure. This chapter is the first opportunity to assess this aspect of policy communities.

Context

The key event in the formation of the modern fire service was the blitz on London during 1940 and 1941, which

> proved conclusively that the wide diversity in such matters as procedure, training, organisation, appliances and equipment that characterised the pre-war brigade was militating against their efficiency in carrying out large-scale operations ... Unified command, with standard operational procedure, became an urgent national need. (Holland, 1977)

Accordingly, the Fire Services (Emergency Provisions) Act 1941 was passed in just nine days. It enabled the creation of a national fire service which absorbed both the local authority brigades and the auxiliary fire service. During the Bill's passage the Home Secretary, Herbert Morrison, said:

> It is the very definite intention of the Government that this is a wartime expedient only ... It is certainly my very definite view that after the war the fire-fighting forces ... should not be permanently run by the State, but should again become a local authority service. [1]

The Act vested responsibility for fire services in England and Wales in the Home Secretary, and in Scotland in the Secretary of State for Scotland. The Act gave them sweeping powers to suspend or modify the powers and duties of local fire authorities, and to transfer functions to the national fire service. According to the Holroyd Report (1970, p. 25):

> The central control imposed by nationalisation had the effect of welding some 1440 fire brigades in England and Wales and some 185 brigades in Scotland into a single operational machine with standardised training, duty systems, uniforms, appliances and equipment and standard arrangements for appointments, promotion, discipline, pay and administration.

For over a year at the end of the war the fire service remained nationalized with no attempt to return it to local authority control. After considerable pressure from the AMC[2] and the Fire Brigades' Union (FBU) in particular, the government's wartime pledge was honoured by the Fire Services Act 1947. The service was not, however, returned to the same local authorities: instead, county boroughs and county councils in England and Wales became the fire authorities, thus reducing the number by 90 per cent from 1,440 to 141. In Scotland the counties and large burghs, except for Glasgow, were required to combine into ten areas served by single brigades and administered by a joint committee of the fire authorities concerned.

Apart from the reduction in the number of fire authorities, the other important differences between the prewar and postwar services were the retention of both central control and of that singular achievement of the war years, the uniform operational machine created by the national fire service. The 1947 Act finally implemented many of the measures for ensuring minimum fire cover standards, greater co-ordination of mutual assistance, standardization of equipment and better standards of training regarded as essential by the Departmental Committee on Fire Brigade Services (Riverdale Committee, 1938) and provided for in the Fire Brigades Act 1938. The legislation not only recognized the need for the Home Secretary to exercise various controls, but also the need for him to act in consultation with fire authorities and fire service representatives bodies through the Central Fire Brigades Advisory Council (CFBAC).

The 1947 Act still sets the legal framework for the fire service.[3] The number of fire authorities was reduced still further, however, in 1974. Following local government reorganization, there are now only sixty-two fire authorities in England, Wales and Scotland. (There is also one fire authority for Northern Ireland, which was created in 1971.) Upon reorganization, county councils (metropolitan and non-metropolitan) in England and Wales were designated local fire authorities. In Scotland, the regional and island councils became the fire authorities, although there are two combined areas and, therefore, only eight brigades in all. (The GLC is also a separate, and indeed the largest, local fire authority.)

Whilst local government reorganization was under consideration by the Royal Commissions in England and Scotland, the Holroyd Committee conducted a comprehensive examination of the structure and functions of the fire service with terms of reference which required it to make recommendations on, *inter alia*, the principles which should govern the organization of the fire service in Great Britain and the relationship between the central government and local fire authorities. The committee welcomed the proposed reduction in the number of local authorities and it recommended that the number of fire authorities in England, Scotland and Wales should also be substantially reduced. The Holroyd Report (1970, p. 70) supported the retention of local authority control over the fire service (the home departments as well as the associations were strongly in favour of this too), saying:

We cannot emphasise too strongly that we have no wish, and see no need, to reduce the freedom of action of local fire authorities.

It also said (p. 64) however, that:

> the power and resources of the Home Departments to provide guidelines for brigades to promote the efficiency of the service are too limited.

The report (p. 70) also commented that both the associations and the Chief and Assistant Chief Fire Officers' Association regarded the relationship between the home departments and local fire authorities as 'harmonious'. The same bodies, however, 'advocated strongly that there should be no extension of the powers of control exercisable by central government'.

Since that date the relationships have not always been so harmonious. There have been differences of opinion between the Home Office and the associations about the Home Secretary's powers in relation to fire authorities.

Actors and functions

It is generally thought that the Home Secretary has a fundamental and general responsibility for the provision of the public protective services such as the fire service. This is certainly the view of the Home Office:

> The Home Secretary has a general responsibility to Parliament for the Fire Service; and under the Fire Services Acts 1947–59 he has certain regulatory powers relating to operational efficiency.[4]

The Home Office distinguishes between an individual local authority fire service and the fire service as a whole. The role of the Home Office is to ensure a national provision to protect the public against fire. In addition to this wide role, the secretary of state has specific responsibilities for the operation of an individual fire brigade: for example, the 1947 Act empowers him (s. 33) 'to hold a public local inquiry into the manner in which any fire authority are performing their functions under this Act, or into the circumstances of, or the steps taken to deal with, any particular outbreak of fire'.

There has, however, long been disagreement between the associations and the Home Office about the latter's interpretation of the Home Secretary's responsibilities. The associations have maintained that the constitutional position set out in the relevant legislation does not bear out the Home Office's claims and does not support the notion that Parliament has placed a general responsibility upon the Home Secretary. Writing in 1979, the (then) under secretaries responsible for fire service matters in the ACC and AMA said they believed that the Home Office construed the Acts as giving the Home Secretary this general responsibility but, they wrote:

We cannot find it: our reading of the 1947 Act is that responsibility for securing an efficient fire service rests directly in the local fire authorities (Section 1 itself says so) and that the Home Secretary has certain carefully defined if extensive powers, including those of making regulations. It is all a matter of balance, of course, but we don't think our friends at the Home Office have got that balance quite right – if we are to believe what we sometimes read. (Roberts and Hodgson, 1978, p. 232)

The associations' view is that:

the statement that the Home Secretary has a general responsibility to Parliament for the fire service can therefore only be true in a non-legal sense.[5]

Section 1 of the 1947 Act p...ced the duty to provide fire cover in their area directly upon local fire authorities. The associations maintain that 'the whole Act is framed on this basis' with the powers of the Home Secretary restricted to making regulations on certain defined matters only. The associations contrast these limited powers both with other legislation in the home policy field (for example, Section 1 of the Education Act 1944, 'which places a direct responsibility on the Secretary of State to promote education'), and with the powers of the Home Secretary with regard to the police service.

To summarize briefly, the Acts controlling the fire service give the Home Secretary statutory powers in relation to the reduction of authorized establishments, closure of stations and the withdrawal of appliances. (For more details see Holroyd Report, 1977, appendix B.) Thus, fire authorities must notify the secretary of state annually of the establishment scheme currently in force. This scheme is not approved by the secretary of state but any variations in it – for example, reductions in firemen or in the number of appliances – which could adversely affect fire cover do require his approval. Additionally, if the secretary of state is convinced that the scheme is unsatisfactory, he may make his own after consulting the fire authority. There are, however, other important areas which although discretionary under the law are the subject of strong Home Office advice, which is 'enforced' through the annual inspection system. The most important of these areas relate to standards of fire cover – for example, manning levels, risk categories, speed and weight of first attendance.

The Acts do empower the secretaries of state to ensure certain standard practices amongst fire authorities, relating to pension and gratuities, and regulations for standard training and equipment. The latter, however, must follow consultations with the Central Fire Brigades Advisory Council (CFBAC) (see below). The 1947 Act also empowers the secretaries of state to make regulations concerning the operational control of individual fire authorities: Section 17 refers to the maintenance of discipline and the ensuing regulations give rights of appeal to the secretary of state against the severest disciplinary decisions of a fire authority. Section 18 of the 1947 Act enables the secretary of state to make regulations concerning the qualifications and standards required for appointments and promotion. The regulations also required a fire authority to obtain the secretary of state's approval before appointing their chief fire officer (see below). All the secretary of state's powers in this respect are permissive, not mandatory: he may make regulations regarding discipline and appointments (and successive Home Secretaries have done so), but he doesn't have to make them.

The 1947 Act lays certain specific duties upon local fire authorities:

(a) to secure the services for their area of such a fire brigade and such equipment as may be necessary to meet efficiently all normal requirements;

(b) to secure the efficient training of brigade personnel;

(c) to provide efficient arrangements for:

    (i) dealing with calls for assistance and summoning members of the brigade;

    (ii) obtaining information required for fire fighting purposes;

    (iii) preventing or mitigating damage to property in the course of fire fighting; and

    (iv) to give advice on fire prevention and related matters.

In order to carry out these duties, local fire authorities are empowered to provide necessary accommodation; to pay retained firemen; to use the brigade outside their own area; and to use the brigade for non-fire-fighting purposes (for example, special services such as assistance at traffic accidents and pumping out of flooded premises). The fire authority can if it wishes charge for such services; in practice charges are levied only for non-humanitarian tasks. The provision of such special services is a discretionary power for local fire authorities – they are under no statutory obligation to provide them. In practice, all authorities do provide such services and indeed they have come to represent an increasing proportion of brigades' total calls.

One other important aspect of the 1947 Act was the power it gave to the secretaries of state to appoint an inspectorate. This inspectorate (HMI) is required to inspect every fire authority and report to the Home Secretary. The main function of the inspectorate is to provide professional advice to the Home Secretary. Its reports are confidential and they have remained so despite a number of representations by the associations that fire authorities be informed of their contents. The HMIs have been described to us as 'the missionaries into the fire service' who are 'more advisers to authorities than anything else'.[6] This advice or forewarnings will be on technical matters but 'they never tread on the political area at all'. Prior to 1959 'their great sanction was the removal of the direct grant of the fire service'.[7] This was a 25 per cent grant. In the words of one chief fire officer, 'their teeth were drawn in 1959'. Traditionally, there is a very amicable relationship between the HMIs and local authorities because they are all former fire service officers (typically chief officers) and therefore senior colleagues of currently serving officers. They are available to advise chief fire officers at any time and contacts are not confined to their regular inspections. They will also generally have been advisers to the associations and thus have very wide experience of relationships within the service at the national level.

Two of the most important provisions of the 1947 Act were those which recognized the two national joint councils for the purposes of consultation, and established the Central Fire Brigades Advisory Councils (CFBAC) — one for England and Wales and one for Scotland. The bodies which make up the fire service, and the formal mechanisms which exist to mediate their relationships, are shown in Figure 8.1.

It was in 1978 that the associations agreed to review the number and extent of government controls over local authorities with a view to seeking the abolition or amendment of those

> which are excessive, result in too much day-to-day interference in the operation of service and impinge on local government's responsibilities for planning and development of services.[8]

The results of this review were set out in *Review of Central Government Controls over Local Authorities*, which was published jointly by the associations in February 1979. Section E of this report deals with police, fire and other Home Office services. As regards Home Office controls in the fire service, the associations referred to a number of instances of financial controls where charges were laid down or recommended by the Home Office which constituted 'over-detailed control and grandmotherly advice' such as:

(a) charges for special calls — e.g. road traffic accidents (S.3(1)e of the 1947 Act); and
(b) penalties for false calls (Home Office Fire Service Circular 13/1967).

The associations called for the repeal of sections 17(1), 18 and 19 of the 1947 Act, concerned respectively with regulations on discipline and appeals; appointments of chief officers, qualifications and promotion; and the approval of establishments.

At a meeting between the associations and Home Secretary on 14

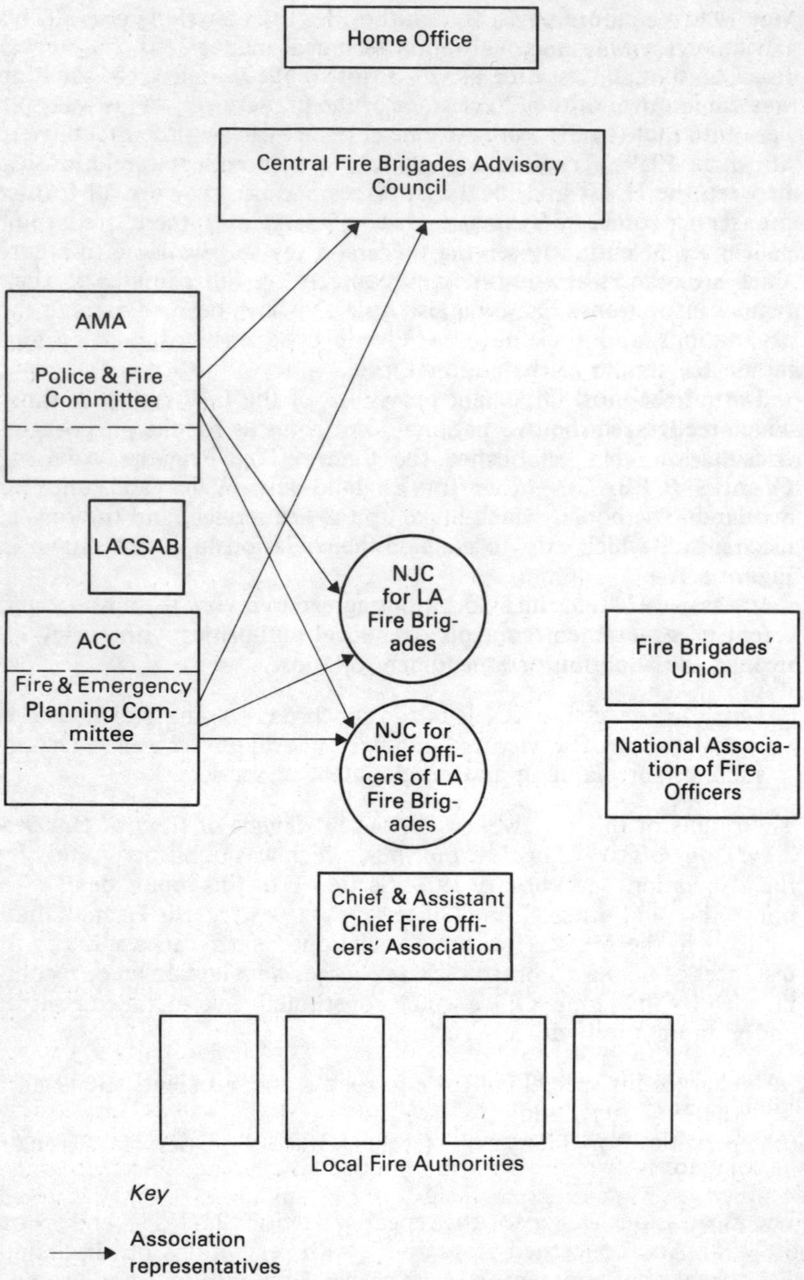

```
                    ┌─────────────────────┐
                    │    Home Office      │
                    └─────────────────────┘

              ┌──────────────────────────────────┐
              │  Central Fire Brigades Advisory   │
              │              Council              │
              └──────────────────────────────────┘

┌──────────────────┐
│      AMA         │
├──────────────────┤
│  Police & Fire   │
│   Committee      │
└──────────────────┘

      ┌──────────────┐
      │   LACSAB     │
      └──────────────┘
                                    ╭──────────╮
                                    │   NJC    │
┌──────────────────┐                │  for LA  │
│      ACC         │                │Fire Brig-│
├──────────────────┤                │  ades    │            ┌──────────────┐
│ Fire & Emergency │                ╰──────────╯            │Fire Brigades'│
│ Planning Com-    │                                        │    Union     │
│    mittee        │                ╭──────────╮            └──────────────┘
└──────────────────┘                │   NJC for│
                                    │Chief Offi-│           ┌──────────────┐
                                    │cers of LA │           │National Asso- │
                                    │Fire Brig- │           │ciation of Fire│
                                    │  ades     │           │  Officers     │
                                    ╰──────────╯            └──────────────┘

                        ┌──────────────────┐
                        │ Chief & Assistant│
                        │ Chief Fire Offi- │
                        │ cers' Association │
                        └──────────────────┘

        ┌──────┐   ┌──────┐   ┌──────┐   ┌──────┐
        │      │   │      │   │      │   │      │
        │      │   │      │   │      │   │      │
        └──────┘   └──────┘   └──────┘   └──────┘
              Local Fire Authorities
```

Key

→ Association
  representatives

Figure 8.1 *Local authority association relationships within the fire policy community.*

May 1979 the latter said he was anxious to avoid unnecessary controls and 'do everything possible to preserve proper local discretion'.[9] Indeed many of the controls itemized by the associations were seen by the Home Office as 'guidance' which was issued after consultation with the CFBAC and, on occasions, at the request of the associations. Nor did the Home Office agree that the controls which did exist were unnecessary or overly detailed. On appointments, Mr Whitelaw argued that it was important for public confidence in the abilities of chief fire officers that the powers of approval and veto be exercised. As regards establishments, the associations argued that control over them was unnecessary and led to damaging disputes between the Home Office and fire authorities. The associations claimed that fire authorities should set standards: HMIs and the secretary of state's power to hold public inquiries could thereafter ensure that they were adequate. The relevant Acts clearly and unambiguously vest provision of fire services in local authorities; and, if they don't meet their obligations, they are answerable to their electorates and liable to answer in the courts for any inadequacies and/or errors. Mr Whitelaw disagreed. He said that it was essential to ensure that minimum standards were maintained in the interests of public safety. HMIs were only empowered to collect information about how fire authorities were performing their functions and their advice carried weight because of the secretary of state's back-up powers.

On the question of disciplinary regulations, the associations expressed the same objections as to control of establishments. Mr Whitelaw, however, replied that the uniformed and disciplined services concerned with public protection (police and fire) were always liable to be called upon to face danger; they were special cases and therefore a national code of discipline with appropriate appeal procedures was essential.

The government's subsequent White Paper, *Central Government Controls over Local Authorities* (Cmnd 7634, HMSO, 1979b), contained only one proposal relating to the fire service: to abolish the requirement for the appointments of chief fire officers to be approved by the secretary of state. And even this was to be replaced by a requirement that local authorities should advertise nationally any such vacancy, consider all applicants, and interview all those who were suitable. The associations regarded this as wholly unnecessary interference and the single proposal as wholly inadequate. They contrasted the comparatively minor contribution from the Home Office with that of other government departments, which had suggested many more amendments (nearly 300 in total). The AMA said it was 'rather disappointed'.[10] The ACC said it was 'most disappointed' with the government's response not least because

the maintenance of central control of establishment is inconsistent

with the government's declared policy of reducing public expenditure by allowing local authorities themselves to determine how
those reductions shall take place. The maintenance of controls
which require central approval for reductions in staff, appliances,
or fire stations is clearly contrary to that declared policy.

It was all the more important

at a time when local authorities require the freedom to manage their
own expenditure in order to give effect to the government's overall
policies in relation to total public expenditure.[11]

This concern was at the heart of the associations' desire to seek reductions in controls – that at a time of substantial public expenditure cuts
and when local authorities were being urged to make significant
manpower cuts it was essential that individual local fire authorities
should be able to set their own standards on establishments. Reductions were difficult to achieve if the controls remained and were enforced by HMIs. The AMA too asked the Home Secretary in July
1979 'to accept that Home Office advice on standards of cover is no
longer relevant in the changed economic circumstances'.[12]

Furthermore, if local authorities imposed manpower cuts they faced
the serious threat of industrial action. Mr Whitelaw was therefore
asked, at a meeting on 30 July with the associations, for an assurance
of government support and assistance in such an event. Mr Whitelaw
replied that

a decision to provide such assistance could only be taken by the
government in the light of circumstances prevailing at the time. It
would be a central government decision and I do not think that we
could appropriately seek to draw up plans in advance with other
interests.

As to the question of relaxation of standards of cover, Mr Whitelaw
said he would

wherever possible – support fire authorities' efforts to reduce expenditure, and ... give full weight to their need to do so in considering
applications for my approval ... to variations in the establishment
schemes for fire brigades. This implies a degree of flexibility as
regards standards of fire cover in appropriate cases but ... I would
not be prepared to approve proposals the effect of which would be
to reduce fire cover provision below the recommended minimum
standards.[13]

The Fire Brigades' Union's (FBU) view is that increasingly the Home

Office in recent years – under the present government – has been agreeing to cuts in establishment for financial reasons. This is strenuously denied by the Home Office, which argues that reductions are only approved when they would not endanger the maintenance of minimum standards.

Mr Whitelaw rejected other criticisms from the associations by reiterating that appointments and promotions were best prescribed centrally so that minimum standards could be maintained. He could make no concessions here and emphasized that regulations promulgated under Section 18 of the 1947 Act could not anyway be made by him without prior consultation with the CFBAC.

Before describing the subsequent (post-1979) dispute between the associations and the Home Office over areas of responsibility and controls, I will now examine the composition, functions and procedures of the CFBAC – itself the object of considerable and long-standing complaint by the associations.

The pattern of contact

The Central Fire Brigades Advisory Council   Under the Fire Services Act 1947, as amended by the Fire Services Act 1959, Sections 29(1) and 36(18), the secretaries of state for the Home Office and for Scotland are required to constitute a CFBAC for England and Wales and for Scotland respectively. The purpose of these consultative bodies is to advise the secretary of state

> on any matters as to which he is required by this Act to consult the Council or any other matter arising otherwise than under Section 17 of this Act, in connection with the operation of this Act which the Council have taken into consideration whether on a reference from the Secretary of State or otherwise.

The secretaries of state are required to consult the councils before making regulations concerning the following:

(1) uniformity in fire hydrants and hydrant indication;
(2) the method of appointment of chief officers;
(3) the qualifications for appointment to any local authority brigade or to any rank therein, and for promotion into any such rank and the method of ascertaining any such qualifications;
(4) standards of training;
(5) design and performance of equipment;
(6) pensions.

Section 17 of the Act deals with discipline and appeals against dismissal on disciplinary grounds. These matters cannot be dealt with by the councils either by reference from the secretary of state or by reference to him. The appropriate consultative bodies for these matters are the NJCs for Local Authority Fire Brigades (LAFBs) and for Chief Officers of Local Authority Fire Brigades.

The secretary of state is also empowered to consult the council on any other matters arising in connection with the operation of the Act and the council itself has power to raise matters with the secretary of state.

The council itself has forty-four seats. It has eight joint committees with a total of over 200 seats as well as subcommittees and working parties. The secretary of state has discretion in the appointment of the Chairman and in the number of members but these must represent two interests: fire authorities and members of fire brigades. The secretary of state also can and does appoint 'independent' experts; that is, not representative of either the local authority employers or employees but of, for instance, the Fire Res. rch Station.

In 1980 the membership of the CFBAC was as follows:

Chairman	Parliamentary under secretary of state, Home Office	
Secretary	Home Office, principal	
Employers	ACC	7
	AMA	6
Employees	Chief and Assistant Chief Fire Officers' Association (CACFOA)	2
	National Association of Fire Officers (NAFO)	8
	FBU	8
*	Home Office	8
*	Chief Fire Officer, London Fire Brigade	1
*	Institution of Fire Engineers	1
*	Director, Fire Research Station	1

*Note: Discretionary appointments

Central government provides the secretariat for the council, prepares its agendas and meets its expenses. The full council usually meets only twice a year, principally to consider reports submitted to it by the many joint committees which carry out the bulk of the work of the council. These joint committees report to both the English and Welsh and to the Scottish CFBACs, and cover the whole range of fire service matters not within the purview of the NJCs. In other words, the CFBAC deals with operational aspects of the service.

Figure 8.2 shows the composition of committees in 1980. The eight main joint committees have developed into permanent standing committees. Beneath them, however, subcommittees and working groups are formed as and when it is found necessary to delegate specific tasks to them. They will normally be wound up once they have reported on their work to the main committees.

The composition of the standing committees aims to reflect the membership of the council itself. This means that the ACC always has one more member than the AMA. In addition to their representatives, each association nominates an officer adviser to accompany them – in the AMA's case two members and one adviser on each committee. The membership of CFBAC working parties or study groups need not be confined to council members. Frequently members will be drawn from other government departments, universities, or industry, depending upon the expertise required. For the smaller working groups concerned with wholly technical matters, the associations commonly appoint only their officer advisers.

Only the council is legally required, not the committees or working parties, but it is the recommendations of these committees which principally set the agenda for the council. The Home Office maintains that it sets the council's agenda only in an administrative sense – that the items arise automatically and that it is open for all parties on the council to propose other agenda items. The associations' complaint, however, is that although many of the agenda items may be substantially technical – and indeed have been accepted as such by the association representatives on the relevant committees – nevertheless when they are considered by the full council they may have financial and/or manpower implications which are unacceptable to the associations (as representatives of fire service employers and managers). The associations complain that the relevant papers arrive so near to the date of meetings that there is no time for adequate consideration by the associations, let alone for consultation between them. More important, the associations consider that there is a gulf between themselves and the Home Office which is wholly inappropriate for bodies which jointly constitute the management side of the fire service.

The CFBAC has been the subject of persistent criticism by the associations and it is clear that it embodies the problems and tensions in the relationships between the various constituents of the fire service.

The council has been variously described to us as 'the Mount Pleasant of the Fire Service',[14] 'a shunting yard'[15] and 'a convenient cloak for the Home Secretary to hide behind'.[16] The associations have long argued that the council is far too big, too cumbersome, unco-ordinated, uncertain of its purpose and bogged down in trivia. As long ago as 1968 the AMC and CCA argued that the council should be halved in size.

One of the principal criticisms from the associations is that in a number of committees there is the wrong weight to representation, and that many of the most important issues discussed in the council are political/management decisions – for example, standards of fire cover. Although voting does not take place, nor is any attempt made to assess the majority view, none the less the association view is that

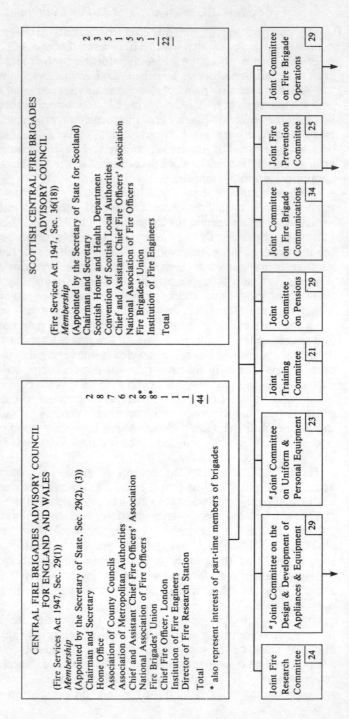

SECRETARY OF STATE FOR SCOTLAND

SCOTTISH CENTRAL FIRE BRIGADES
ADVISORY COUNCIL

(Fire Services Act 1947, Sec. 36(18))

Membership

(Appointed by the Secretary of State for Scotland)

Chairman and Secretary	2
Scottish Home and Health Department	3
Convention of Scottish Local Authorities	5
Chief and Assistant Chief Fire Officers' Association	1
National Association of Fire Officers	5
Fire Brigades' Union	5
Institution of Fire Engineers	1
Total	22

SECRETARY OF STATE

CENTRAL FIRE BRIGADES ADVISORY COUNCIL
FOR ENGLAND AND WALES

(Fire Services Act 1947, Sec. 29(1))

Membership

(Appointed by the Secretary of State, Sec. 29(2), (3))

Chairman and Secretary	2
Home Office	8
Association of County Councils	7
Association of Metropolitan Authorities	6
Chief and Assistant Chief Fire Officers' Association	2
National Association of Fire Officers	8*
Fire Brigades' Union	8*
Chief Fire Officer, London	1
Institution of Fire Engineers	1
Director of Fire Research Station	1
Total	44

* also represent interests of part-time members of brigades

| Joint Fire Research Committee | 24 |

| "Joint Committee on the Design & Development of Appliances & Equipment | 29 |

| "Joint Committee on Uniform & Personal Equipment | 23 |

| Joint Training Committee | 21 |

| Joint Committee on Pensions | 29 |

| Joint Committee on Fire Brigade Communications | 34 |

| Joint Fire Prevention Committee | 25 |

| Joint Committee on Fire Brigade Operations | 29 |

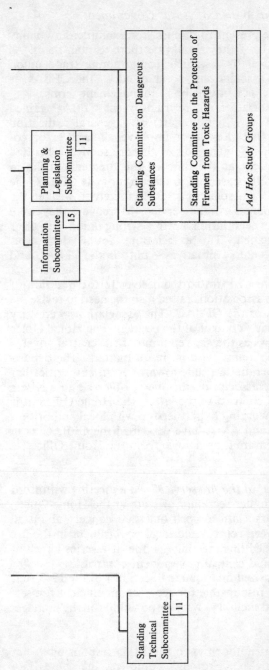

Note: [a] Merged in 1982 to form the Joint Committee on Appliances, Equipment and Uniform.

Figure 8.2 Structure of the Central Fire Brigades Advisory Councils, 1980.

the unions should not be present to discuss, for example, how many appliances there should be – they should be there to man them. As it is, however, the council 'is a vehicle for attaining trade union objectives'.[17] From the associations' point of view, the CFBAC is therefore not as effective as it might be in management terms.

The moves by the associations to restructure the CFBAC gained momentum in 1979 and were symptomatic of a general realization within the associations that they must improve all aspects of co-ordination within the management side of the fire service. This had been made all too apparent at the time of the firemen's strike in 1977–8. It had long been the case that in meetings of the CFBAC the often disparate views of the associations served merely to weaken the local authorities as managers of the service. Moreover, they were faced (as they were in pay negotiations) with a strong union with clear policies uniformly presented. The associations found themselves perpetually responding to unio.. initiatives – both in the CFBAC and NJC for LAFBs.

At the same time as they addressed themselves to the question of government controls, the associations raised also the need to revise the structure and operations of the CFBAC. The associations were very critical of the Home Office's control of the council. The Home Office was described in interviews as the very epitome of the central government view that it has the innate wisdom in all matters. The department's 'notoriously autocratic' attitude towards local authorities has been contrasted by many association members, officers and advisers with that of the DoE. In contrast to the latter, the Home Office, it is claimed, has no sense of working in partnership with local authorities. Advisers from the ACC and AMA have described the CFBAC as in practice serving 'as little more than a voice from the Home Office'.[18]

Post-1979 and the 'future' of the fire service   At a meeting with Lord Belstead (parliamentary under secretary of state at the Home Office) on 25 March 1980, the associations spelt out their concern about all aspects of relations between central and local government in the fire service. The AMA regarded this meeting 'as one of a series aimed at decreasing bureaucracy and central government controls'.

The associations emphasized first, quoting Section 1 of the 1947 Act, that fire authorities were responsible for securing an efficient fire service in their areas; elected members were responsible for the management of the service:

> However, the ability of authorities to fulfil this responsibility has been and is being impaired. Prominent amongst the causes is a misconceived view of the Home Secretary's proper role in relation to the fire service.

The associations said that that role should be restricted to providing technical oversight and they wanted 'reasoned arguments for any contrary view'.[19] In particular the associations questioned the Home Office's view that the Home Secretary's role in relation to the fire service is constitutionally different from the position of other ministers in relation to other local authority services. Lord Belstead repeated the line that is always held by Home Office ministers and officials – that the Home Secretary indisputably has a general responsibility for the service. Home Office officials insist on this interpretation, citing the Holroyd Report's (1970, para. 15) statement that 'The Secretary of State for the Home Department ... [has] central responsibility for the fire service in England and Wales' as well as the powers listed in appendix B. However, the Holroyd Report (1970, p. 72) also recommended

that the Home Secretary and the Secretary of State for Scotland be given a specific statutory responsibility for promoting the efficiency of the fire service throughout Great Britain and for providing research and management services, both to assist in the discharge of this responsibility and for the guidance of local authorities in the performance of their statutory functions

Whether this recommendation is merely a *restatement* of the secretary of state's powers or an extension of them is yet another stage in the dispute.

At their meeting with Lord Belstead the associations also questioned whether Home Office controls 'are really necessary or consistent with the essential nature of the fire service as one that is locally provided'. On the issue of union involvement in fire service policy-making, the Associations argued that local authorities.

should not be required to negotiate with trade unions on the variation of authorised establishments or standards of fire cover, that consultation with the unions should be at the authority's discretion, that there should be no unilateral negotiations or consultations between the Home Office and the unions; nor should direct administrative arrangements be made with them falling within the local managerial province.

In reply, Lord Belstead acknowledged the competence of the authorities to consult with unions locally and said the Home Office

would not consult the unions nationally but would wish to know that consultations had been carried out by the local authority before being prepared to approve, for instance, a variation in establishments or to advise in certain circumstances.[20]

Finally, at the meeting the associations indicated that a number of suggestions could be made for improving the work of the CFBAC. The minister indicated that he would be willing to discuss any such suggestions.

Subsequently the associations' fire service advisers made the following recommendations. First, that pensions should be removed altogether from the CFBAC and instead come within the purview of the NJC:

> Why should the Home Office have a role in that area in circumstances where by common consent government is not welcome in other aspects of conditions of service negotiations?[21]

Second, the council's committee should be simplified by amalgamating the uniforms joint committee and the design and development joint committee; and by abolishing standing subcommittees and working parties. Instead, the advisers recommended small *ad hoc* working groups reporting back on specific problems. Third, the financial consequences of all proposals put to the council should be specified. Fourth, the numbers on committees should be cut either by reducing the numbers representing certain bodies (for example, the Home Office's 'top heavy' representation on the fire prevention and communications committees) or by ending representation altogether (for example, the 'altogether unjustified' representation by the FBU and NAFO on the fire prevention and communications committees). Finally, the advisers recommended setting up a joint association working party to formulate comprehensive proposals for restructuring the council.

These suggestions were endorsed by the associations' respective fire committees and a joint officers working party was quickly set up. It first met on 4 February 1981 and comprised not only advisers to the two association fire committees (three chief fire officers – one ACC, one AMA, one GLC – and five other chief officers) but also the two members of the associations' secretariats responsible for the fire service, and one member from the LACSAB secretariat.

The associations' principal aim had been to persuade the Home Office to consult with them – as, jointly, the management side of the fire service – prior to CFBAC meetings. The council itself, and union involvement in it, should be reserved for 'minor' technical matters: when occasional matters of importance are discussed the CFBAC, the associations claim, is not an effective substitute for direct consultation. The associations may have been seeking to alter the CFBAC to facilitate future co-operation over policy-making in the service, but they felt that their efforts were severely hampered. In June 1980, two months after the meeting with Lord Belstead, the Home Office produced a document which had been prepared without consultation with the associations, and outside any prior CFBAC remit or consideration. This document was the Green Paper entitled *Future Fire Policy* (backed by the report *Review of Fire Policy*, upon which the recommendations in the Green Paper were based). The review was a wide-ranging study affecting many interests and the Home Office argued that it would not have been practicable to consult each organization independently and separately, or to take account of divergent views. Rather, it decided to publish the study in the form of an open consultative document. The associations remained unconvinced: other departments did not find the practical problems insurmountable. They felt that the agenda for reform had been unilaterally determined and the scope for association initiatives constrained. It was no comfort to them to know that the FBU, National Association of Fire Officers (NAFO) and Chief and Assistant Chief Fire Officers' Association (CACFOA) had also been ignored in the preparation of these documents. All of these bodies, and especially, the FBU, were extremely critical of the lack of consultation.

There is a general belief amongst both management and employees that this review was carried out principally to justify cuts in the fire service (see CACFOA, 1980, p. 5). The review's main purpose was to promote the efficiency and the effectiveness of 'the future attack on fire'. Whilst additional expenditure may be necessary in certain areas, 'significantly more substantial savings would be in prospect' from, *inter alia*, the proposed review of fire cover standards.

Thus, by 1981, this issue, crucial for the future of the service, was being dealt with by the CFBAC (a special committee of the council) – typically, in spite of calls by the FBU for a full public inquiry and by CACFOA for a Royal Commission. The outcome of these deliberations, and the future relationship between the associations, the CFBAC and the association, remain to be seen and will have to form part of some other account of the fire service. For the 1970s, one point is clear: the associations never established their claim to the joint management of the fire services.

CONCLUSIONS

At this stage it is important to note, however, the interests encompassed by the fire policy community:

1 the local fire authorities, as employers and managers of the service, represented by the associations (and CACFOA);
2 the employees of the service, as represented by the FBU and NAFO;
3 the Home Office, which seeks to maintain an aloof impartiality designed to secure the best possible service in the interests of the

community at large (consistent, of course, with any changes in policy deemed appropriate by the government of the day).

It is not possible to describe these three interests as permanently in conflict. Most notably, chief fire officers — although obviously employees in the service — occupy the position of managers of the service as advisers to the associations. They also seek, via CACFOA, in a consciously disinterested fashion, to further the broadest interests of the service in general, as they perceive it as professionals. Clearly, too, HMIs share a common experience with chief fire officers, and it is one of the strengths of the fire service that it is a single-entry profession with a shared work experience: all chief fire officers (and HMIs) will have begun as ordinary firemen.

The FBU also seeks to promote the interests of the service in general as well as promoting the narrower trade-union interests of its members. Many improvements in operational efficiency, and particularly in safety, have derived from FBU pressure in the CFBAC. The conflict of interest between the FBU and the employers derives from the simple fact that the latter are concerned with the resource implications of change. The FBU regard this concern as too often exercised at the cost of efficiency and safety. The union would be horrified at the thought that local authorities should ever be able to determine their own standards of cover; in the union's view this inevitably would lead to a drastic reduction of standards.

The local authorities' response is that all they seek is the ability — especially at a time when they are being not merely exhorted but forced to implement drastic expenditure cuts — to determine priorities locally across all services. In other words, they want the right to decide whether cuts, if they are necessary, should be made in the fire service rather than, for example, in the provision of homes for the elderly (Stevenson, 1982, p. 21). The Home Office view is simply that the fire service is an essential service which the government is obliged to ensure is provided to certain minimum, and nationally determined, standards. Their view is that local authorities do contribute to the setting of these standards through the associations' membership of the CFBAC.

It is a measure of the FBU's disillusionment with the local authority employers that since 1977 they have campaigned for the service to be nationalized. Needless to say, the associations would resist such a move to the utmost. There was, therefore, considerable consternation within the associations when CACFOA advocated nationalization, albeit very cautiously, in its response to the government's *Review of Fire Policy*. CACFOA (1980, pp. 52 and 54) objected to partisan considerations taking precedence over the efficiency of the service and 'the total needs of society'. Regretting the low morale of the service, CACFOA added:

We believe consideration needs to be given to whether or not the Fire Service should remain a part of local government and if it does what provision should be made to ensure that the safety of society is not prejudiced by a change of political influence in employing authorities.

Chief fire officers have significant access to government via CACFOA in the way in which chief constables have via the Association of Chief Police Officers (ACPO). However, for chief constables their professional association is the channel of access to the Home Office. For chief fire officers, CACFOA is a constrained channel of communication. Most important, their views have to confront other, often different, interests, which also have significant access. In an era of retrenchment and its attendant partisan disputes, professional considerations have been challenged by the associations' concern with the financial implications of po.cy. The challenge has not always been welcomed − hence the desire to insulate the fire service from partisan conflicts by nationalization. But to note limits to the influence of chief fire officers is not to deny they have such influence, especially on the operational aspects of the service.

The associations have been dissatisfied with their relations with the Home Office for a number of reasons. First, especially in the eyes of the associations, consultation is often nugatory because of the Home Office's 'autocratic attitude' (a charge to which Home Office officials are well accustomed and for which they account by virtue of the special nature of the services for which they are responsible − police, fire, probation, immigration, prisons). The associations feel that they are treated by the Home Office as an administrative convenience. One Home Office respondent considered this comment 'offensive' and 'inaccurate' but it is certainly an accurate summary of the views expressed by association political leaders and officers. Equally, other central departments − for example, DES, DoE − adopted a far more open consultative style. For example, they consulted the associations before studies were undertaken and even on the drafting of White Papers.

Second, because it has an inspectorate, the Home Office has an alternative channel of communication with individual local authorities, enabling it to keep abreast of local practice and developments and decreasing its reliance on the associations for information and advice.

Third, because there are far fewer local fire authorities than local authorities, it is relatively easy for the Home Office to consult local fire authorities individually and to obtain the needed information and advice. It does not act 'over the heads' of the associations − the Home Office claims that it always seeks the associations' views about potential financial implications of policies − but it is not dependent on them for data on the management of the service.

Finally, some dissatisfaction on the part of the associations seems inevitable, given the dispute over the powers of the Home Secretary. The associations' own view of their role is that:

> Fire authorities, as local authorities, have set up national Associations – the Association of County Councils and the Association of Metropolitan Authorities – to act as their voice on the national aspects of all local government service matters. The Associations are therefore the representative voice of fire authorities on fire cover matters. As a matter of practice (but not of law) the Associations have accepted a role for the Home Office on this question and have co-operated in any national discussion.[22]

Unfortunately the problem for the associations is not just to get the Home Office to accept this role, but to get their own members to accept it. In a letter written in 1980 setting out a possible future framework for improved co-ordination amongst the fire service employers, a LACSAB official argued that:

> I believe that in practice an authority has only one *effective* channel, through the local authority association to which it belongs, any other channel is a waste of time and if it continues to be used becomes counter-productive – the 'not them again' syndrome which, in a tight community like the Fire Service, can quickly gain the authority a bad reputation.
>
> The message must be rammed home that if an authority wishes to raise a policy matter, whether to amend present practice or introduce new practice, it *always* makes its approach through its association.[23]

Even if this message was taken by local authorities it would not necessarily lead to co-ordination amongst the employers' side, nor thereafter to co-operation between the employers and the Home Office. Community there may be in terms of institutions, procedures and frequency of contact, but not in terms of shared interests. The 1970s saw the associations searching for a more effective say in the fire policy community with no conspicuous degree of success.

With the advent of the 1979–83 Conservative government and the cuts in public expenditure, it might be anticipated that the relationship would be subjected to even greater stresses and strains. However, the fire service has been *relatively* protected from the cuts and a number of the initiatives canvassed by the associations have been acted upon. After a series of meetings during 1982 the structure of the CFBAC has been simplified, new procedures for the circulation of papers and minutes have been agreed and undertakings about closer consultation between the Home Office and the associations have been given. These changes were welcomed by the associations and may well represent the sought-for status as joint managers of the service: it is far too early to assess the impact of the changes. Whatever the outcome, it is clear that the relationship between the national community and the fire policy community has been characterized by the search for greater involvement by the national community.

THE EDUCATION POLICY COMMUNITY [24]

Context
In his analysis of educational policy-making, Kogan (1975, p. 238) concludes:

Pluralistic, incremental, unsystematic, reactive – how untidy the total system is.

Sir William Pile (1979, p. 41), former permanent secretary at the Department of Education and Science (DES) opines that:

It is probably fair to say that the Department is as conscious as any department of central government of the need to promote continuous consultation with its local authority and other partners on all major issues of policy and resource allocation.

And in his evidence to the Expenditure Committee he elaborated:

'there is a whole network of interfaces, confrontation and arguments conducted at the highest level of Ministers'. In addition, he spoke of 'what is generally intended to be the open door in the Ministry . . . that anybody can come and tell us what they think and feel'. (Cited in Lodge and Blackstone, 1982, p. 23)

However, this perception is not shared by all those consulted. The National Union of Teachers (NUT) has complained that:

There have been a number of occasions in recent years when the Union has had cause to make strong complaint to the Secretary of State at what it considered a failure to carry out full and proper consultation with the Union and with other professional and educational interests. (Cited in Lodge and Blackstone, 1982, p. 23)

Nor is the consultation between equals. Kogan (1975, p. 238) qualifies his description of educational policy-making as pluralistic by commenting that:

The DES denies it has power to aggregate or lead yet it plainly does so ... The only certainty is that the DES wields determinant authority and great power.

In a similar vein Lodge and Blackstone (1982, p. 18):

> seek to establish that officials of the ... DES are a vitally important source of influence on policy-making – indeed, in some instances the single most important source of influence.

And in its report on British educational policy-making the OECD (1975) concluded that the DES was

> the most important single force in determining the direction and tempo of educational development.

To identify the DES as the key source of policy initiatives is not, however, to consign other actors to oblivion. Regan (1979, p. 35) argues that:

> the DES has much more power than the old, pre-war Board of Education, and more than most government departments today over their respective services ... In any case there are substantial areas of education where no DES control exists ... Partnership is a hackneyed term and does not fully convey the flavour of central–local relationships in education. Nevertheless no other term would do as well. The partners may not be equal ... The contribution of both is, however, equally indispensable and both sides know it.

Out of this interdependence springs a 'consensual network'. Educational policy-making

> is generally assumed to be strong, largely continuous and consensual in its workings and in its assumptions.

The assumptions are

> sustained by an authority and power network not easily paralleled in any other area of public life.

The continuity depends upon

> interaction between three main sets of agents, central government, local authorities and teachers, who both sustained the continuity and produced change. (Kogan, 1975, pp. 72, 101)

The influence of these actors varies from issue area to issue area. Sir

Toby Weaver argues that the secretary of state's control is greatest in the sphere of individual and social opportunity and resource allocation whilst the teachers' influence is greatest over the curriculum and the local education authorities' (LEAs) influence is greatest on organization (cited in Ranson, 1980, p. 5). Not all authors are willing to specify which actor has determinant authority in the system but it is widely conceded that the focal point of the network is the DES and Lodge and Blackstone (1982, pp. 20, 33, 34 and 35) extend this conclusion to argue that there is a clear 'departmental view' of policy: 'it is like joining a good ship in the navy'. In a similar vein to Kogan, they stress the consensual nature of the system: the DES is 'pragmatic, conservative and evolutionary', reacting to 'the logic of the education service as it was developing' and 'going where the arithmetic leads'. And implicit in Griffith's (1966, pp. 522–4) characterization of the DES as promotional in its dealings with local authorities is the notion that there is a departmental view to promote.

This stress on consensus and the departmental view should not obscure the real differences of interests between the major actors – differences which are for the most part obvious.

The associations share an interest in limiting the size of pay increases and a commitment to education as 'a local government service' – a phrase with two distinct meanings. First, it refers to the view that education is one, albeit the largest, local government function linked with the other services. Especially in an era of public expenditure cutbacks, any suggestion that education should receive special treatment is strongly resisted, although this stance predates the era of cuts. Second, it refers to the determination to resist any increase in central control of education. Both these interests are potentially a source of conflict. The associations and the DES may wish to limit pay increases but, self-evidently, the teachers' unions do not. With increasing union militancy such differences have become sharper and are not limited to the annual pay round, now encompassing conditions of work (negotiated outside the Burnham structure, see below), the curriculum, definitions of the teachers' role and falling school rolls, cutbacks and redundancies. Similarly, the commitment to education as a local government function can generate conflict with both the DES and the unions, especially on such questions as hypothecating the education element in general grant. Nor can it be assumed that the associations necessarily present a united front to their education 'partners'. Historically, the rural and urban interests of the two associations have led to divergent policy preoccupations and, if the reorganization of 1974 muted these differences by merging the urban and rural authorities within county areas, it also exacerbated relations as the associations became more politicized. Finally, the 'professional' interest in education (manifested not only by the teachers' union but also by such bodies as the Society of Education Officers) leads not only to a 'national' perspective (as in the concern for disseminating information and advice on best professional practice) but also to conflict with the political parties, which can and do have different educational priorities.

In sum, policy-making in education has been described as consultative and consensual, with the DES taking the initiative and promoting a conservative departmental view. However, the consensus

> has had a narrow basis ... because only a small fraction of the formally defined constituency of educational government has been consulted on any particular issue. (Lodge and Blackstone, 1982, p. 40)

Pre-eminent amongst those consulted are the teachers' unions and the associations, which, in spite of differing interests, constitute with the DES the co-operative, tripartite nexus of educational policy-making. Table 8.1 on the interest groups in education provides both a summary statement of the range of actors and clearly illustrates the prominence of teachers and associations in the education policy network.

Actors and functions

At the outset, it will be useful to sketch the extent of the associations' involvement in educational policy-making. Figure 8.3 covers the major institutions of government in education and shows the links between the associations and other institutions. Descriptions of the functions of the DES and the inspectorate are easily available and are not provided here (see the publications listed in note 24).

Quite simply, the associations are firmly embedded in the network of educational governance and their involvement is not limited to discussions with the DES, lobbying Parliament or even sending representatives to consultative bodies, but includes the establishment of their own joint body and the provision of funds, most commonly Section 2(7) monies, for a range of advisory bodies.

Council of Local Education Authorities (CLEA)   CLEA's function

is to act as the body through which all local education authorities (LEAs) discuss matters of interest. It was established in 1974 following reorganization and it is responsible to the education committees of the ACC and AMA. The objective was to provide 'a strong, single voice for education without being divorced from the main stream of local government'. The ACC and AMA education committees are responsible for:

(1) Major educational policy issues, including those 'across-the-board' policies involving other functions in addition to education.

Table 8.1 Educational Interest Groups: a Summary

Government-sponsored	Managerial and legitimized	Non-managerial and legitimized	Non-managerial Non-conflictual	Conflictual
Schools Council	Association of Metropolitan Authorities	National Union of Teachers*	Advisory Centre for Education	National Union of Teachers*
Section 2(7) bodies (e.g. National Foundation for Educational Research)	Association of County Councils	National Association of Schoolmasters*	Confederation for the Advancement of State Education	National Union of Students*
Advisory committees	Council of Local Education Authorities	Joint Four	Nursery Schools' Association	Society of Teachers Opposed to Physical Punishment
Consultative Council on Local Government Finance	Inner London Education Authority	Head Masters Conference		National Association of Governors and Managers
Burnham Committees	London Boroughs Association	Denominations		National Association of Schoolmasters*
	Welsh Joint Education Committee	Research Community		Child Poverty Action Group
		Educational Press		
		Private Foundations: Nuffield Foundation		
		National Children's Bureau		

Note: Some groups which are both legitimized and non-legitimized, conflictual and non-conflictual, are marked with an asterisk.
Source: Modified from Kogan, 1975, p. 232.

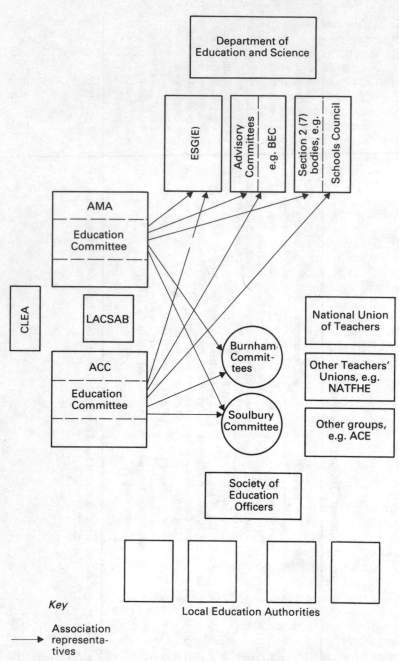

Figure 8.3 *Local authority association relationships within the education policy community.*

(2) Parliamentary activities.

(3) Discussions at ministerial level.

(4) Appointments and general policy co-ordination in relation to Burnham and other negotiating bodies.

(5) Other policy matters not specifically referred to the ... Council of Local Education Authorities and matters referred to the Association by their constituent members and by government departments.

(6) To provide information and advice to their constituent local education authorities (other than LAHEC matters and salary and conditions of service) and to co-operate with each other (ACC/AMA) in this service.

CLEA is responsible for:

(1) Policy decisions and matters specifically allocated by ACC/AMA committees to CLEA.

(2) Consideration of matters referred to CLEA for (a) decision, and (b) implementation or administration of ACC/AMA committees' policy.

(3) Joint discussions with Ministers arising from (1) and (2) above.

(4) Preparation of reports and submissions to the ACC/AMA Policy Committees.

(5) Service to and liaison with elected members serving on education organisations.

(6) Co-ordination of the provision of information and advisory services by the Associations to all local education authorities and development of joint action thereon.

(7) Annual education conference and other special conferences.

(8) Publications.

(9) The Local Authorities' Higher Education Committee and the LAHEC specialist staff.[25]

The simple reason for quoting these terms of reference is that they demonstrate clearly the circumscribed nature of CLEA's remit. Policy is the responsibility of the associations and not CLEA and when there is any disagreement, on any matter, it must be referred back to the associations' education committees. This tight control of CLEA betrays the origins of the organization.

The relatively neutral objective of a 'single voice' in education does not convey the full flavour of the ACC/AMA intentions: they wished to extend their influence and curtail the influence exerted before reorganization by the Association of Education Committees (AEC). From its formation in 1904 until its demise in 1977, relationships between the AEC and the associations were seldom cordial and often strained. The AMC expressed regret that the AEC was ever formed

(AMC, 1972, p. 7). In representing the interests of a single service the AEC was testimony both to the power of that service and to the limited influence of the associations within that service. There was a 'very deep-seated resentment about the separateness of education in local government' and about the AEC 'giving a purer education view unsoiled by any other considerations'.[26] The newly formed ACC and AMA determined, therefore, 'to see education as a part of the totality of local government not as a separate entity ... it is illogical for an authority to be in membership of two national organisations each concerned with the same function'.[27] They were particularly exercised by the finance of education and its links with other services: it was the era of corporate management. The transition was rarely less than acrimonious and exacerbated by personality conflicts. The secretary of the AEC, Sir William Alexander, commanded considerable respect in the education world and was the dominant figure within the AEC and, in the opinion of some, within Burnham. In the words of Edward Boyle, 'Now and then rather absurd attempts used to be made by other association leaders to be sort of equal with Sir William. Well, I mean, they just weren't.' He was seen as 'larger than life' and 'a formidable man' (Kogan, 1971, p. 135; 1975, pp. 81–2 and 89). Curbing Sir William Alexander and the AEC was an attempt to substitute association and party control of education for personalized, professional control.[28] The death knell was the decision by the Secretary of State for Education and Science, Reg Prentice (Labour), to remove the AEC from Burnham: 'It cannot be disputed that the responsibility for education rests by statute upon the LEAs and not education committees' (*Times Educational Supplement*, 24 May 1974). Within weeks AEC membership had fallen to 35 (out of 104) and in 1977 it was disbanded finally. This backcloth explains the emphatic control of CLEA by the ACC and AMA.

The ACC and AMA were equally represented on CLEA, each nominating twelve elected members and five officer advisers. The secretaries of the two associations are the joint secretaries of the council and the education officers of the two associations are CLEA's joint education officers, both being hierarchically superior to CLEA's own staff. It would be a mistake, however, to assume that detailed supervision remains the norm.

With the principle of policy control firmly established and as the keener edges of memory blur, informal liaison or 'a multiplicity of contacts' has become ever more prominent. At the outset, the following kind of comment was not atypical: 'What's the point of CLEA. You don't have any real clout at all and there are no delegated powers. You have this conference and you come across with the occasional press release but it doesn't amount to much.'[29] But over the years recognition has grown. 'I don't think it's as a result of any identifiable achievement, single identifiable achievement, it's just the way time has a way of bringing about change in people's attitudes ...'[30] If stress and suspicion characterized CLEA's origins, 'a close working relationship' captures the normality and informality of its relations in 1980. Trust has replaced suspicion and now CLEA not only participates in joint discussions with ministers on matters referred to it by the ACC and AMA, but it participates also in informal ministerial discussions and meetings.

Section 2(7) bodies   Here, only those education bodies in receipt of Section 2(7) monies are considered (see Chapter 3, pages 69–71 above). All claims for such monies are vetted by CLEA and in 1978/9 comprised:

	£(000s)
Schools Council for Curriculum and Examinations	1,221
National Foundation for Educational Research	304
Further Education Staff College	220
National Council for Audio-Visual Aids in Education	154
National Institute for Adult Education	54
Field Studies Council	50

Since 1978, the claims have then been submitted to a joint subcommittee of the three associations – a subcommittee of their policy committees, to which it reports. To illustrate the scale of expenditure, CLEA's income in 1978/9 was £22,000, and the AMA's income was £939,000. The importance of the associations as a source of income for these bodies varies. They provide 50 per cent of the Schools Council's income, 67 per cent of the NFER's income and 100 per cent of NIAE's income, whereas the FSC is self-financing, apart from its central administrative costs.

It is not the objective to describe in any detail the functions of the wide range of educational bodies – they are, for the most part, obvious from their titles. It is sufficient to draw attention to the simple fact that the associations fund several such bodies as well as nominating representatives to their councils: it provides a crude but none the less effective indicator of the extent, as well as the range, of association involvement.

Advisory committees   This term refers to official committees, including those with a statutory basis. The objective is not to provide a complete listing of such committees but to illustrate the range of association involvements.

Section 4 of the Education Act 1944 established permanent central advisory councils for England and Wales. Their function was to advise the minister 'upon such matters connected with educational theory and practice as they think fit and upon any questions referred to them by him'. Since 1967 secretaries of state have ignored their statutory duty to reconstitute the councils. Although responsible for a number of major reports, the councils only acted on ministerial initiative and they would not be worth mentioning here but for one simple fact: in statutory basis, terms of reference and composition they bore a marked resemblance to the Central Fire Brigades Advisory Council (CFBAC). However, whilst the Home Office has continued to work with and through the CFBAC, the DES has preferred to work through *ad hoc* committees and working parties with more specific remits (Fenwick and McBride, 1979, p. 48; Pile, 1979, p. 38).

The demise of the central councils did little to simplify the patchwork quilt of advisory bodies. The permanent or standing bodies include the Business Education Council, the Careers Service Advisory Council, Advisory Council on the Supply and Training of Teachers, Council for Educational Technology and the Technician Education Council. The associations send representatives to all these bodies.

The Schools Council, although listed as a Section 2(7) body, is also a standing advisory committee and it is probably the most important of all the organizations noted to this point. Its distinguishing features include its independence from the DES and the controversy which has surrounded it. Established in 1965, its primary task is to review the curriculum, teaching methods and examinations in schools. The teachers' organizations have called for more substantial LEA representation. However, the DES has wanted a more direct involvement in curriculum and examination questions. The Labour government published a Green Paper in 1977 and revised the Schools Council's constitution in October 1978 but it was left to Sir Keith Joseph to remove 'the thorn in the flesh' by closing the council in April 1982 (*Times Educational Supplement*, 30 April 1982). Whether these changes represent 'growing public insistence' (Pile, 1979, p. 80) that the DES should be more directly involved or the DES's 'intense dislike of outside councils and committees' (Lodge and Blackstone, 1982, p. 26) is arguable. It is clear that DES involvement in curriculum questions has grown.

Expenditure Steering Group (Education) and Burnham. The creation of the Consultative Council on Local Government Finance (CCLGF) was an innovation of major importance for the education policy community, not only because financial constraints were an important problem for the service but because, under the umbrella of the CCLGF, a series of consultative forums, known as steering groups, were created. Established in 1976, the function of the groups was to assess the implications for local government services of forecast trends in present expenditure policies: the Steering Group — ESG or pronounced 'ez-gee' — was one such group. Curiously, its role is not widely discussed in the education literature. Pile (1979, pp. 41 and

50–51) mentions its existence but describes grant negotiations without mentioning it by name. Kogan (1981, p. 159) notes its importance for the discussion of cuts in expenditure, but for the most part it receives scant attention.

The position of ESG(E) within the CCLGF is shown in Figure 4.2. It is composed of officials from the DES and the associations. In 1979 the ACC sent seven officer advisers and two members of the secretariat to ESG(E); the AMA sent three officer advisers, two members of the secretariat and two ILEA officers; and the LBA sent three officer advisers. The DES was represented by senior officials, whose numbers fluctuated from meeting to meeting, depending on the agenda, although the principal finance officer was invariably present to ensure continuity.[31] The education subgroup's primary task is to make technical assessments of PES White Paper figures, including forecasts of outturn figures for the previous year. The education steering group assesses the implications of these figures for the service, sets out the preferred distribution of expenditure for its services and comments on the balance between capital and current expenditure. Indeed, ESG(E) has stressed the problems which will be caused by cuts in educational expenditure. Along with other steering groups, it has been accused of making no genuine effort to find savings (see Chapter 4, pages 127, 140–1 and 145–6 above) and its reports have been singled out as 'prone to exaggerations'.[32] However, as Peter Shore noted, their views committed neither side. But the reports of ESG(E) to the CCLGF are not its most important function: rather, ESG(E) itself can be described as 'the consultative council for educational finance' for it has played this role for the DES. Interview notes record the following reaction:

Because time was pressing, I asked him if we could talk about ESG(E). I said a number of our respondents on the CCLGF case study had described ESG(E) as a consultative council for the DES – and I asked if this was an accurate description. His answer was an emphatic 'Oh yes' – as if it was a blindingly obvious point.[33]

As it transpired, the point *was* obvious. Up to half of ESG(E)'s work is on matters of education policy not directly related to the CCLGF. The information and advice generated is one of the important inputs to the tripartite nexus of educational subgovernment. The DES respondents even agreed that the ESG(E) reports had limited impact on the CCLGF and the Treasury: it was seen as the 'educational lobby', overemphasizing the damage from the cuts. Potentially, of course, the associations could have objected to this development; they have always objected to the centre's involvement in the distribution of general grant between and within services. However, such objections to hypothecating general grant were seen as a 'ritual' and association spokesmen were said to 'fully participate' in the discussion of expenditure priorities within education. Indeed, there was considerable agreement about 'the way to move'; the relationships within ESG(E) were described as 'cosy' and it was claimed that the DES's relationships with the associations 'were closer than those of any other department'. In short, ESG(E) was the principal forum for the management side of the education service.

The immediate caveat to this general conclusion about ESG(E) is that, whilst it may have 'no precise terms of reference', its focus is on educational resources. The other key resource is, of course, manpower and, in this context, the Burnham Committees are of key importance: they constitute *the* forum for union–LEA pay negotiations.

The present Burnham Committees are constituted under the Remuneration of Teachers Act 1965. Their remit is limited to pay negotiations, CLEA being responsible for conditions of work. Amongst other provisions, the Act requires the secretary of state to establish one or more committees, to nominate DES representatives and to appoint an independent chairman. On the Burnham Primary and Secondary Committee, the employers' side or management panel has twenty-seven representatives, appointed predominantly by the ACC and AMA but including two from the DES. The employees' side (the teachers panel) numbers thirty-two representatives (from seven unions/professional associations), of which sixteen represent the National Union of Teachers. In the Burnham Further Education Committee the management panel has seventeen representatives, again predominantly appointed by the ACC and AMA. The teachers panel has sixteen members, representing four staff associations, twelve of whom represent the National Association of Teachers in Further and Higher Education.

In short, the associations are deeply involved in the negotiating process for a key national educational resource. Without attempting to provide a synopsis of teachers' pay negotiations, it is clear that the associations' discretion is not unfettered – for example, by government pay policy. None the less, to return to an early theme, one of the issue areas within which the associations play a prominent role is that of educational resources. As key actors on the management side, it is scarcely surprising, therefore, that the associations should have such intensive formal involvement in both ESG(E) (for grant) and Burnham (for manpower).

Other groups   Given the specific focus of this section, the role of teachers' organizations will not be discussed in detail. Table 8.1 provides a list of the major organizations. It is important to note, however, Lodge and Blackstone's (1982, p. 24) assessment that 'the NUT is the most important source of professional comment on the process of policy-making'. The teachers' unions are not, however, the only source of professional advice. The Society of Education Officers (SEO) and the County Education Officers' Society (CEOS) are also members of the educational policy community, providing advisers for the associations' education committees, for the management panel of Burnham and for ESG(E). In the case of the ACC, the County Education Officers' Society nominates the advisers, whereas the AMA makes its own nominations. Whilst the bulk of their input to the policy process is indirect − that is through the associations − they also have direct contact with the DES, for example, on the 'organic change' proposals. There is an important difference between the society and the other educational professions: they are members of the employers', not the employees', side of Burnham whilst assuming the employees' mantle for their own pay negotiations. The SEO does not command the high visibility of the NUT but its members hold key positions within the management side of the educational policy community.

However, under the heading 'other groups' the main objective is to draw attention to the range of groups which participate, albeit inter-mittently and even ineffectively, in educational policy-making. Kogan (1975, ch. 8) distinguishes between parental groups (for example, the Confederation for the Advancement of State Education (CASE), Advisory Centre for Education (ACE), Nursery Schools Association; denominational groups (for example, Catholic Education Council); the intelligentsia, including the press and a range of research bodies (for example, National Children's Bureau); and private foundations (for example, the Nuffield Foundation). As Fenwick and McBride (1978, p. 47) comment:

> Although other lobby groups may not be within the quasi-official advisory network, bodies such as the Advisory Centre for Education and the Confederation for the Advancement of State Educa-tion are sometimes able to impress their advice on the Department directly or at one remove, through official advisory bodies to which they may submit evidence.

But, most important, 'the interests developing around education . . . were various and often important and strong' (Kogan, 1975, p. 146). Although the associations would not send representatives to the controversial, promotional groups, such as CASE and ACE, they have to recognize the plethora of interests and organizations in educa-tion. Out of a hundred and fifty-eight organizations for which the ACC listed nominees in 1978/9, thirty-two − excluding examination boards − were in the field of education: for example, the Adult Literacy Resource Agency and the Christian Education Movement.

In short, the associations are embedded in an extensive network of organizations and they are key actors in the more important con-sultative bodies, especially ESG(E) and Burnham. But this focus on actors and contacts tells us little about the substance of consultation. The next section sketches the range of issues upon which the associations are consulted and discusses the nature and efficacy of such contact.

Patterns of contact

Kogan (1975, p. 83) analysed the minutes of the associations' education committees, recording the number of times topics were referred to in order 'to see which issues they initiated, at least at the recorded and formal level, and on which issues their role was primarily reactive'. This analysis was replicated for the years 1974–80. In addition to providing some data on association initiatives, this analysis also permits, first, an assessment of the changing pattern of issues confronted by the associations before and after reorganization; second, a comparison of the educational interests of the associations; and, finally, an assessment of the changing patterns of contact within the extensive network of bodies described in the previous section. Tables 8.2 and 8.3 show the main topics discussed before and after

Table 8.2 *Main Topics Discussed by the CCA, AMC and AEC*

Topics	CCA (1960–72)	AMC (1963–72)	AEC (1960–73)
Teachers (training, conditions of service)	127	83	248
Educational building costs and programmes	35	42	56
Further education	37	47	93
Schools Council, NFER	50	63	45
Universities and students	65	39	90
School meals and milk	30	36	57
Schools (libraries, equipment, valuation of sites)	69	49	*a*
Agricultural education	30	1	10
Inter-authority expenditure	34	2	16
Polytechnics	11	33	8
Youth leaders and community wardens	4	0	39
Industrial training (including day release and the Industrial Training Act)	19	26	35

Note
a It is difficult to compare the AEC with the CCA and AMC as they discuss a greater variety of 'school' subjects.
Source: M. Kogan, 1975, p. 88.

Table 8.3   *Main Topics Discussed by the ACC, AMA and CLEA*

Topics	ACC (1974–7)	AMA (1974–7)	CLEA (1974–80)
Teachers (training, conditions of service)	45	28	38
Educational buildings costs and programmes	11	14	1
Further education	47	21	77
Schools Council/NFER	11	5	2
Universities and students	31	23	30
School meals and milk	13	7	2
Schools (libraries, transport, valuation, equipment)	22	7	4
Agricultural education	27	1	1
Inter-authority expenditure	6	2	—
Polytechnics	2	1	10
Youth leaders and community wardens	10	6	—
Industrial training	14	9	—
Schools (standards, curriculum, discipline, attendance, etc.)	22	12	11
Nursery education/Under-5s	8	5	—
Careers service/youth unemployment	23	11	1
CLGA	35	10	—
S2(7) bodies	7	3	15
Race relations/ethnic minorities	6	9	1
Adult illiteracy	8	2	—
Youth service	13	2	—
RSG/educational expenditure	9	11	5

Source: Committee minutes.

reorganization. Tables 8.4 and 8.5 identify the initiators of committee discussions. (On the methodology, see Kogan, 1975, pp. 83, 87 and 88–9.)

The major items considered by the associations reflect their different educational interests. Thus the ACC is particularly concerned with agricultural education. CLEA is primarily concerned with teachers' conditions of service, further/higher education and Section 2(7) bodies – all matters specifically allocated to it. In his pre-reorganization study, however, Kogan (1975, p. 84) pointed to 'the differences in educational interests between rural and city areas'. Such differences remain but in a more muted form because of the amalgamation of urban and rural areas in the 1974 reorganization. Thus the AMA is no longer distinguished by its interests in industrial training or further education. Indeed, further and higher education is

Table 8.4   Initiators of Committee Discussions, 1960–73

Groups which initiate action by the AMC, CCA, AEC	CCA (1960–72)	AMC (1963–72)	AEC (1960–73)
DES letters, circulars, memos	175	123	384
Evidence to government and parliamentary committees	48	41	43
Acts/Bills	13	14	39
Parliament	7	5	13
White Papers	16	18	20
Government and DES committee reports on education	24	29	67
Local authorities (individual)	77	—	351
CCA (letters)	—	1	7
AMC (letters)	44	—	5
AEC (letters)	10	7	—
NUT (letters and actions)	5	4	21
Other groups (main groups that are mentioned in the text)	45	29	69
Miscellaneous groups	48	17	136
Schools Council/NFER	33	43	21
Burnham	12	8	22
Public Schools Commission	1	8	11
Other government departments	11	8	38
Initiated indirectly from outside	207	159	344

Source: M. Kogan, 1975, p. 89.

one of the prominent issues common to all associations, along with teacher training and conditions of service and building programmes.

Of greater significance than differences between the associations – which have indeed receded post-reorganization – are the differences in the prominent issues before and after reorganization. Thus, school standards, discipline and curriculum, careers service/youth employment, race relations and rate support grant have all risen to prominence on the agenda. It requires little or no ingenuity to explain such changes – the declining fortunes of the British economy and the intensification of the problems of unemployment and the inner city coupled with cuts in government expenditure. But the emergence of these issues is revealing of the changing role of the associations. Before reorganization Kogan (1975, p. 84) commented that 'there are some surprising omissions from the papers, particularly those of the AMC', itemizing comprehensive education, positive discrimination and educational priority areas. No such conclusion is possible after reorganization. Both in terms of topical issues and indeed sheer range of issues – there are twenty-one categories in my listing compared to twelve in Kogan's analysis – the associations cannot be accused of sins

Table 8.5   *Initiators of Committee Decisions, 1974–80*

Groups which initiate action by the ACC, AMA and CLEA	ACC (1974–80)	AMA (1974–77)	CLEA (1974–80)
DES letters, circulars, memos	98	61	28
Evidence to government and parliamentary committees	20	13	2
Acts/Bills	17	14	4
Parliament	8	3	1
White Papers	11	7	3
Government and DES committee reports on education	12	4	7
Individual member local authorities	85	41	11
ACC	32[a]	3	4
AMA	4	32[a]	9
CLEA	34	10	30[a]
NUT	4	2	6
Other main groups (mentioned in the text)	41	20	20
Miscellaneous groups	46	20	30
Schools Council/NFER	11	6	2
Burnham	12	3	33
Public Schools Commission	—	—	—
Other government departments	38	23	7
Initiated indirectly from outside	54	28	32

Note
[a] Refers to items referred by another committee within the association.
Source: Committee minutes.

of omission. This change reflects the growth in the size of the associations' staff, the fact that all AMA members are now LEAs (compared to one third in the AMC), the concentration of educational policy issues in the education committees with replacement of the AEC with CLEA, and the increasing party politicization of both associations. At the time of his analysis, for example, Kogan (1975, pp. 94, 97 and 84) commented that the CCA was 'overtly non-partisan'; that, at the AMC, 'education was not given priority'; and that 'until 1974 the AMC did not have an education officer'. As Kogan (1975, p. 97) anticipates, none of these comments is correct for the post-reorganization associations: 'it would be surprising if the new arrangements did not quickly move the AMA into a more positive and active role'. They did and they have. Whether or not this more active role extended to policy initiation is something that can be examined using Tables 8.4 and 8.5. They show which groups initiated discussions in the associations' education committees and this indicator, if not exhaustive, does at least show the formal interactions which might have affected their reactions to policy proposals.

As in the pre-reorganization period, the associations have a great deal of contact with the DES. Indeed there are only two major changes in the pattern of contacts after reorganization. First, with the abolition of the AEC and the new arrangements at the AMA, the extent of association contact with individual member local authorities has increased sharply, although neither approximates to the scale of the AEC. Moreover, this function has been assumed by the associations and *not* by CLEA. Kogan (1975, p. 87) concluded that the associations 'are under a great deal of pressure from individual local authorities and also from a wide range of groups which are on the periphery of the education world' – a conclusion supported by the analysis of the 1974–80 period. Second, one of the reasons for the new arrangements at the AMA and for the replacement of the AEC was to strengthen links between education and other local government services. Kogan's original analysis does not include agenda items initiated by committees within an association. Table 8.5 clearly shows that a substantial number of issues on the education committees' agendas were initiated by other committees. Formally, at least, integration between services has been strengthened.

In short, the associations in the post-reorganization period have become concerned with a broader range of issues and the unrivalled representatives of the LEAs in an extensive network of contact. It would be difficult to conclude, however, that the several changes identified have led to any dramatic change in the nature and efficacy of the associations' activities. In spite of improved formal committee integration, the issues discussed remain initiated directly or indirectly from outside. The associations are prominent, legitimized 'partners' in education policy-making but they participate in a consensual decision-making process and, therefore, they are

> explicitly and unashamedly reactive rather than innovative. They are an important example of the consensual network and inasmuch as they break consensus it is for obvious sectional interests. (Kogan, 1975, p. 101)

I would not demur from Kogan's assessment, nor would many of our interviewees.[34]

Amongst members, the associations were seen as useful: for example, commenting upon and amending legislation. In some cases, for example on Burnham pay negotiations, they were seen as essential. Some members felt, however, that the associations were 'more informative' for the DES: 'the collective voice carries weight' and it helps DES to avoid 'exacerbating regional differences and imbalances which exist even now'. As ever, the associations 'could do more', although it is rare for the 'more' to be specified and common to enter the caveat that 'it is a double-edged sword – despite the benefits there are dangers that if you do too much down in London you might get removed from local problems'.

Amongst education officers, opinions about the associations taking the initiative were both adamant and negative: 'frankly, I don't think the AMA should be in the business of issuing advice to individual local authorities'. Or 'the AMA exists entirely and solely to pursue issues of national interest on behalf of member authorities' and if it was given more resources there would be 'the dangers of the association developing views of its own – they're occasionally apparent now'. Or again, more pungently: 'We don't look to the ACC for the initiative.' Still in a critical vein, but a shade more sympathetic, concern was expressed about links with the DES: 'I'm sure the association is too responsive to government but I accept that with the size of its staff and as presently organized it is difficult to be less so.' Similarly, 'of course, there are dangers in proximity to government, but it's a fine line'. But none of the members or officers disputed the important role of the associations on national or general educational issues. Indeed a number contrasted the separateness of education before reorganization with subsequent developments:

> Yes, there was, pre-reorganization, a strong separate education community with strong links to Whitehall. And undoubtedly the associations have now broken that separateness – there are still very good links to DES but now they run through the AMA and ACC.

And the same respondent adopted my terminology to argue:

> It would now be wrong to say there was an education policy community separate from any national community – the education community now speaks through the national community: they are inseparable.

A note of nostalgia creeps into these remarks, not to mention invective about corporate management, and another respondent recalled earlier years as follows:

> The important thing is that the education under secretary is more assertive with the DES and MSC – in other words as near an approximation to Alexander as possible.

From the standpoint of the centre, the role of the association is seen rather differently. Officially, the DES

> recognises the importance of associating ... other parties and the local authority associations closely with the planning process, the results of which are often vital to their interests. There are

difficulties about this – not least the fact that decisions arising from the need to reduce the rate of growth of public expenditure often have to be taken on a short time-scale. This points to the importance of developing further the process of consultation, whether formal (e.g. through the Consultative Council on Local Government Finance ... and the Council of Local Education Authorities), or informal (e.g. through involvement in the Rate Support Grant negotiations). (Pile, 1979, p. 41)

Unofficially, DES views are more emphatic. Thus on public expenditure:

We take local authority views on total expenditure seriously but more importantly their views on its distribution between different parts of the service.

On grant and pay negotiations the associations are viewed as key partners in the management of the service, a point emphasized in the earlier discussion of these areas. However, on other policy issues, assessments of their role are more cautious. Thus, Michael Stewart (secretary of state, 1964–65) commented that '... over major controversial issues, they follow, rather than lead' – an opinion confirmed by Sir Toby Weaver, formerly deputy secretary, DES. The associations are legitimized, managerial groups and it is scarcely surprising, therefore, that the view from the centre should emphasize this role. At times the associations have railed against the limits to their influence on the DES. The AMA claimed in its evidence to the Expenditure Committee (1976, p. 70) that

the DES traditionally consults too little, too late and with too closed a mind. It has plenty of channels open if it wished.

However, such a judgement seems harsh. As Lodge and Blackstone (1982, p. 24) argue:

On occasions the DES may even consult too much, and in general its record on consultation is much better than those of other government departments.

Clearly one of the senior partners in the educational policy community, it would be easy to overstate the influence of the associations. However, as Kogan (1975, p. 35) persuasively argues:

The sources of policy generation are so difficult to locate, let alone place in any logical pattern, that detecting the changes in values, or the pressures by which change is effected, is more a matter of art than analysis.

None the less one of the distinctive features of educational policy-making is clear: it is policy-making by 'educational sub-government' (Manzer, 1970, p. 3) – by bargaining between DES, teachers and associations. Their search for consensus may break down and the participants may launch public campaigns but such political tactics are, for the most part, abjured. Educational subgovernment is substantially if not wholly confined to administrative arenas.

CONCLUSIONS

Characterizing educational policy-making as 'subgovernment' immediately raises the question of whether or not the pattern has changed or is changing. For example, Ranson (1980) argues that the early postwar period until the mid-1950s was a period of central dominance; that the middle postwar period until the early 1970s was a period of local dominance; and that recent years have seen an increase in central control, particularly over resources. Kogan (1978, pp. 39–48 and part 2) has argued that the 1970s saw challenges to the educational consensus, whilst Crispin and Blackstone (1980) strongly criticized the cuts in expenditure, arguing that, in spite of falling school rolls, there remain unmet needs of high priority. However, the scale of cuts in educational expenditure between 1979 and 1983 was frequently overstated. Williams (1981, p. 196) argued that the changes were not dramatic, talking of 'evolutionary change' and 'the continuation of broadly consensual policy-making'. In a similar vein, Kogan (1981, pp. 161, 168) suggested that 'the traditional consultative process is hardly geared to making quantum cuts' and concluded:

> In 1971, Edward Boyle could say that educational policy is largely decided as a result of pressures inside the education world. It would appear that that statement remains largely true.

Cuts in educational expenditure and challenges to the educational consensus have not affected any major transformation in the educational policy-making nexus of DES, associations (LEAs) and unions. As Rhodes (1984) noted for the cuts more generally:

> The cuts were selective, falling on capital not current expenditure, on local not central departments. The resistance of central departments, and the policy communities, lie at the root of this disparity. It would seem that at least some of the policy communities have been able to mount a rearguard action of some consequence.

Undeniably there were challenges and the ground conquered in the 1960s had to be defended anew but education was able to mount a rearguard action on public expenditure cuts and, arguably, the greatest challenge to the educational policy community came from policies on vocational training and youth employment (see Hinings *et al.*, 1982, appendix C).

It was also argued earlier that the period 1979–83 saw the national community's relationship with the policy communities shift from involvement to disengagement. Clearly, the 'subgovernment' of education was not displaced and the associations remained legitimated participants. None the less there were signs of estrangement. Under the impact of severe restraint on local expenditure, ESG(E)'s importance declined. The call for a specific education grant was voiced on the presumption that it would strengthen the education policy community in its negotiations with the Treasury. The initiative was resisted by the national community but it reappeared in the guise of an earmarked component of block grant – that is, 0·5 per cent of total local expenditure on education – to fund initiatives approved by the secretary of state. The national community itself no longer aspired to become the intermediate tier of representation but to fight a rearguard action over the ever-changing grant system and reductions in the level of local expenditure. In these circumstances, involvement in any service-specific policy community ceased to be of high priority. 'Separateness' had become the order of the day and the integration of the educational policy community was subjected to stresses and strains on a scale rarely encountered throughout the 1970s. That it survives attests to the strong foundations of educational subgovernment: to the interdependence of its participants.

CONCLUSIONS: POLICY COMMUNITIES AND THE
NATIONAL COMMUNITY COMPARED

The similarities and differences between the fire, education and national communities can now be summarized.

First, a distinct feature of education, as of fire, is the tripartite nexus of central departments, associations and unions, each with distinct interests.

Second, and in sharp contrast to fire, the range of educational organizations involved in consultations is wide, even if many are peripheral, and there is no single apex institution in education paralleling the CFBAC. The limited organizational span of the fire service is a product of that service's characteristics – an emergency service with semi-skilled manual recruitment and on-the-job, internal training and promotion.

Third, central departmental styles are markedly different between the two policy communities: the Home Office is seen as autocratic; the DES can only be described as consultative. As a result, there is no demand by the association for recognition as joint managers of the education service; the DES has conceded that which the Home Office refuses to recognize.

Fourth, in both policy communities, the associations have sought to strengthen their position as the central presence for local government – an aspiration revealed most clearly in education by the demise of the AEC and the formation of, and subsequent control over, CLEA. Equally, central departments have encouraged and supported this aspiration, if not always with the hoped-for degree of success.

Fifth, the interests within both policy communities are not in perpetual conflict. Indeed, the search for consensus is a distinctive feature of policy-making within education and illustrates the importance of a shared appreciative system or ideological integration for a complex network of organizations.

Sixth, the role of the teachers' and fire brigade unions indicates the need for some care in discussing the role of local government professions. The description has two discrete senses: the professions as chief officers' societies which play a prominent role in both the national community and the policy communities, and the professions as trade unions which are represented only in the policy communities. And the term 'profession' remains relevant. The teachers' unions are seen by themselves and by others as speaking for a profession, and their concern extends well beyond pay and conditions of work. But, such subtleties to one side, the bald conclusion is that professions are key actors in policy communities.

Seventh, the participation of the associations in policy communities is focused primarily on pay and grant negotiations and those policy decisions with substantial manpower/financial implications.

Eighth, in both policy communities any bargaining is not between equals. Even in the consultative educational policy community, the DES has determinant authority and wields considerable influence in determining both the agenda for and timing of consultation.

Ninth, the potential for manipulation by central departments of policy communities is considerable – a conclusion vividly illustrated by the earlier analysis of pay negotiations and by both the enhanced role of ESG(E) and the review of fire policy.

Tenth, the differences between the two policy areas cannot be viewed as wholly a product of different departmental styles. A formal analysis of patterns of contact is inappropriate for exploring differences arising from policy content but it seems likely that the different styles of the departments are related to differences in substantive policy.

Eleventh, given the range of contrasts between the education and fire policy communities, and indeed the 'policy community' for local government, it is clear that the comparison of policy communities and their different styles is crucial to the analysis of intergovernmental relations.

Twelfth, the national community of local government differs markedly from the policy communities both in issue scope and range of access and, therefore, warrants a separate label.

Thirteenth, relationships between the national community and the policy communities cannot be adequately characterized as conflictual. The most distinctive feature is the penetration of a wide range of policy communities by the national community coupled with the shifting nature of the coalitions to which it is party within each such community.

Moreover, in so far as there is conflict, it is not simply between the national community and particular policy communities. The appropriate functional committees *within* each association also have a dual allegiance – to the association and to 'their' function-specific policy community – with attendant conflicts of loyalty.

Fourteenth, the national community is not constrained by narrow 'issue scope'. Rather, membership of a range of policy communities is both a constraint and an opportunity for the national community. In order to foster its central interests on grant and pay, participation in the policy communities is essential because decisions on fire and educational policy can have major repercussions for these interests. In this sense, the issue scope is broad and participation is an opportunity. But the wide ranges of actors (and interests) in the policy communities, the intermittent contribution of the associations – not all policy decisions are of key importance to them – and their wide-ranging commitments, coupled with limited time and resources, all limit the effectiveness of their involvement. In this sense, the associations can only attend to a limited range of issues and participation is a constraint: it diverts time, staff and money away from central interests with no certainty that the national community's voice on specific policy issues will be heeded. Dispersion of effort across, multiplicity of interests within, and not exclusion from, policy communities constitute the major constraints.

Fifteenth, for both policy communities and the national community their capacity to exert effective influence is constrained by the government's economic policy. Decisions on the aggregate of public expenditure or even on the aggregate of local expenditure are unilaterally determined by central government. Any bargaining takes place within such predetermined ceilings. In a highly concrete sense, therefore, the communities could be said to be confined to ordinary, albeit important, issues: namely, the between- and within-service disposition of the aggregate. Thus, in spite of its importance for the associations, ESG(E) works within *given* public expenditure White Paper figures.

Finally, *all* the policy communities have had to adjust to the exigencies of economic decline. The fire service has been substantially 'spared'. Education expenditure has fallen but the 'cuts' have not been so severe as those experienced by housing and, in some respects, for example, staff–pupil ratios, it could be argued that the standard of educational provision actually rose! Be that as it may, the education policy community was able to soften the impact of government public expenditure policy on 'their' service. In straitened times, such resilience is notable and it was not a prominent feature of the relationship between the policy community and the national community which began to show signs of estrangement.

The relationship between the national community and the policy communities has fluctuated over the past decade primarily under the impact of government economic policy. The national community has been constrained not only by particular relationships – namely, with the national government environment – but also by the sheer range of relationships within which it is embedded. But to this point individual local authorities have been conspicuous primarily for their absence – an omission rectified in the next chapter.

NOTES AND REFERENCES: CHAPTER 8

1 *Hansard*, 20 May 1941, col. 1429.
2 According to C. A. Cross, 'The AMC: a study of its structure' (unpublished MA thesis, University of Manchester, 1954), the AMC 'exercised an appreciable influence on the form and substance of many of the provisions of the Act ... the service might well have been nationalised on a permanent basis but for the constant pressure against the Government to redeem a promise'.
3 The other major subsequent Acts governing the operation of the service are the Fire Services Act 1959 and the Fire Precautions Act 1971. The former deprived the secretary of state of his responsibility for pay and conditions of service and modified his control over establishments. The latter was designed to strengthen and rationalize the existing law on means of escape in case of fire.
4 Note on fire service responsibilities from the Home Office to the local authority associations, 22 June 1978, p. 1; a view also confirmed in interview with senior Home Office officials.
5 ACC and AMA, Note on the legal relationship between the Home Office, the associations and the NJC for LAFBs.
6 Interview with Deputy Commandant, Fire Service College, transcript.
7 AMA police and fire committee report no. 4/1978, 29 June 1978.
8 AMA police and fire committee report no. 4/1978, 29 June 1978.
9 Letter from Home Office to associations, 18 September 1979.
10 Letter from Councillor S. T. Moss, police and fire committee, AMA, to William Whitelaw, Home Secretary, October 1979.
11 Letter from secretary, ACC, to assistant secretary, Home Office, 27 September 1979.
12 AMA notes for a meeting with the Home Secretary, 25 July 1979.
13 Letter from William Whitelaw, Home Secretary, to Councillor M. Brannan, chairman, fire and emergency planning committee, ACC, and Councillor R. A. Wootton, chairman, police and fire committee, AMA, 28 October 1979.
14 Interview with Deputy Commandant, Fire Service College, transcript.
15 Interview with Councillor M. Brannan, chairman of fire and emergency planning committee, ACC, transcript.
16 Interview with assistant secretary, AMA, notes.
17 ACC/AMA, 'Future aspects of the fire service – review of the CFBAC: a discussion paper', 28 August 1980.

18 ibid.
19 All preceding quotes from, AMA police and fire committee report no. 3/1980, 16 April 1980, p. 3.
20 ibid.
21 Report dated 28 August 1980.
22 ACC/AMA, Note on the legal relationship between the Home Office, the associations and the NJC for LAFBs.
23 Adviser, ACC, private correspondence.
24 There is an extensive literature on education policy-making covering the context of policy, the roles of participants and the major institutions. It is not summarized here. The major sources for this section include Byrne, 1974; Coates, 1972; Fenwick and McBride, 1979; Halsey *et al.*, 1980; James, 1980; Kogan, 1971, 1975 and 1978; Lodge and Blackstone, 1982; Pile 1979; Regan, 1979; Saran, 1973; and Expenditure Committee, 1976. The minutes of the education committees of the ACC and AMA and the minutes of CLEA were also consulted and a limited number of interviews (ten) at central, association and local levels were carried out. The analysis covered the period 1974–80 and focused on primary/secondary education.
25 ACC and AMA, 'Joint arrangements for education: establishment of a local government central council for local education authorities', policy statement, 21 November 1973.
26 Interviews with principal administrative assistant, CLEA, transcript; and education officer, ACC, notes.
27 CCA, minutes of the association, 1974, p. 31.
28 The selfsame point was made in an interview with principal administrative assistant, CLEA, transcript.
29 Interview with education officer, ACC, notes.
30 Interview with principal administrative assistant, CLEA.
31 *Rate Support Grant 1979–80* (London: ACC, AMA, ADC, LBA and GLC, February 1979).
32 Interviews with secretary to CCLGF (DoE) and under secretary, DES, notes.
33 This and subsequent quotations are all from interview notes with DES officials. The interviews were on a not-for-attribution basis.
34 As usual, interviews with officials (and some members) were on a not-for-attribution basis.

Chapter 9

THE NATIONAL COMMUNITY AND ITS MEMBERS

INTRODUCTION

In theory at least, any presssure group should articulate the demands of members and strive to protect their interests. In reality, the relationship between a group and its members is rarely so straightforward. The foregoing case studies have demonstrated a clear trend towards aggregation. Central departments have pursued a strategy of building up the associations into the peak representative bodies of local government. The creation of the CCLGF and the joint manpower watch both provided institutional support for the position of the associations. Less conspicuously, the continuous involvement of central departments with LACSAB and the associations in pay negotiations similarly reinforced local government representatives at the centre. Nor are these case studies the only source of evidence for this trend. Central departments also funded specific initiatives within the national community – for example, the creation of LAMSAC – and some respondents argued that funding through Section 2(7) weakened member influence over the joint bodies and strengthened the associations.

Throughout the 1970s the associations were willing partners in the majority of these developments. They sought involvement in PES and incomes policy long before the government had tabled any proposals. And the views of members were not necessarily sought prior to any initiative. On participation in the CCLGF and in joint manpower watch, there was limited discussion outside the national community. Members were also encouraged to work with and through the national community even on matters specific to a local authority. Thus:

if individual local authorities are to influence the way [grant related expenditure] GREs are calculated they are virtually obliged to go through the associations. The AMA welcomes individual authority contributions to the debate, and then gets the authority involved in the negotiations. Often submissions made directly from a local authority to the DoE will not be properly considered, but the AMA can always ensure that an idea is subject to a full debate. (Hughes, 1982, p. 151)

And the DoE provided explicit support for such channelling of contacts. Internal Circular HOD 40/80, on consultation with local government, states:

> The Association of County Councils, the Association of District Councils and the Association of Metropolitan Authorities are the accepted and accredited representatives of their class of authority and ... speak for local government as a whole in England and Wales. Consultations on all matters relating to local government or local authority services generally should be carried on through the Associations.

And the CCLGF has a special status extending beyond local government finance: it

> provide[s] a central forum for consultation on issues affecting local government finance *and other general topics affecting local government as a whole*. (My italics)

There are special arrangements for London (see Chapter 7, pp. 267–8) but

> Consultation documents should not ... be sent separately to local authorities in metropolitan areas other than Greater London.

Similarly for professional societies:

> Such bodies do not speak for local government as a whole and they cannot be consulted as bodies representative of local government or on policy matters. [1]

And this circular was sent also to the DES, DHSS, Home Office, Department of Trade, MAFF, Department of Employment and Department of Industry. Intent and reality may diverge but the intent is clear: the associations are the 'accredited' representatives *and*, for both central departments and individual local authorities, contact should be channelled through them. [2]

It would be misleading to suggest that the associations wilfully disregarded members' views. For both organic change and pay negotiations, elaborate soundings were taken. Additionally, the associations provide members with considerable amounts of information through their journals, circulars and letters to chief executives. They also answer many queries from individual local authorities both over the telephone and in writing. But, with the trend towards the aggregation of local government's interests, it is obviously relevant to ask how relationships with members have changed, if at all. This chapter has two objectives, therefore: to describe the relationship between the associations and their members, focusing on who participates in the associations, the dissemination of information and members' evaluations of the relationship; and to analyse the relationship, focusing on explanations of variations in the relationship and the changes between 1976 and 1983.

To this point, the analysis has focused on the relationship between the national government environment and the national community of local government and on relationships within both the national local government system and the national community. On this occasion, continuing the journey away from the centre, attention is switched to the relationship between the national community and individual local authorities (see Figure 2.3). For the first and only time, centre–local relations take precedence over centre–centre relations.

The analysis is based on a survey of local authorities which encompassed variations in size, geographical location and type of authority as well as a variety of formal positions, service affiliations and party allegiances within individual local authorities. No equivalent survey has been published before and, if many of the findings confirm existing opinions, the conclusions are based on hard information. (For a detailed description see Rhodes, 1982, and Rhodes, Hardy and Pudney, 1983c ch. 2.)

THE RELATIONSHIP DESCRIBED

Table 9.1 reports a series of items on formal contact between the respondents and the associations and clearly demonstrates that the relationship can be described as 'distant'.

Thus, 44 per cent of those interviewed had no formal position within an association and, it should be noted, the sample included only senior members and officers. Of those interviewees who had a formal position, 48 per cent were chairman of the council or leader of the council and 51 per cent of the advisers were the chief executive or director of finance. In short, participation in association affairs was the prerogative of the most senior members and officers of the local authority. Moreover, many members and officers had participated for a considerable period of time: 47 per cent of all respondents who held some formal position had served for more than three years, although turnover of members was greater than turnover of officers.

The exclusive nature of participation in association affairs becomes even more marked when attention is turned to other forms of contact. An even smaller proportion of those interviewees who held any position were also members of any joint body, major or minor (25 per cent). With the exception of the one association chairman in the sample, none of the members contacted the association secretariats directly for information. Invariably, they would contact their own chief officers who, if necessary, would then contact the association.

Table 9.1   Patterns of Contact between the Associations and their Member Authorities

	ACC	ADC	AMA[a]	Totals
Formal position in association				
Chairman	—	1	—	1
Committee member	2	1	7	10
Representative	3	—	7	10
Advisor	7	1	16	24
No position[b]	7 (5)	3 (2)	13 (6)	23 (13)
Years of service on association[c]				
< 1 year	— (0)	1 (1)	3 (0)	4 (1)
1–3 years	6 (1)	— (0)	8 (3)	14 (4)
> 3 years	2 (5)	— (0)	6 (8)	8 (13)
Membership of joint body[d]	4 (5)	1 (0)	3 (4)	8 (9)
Nil	12 (7)	4 (3)	24 (18)	40 (28)
Contact with secretariat for				
Information[e]	0	1	0	1
Nil	16	4	27	47
Average number of advisers				
per authority[f]	1·8	0·5	1·8	1·4
Formal requests for action				
Never	3	0	13	16
< once a year	6	2	3	11
Once a year	1	1	4	6
> once a year	3	2	2	7

Notes

[a]   Includes LBA and GLC.

[b]   Includes 2 members and 2 officer advisers on SACLAT from Derbyshire CC which is no longer a member of the ACC.

[c]   Includes all respondents who had served on associations and not just current representatives.

[d]   All figures in brackets from here on refer to officers.

[e]   The figures refer to elected members only and *exclude* information from the association journal/minutes which were circulated to all local authorities. All members said they looked at the journal.

[f]   All officer advisers are in contact with the secretariat and this item gives an indication of the extent of this contact per authority.

67·5 per cent of all respondents claimed that they never (or less than once a year) made any such request.

The links between officers and the associations can be explored simply by examining which local authorities provide advisers. As noted earlier, the 'topocratic' professions provide a disproportionate number of advisers and are appointed for all association committees. The distribution of officers between member authorities is not skewed to the same degree. All associations take pains to ensure that as many local authorities (and professions) as possible provide advisers. Thus, fifty-five of the AMA's seventy-seven members provide at least one adviser. The AMA and the ACC attempt to get an even distribution of advisers both geographically and between the various types of authority in membership. For the AMA, the metropolitan counties form just under 8 per cent of the membership but they provide 23 per cent of the advisers, whereas the districts with 47 per cent of the membership provide 46 per cent of the advisers. These ratios are counterbalanced, however, by the greater number of advisers appointed from the districts. The ACC has an even geographic distribution. South-east or home counties advisers do not predominate, with care taken to appoint from the counties furthest from Sloane Square.

For the ADC, the problem of achieving an equal distribution of advisers is intractable. Only forty-eight authorities (14 per cent) provide advisers and fourteen (4 per cent) supply virtually half the advisers. And the 'big eleven' are favoured by the system for appointing advisers, providing thirteen (20 per cent) advisers in total – only three of the 'big eleven' provide no advisers. Ensuring the selection of advisers from the largest district is 'almost one of the tablets of stone' in the ADC, principally for political reasons. The 'big eleven' are frequently Labour-controlled, and, although they are guaranteed representation on the council, their leaders do not get chairmanships and vice-chairmanships. The secretariat and the Conservative leadership of the ADC always ensure that the largest districts provide advisers 'to counteract any loss of weight at the political level'.[3]

The pattern of contact for officer advisers appears to differ sharply from that of members. 55 per cent claimed that they attended association meetings frequently (that is, at least quarterly) and the secretariats were numbered amongst those whom they would consult when preparing reports. However, the most distinctive feature of such consultation was the range of individuals consulted, including association chairman, group leaders, the relevant under secretary, other advisers, and members of their own department. However, even for advisers the relationship with the associations cannot be described as close. 27 per cent claimed that they consulted no one in drawing up their reports, a further 27 per cent consulted only within their departments and 86·5 per cent considered that there was no need to keep the secretariat informed of their deliberations prior to reporting. And, when asked to rate the frequency of all forms of contact, only 43 per cent said that it was frequent (that is, more than once per month). Whilst advisers were in closer contact with the associations than members, such contact cannot be described as intense or of a markedly high frequency.

Infrequent contact and limited participation are not necessarily indicators of a defective relationship. If the rest of the local authority is fully informed about association business, and if the association is contacted on all relevant matters, there would be little reason for comment. Table 9.2 reports on the extent to which knowledge of association business is disseminated within individual local authorities.

Quite clearly, the circulation of information is limited. Neither members nor officers reported back on their activities systematically or regularly. Only 16 per cent of advisers reported back to anybody, predominantly members of their own department, and, whilst most members reported to someone, characteristically it was to their chief officer and on selected items only. On items of particular importance to the local authority, a report would be presented to the majority party group but even such items were rarely included on the agenda of the full council. In short, participation was limited to the few who reported to the many at their discretion and only on selected major items. Parenthetically, a number of chief executives were prompted by our questions on reporting back to note the lack of any procedures and to raise the matter subsequently with their colleagues. Whatever the outcome of any such deliberations, this portrait of the relationship (or lack of it) between member authorities and associations might suggest that members would be critical. In fact, any such suggestion would be wrong.

Table 9.2 *Involvement with the Associations within Member Authorities*

	ACC	ADC	AMA	Total
Association items on council agenda:				
never	5	1	9	15
< once p.a	6	3	17	26
> once p.a.	—	1	—	1
Association proceedings reported to[a]:				
council/committees	1	2	4	7
group	5	—	7	12
officers	—	4	—	4
no procedures/not applicable	9	3	12	24
Advisers report back to:				
council/committee and/or				
other chief officers	1	1	4	6
no one/not applicable	11	2	18	31

Note
 [a] The responses to this question exceed the number of members who held formal positions because respondents volunteered more than one answer.

Table 9.3 *Evaluations of the Relationship with Associations*

		ACC	*ADC*	*AMA*	*Total*
Is representation adequate?	Yes	11	1	21	33
	No	5	4	5	14
Are the needs of this particular local authority met?	Yes	8	1	15	24
	No	7	4	10	21
Is the time spent on association business excessive?	Yes	6 (0)	0 (0)	4 (0)	10 (0)
	No	8 (9)	5 (5)	22 (17)	35 (31)
Is the subscription value for money?	Yes	7 (4)	3 (2)	23 (17)	33 (23)
	No	8 (2)	2 (1)	4 (2)	14 (5)
What is the proper scope of association activities?					
local government in general		8	3	19	30
the specific local authority		1	1	3	5

Note
Figures in brackets refer to responses of officers.

As Table 9.3 suggests most members were satisfied with the relationship: 70 per cent of all members thought that they were adequately represented; 53 per cent thought that the needs of their particular authority were met; only 22 per cent thought that excessive time was spent on association business; and 70 per cent thought that the subscription was value for money. The same general picture emerges for officers: for example, no officer felt that the time spent on association business was excessive, even though only 13·5 per cent had a member of staff assisting with the work. In addition, advisers were satisfied with their work for the associations: 62 per cent described their work as compiling or commenting upon policy documents and 65 per cent considered the division of functions between themselves and the secretariat satisfactory. Nor did they consider that their function was limited to acting as a 'sounding board' for the secretariat, arguing that their involvement with members necessarily required a more general advisory role.

At first sight, there would seem to be a sharp contradiction between the 'distant' relationship and the general expressions of satisfaction. The contradiction is more apparent than real and the final item in Table 9.3 suggests why: respondents had a clear perception of the precise functions of the associations. Their task was to represent the general interests of their class of local authority (86 per cent). The associations had no part to play in the specific problems of a particular local authority. And, if the associations are limited to general issues spanning a large number of local authorities, it is scarcely surprising that they do not loom large in the daily life of a particular local authority. The respondents were satisfied with associations because their expectations were being met. They neither expected nor wanted day-to-day contact and detailed involvement.

In short, the survey presents a highly uniform picture of member–association relationships. The relationship is distant but meets member expectations. However, whilst it is relevant to present such a broad-brush impression, it inevitably minimizes variations. It is now important to explore variations in the relationship and to add more detail to the general account. In so doing, it will be argued that the uniformity in behaviour and expectations is a product of a variety of factors, including size, geographical location, party and type of authority. If the opinions of local authorities on the association are uniform, they are so for very different reasons.

THE RELATIONSHIP ANALYSED

In the first instance, a statistical analysis was carried out to determine the effects of party, size, location and type of authority on patterns of contact, involvement and evaluations. The results of this analysis showed a weak relationship between the independent variables and patterns of contact and no relationship between the independent variables and involvement and evaluations. However, the bulk of the data collected was qualitative, focusing on evaluations of the associations, and my analysis concentrates on this material. To facilitate comparison with the previous section, the discussion centres on patterns of contact, internal involvement and evaluations.

Patterns of contact

The reasons given for the limited contact with the associations were many and varied. Respondents in two northern district councils said, as anticipated, that they were unique because of their geographical location.[4] Not surprisingly, a number of authorities pointed to their different interests compared with the bulk of the membership. One West Midland metropolitan district suggested that AMA members had no shared needs and that it was largely superfluous. It was far more important to maintain direct links with government departments. The GLC similarly felt that it was out of place within the AMA – a comment which *cannot* be viewed as another 'Red Ken' eccentricity. It was unique because of its size, finance and political situation as the capital city. It also had better channels of access than the AMA (see Chapter 7, p. 268). Such protestations of different interests were not unique to the AMA. Norwich did not wish to be a district council and it felt that ADC was not geared to city interests.[5] And the existence of the 'big nine' and the 'twenty-two' (or former county boroughs and medium-sized cities) within the ADC attests to the different interests within that association. Without denying that such authorities have distinct interests, their views on the ADC were coloured by the system for electing representatives. The medium-sized cities were effectively denied representation and repeated attempts to reform the system had, by 1983, borne no fruit. In such circumstances, it is scarcely surprising that contact is limited. Finally, political factors have affected contact. For example, Derbyshire County Council withdrew from the ACC because 'it had never done anything for Derby' and because it was 'politically biased'. Derbyshire was not the only authority to comment on the influence of political factors on contact. One northern district felt that changes in local political control 'violently' affected contact with the ADC and, although it was a secondary consideration, Norwich felt that the benefits they could expect from contact with the ADC would be limited because of their different political complexion. Conversely, one Conservative-controlled county argued that the influence of the ACC was under-estimated because it had strong party links with the government and, in reality, it was the prime channel of communication.

In short, large local authorities with distinct interests had separate channels of communication from the associations whilst small, geographically remote authorities had limited contact with them. When allied to difference in political control between locality and association, the recipe seems guaranteed to produce infrequent contact and limited participation. However, interviewees also identified two additional reasons for limited contact. First, as one chief constable pointed out, relationships vary from service to service. Because he was 'operationally distinct and independent from both local authorities and the Home Office' he cannot 'provide the same sort of advice for the ACC' as other chief officers. Indeed, his 'constitutional position would mean it was improper to promulgate advice'. As a result the main channel of communication was the police policy community based on ACPO, the Home Office and their joint working parties. Second, some local authorities are 'parochial and fairly backward' – a comment which illustrates how easy it is to miss the obvious. Not only did some local authorities have limited contact with, and knowledge of, the associations, they did not want more contact or knowledge. Other authorities could get involved if they wanted, but some did not wish to look beyond local matters.

If contact with the associations is 'peripheral', there is no one alternative channel of communication with the centre. A large number of respondents stressed the importance of direct links with central departments, both ministers and permanent secretaries. It was suggested that the AMA was useful for smaller authorities, although which authority in the AMA could be described as 'small' escaped this interviewer.[6] The 'large' authority could contact the regional offices of central departments, MPs, Whitehall and, ultimately, ministers. A surprising number of respondents mentioned MPs: 'AMA does not open doors, local MPs do this when necessary'. They were seen as a 'link to the minister', especially for political issues.

These comments were not intended as criticisms of the associations. Rather, respondents were emphasizing that it was 'one of many channels of communication'. Which one was used 'depends very much on the issue' and the associations were 'a vital link in the chain with the DoE'. However, the DoE is only one of several central departments with which local authorities have contact. Under the Thatcher government, it would be foolish to deny that the comments of many respondents had a tinge of cynical resignation: the AMA may be a useful channel of communication but 'it means bugger-all anyway'.

Internal involvement
Respondents were remarkably unconcerned about the dissemination of information within the local authority. The comments elicited fall into four categories. The first group blame it on association representatives. This batch of comments includes such remarks as: 'I'm totally unaware what the reps do'; 'they need to talk about real people and real money'; and 'X loves to say "I saw the minister yesterday ..."'. The second group simply don't admit there is a problem: 'if this is happening, it may be that it is not really that important'. The third group point to the different time scale of centre and locality: 'on an immediate issue, it takes too long. It would be dead before it was considered'. Or more succinctly, 'progress is slow'. In short, by the time the associations have deliberated upon an issue, all interest in the local authority has evaporated. Finally, many respondents had no personal contact with the associations, their authority had no representatives or officer advisers, and as a result they saw the associations as 'none of their business'. In a few authorities, the former majority party leaders had a similar attitude. Involvement with the association was not the responsibility of the opposition.

The same lack of concern was manifested over the selection of representatives or, to be more accurate, the self-selection of representatives. 'No one else would go' would seem an appropriate motto for all local authorities. We found *one* instance of election (by the majority group). If the leader wasn't a representative, he nominated someone else. Such procedures were seen as perfectly satisfactory.

The dominant attitude amongst all local authorities was 'don't tell me unless it's important'. As an ex-leader of the GLC put it, 'if everything's going alright, I don't want to know'. In these conditions any elaborate system of reporting back would be, at best, irrelevant and, at worst, an object of scorn. This dominant attitude is consistent with the patterns of contact described earlier and occurs for the same reasons.

Evaluation
The range of views expressed on the costs and benefits of membership was very wide. The discussion of patterns of contacts identified a range of factors which limited participation. Of these factors, political party exercises a major influence on respondents' evaluations.

At the outset, it will be helpful to discuss members' perceptions of the roles of the associations for they have a great influence on the evaluations. It is tempting to try to classify the associations as channels of communication of either the first or last resort. Indeed, some respondents discussed them in these terms. However, they are best described as channels of convenience and they are convenient on general issues. This conception of their role was expressed in a variety of ways. For one county, the ACC was useful 'where muscle and support is required' and for another where there was 'a consensus view on national not particular issues'. One northern metropolitan district felt that the AMA could 'highlight problems and deficiencies', although it did not initiate discussion of such problems. One London borough suggested that the AMA was useful 'where a solution is impossible any other way'. Other authorities highlighted particular policy areas – for example, pay and conditions of service, technical issues surrounding block grant. Whilst some authorities felt that it was difficult to identify association issues and others were downright cynical – 'a weak case, use the AMA' – the bulk of the sample would accept that the association 'exists entirely to pursue issues of national interest on behalf of member authorities'. They were equally certain about the matters which were not the concern of the associations – local issues and decisions.

This description should not be equated with the trivial or the parochial. It refers to issues specific to that local authority and encompasses such matters as the sale of council houses and the decline of the textile industry. Nor is the problem necessarily one that can be dealt with exclusively by the local authority. Many authorities mentioned discussions with regional offices as well as the central department and two authorities talked of their current efforts to amend legislation and remove anomalies.

Before examining the success or failure of the associations in pursuing national issues, it is important to note a number of incidental benefits of membership: the associations are a means of keeping up to date, of providing links with national government for isolated areas, of linking local authorities throughout the country and encouraging 'the cross fertilisation of ideas'. These remarks are all from small districts and demonstrate the particular benefits they derive from membership. However, many others noted the benefits of the associations as a 'forum'. They were described as a 'broadening experience'; a means for 'discussing common problems'; providing 'a cross-section of views and experience'; 'a good alerting system'; and as providing 'contacts which would not be available direct'. In addition, the role of the associations in specific policy areas such as grant and pay negotiations was valued by a range of authorities, many of whom pointed to their technical nature and the problems they would pose if the preserve of individual local authorities. If small remote authorities are particularly conscious of these benefits, they are equally valued by large and small, near and far, Labour and Conservative.

There was a similar consensus about the provision of advisers for the association. It was said to 'broaden officers' experience'; to make officers 'capable of sounder judgements by being better informed'; and to benefit the individual officer and, therefore, indirectly the authority. It was also said to raise morale because the officer recognizes that other authorities face the same problems. And, if the authorities benefit from the information and expertise thus acquired, the associations are said to benefit because advisers 'keep them in touch with reality and local problems'. Not all local authorities were convinced of the benefits. A few felt that the demands on an adviser's time were excessive and detrimental to his work in the authority. But the note of criticism becomes considerably more pronounced when one moves away from the incidental (although real and valuable) benefits of membership to the major role of the associations of representing members to central government.   .

Some district councils felt that the ADC provided easy access to government and that the government would take notice of the ADC whereas it would disregard individual local authorities. Members of the ACC also felt that the association could influence government by providing 'a united voice'. Similarly, members of the AMA felt that it not only gave them a united voice but also 'added teeth'. The associations were seen as 'co-ordinating views and reactions' or 'achieving a common approach' which gave them 'considerable clout' in meetings with ministers. Other respondents, whilst not critical, felt that there were few direct and immediate benefits accruing to the local authority: the associations 'furthered the interests of local government in general'. Membership was justified by the 'potential influence' of the associations. Surprisingly, few authorities mentioned the ability of the associations to influence legislation if only at the technical, implementation level, although some did point to the 'ignorance of civil servants' on local affairs and on the need to advise them. One metropolitan district pointed out that civil servants 'welcome advice'.

Virtually no authority could point to direct and immediate benefits. Indeed, their eloquence was reserved for criticisms of the associations.

The criticisms of the associations are almost as many and varied as their membership. Every association was criticized for its lack of awareness of local needs – at times such comments seemed to be an automatic reflex – and for its involvement with central government. The term 'London', in the pejorative sense beloved of northerners, figured predominantly in comments – from the polite 'London-dominated', through the insecurity of 'I feel out of place' to the anger of 'bloody cockneys'. On the 'cosy relationship' with government, comments included: the ACC 'does too much of the government's work' (shire county); the AMA 'is too used to Whitehall; its perceptions are dulled by familiarity' (metropolitan county); the ADC was 'a vehicle by which government governs' and 'too close to government to be effective' (shire district). Many also commented on the lack of success: 'the AMA never wins an argument' (GLC); 'I can't mention one issue as an ACC success' (Conservative shire county).

The great bulk of these comments were as expected before the survey was carried out. The volume of criticism directed at the internal workings of the associations was surprising. Many representatives felt that the meetings were 'a waste of time' and some described them as a 'farce', 'not worth the time travelling', 'lasted only five minutes', and complained that they were never held outside London. The political leadership attracted some caustic remarks. Committee chairmen were said 'to keep information to themselves' so members were unaware of the AMA's purposes and power and did not respond as they might. Leading members were alleged 'to agree matters amongst themselves' and 'to present a consensus view to members'. Power and functions were 'concentrated in too few hands'. They are too aware of their own kudos. 'I've been doing this but can't tell you'. These comments are from several authorities and all refer to the AMA. In part, they reflect whether or not an authority had a representative on the policy committee: those not so represented tended to be more enthusiastically critical. Whilst the AMA was the one association thus criticized most frequently, it was by no means unique. A representative from a shire county commented that, 'one feels totally excluded' and the ADC was decribed as 'unrepresentative' not only by the 'urban interests' but also by the 'rural interests' conscious of the 'status difference' between former county boroughs and themselves. And, although the numbers involved are small, those districts which had no representatives or advisers were considerably more critical.

The association secretariats seem to be exempt from this kind of criticism or, when they were criticized, the blame was laid at the feet of member authorities: 'the solution lies in the hands of local authorities'. And most of the comments have been heard many times before: 'They should originate more'; 'too docile'; 'progress is too slow'; 'the staff aren't up to it'. More commonly, authorities pointed either to the lack of resources or to the secretariats trying to do too much with the limited resources at hand.

Curiously, given the frequency with which it has been used to advocate reform, very few respondents referred to the clash of interests between associations. A few authorities talked of the need for *a* national body representing local government but, in so far as divergent interests were seen as a problem, most authorities referred to intra-association divergences. Nor was the 'impossible federation' of the AMA unique: such clashes were noted for all associations.

No doubt reflecting intemperate climes, one source of tension both within and between associations was singled out repeatedly: party differences were said 'to hinder a positive approach' and to make one feel 'like an outsider'. Across the board, authorities felt that party politics had become more important since reorganization: 'It is a fact of life that the associations are politically controlled and that Conservative councils support Conservative governments.' The influence of an association was seen as dependent on party political control and it was felt that the ACC ought to have good access under a Conservative government. Needless to add, such access was criticized: 'they now kowtow to the government'; enable 'legislation to be passed through more effectively'; and because of political allegiance they have 'ceased to exert pressure on government'. Many authorities felt that the increased salience of party politics had had an adverse effect on all the associations: 'real discussion went out of the window with the advent of party group meetings'. There were a number of calls for an association to be a more effective pressure group – 'if it's not a pressure group, it's nothing' – and effectiveness was said to require unity at least within an association.

Suggestions for improving the associations' effectiveness tended to concentrate on closer contacts with member authorities and on taking the initiative. Thus it was said that the associations need to 'make more effective use of member authorities'; 'to visit the regions' and to promote 'information exchange on a range of issues'. They should be far less a 'talking shop' and 'take decisions'. Advisers should be used 'to provide policy initiatives' and the secretariat should 'collate views of specialists *now* rather than referring back to *when they were specialists*'. Doubts were expressed about increasing the resources of the associations. 'The shortage of resources makes the ... bureaucracy responsive' and any increase 'might go against the smaller local authority in favour of larger who could supply specialist staff'.

To summarize the variety of comments briefly is a daunting task but two remarks seem to capture the kernel of the criticisms of many respondents:

a necessary bridge but a lowest common denominator type of institution. (Metropolitan district)
They receive professional advice and look at a service from a position within the service, they never see the customer side at all. They do not equate with a ... slum. (Shire county)

And, in this welter of criticism, it is crucial to remember that the overwhelming bulk of the membership were satisfied with their associations.

At various junctures several factors which influence the relationship between the associations and their members have been identified – type of authority (interests), size, geographical location, political party, parochialism and policy area – but in spite of this range there is remarkable uniformity in the behaviour and expectations of members. Members expect their association to represent them on a relatively small number of general issues and become involved only to the extent necessary to sustain this limited role. If the associations are clearing houses or post offices for government departments, they are flags of convenience for individual local authorities. Or, to mix metaphors, they are in the no-man's-land of trench warfare, vulnerable to bombardment from both sides.

Individual local authorities have limited expectations of the associations for a variety of reasons. The large local authority with distinct interest, the small, geographically remote authority, the authority controlled by the party in opposition within the association, the service chiefs oriented to their policy community – all have limited contact with the associations. This conclusion immediately raises the questions: 'Why are expectations uniformly low?' and 'Is this situation a recent development?'

The answer to the first question lies in another question: Is a *national* community of *local* government a contradiction in terms? (Stewart, 1977, p. 35). The major cause of the low expectations is the simple fact that the main interests of local authorities lie in local problems whereas the associations have to generalize across local authorities and identify the national aspects of a problem. This is a fundamental divergence of interest which inevitably limits the extent of involvement of individual local authorities in association affairs. The comments of many interviewees demonstrate an awareness of the difference. Not only did they have a clear conception of the associations generalizing function, but they also criticized them for lack of contact with the grass roots. It is perhaps inaccurate to describe the expectations of members as 'low'; they could be described as 'realistic'. It would be more noteworthy if member participation were not intermittent. And it is worth stressing that describing participation as intermittent and the relationship as distant does not mean the associations are unresponsive. It simply means that the range of issues upon which members choose to participate is limited. The case studies do *not* support the contentions either that the associations act independently of members or that members fail to hold the associations to account. There is a contradiction in the national community of local government: legitimacy resides in the locality, in local elections and local decisions on local problems. The national component of such local action is not of paramount importance to members of the associations.

It is more difficult to determine how this situation arose and how it is changing, because no data on expectations and behaviour in earlier years exist, although no one appears to have suggested that participation was ever more than intermittent. However, in the course of the interviews, two changes were repeatedly impressed upon us: the dissatisfactions arising from the politicization of the associations and the attempt by the DoE to support and strengthen the role of the associations. Both of these changes can be illustrated by Derbyshire County Council's resignation from the ACC.

On 7 July 1981, Derbyshire resolved to withdraw from the ACC on the grounds that 'there is little evidence to suggest that membership of the Association shows any benefit to Derbyshire and that the County Council could have a greater impact by submitting representations and comments direct to Government rather than through the machinery of the Association'.[7] In interviews, it was made crystal clear that Labour-controlled Derbyshire objected to the attitudes and behaviour of the Conservative-controlled ACC towards the Thatcher government: 'it was not properly representative and was politically biased', 'it only represented the Conservative majority'. Subsidiary complaints included: cost, which, with officers' time, was nearer £100,000 per annum (compared with the subscription of £35,000); time wasted at committee meetings; the need for officers to serve Derbyshire; and membership was described as a 'perk'.

Whilst Derbyshire's actions may seem atypical, similar discontents have been expressed by other authorities and not just within the ACC. Avon County Council has resigned and threatening noises emerged from Humberside and Cornwall.[8] Within the other associations similar rumblings can be detected. Labour authorities have resigned from the Conservative controlled LBA and set up the Association of London Authorities. Bromley LB has resigned from the AMA, which also has to fight proposals to abolish the metropolitan counties knowing that some members consider their abolition long overdue. The ADC continues to face demands from the 'twenty-two' in particular for both a reallocation of functions between counties and districts and for constitutional amendments to guarantee the medium-sized cities a role within the association. And it too has had resignations (for example, Basildon).[9]

The reaction of the DoE to developments in Derbyshire reflects their policy that consultation should be focused on the associations. They replied to Derbyshire's request for direct consultation by pointing out that:

> Your Council's withdrawal from the Association of County Councils will not, of course, affect existing arrangements for consulting your Council in circumstances where the Department would seek direct contact with individual authorities, or where the Department would wish to have the benefit of the views of your Council or its officers. Where, however, the Department is seeking the views of local government at large, or particular classes of authority, it has been long-accepted practice that consultation should take place through the Associations ... These consultation arrangements reflect the firmly expressed wishes of local government that the Associations, as the bodies set up to represent their collective views, should be regarded by central government as the accredited organisations to express views on behalf of local government generally, or the class of authorities that each represents.
>
> I regret therefore that the Department does not feel that it can accede to your Council's request.[10]

The Department of Industry, Office of Fair Trading and the Home Office all replied in a similar vein. The replies from the DES and DHSS were not available. In short, the explicit policy of the DoE was to aggregate the interests of local government. To resign, therefore, is to incur the sanction of non-consultation, although no Derbyshire repondent felt that such a loss was of consequence.

It would seem plausible to suggest, therefore, that the trends in member–association relationships have reinforced rather than weakened the distance between the two. Politicization has bred dissatisfaction amongst minority groupings within associations and led to the claim that party takes priority over the interests of local government. Central government support for the associations has served to reinforce perceptions that they are too close to government. The distance which characterized relations for the bulk of the period under study gave way to discontent and all the associations became concerned about their links with members. But it is worth remembering that such tensions are not peculiar to the associations. From Michel's pioneering thesis on the 'iron law of oligarchy' in political parties to secret ballots of union members before strikes, the relationship between members and leadership in voluntary organizations has been characterized as undemocratic, unaccountable or whatever pejorative term happens to be fashionable. The associations provide but one more example of an ever-present phenomenon.

CONCLUSIONS

At this juncture, the major findings of the survey are summarized.

Participation in the associations was the prerogative of senior members and officers and, even for this group, infrequent and limited in scope.

The overwhelming proportion of members and officers have no formal position within, no contact with, and their councils rarely request action from, the associations: the relationship was 'distant'.

The circulation of information on association business within local authorities was limited.

The overwhelming bulk of members and officers were satisfied with the work of the associations primarily because they did not expect the associations to do a great deal.

The uniformity of expectations and behaviour has several, discrete causes, including geographical location, size, party, type of authority and policy area.

The associations were but one of several channels of communication which were used as convenient, usually for issues of national scope affecting all member authorities.

As well as conventional pressure group activities, the associations offered members a series of incidental benefits – including keeping up to date, sharing information and discussing common problems – which, although valued by all members, were of particular benefit to the smaller, remote authority.

The associations were criticized on a large variety of grounds, especially by local authorities which had no representatives or officer advisers. Grounds included lack of local contact, involvement with central government, lack of success, centralized internal policy-making and, most notably, politicization.

Members had low (or realistic) expectations of the associations because their prime concerns were local, not national, problems, specific, not generalized, issues.

Two trends were reinforcing the distance between members and their associations and breeding discontent – increased party politicization was isolating minority groups within associations, and central government support for consultation only with the associations was reinforcing involvement with the centre.

Many of these conclusions are not new, nor is the distant relationship between members and associations peculiar to local government pressure groups. The last word is left to one of my respondents:

A good service for the little it has to do.

Ten words which capture both member satisfaction and the reasons for it.[11]

NOTES AND REFERENCES: CHAPTER 9

1   Department of the Environment, Heads of Division Circular 40/80, 'Consultation with local government in England and Wales', 3 November 1980.
2   See also Alexander, 1982, p. 164; and CPRS, 1977, p. 38. For a normative critique of this strategy see Rhodes, 1983.
3   Interview with deputy secretary, ADC, transcript. For the detailed statistics on the distribution of officer advisers see Rhodes, Hardy and Pudney, 1982b, pp. 121–6.
4   For ease of exposition, individual councils are treated as the respondents. Self-evidently, the views expressed by members/officers in a particular local authority can differ widely. As this section is concerned precisely with such variety, it seemed pedantic to preface every remark with 'As one respondent in ...' or some such phrase.
5   Both Norwich and the GLC are named with permission.
6   The smallest authority has a population of 166,000 (South Tyneside).
7   Derbyshire County Council, report and minutes of the policy committee, 7 July 1981.
8   See *County Councils Gazette*, January 1983, pp. 336–7; and March 1983, p. 394.
9   On these various internal conflicts see Chapter 6, pages 213 and 247–8, and Chapter 7 page 267. On the proposals to abolish the GLC and the metropolitan counties see HMSO, 1983b. A voluminous literature has emerged on this latest bout of reorganization. For surveys of recent developments and a guide to the literature, see Forrester, Lansley and Pauley, 1985; and Flynn, Leach and Vielba, 1985.
10 Letter from assistant secretary, DoE, to clerk and chief executive, Derbyshire County Council, 4 August 1981.
11 I would like to thank Melvyn Read for his help in analysing the returns.

PART FOUR

———◆———

CONCLUSIONS

Chapter 10

ASSESSING THE INFLUENCE OF THE
NATIONAL COMMUNITY

INTRODUCTION

At the outset, I presented a framework for analysing relationships both between the national government environment and the national local government system and within the national local government system. Taking the national community of local government and its constituent public interest groups as the central units of analysis, these relationships have been explored in a series of case studies covering the 1970s. The terminology introduced in Chapter 2 has been deployed throughout the book and the major conclusions of each case study have been summarized. But the conclusions from each case study have not necessarily been consistent with each other and the links between the different levels of analysis have not been explored. Equally, although the constraints and cleavages within the national community have been described at several points, they too have not been considered as a whole and their consequences for the effectiveness of the national community have not been assessed.

The objectives of this final chapter are therefore to provide a summary interpretation of the changing relationships of the national local government system, and to assess the effectiveness of the national community of local government. The format of this discussion parallels that of Chapter 2 and Figure 2.3 with one amendment: it proceeds from the macro-level of interventions by the national government environment through the meso-level of relationships between policy communities to the micro-level of power-dependence (or exchanges between organizations).

A SUMMARY INTERPRETATION

Trends and processes in the national government environment

Trends There were three distinct trends in intergovernmental relations in the 1970s: bargaining, incorporation and direction. (This section draws upon Dunleavy and Rhodes, 1983, pp. 122–32.)

BARGAINING Consultation was the 'normal' style of central–local relations throughout the post war period until the mid-1970s. For most of this time local service spending was buoyant, and the numbers of local authority employees grew fairly regularly. Central governments of both parties kept an eye out for electorally damaging slippage or non-performance by local government in areas of key importance. For example, slum clearance and rehousing were major public concerns for most of the 1950s and 1960s. A set of expectations about reasonably consensual dealings between Whitehall, the national community and local councils were embodied in the concept of partnership. Ministers often went out of their way to choose modes of implementing policy that maximized voluntary local authority cooperation.

In these years, the national community of local government, although ostensibly weak in comparison with its position in the 1970s, bargained over the total level of expenditure, the rate of growth in central grant and the distribution of government grant between different types of local authority, achieving changes at the margin in all three areas of negotiation. Up to 1974, the national community can be described as 'loosely coupled': that is, its structure was disconnected in terms of its functions or tasks and these tasks were disconnected from their effects (Meyer and Rowan, 1978, p. 79). In other words, although its task was to represent local government as a whole, there was extensive competition between the constituent organizations, each representing specific interests, and yet this rivalry did not manifestly weaken local government's bargaining position.

This bargaining phase lasted throughout the Heath government's period of office, despite some selective attempts by the Conservatives to develop more stringent controls over council policies. The government enforced changes in council housing finances against strong resistance but elsewhere was more cautious. Sales of council housing were successfully obstructed by all Labour councils. With much opposition from councils destined to lose many of their powers, the government adopted a two-tier system for local government reorganization which was more popular with existing councillors and officers than previous Labour proposals for unitary authorities. Staffing and financial arrangements for the reorganization were tailored to minimize opposition and, coupled with its determination to increase public expenditure as a means of reducing unemployment, the Heath government in fact presided over a bigger four-year growth in local service spending than any 1960s administration, a record that fitted oddly with the hard-faced 'Selsdon man' image with which it began its life. Indeed, the whole of this period can be characterized as the era of the policy communities: central spending departments and their associated professions had a vested interest in increasing service expenditure. Indisputably the treasury as 'guardian' of the purse strings fought a rearguard action against dominant policy communities, the 'advocates' of spending (Wildavsky, 1975, pp. 7–9). The period is characterized by the competition for resources and the relative insulation of the national community and the single-function policy communities.

THE STRATEGY OF INCORPORATION 1974-9   Throughout this period, the Labour government adopted strategies of aggregation and incorporation. Quite deliberately this trend has not been described as a 'corporatist' system because of that term's multiple, conflicting and contiguous meanings. Assuming that Schmitter's (1979, p. 13) list of characteristics is distinctively corporatist, those characteristics cannot be applied to this phase of central–local relations without adding to the already long list of adjectival qualifications to corporatism. The associations did not and could not regulate their members; they never held a monopoly of representation; membership of an association was never compulsory; and there was competition between the constituent organizations of the national community. Any further examples would be superfluous. Clearly, the description 'corporatist' would be highly misleading. But equally clearly the Labour government did make a sustained effort to introduce a kind of top-level integration in its dealings with local authorities.

The key innovations were the explicit recognition of the associations as peak associations, actions designed to foster integration within the national community of local government and its incorporation into central decision-making on public expenditure. This strategy of incorporation differed markedly from earlier central attempts to manage relationships with local government. For the first time, Whitehall set up a forum in which to discuss the long-run future of local spending with the national community of local government. The CCLGF was remarkable for bringing the Treasury and local authority representatives into face-to-face contact for the first time, and in explicitly integrating the planning of local expenditure into the PES system. The government's objective was that by involving the national community of local government in policy making affecting local government they would be able to persuade them of the 'realities' of the economic situation and thus enlist them as allies in the battle to keep down the growth of local spending.

This initiative was welcomed by local government. Indeed they had trailed the idea of involvement in PES for a number of years. Nor was incorporation limited to grant negotiations. Pay became increasingly entwined with the government's macro-economic strategy. The associations became acutely aware of the 'knock-on' effect of pay settlements for grant negotiations in an era of cash limits. The government sought to regulate pay settlements as part of its counter-inflation measures. Both sides welcomed closer involvement and the associations' aspiration for the status of peak associations served to generate constraints on local government's rights to decide pay for itself. There was no institution equivalent to the CCLGF for pay but the degree of incorporation was in no way reduced by this 'oversight'.

In charting the twists and turns in the fate of the CCLGF, three features stand out. The primacy of macro-economic considerations in determining central policy on local expenditure; the ability of central government to change the relationship between the two levels of government; and the inability of the associations, in the face of determined central government, to wrest anything but minor concessions for their members. Certainly it would be an incorrigible if not Panglossian optimist who concluded that the CCLGF had limited the freedom of central government to introduce reforms and enhanced the influence of the associations (cf. Foster, Jackman and Parlman, 1980, pp. 3, 351). The achievements of the CCLGF are not, therefore, as clear-cut as might be imagined. Many of its members argue that it was successful in getting the national community to persuade member local authorities to behave with restraint. But there were other pressures working in the same direction. The council was set up at the same time as a system of strict cash limits on central grants to local authorities was introduced. And, under a Labour government, many of the naturally high-spending councils could be persuaded to stay close to government guidelines out of a feeling of party loyalty and concern not to rock the boat. In addition, the swing against Labour in the mid-term local elections meant that the government's policy of restraint dovetailed neatly with the natural inclination of the new Conservative-controlled authorities. But the council did succeed in increasing the volume of knowledge in local government of Whitehall's problems.

If the council's effectiveness in reducing local expenditure is difficult to judge, there was one clear achievement: it promoted the associations into greater prominence than before. Their new role revolved centrally around financial, 'manpower' and economic issues, and the main bodies that found their influence decreased by this change were the many different policy communities promoting increased spending in one issue area or another. Whatever else it accomplished, the council helped along a shift of influence within local government away from service-oriented councillors and officers (for example, the education lobby) and towards local politicians and finance directors more concerned with 'corporate planning', increased efficiency and financial soundness. In effect, the council was a Whitehall attempt to build up the influence of the local authority associations and local government finance managers, in order that they would be better able to control the rest of the local government system in return for consultation and a direct voice in future planning.

DIRECTION   By contrast, the Thatcher government elected in May 1979 had little faith in consultation mechanisms, still less with 'corporatist' devices. The new right (and 'dry') wing of the Conservative Party argued instead that government must act with authority, without muddying its responsibility or intentions. And this authority has been primarily deployed in the service of a monetarist economic strategy which argues that government's overriding priority must be to control the money supply in order to reduce inflation. The main influence on the money supply is, in turn, the public sector borrowing requirement, so that all forms of government activity that tend to push up the central government's need to borrow money must be firmly cut back. Any kind of central government spending may do this, but in local government only capital spending (on buildings or plant) has any implications for overall government borrowing. On day-to-day local spending the central government can simply cut its block grant to councils without worrying about what happens to total spending; if local authorities make up a loss of central grant by raising their own property taxes (the rates) this does not increase the money supply, nor is it necessarily inflationary (since total spending in the economy remains the same).

Given this background it was inevitable that the Conservative government would crack down hard on local capital expenditure. By 1979 the Conservatives were fiercely critical of council-housing programmes, and this service has accordingly borne the brunt of the capital cutbacks. What came as more of a shock for local authorities of all political complexions was the determination of the new DoE minister, Michael Heseltine, to control *all* council revenue spending, whether Whitehall was picking up the tab for it or not. Heseltine's first Act in 1980 gave the DoE unprecedented powers to assess how much they thought each local authority should spend in total, and to withdraw grant at a penalty rate if the council overshot this limit. The government unilaterally changed the rules of the game. Local expenditure is now seen as part of the national public expenditure survey and not as a matter for local decision. The government seeks to impose nationally determined targets on local authorities. Most significantly, they have moved from control at the aggregate level to control over the expenditure decisions of individual local authorities. These changes were already mapped out by earlier developments but indisputably the Conservatives intensified the search for control by unilateral, not negotiated, means.

The period after 1979 saw a general deterioration in central–local relations, largely but not entirely because of the changes in financial controls. The associations saw their special position slip away, and the CCLGF was converted solely into a forum where ministers announce hard-and-fast decisions to unavailing protests by the local government representatives. Some of the council's technical working groups remain important in spite of increasing restrictions on their work, but virtually all of the local government organizations at national level have been permanently on the defensive, stigmatized by Whitehall as promoters of profligacy rather than as potential allies or partners. There have been some exceptions to this pattern, most important among which is the ability of some policy communities to mitigate some of the government pressure for cutbacks. Spending has fallen sharply in some services, such as council housing, but risen in others, such as police authority funding. Cuts have been selective, therefore, and central departments and policy communities in different areas have been able to mount a rearguard action of some significance.

What remains in doubt is how much the new directive strategy in central–local relations has achieved, even in terms of the government's own policy objectives of reducing local government spending. Apart from its success in cutting capital expenditure the Conservative government did not have as much success in implementing cuts as is widely perceived. For example, current expenditure grew by 9 per cent in real terms between 1979 and 1983. For central government the result of the new style of central–local relations has been a series of unintended consequences, amongst which the constant changes in the grant system must be numbered the most serious. Consequently, in 1984, a new phase in central–local relations is imminent: centralization. Dissatisfied with its ability to control local expenditure, the government has decided to control local income by fixing a ceiling on the rate levied by local authorities: 'rate-capping'. Quite explicitly it has been determined that *local* income and expenditure must conform with *national* decisions. If the past two decades reveal an inexorable move towards central control, the steps along this road have been faltering ones. Intention and achievement have diverged frequently.

Processes The national local government system has clearly been subject to dramatic transformations in the 1970s and the role of the national community has varied accordingly. The most obvious cause of these changes was the continuing economic decline of the United Kingdom but it was not the only process of significance. In addition, the fragmentation (and organizational inertia) of British government coupled with the tradition of executive authority (and the associated intensification of partisan, ideological conflict) serve to explain not only the changes but also the contradictory results of government initiatives.

The period prior to 1973 can be seen as the era of the professional. With the continued expansion of the welfare state the policy communities were dominant and the 'loosely coupled' national community played a secondary role. But, with intensifying national economic problems, the Treasury restrained expenditure: the 'guardians' challenged the policy communities or 'advocates' of expenditure. But the fragmentation of policy-making was an important obstacle to such intervention. In response to this problem, means were sought to aggregate demands. Thus, the demands of local political elites were articulated and interpreted – even supplanted – by the national community of local government. With the expansion of welfare programmes, the imperatives of rationalization – the need to co-ordinate interlocking policies and networks of organizations – became more acute and the pressures for aggregation, this time *in the interests of the centre*, were accelerated. This process strengthened the degree of integration within function-specific policy communities and further institutionalized the professions. Not only did the centre seek to create an intermediate tier of representation for local government but it also reduced the number of local authorities with which it had to deal in the reorganization of 1972.

Paralleling this development was the growing integration of the national community of local government for not only grant but also local pay negotiations. Increasingly it sought involvement in particular policy communities. Given the increasing pressure to control the level of expenditure, given the built-in tendency of policy communities to promote expenditure, it is not surprising that a second prong in the attack on expenditure should be to promote those representative bodies not specifically committed to a single service. Increasingly the centre sought (and the national community concurred) to funnel contact through an intermediate tier. Just as the Treasury represented guardianship at the centre, so the national community was an obvious ally in retrenchment: in theory at least their interests encompassed local government in its entirety, and they could be expected 'to see the problem in the round'. That they espoused the ideology of retrenchment prior to 1979 is clear.

This shift of advantage to the national community represented a marked change in the pattern of relationships but it was not to last. The Conservative government of 1979–83 abandoned incorporation for direction, with retrenchment as the dominant theme of its economic policy. The change was not, however, a change in economic strategy alone. There has been a resurgence of ideological politics with the Conservative Party asserting the virtues of social market liberalism and consequent restrictions upon the role of the state. This political component of the strategy required the government to act with authority and decisive action has been a keynote symbol of the 'dry' wing of the Conservative Party. The desire for an unambiguous reassertion of authority was translated into action with some ease for, as noted earlier, the government has structural power: that is, the relationship between centre and locality is that of constitutional superior and subordinate and the centre can unilaterally abrogate the existing rules of the game. Indeed, the decision to deploy strategies of incorporation was a central decision. However, this strategy sought compliance: the centre sought agreement to its proposals for reductions in expenditure. The Conservatives' unilaterally decided strategy sought to direct and control (not influence) the expenditure of individual local authorities and bypassed the national community. The government's policy was anti-corporatist. If local authorities complied voluntarily, if the national community supported the strategy, then control would be facilitated but compliance was not a precondition of the strategy. Indeed, one strand in the government's policy could be described as an attack on the national community – part of a more general rejection of corporatism.

It was an attack which, in the case of local government, had an easy victim. The cleavages within and the constraints upon the national community had always rendered incorporation a short-term strategy. It had never been possible, for example, to regulate the national community's membership. Aggregation, integration and incorporation could not overcome the institutional weakness at the heart of the projected intermediate tier of representation. The national organizational networks of local government have been reluctant tools in the hands of both centre and locality.

But bypassing the national community and rejecting corporatist strategy in favour of direction forced the government to confront the problem of interdependence in fragmented service delivery systems. Recalcitrance and unintended consequences were as prominant outcomes as expenditure cuts. Not all local authorities reacted to direction with recalcitrance. The majority of district councils were Conservative-controlled and 'responsible', accepting the government's targets. Equally, recalcitrance was not limited to Labour-controlled metropolitan authorities. Conservative-controlled county councils were penalized for 'overspending'. If many continued to accept, as in the past, the government's right to stipulate the level of public expenditure, none the less dissatisfaction became widespread, with the Conservative-controlled ACC experiencing internal dissension on an unprecedented scale whilst relationships between the associations also deteriorated markedly.

The hoped-for integration of the late 1970s had developed fissures and, if continued government attempts at control led to a papering over of the cracks, their re-emergence is but a White Paper away. And as the fissures emerged, as the national community's intermediating role receded, so disengagement characterized its relationships with the single-function policy communities: its involvement became more limited. Similarly, relationships with members, always remote, became marred by discontent, with local authorities resigning from the associations. The fate of the national community contrasts markedly with that of some policy communities, which were able to mitigate the calls for cuts. The government's policy encountered the inertia created by the institutionalization of professional interests in the structure of government: that is, in policy communities. In short, retrenchment (and its associated ideology) and executive authority conflicted with professionalization and the imperative of rationalization, generating rapid and marked fluctuations in the pattern of relationships. And the instability thus engendered was not accompanied by expenditure cuts on the scale envisaged or desired. If the targets imposed on local authorities were, to a degree, 'symbolic', if the government never expected 'real' cuts on the announced scale, none the less *cuts* in public expenditure in general and local expenditure in particular were expected. But between 1979 and 1983, with the exception of local capital expenditure, there was *growth* in real terms in national and local current expenditure.

Thus, the government's ability to acquire new formal powers of control had not, by 1983, proved to be a stable substitute for strategies directed at securing the compliance of policy communities and the national community of local government. These communities or networks of resource-dependent organizations were manipulated by the centre (in this context, the Treasury) and subjected to different strategies of intervention. But the contradictions in the context of these relationships constrained the effectiveness of any strategy. Whatever its formal powers, the government was dependent on the communities for policy implementation and on professionals for expertise. Obviously, the degree of dependence varied from policy area to policy area but, even in more diffuse issue networks, compliance was a prerequisite of effective policy-making. Institutionalizing interests to facilitate implementation served to institutionalize opposition. Aggregating interests to facilitate consultation and to manage political demands reinforced the constraints on the government's own actions. Its capacity to take unilateral decisions – to exercise structural power – proved to be a short-term palliative which intensified the initial problem.

After four years of direction and control, the Conservatives returned to office facing a choice between intensifying direction and a more conciliatory mix of strategies designed to win compliance. It has chosen to intensify direction. This new phase of explicit centralization involves rate capping and abolishing the 'worst over-spenders' – that is, the GLC and the metropolitan counties (see HMSO, 1983a, 1983b). Developments over the past decade suggest that, when control is the preferred strategy, the outcome will be unintended consequences, recalcitrance, instability, ambiguity and confusion: in short, the policy mess that has become the defining characteristic of British central–local relations.

In brief the national community changed from a loosely coupled set of competitive organizations into an integrated community with 'peak associations' and the status of an intermediate tier of representation. By 1983, however, the national community had 'fissured'. The compromises which public expenditure growth between 1966 and 1974 permitted were now denied to the associations and replaced by inter- and intra-association disputes. Any future unity will have a fragile base and be vulnerable to the imperatives of party loyalty and the interest of each type of authority.

This panoramic review of the 1970s has the advantage of simplifying a complex series of events and the disadvantage of overstatement. The relationships between the national government environment and the national local government system oscillated wildly and, on occasion, the constraints on government action were considerable. The trends and processes have to be unpacked in order to appreciate the fluctuating quality of the relationships. The national government environment sets the boundaries to centre–centre relations but it does not invariably determine policy outcomes. Against the backcloth provided by this section, the role of the policy communities (including the national community) requires further exploration.

Policy communities, professionals and political parties

At the outset, it was argued that the policy communities would be relatively 'closed' to each other and that the relationship with the national community would be conflictual. In fact, the relationships were far more complex than this characterization suggests.

The starting point for the discussion has to be the Treasury, or the Whitehall expenditure community, because it has exercised such an important influence on developments over the past decade. Changes in relationships were largely due to the government's perceptions of changes in the national economy. Obviously these perceptions were influenced by party ideology but the values, beliefs and professional judgements of the government's advisers, especially within the Treasury, had a significant influence. The Treasury was increasingly concerned with the rising trend of local authority expenditure, and perceived a need for both restraint and a new approach. However, as a department, its decision-making powers were limited; it is the department's view that it 'does not make decisions, it influences them'. But even its powers of influence over local government were limited because direct contact with the associations was scrupulously avoided. Contact was made only through the DoE; and, although the Treasury could influence the DoE, the two departments did not always agree on economic issues. The Treasury, therefore, regarded it as essential to enlist the political co-operation of local government and promote a better understanding between local and central government.

Enlisting local government support was, however, only part of the problem. For the Treasury the problem of a fragmented central government was as great as relative lack of control over local government. The combination of economic decline, increasing growth rates of national and local government expenditure, lack of Treasury influence or direct contact with local government, and the prevalence of departmentalism in central government prompted the Treasury to seek integration through the CCLGF. Through this machinery the Treasury sought to explain the national economy to both central departments and local government, to make direct contacts with the associations, and to establish a coherent central government view. To assist in this task the Treasury was present in the consultative council and in the officer groups (the OSG, the expenditure subgroups and the grants working group) not just to keep informed, but also to caution against unrealistic commitments, and to explain the national economic context.

Incorporation was seen as the most effective method of controlling the growth of public expenditure by giving local government access to economic decision-making, explaining the importance of their position and role in the national economy, and gaining their agreement on the appropriate measures. It was not a substitute for bargaining, but rather an additional, complementary dimension. It was stressed at the establishment of the CCLGF that the council would not affect existing relations between central departments and local government. Since its creation in 1970, close links had been developed between the DoE and the associations, with frequent off-the-record discussions. The new approach was to build on that co-operation and bring the two sides of government closer together on an organized and formal basis to face the problems of the national economy. However, for at least one Treasury official, *the* major benefit of the CCLGF was the improved co-ordination in Whitehall. For the first time ministers were forced to consider local government as a whole, helping central government to speak with one voice instead of two or more. Not only was this appreciated by the Treasury; it was appreciated by local government as well. There were few other benefits for local government. The promised involvement in PES never materialized. Indeed, 'involvement' never meant more than the provision of information by local government which would be 'considered' by ministers and civil servants in the next round of PES deliberations. The expenditure community was truly closed to all outsiders, including those of long standing respectability like the associations. The bargain – if it can be so labelled – which underpinned the creation of the CCLGF was one-sided. The Treasury's view was explicit. If the required co-operation was not forthcoming, more direct controls would be sought. The creation of the CCLGF presaged developments between 1979 and 1983.

Not all policy communities are as immune to outside influences. Indeed the expenditure community is highly distinctive because it is not built on long-standing consultation between government and interest groups. Notwithstanding the voluminous material on the 'Social Contract', all groups are outsiders to the central budgetary process. The various bargains on economic policy struck by governments are an input to that process – inputs which can be substantially renegotiated in the absence of one of the parties.

The organic change case study provides a useful counterbalance to the easy assertions that central government is pre-eminent in central–local relations or that the policy communities are closed. A unified and determined government with an agreed policy can override any and all objections from local government. But not all policies have a high political priority, nor are they specific to one department. Where agreement between several departments is necessary but not forthcoming, then there will be opportunities for influence. If a central department becomes an ally of an association, its chances of some degree of success are enhanced. Above all, the degree of bargaining is not just a function of the context of intergovernmental relations but also of the specific policy area. The CCLGF may illustrate co-option by government and the ability of the government unilaterally to change the rules of the game when faced by economic crises. Organic change, on the other hand, illustrates the normal rules of consultation in operation.

These comments are aimed at redressing a balance: they should not be interpreted as arguing that any bargaining is between equals. Peter Shore at the DoE insisted on a policy of reallocating functions and, in a form, attained his objective. The modifications to the policy were won by ministers in Cabinet committees, the existence and discussions of which are 'secret'. But to recognize that national policies are taken by the government is not to deny that the national community and the several policy communities can exert some formative influences. In addition these comments are also designed to caution against the easy generalization that influence is limited to the implementation stage of policy-making. In many instances, this may well be true but it is not an inviolate rule. Organic change illustrates the range of channels of influence that can be used before the government has made a firm commitment. Nor do all policies pose issues of national economic management. In the case of the 1972 reorganization, aggregation may have been a spur to action by the government to improve control of local expenditure. For organic change similar motivations can only be detected in the desire of central departments to protect what they already had. But a more 'economical' explanation of the behaviour of the DES and the DHSS would seem to lie in institutional inertia rather than seeking to relate all policies to macro-economic developments.

The simple fact that organic change spanned several policy communities highlights a characteristic feature of central policy processes – fragmentation. The opportunities for the associations to influence central decisions are greater when they can exploit the divisions between departments generated by fragmentation than when the policy is limited to a single policy community. In the latter case, the dominant pattern is one of subgovernment – of intensive consultation between department and groups. Such consultation does not mean that the policy communities are 'open'. As both the education and fire policy communities demonstrate, consultation may be intensive but it is not extensive. Relatively few groups command the privilege of continuous access. Of these groups, the several local government professions are amongst the most prominent.

There are marked differences in the respective compositions of the national community and the single-function policy community: the former excludes trade unions. Any sharp distinction is blurred, however, by the dual role of chief officers. They act as both employers in pay negotiations and as employees in their own negotiations. This simple fact suggests that it is more accurate to talk of the professions as chief officer societies, prominent in both the national community and the appropriate policy community, and as trade unions, prominent only in the policy communities. And the latter are not limited to 'trade union' issues. Although firemen are not normally described as professionals, their concerns are extensive and they are consulted on a range of issues by the Home Office. Moreover, any characterization of the relations between the national community and the policy communities has to recognize the multiple interests of many of the actors.

To continue with the fire service example, officer advisers in the CFBAC speak for both their service and for local government. Members nominated by the associations can be representatives of those associations, spokesmen or negotiators for a joint body, the leader of a local council and the advocates of a particular service. Multiple loyalties not only generate conflicting expectations but also shifting coalitions of interest. Thus, association representatives, chief fire officers and the Home Office can be aligned against FBU and NAFO; association representatives, members and chief officers can be aligned against the Home Office (for example, chief officers' pay anomaly rectification). Association representatives, chief officers and FBU and NAFO can be aligned against the associations and the Home Office (for example, the 1980 pay settlement). The conflict between the service interests in local government and the interests of local government indubitably exists but the several actors are not limited to the defence of one or other interest.

The role of the professional societies has a number of similarities with that of the associations. For example, they provided briefs on the practical problems and the consequences of organic change. They did not mount publicity campaigns nor did they lobby Parliament. The most distinctive feature of their activity is the great number of opportunities to try and exercise influence. The Association of Directors of Social Services submitted memoranda to the DHSS, met officials to 'clarify' points, invited the secretary of state to their annual conference, gave their views wider currency through professional journals such as *Social Work Today*, provided advisers to the ACC social services committee and contributed to the ACC's submissions to not only the DHSS but also the DoE. And there were separate submissions to the DHSS as well as the several, general memoranda of observations submitted to the DoE, all of which contained a discrete section on the personal social services. Nor should it be thought that any or all of these activities mark out the ADSS as exceptional. Its role was routine. Every local government professional society of any note has equivalent opportunities to make its views known.

The organic change case study does not suggest that the societies had a decisive influence on organic change. Undoubtedly, they contributed to, and reinforced, the doubts of the central departments about the policy. As with the 1972 reorganization, they shared with the central departments a preference for large authorities. They were a substantial part of the institutional inertia that this policy initiative had to overcome. As members of both their service's policy communities and of the national community (as association advisers), it is clear, however, that the societies are particularly well placed to air their views even if they are not on all occasions decisive. In this instance their main contribution was negative: their opposition was a concrete problem for the central departments involved – neither the DES nor the DHSS wished to incur needlessly their wrath for another department's policy – and, consequently, it provided further grounds for extended discussions of the practical problems and further impetus in designing safeguards for the transfer of services. With the ACC to the fore, acting as a (willing) conduit for their views, overt lobbying was not required. The ADC was at some disadvantage in this respect as, with the exception of the planning profession, few if any societies associated with district level functions were directly affected by the policy.

The opposition of the central departments and the professional societies illustrates one of the major themes of the 1972 reorganization – the need for large local government units. Both the DES and the DHSS were concerned to preserve the gains of the 1972 reorganization and the same concern was echoed by the professions. 'Functionalism', or the belief in the effectiveness of large units, was the dominant theme of their evidence to the Royal Commission in 1967 and 1968, and was the dominant theme in their objections to organic change. The interests of service management still prevailed over the interests of urban areas. In short, the 'technocratic' professions acted to defend their specific service interests.

This focus contrasts sharply with the role of the 'topocratic' professions of chief executives and directors of finance, which encompasses the full range of policies. Not only do they provide advisers for *every* association committee but they are intensively involved in grant and pay negotiations. The professions may be prominent but they are a disparate group of organizations, some of which are more equal than others. The case studies provide little evidence about the actual impact of professionals. No policy was crucially altered by the intervention of a professional body. Their influence resided in their continuous involvement and the ideologies they articulated. The 'topocratic' professions expounded the 'responsibility ethic'. The 'technocratic' professions espoused 'functionalism'. Within particular policy communities, the 'technocrats' supported the shared appreciative system – for example 'the logic of the arithmetic' in education. These beliefs served to foreclose the range of options considered. The professions exerted a negative or conservative influence on policy-making. A far more decisive role was played by the political parties.

Initially, the policy communities were seen as professional-bureaucratic networks which had supplanted party political channels of communication and influence. Any danger that the role of parties would be 'relegated' to that of articulating a broad, overarching strategy quickly evaporated with the detailed case studies. Party was at times a complementary and at other times a rival channel of influence to the policy communities (including the national community) but it was at all times a prominent feature of relationships and an important influence on policy-making. This conclusion applies to relationships within the national community and between the policy communities. For example, although all the associations attempted to cultivate bipartisan approaches to pay negotiations for the bulk of the period of study, none the less internal and external relations were periodically subjected to stress from party political cleavages. The attitude of an association to LACSAB varied with party control both of the association and of the government. The conflict between the ACC and the AMA over control of LACSAB was firmly rooted in party differences. It may have remained latent but it was probably the most serious obstacle facing the reforms, *pace* the ADC's successful opposition. In short, LACSAB's constitutional crisis cannot be reduced to a simple disagreement over accountability: it mirrors the political cleavages within the national community.

Formally the main Conservative Party linking body is the National Local Government Advisory Committee. Although since 1979 there has been frequent contact with the leaders of the ACC this channel of communication is regarded by rank and file ACC members as weak and not presenting adequately a local government view. Formally the Labour Party appears to have clearer party links through its National Executive Committee and its Regional and Local Government Sub-Committee, and a greater proportion of its MPs have a local government background. Both formally through their vice-presidents and informally, the associations can attempt to influence governments by lobbying MPs.

The effectiveness of this strategy varies both from issue to issue and with the political complexions of the government and the associations. For both pay and grant negotiations generally informal contact was of considerable importance. Through such contact, ACC opposition to the 1980 Bill was overcome but the link is not always the obvious one between governments and associations under the control of the same party. Thus, confrontation between the major political parties played a limited part in organic change – at least in the conventional sense. Given that a Labour government was attempting to return functions to Conservative-controlled cities, this is unsurprising.

There was an adversary element to organic change. Michael Heseltine and Keith Speed attempted to blunt the demands of the cities for the return of functions, seeing the attacks on the 1972 Act as 'unwelcome'. The adversary strategy required united Conservative opposition to organic change and unity was only forthcoming on the eve of a general election and after Michael Heseltine had conceded the need to change the allocation of planning responsibilities and to review agency arrangements. The problem for the Conservative Party was further compounded by the differences between the shire Tories and their urban counterparts. Born and bred on disciplined party politics, the urban Conservatives are a rather different breed from their independent and squirearchy-influenced shire colleagues. Awareness of this difference can be found in both the ADC's desire to avoid special treatment for the big cities and the latter's disdain for the Conservative-controlled counties. In calling for party to take precedence over local allegiances, Michael Heseltine was recognizing not just the different interests of various types of local authority but also the different breeds of Conservatives. Organic change may have generated party political differences at the national level but not so within local government. Here the differences lay between Labour and the urban Conservatives on the one hand and the shire Conservatives on the other.

For the Labour Party, the major tension arose not between the party and Conservative-controlled associations, nor between the parties in Parliament, but between the party and the Labour government. The party accepted organic change only reluctantly and with the proviso that it should be seen as a step towards a more fundamental restructuring of local government. Peter Shore had to persuade the National Executive Committee and the Regional and Local Government Sub-Committee that the two proposals were compatible: that organic change was the first step on the road to radical reform. Equally important, the Labour Party machine was the channel through which organic change was put on the policy-making agenda. Individual local authorities took the initiative, the ADC followed, and the party was seen as the efficacious means for getting government action.

Although organic change does not provide a straightforward illustration of adversary politics in British policy-making, it none the less demonstrates the impact of party politics. There were clear partisan benefits in the positions of the two major parties. The *status quo* favoured the Conservatives whereas organic change would have benefited the Labour Party. Many of the 'big nine' may have been controlled by the Conservatives at the time of Peter Shore's initiative but Labour could and would win control of these cities in the future whereas it would never (or rarely) win control of many county councils.

The simple description 'adversary politics' is itself misleading. It emphasizes the confrontational style, ideological character and national component of party politics. The affect of party is far more pervasive. It spans levels of government and functions as a channel of communication for a range of interests. Its policy-initiation function is not limited to annual conferences and party manifestos when the party is in power. Most important for this study, it spans policy communities. If the policy communities are closed, party is one of the means for prising them open. Obviously the government of the day influences the relative saliency both of policy communities and of issues within them. Thus, the Labour government, by supporting the emergence of an integrated national community, was asserting the primacy of financial interests over the service interests of government. But party is also the grit in the molluscs of Whitehall-based policy networks. It disrupts the consensual expectations and dealings of the policy communities. The Conservative government of 1979–83 is one clear example of this phenomenon. On a less elevated plain, the Conservative-controlled AMA's disruption of local government pay negotiations is another. If the professional-bureaucratic complexes described here as policy communities are a source of institutional inertia, the parties are a source of change.

Once stated, this conclusion must be qualified. British government cannot be reduced to the simplistic dualities of party versus bureaucracy, minister versus civil servant. But the fluctuating relationship between party and policy community is central to understanding the policy process. This study has emphasized the importance of policy communities because its prime objective is to analyse one such community. It is important, therefore, to stress at this stage the impact of party politics. Both party and policy community can, by turns, initiate and frustrate. Both can act to integrate government action or they can sustain governmental fragmentation. It is the interweaving and interpenetration of the two – with all its twists, turns and reversal of roles – which should be emphasized and not the particular role adopted on a specific issue or within one policy community. Political parties are not one of the constituent organizations of the functional policy communities (although they are prominent in the national community) but they are a major influence upon them both ideologically and more prosaically as a channel of communication and a means for articulating interests.

The impact of party is not the only omission or inadequacy in the initial discussion of policy communities. It was also suggested that the issue scope of policy communities would be limited to ordinary issues. The problem is that such policy areas as grant or pay simply cannot be categorized in this way. The level of grant or of pay settlements has a direct relationship to the government's policies for the management of the economy. The 'corporatist' approach favoured by the Labour government and the 'market' approach of the Conservatives both address themselves to the question of the role of state intervention in the management of the economy. If these policy differences cannot be categorized as 'grand issues' it is difficult to know what constitutes such an issue. In other words, the national community was not limited to ordinary issues. It may not have been an influential participant. It may have set no agendas, initiated no policies and decisively affected no outcomes. The policies may have been antithetical to its interests. But it was involved. Consultations took place on a range of macro-economic issues and yet in theory, because of their very nature, 'grand issues' are not the stuff of such pressure politics: they are left off the agenda. Indeed, it is the lack of a consensus – heavily indoctrinated or not – which has generated the instability in relationships described in this study. Economic decline and the resurgence of ideological politics has discomfited the policy communities because the role of the government of which they are such a central part has itself been an issue. The influence, not the issue scope, of the policy communities is limited. And care must be taken not to overstate the case. Some policy communities fought effective rearguard actions and neither the scope nor the cost of their functions were reduced.

It is tempting to speculate that the capacity of some policy communities to resist retrenchment is related to their client groups. A community with a large, organized clientele can draw upon it for support whereas the national community has no such groupings to mobilize in its defence. Children and patients have far more appeal (and supporters) than local authorities. There are other important differences between the policy communities and the national community. Not only is the membership of the national community distinctive, encompassing political parties as well as units of government whilst excluding the trade unions, but its issue scope covers governance, resource and service policies (see Chapter 3, page 62 above). The difference is one of emphasis. The policy communities also encompass a range of issues but service policies predominate. For the national community governance and resource policies are of central importance *and* it is involved in a range of service policies. Its horizontal linkages are correspondingly extensive. These differences do not mean, however, that the interests of the national community are necessarily antithetical to those of the policy communities: they are often complementary. 'Technocratic' and 'topocratic' interests are distinct but interwoven.

With these important caveats about the role of parties in, and the issue scope of, policy communities to one side, this study provides many illustrations of the characteristics identified in Chapter 2. Thus, relationships within policy communities are asymmetric – for example, reform of the grant system, review of fire policy; policy communities are manipulated and constituted by central departments – for example, the 'creation' of an intermediate tier of representation based on an integrated national community; the policy process varies considerably between policy communities – cf. the fire and education policy communities; the professions are key actors (pp. 385–7); and policy content is a major influence on relationships – cf. the Home Office's autocratic style compared with the DES's consultative style. A more detailed comparison requires an analysis of the structure of power-dependencies within policy communities – of the rules of the game, strategies, resources and appreciative systems.

Rules of the game, strategies and power-dependence
For the period and the policy areas under study, the following rules of the game can be identified (see also Richardson and Jordan, 1979, pp. 103–5, Heclo and Wildavsky, 1974, pp. 14–21; Lijphart, 1968):

1 *Pragmatism* doctrinal, especially party, disputes should not prevent the work being done.
2 *Consensus* agreed settlements are preferable to imposed solutions.
3 *Fairness* the parties affected by proposed policies, even known opponents, should have the opportunity to state their case.
4 *Accommodation* where agreement is not possible, the 'loser' is not antagonized, a special case of the British love of the under-dog, and pains will be taken through consultation over the details – to minimize losing over the principles of policy.
5 *Territoriality* actors do not extend their demands beyond their known remit. Thus, there is a 'lead' department for issues and other central departments (for example, the Treasury) should not intervene. Similarly the national community is constrained in its interventions in policy communities.
6 *Secrecy* discussions should be private and limited to the affected parties and not open to wider public scrutiny.
7 *Depoliticization* issues should be subject to technical rather than political criteria as in the case of grant distribution.
8 *'Summit diplomacy'* decisions should be taken by elites, meeting in secret, and be a product of direct, face-to-face discussion. Thus, Tony Crosland met the political leaders of the associations.
9 *Local democracy* local authorities as elected units of government have a legitimate sphere of competence which is 'out of bounds' to central departments.

10 *'The right to govern'* certain matters are in the national interests and the centre has both the right to intervene to preserve that interest and a monopoly of legitimate coercion to impose its definition of the national interest.

11 *'Trust'* access to discussions, secret and otherwise, and effectiveness in these discussions hinges on assessments of reliability. If and only if a group is deemed reliable, as in the case of the associations, will it command an entrée and attention.

As these rules are 'conventional' and set approximate limits to discretionary behaviour, they were not immutable. Not all rules were operative for the period under study and they varied in their relative importance – a point discussed in more detail below.

In exactly the same manner, it is possible to specify the range of strategies available to the participants. (See also Cawson and Saunders, 1983; Dunleavy, 1983a; Elkin, 1975; Fox, 1983; Offe, 1975; Saunders, 1980 and 1981.)

1 *Bureaucratic* through its command of resources, especially legal resources, government can authoritatively determine relationships between public sector organizations. Such actions can be positive – requiring local authorities to undertake certain activities (that is, direction) – or negative – preventing particular actions (control).

2 *Incorporation* the co-option of local government into central decision-making processes, a strategy which can generate 'clientelism' or the identification of departments with the interests of groups and shared priorities.

3 *Consultation* central government initiates discussion of its proposals with local government without committing itself to any modifications.

4 *Bargaining* each unit of government commands resources required by another or others and they attempt to agree the terms of any exchange.

5 *Confrontation* local authorities defy central government either by breaking the law and refusing to terminate an illegal policy or by failing to implement a statutorily prescribed policy or by adopting policies expressly (if not legally) rejected by the centre.

6 *Penetration* the reverse of incorporation, and the attempt by local authorities to find allies amongst one or more central departments for their view of a policy, weakening central determination to adopt the policy by a process of divide and rule.

7 *Avoidance* the units of government cannot agree on policy so each deploys its own resources to achieve its own ends, ignoring or vetoing the other party or parties.

8 *Incentives* the offer of financial or other inducements to foster the adoption and implementation of policy.

9   *Persuasion*   literally, to cause actors to accept that the facts are as stated by a variety of means, including rational arguments, lobbying, advice, and the promotion of ideas in good currency – that is, 'best professional practice'.

10 *Professionalization* the creation of single-issue policy areas (not necessarily by unilateral central action) wherein professional criteria, interests and values dominate conventional political processes.

11 *Factorizing* the simplification of problems by subdivision and allocation to subnational, appointed units of government (for example, quangos, regional institutions).

Not all strategies are equally available to all actors. Thus, the bureaucratic, factorizing, consultation, incorporation and incentive strategies are means open to central departments, not local authorities or the national community, whereas the confrontation, penetration and avoidance strategies are primarily the preserve of local government. Other strategies are open to both levels of government. And, as before, not all strategies were used throughout the period under study. It is these changes in the rules and strategies which are of prime importance.

Not surprisingly, the stated policies of the 1979–83 Conservative government attracted considerable adverse comment, provoking such descriptions as 'constitutional crisis' and 'the demise of local government'. But, as the case studies of grant and pay negotiations demonstrated, unilateral changes in the rules of the game are not a new phenomenon. The Labour government consulted no association before creating the CCLGF or before instituting its detailed vetting of local government pay negotiations. These innovations still sought local government's agreement but they were none the less unilateral changes in the rules of the game. And they were *not* the most important changes. Of far greater significance was the explicit treatment of local expenditure as a matter for decision within PES. This reclassification meant that PES and RSG figures could now be reconciled and, implicitly, the government was setting expenditure targets for local authorities. In addition, the introduction of cash limits provided an additional major tool for influencing (if not controlling) local expenditure. Allied to reductions in grant, the government had a range of means for inducing compliance with nationally determined figures.

These changes were the first firm steps down a road which the Conservative government was only too happy to tread. They moved from aggregate control to control of the individual local authority; from the control of expenditure to, at first implicitly and then explicitly, the control of local income. The air of inevitability which surrounds this chain of events – spanning, as it does, a decade and governments of both major parties – suggests that no one party can be said to be responsible for the demise of local government. Rather, these events illustrate the vulnerability of local government in a system characterized by economic decline and a tradition of executive authority.

Just as the government can unilaterally change the rules of the game, so it has the luxury of choice in the strategies it can deploy. If consultation and bargaining were typical of the 1960s – and, as in the case of the reorganization of local government, the government was prepared to adopt, even in this era, bureaucratic strategies – then incorporation, direction and control typify the 1970s and 1980s. The national community adopted a reactive stance, deploying its more limited number of strategies as best it could. In grant negotiations, its options were severely constrained and perhaps the clearest illustration of its impotence can be found in the resort to public campaigns, normally the last refuge of the associations in any strategy of persuasion. Confrontation is the order of the day for the AMA, although this strategy can be most effectively deployed by the individual local authority prepared to increase rates to offset grant penalties.

Too much gloom and despondency would be misplaced. The national community has had its 'successes' even if they are unspectacular. The case study of organic change illustrates the varying fortunes (and roles) of the individual associations. Their roles differed not only with the different stages in the policy process but also with their stance on organic change. Many of the comments that can be made are trite: for example, the ADC played a role in initiating the policy whilst the ACC did not. The roles and strategies of the protagonists differed sharply. Although the ACC was prepared to use the normal channels, it forsook them when it was convinced that the government was set upon legislation, even if the precise form of that legislation remained unclear. Indeed, it would have been difficult to abandon its traditional consultative role, because the DoE wrote direct to their members suggesting that they send their comments to the ACC. But it was unusually active in issuing press releases, holding press conferences and cultivating support from professional societies and the 'distinguished'. The use of outside consultants – both academic and commercial – was also distinctive. If the policy formulation stage is broken down into the intelligence, or problem search stage, and the design stage (Simon, 1960, p. 2), then the ACC strategy of getting independent policy advice was to pay handsome dividends at the design stage. The Stewart report had an important effect on the negotiations between central departments. Similarly, the use of the Society of Public Relations Officers and PR consultants reveals an aggressive public relations posture which is rarely seen in the associations.

The ADC's strategy was considerably more low-key and in conformity with the usual style of all the associations. It concentrated upon consultation and the preparation of briefing papers for the government. The most noteworthy event was the informal meeting with Peter Shore to discuss in some detail 'the way forward' on organic change. In submitting its supplementary evidence to the Royal Commission on the National Health Service, the ADC clearly revealed its intention of playing the role of staunch ally to Peter Shore. In pressing the government to legislate quickly and to drop the use of population criteria in the reallocation of functions, the ADC never resorted to strategies of high visibility. It simply attempted to make its points as authoritatively as possible without compromising its position as supporter of the secretary of state.

The number of meetings with ministers was large. Both the ACC and the ADC seemed to have unlimited access. The DoE consulted only the main associations in the later stages, suggesting that the associations are now, to a greater degree than before reorganization, *the* peak associations of local government. Certainly, no professional society or individual local authority commanded equivalent access, although for less contentious issues there can be greater flexibility about who is consulted and at what stage in the policy process.

Whether the role was that of bystander (AMA), aggressive lobbyist (ACC), or ally (ADC), it would be misleading to ascribe too important a role to the associations. The fact that they had any role is a function of the fragmentation at the centre. But the future shape of organic change emerged from the essentially private negotiations between ministers and civil servants primarily at the DoE, DES and DHSS. The strategies of the departments were straightforward. The DES and DHSS fought a rearguard action on the practical problems of implementation whilst the DoE conceded as little as possible. Any concessions were invariably the express decision of ministers: they were not faced with *faits accomplis* negotiated by their civil servants. The length of time taken to negotiate the White Paper, in spite of the fact that legislation was announced in the Queen's Speech, attests to this fact. Quite simply, the policy was simultaneously ambiguous and contentious and delay was inevitable.

However, the strategies of central departments cannot be described simply as consultative. They vary depending upon the extent of conflict, the stage of the policy process and the status of the participants. Thus, the DoE bargained with other central departments because it needed their agreement if the policy was to proceed but it consulted with the associations and 'noted' any objections. Some professional groups were only formally consulted – for example, the DES letter to the twenty-four bodies – whereas the associations had regular informal discussions. Some bodies – the 'big nine' – had extensive access in the earlier stages but, as the policy was being finalized, they were denied access altogether, primarily to minimize the extent of conflict. This picture of multiple goals and alliances suggests the conclusion that policy-making was fragmented but, additionally, it is worth remembering that the 'outsiders' were the peak associations of local government and a relatively small number of professional societies.

If organic change saw the associations intensively consulted, the perennial complaint from the national community concerns the lack of consultation. The following comment could have been made at any time or for any policy: 'there is still a tendency for Government to consult too little and too late on the effects of proposed legislation'. In addition, there is the problem of timetabling and the circulation of papers, particularly if a matter is referred to a minister for political decisions. Though the local government side occasionally believes that such delays are engineered to 'bounce a committee', such tactics are disapproved of in Whitehall. Nevertheless, papers are frequently circulated so late that advisers have insufficient time to prepare considered responses or to brief members. Finally, and often linked to the previous points, the associations consider that the growing publicity both before and after meetings is undesirable. Often the associations attend meetings unprepared to respond in detail, hear the government's views, and then the minister holds a press conference to announce that 'after consultation with the associations, I have decided that . . .'. This situation both creates constraints for the associations and generates pressures for their members to conform to the decisions even though the discussion may have been superficial. Such complaints were voiced regularly about the CCLGF but the best examples arise from the case study of pay negotiations: that is, the settlement of the manual workers dispute, the '14 day rule'.

Consultation is at the centre's behest and many of local government's specific complaints are manifestations of this central fact. At its crudest, consultation means that the centre decides on the agenda, the participants and the timing, with no prior commitment to modify the policy. Obviously, there are circumstances in which consultation is required by statute. Equally, the centre may welcome local government's contribution and make few or no attempts to regulate the process of consultation. But the ground rules remain the same: consultation is on the centre's terms should it so choose.

The capacity of central departments to choose between the range of available strategies is a function of the resources at their command and their appreciative systems. Indeed, it was argued in the case study of pay negotiations that the styles of central departments were an important influence on relationships. Thus, the Home Office was directive, the DoE was consultative and the DE was a handmaiden. Similarly the case studies of the policy communities contrasted the directive style of the Home Office with the consultative style of the DES. Such sweeping generalizations have to be treated, of course, with some caution. No one style permeated a whole department for all policies. None the less, it is indisputable that the central departments were seen as adopting distinct mantles by the national community. Its expectations about a department's behaviour tended to surround relationships with an air of self-fulfilling prophecy: the departments behaved as they were expected to behave. And certainly the national community's own appreciative system was a major influence on relationships.

For the era of the consultative council and for pay negotiations, the efficacy of government policy hinged on local government's 'responsibility ethic': on the acceptance of central government's definition of national economic problems. The policies of the Thatcher government have sorely strained this ethic but it persists in many shire county and district councils. Indeed, it often appears that this self-imposed control was the centre's major weapon in controlling local expenditure. And espousing this ethic was not a sign of weakness in the national community but directly in its interests. As the voice of responsible local government it was laying claim to pre-eminence in the relationship between central and local government and asserting the primacy of financial managers over specific service interests. Self-interest, not altruism, lies at the roots of the responsibility ethic.

The evidence supporting the argument that the national community shared an appreciative system is mixed. For example, in the case study of organic change, any such consensus was particular to the functional policy communities: the national community was deeply divided. Similarly there were acute differences between the ACC and the AMA over the means for distributing central grant and between the associations and LACSAB over the latter's role. These examples do not mean, however, that there is no shared appreciative system. Thus, during the LACSAB constitutional crisis, it would seem that there was no shared appreciative system and that member authorities were able to influence events. However, the associations continued to share a commitment to strengthening local government's national presence. The LACSAB constitutional crisis illustrates disagreements about the means to this end but not disagreement on the end. Similarly, member authorities objected not only to the specific reform proposals but also to 'centralization'. The criticisms of funding through Section 2(7) were misplaced but they do reflect a concern to limit the ambit of the associations. Such funding does not raise the possibility of greater control by central departments but it does increase the potential for control of LACSAB by the associations. By insisting on a range of inputs, the member authorities were criticizing centralization by the associations and commenting on the distance not only between the associations and members but also between LACSAB and members. The national community may not be 'closed' to member authorities but the 'distance' between the two can be considerable, in spite of attempts to improve consultation, especially in pay bargaining.

Moreover, the goal of creating 'peak associations' was not shared outside the national community. To this extent, therefore, there is a shared appreciative system which serves to separate the national community from members.

Just as important as the shared values of the national community are the multiple constraints and cleavages. The aspiration towards the status of peak associations was a feature of the national community for a relatively short period of time, primarily the period 1975–9. Both before and after these dates, division, not integration, was perhaps the most distinctive feature (see below). The national community is most accurately seen as a confederation. As a result, it cannot be described as 'closed' to its members. The case study of organic change shows that both the ADC and the ACC took particular care to brief their members and to collect their opinions prior to submitting memoranda of observations. It was the awareness of potential conflicts of interests between sections of the membership which prompted the ADC to seek a reallocation of functions for all districts rather than the 'big nine' or the 'twenty-two'. The ACC used its membership as a resource for marshalling information and arguments with which to counter the government's and the ADC's proposals. Conflicts of interest internally and/or with another association may serve to remind the associations of the existence of their members but, whatever the stimulus, organic change illustrates the associations defending them. If a single word describes the relationship between members and the associations it is 'distant', not 'closed'.

Equally, it cannot be assumed that there was a single, if relatively opaque, appreciative system for the national community. LACSAB's conception of pay negotiations coupled with its own direct links with individual local authorities mark a distinct appreciative system which led to a gulf of misunderstandings with the associations. Similarly, the service-specific policy communities also had distinct appreciative systems – most notably education – and the associations were members of these communities. The functional committees of the associations have close links and shared values with the appropriate policy community and the history of the AEC and CLEA, or of the reform of the CFBAC, both demonstrate the efforts of the associations to counter particular service interests. The differences of interests and conflicts between the national community and policy communities are internalized in the associations' committee structures. And, if sections of the national community have a shared appreciative system with policy communities, the national community itself shares values with the government of the day. The 'responsibility ethic', or agreement that the level of pay settlements ought to be minimized, illustrates that the two levels of government can and do have shared goals. Just as there are diverse appreciative systems within central government so there is no one set of expectations and values within the national local government system or even within the national community.

At the heart of the power-dependence model of central–local relations is the control of resources. Central government's ability to initiate change lies in the inequalities in the distribution of resources. It has a virtual monopoly of authority or constitutional-legal resources and, should it choose, it can legislate on all aspects of central–local relations. It also has a preponderance of financial resources.

For its part, the national community possesses, as do central departments, informational, organizational and political resources. The amount of influence they bestowed varied from issue to issue and from policy area to policy area. Thus the associations provided a considerable amount of information and expertise to the DoE on local expenditure and yet it has remained the junior partner in this policy area, frequently bemoaning its lack of resources – for example, staff, technology. Control of information and expertise enabled the National Farmers' Union to contain the diversity of interests within its own ranks and thereby facilitate its influence on government policy (Self and Storing, 1962). The associations are not so adept. For grant negotiations, the associations depend on the DoE for information provided by individual local authorities.

The situation in other policy areas is less perverse. For organic change, the associations did provide information on the likely pitfalls of implementing the policy, although this information did not necessarily enable the associations to influence the government. The most appropriate metaphor is the associations having a great deal of ammunition but no way of firing it. They relied on the central departments to provide the gun – hence their influence was indirect. Certainly the departments needed the information but the associations did not have a monopoly. The professional societies were also a valuable source. Thus, to a significant degree, the ACC could be viewed as a resource of the DES in its bargaining with the DoE. Information by itself only enables the associations to make life unpleasant for central departments: in no sense does it enable them to impose binding constraints.

Because the DoE had strong opponents in the DES and the DHSS, there was some scope for the associations to influence the policy of organic change. In particular, the ACC could attempt to brief opponents of organic change, which is precisely what it did. Although the Stewart report, with the DES as its sponsor, penetrated to the highest levels within government, it was enthusiastically sought and used because it supported predetermined positions. Its intrinsic merits were of less importance than the context into which it was introduced. The relationship between central departments and the associations did not, in the case of the DES, spring from their dependence upon the associations for information and expertise. The DoE, however, depended upon the associations – both the ACC and the ADC – for practical information about the problems of organic change, and if the ACC was not forthcoming with solutions the ADC was prepared to supply both.

Less obvious, but of considerable importance, were the political resources of the associations – or, to be precise, groupings within the ADC. Local political leaders commanded access to government not only through the associations but also through the political parties. For the 'big nine' and the 'twenty-two', the Labour Party was an invaluable avenue for pursuing their demands. The Regional and Local Government Sub-Committee, the local government conference and the regional consultations provided formal venues for discussions. Equally, they facilitated informal contacts at the highest political level. It is difficult to assess the positive gains which can be attributed solely to this channel of access but, at the very least, it ensured that demands could not be ignored or rejected by default.

The associations may have some needed resources but they have no monopoly and, indeed, within the national community itself, they are not necessarily the paramount organizations. LACSAB was an organization with an equivalent range of resources. The informational resources of the individual associations in industrial relations are limited, not because they lack the necessary competence, still less because they are ignorant of the negotiating process, but because they have neither the staff nor the time. It is not being implied that LACSAB has a surfeit of resources, only that it has relatively more resources. As its role has developed, LACSAB has been under considerable strain. It is not concerned with pay negotiations alone but also with advising local authorities on all aspects of manpower and industrial relations. The associations were slow to recognize the increasing salience of pay and manpower issues – a state of affairs reflected in the relatively recent changes in their own internal arrangements, in their reluctance to approve staff increases for LACSAB, and in their appointment of relatively 'junior' representatives to the board.

It was reasonable to presume, therefore, that LACSAB would be able to defend its interests to some effect and this proved to be the case. And, without wishing to minimize the importance of its independent financial resources, a decisive factor in the constitutional crisis was LACSAB's political resources. The associations' political leaders could not claim to be *the* representative voice of local government in calling for reforms and their case was correspondingly weaker. Of all the other organizations within the national community, only the LGTB and LAMSAC have the resources to mount a challenge to the pre-eminence of the associations should the need arise, and it is not obvious that they could do so as effectively.

One point seems crystal clear: in a direct, tangible sense LACSAB was independent of the associations. Multiple constituents and sources of income, control over informational resources on industrial relations, its own political resources, distinct geographical location and the nature of the pay bargaining process virtually guaranteed that LACSAB's actions would conflict with the interests of one or other of its constituents. This capacity for independent action has to be clearly distinguished from the accountability of LACSAB. The mechanisms for holding LACSAB to account for its action have always existed, even if they have not been invoked. Independence and accountability became indistinguishable during the constitutional crisis not because of any change in LACSAB's behaviour but because of the increased salience of pay negotiations for the associations.

In short, for all their resources, the associations were not necessarily pre-eminent within the national community. Resources may admit one to the game but they are a minimum condition of effectiveness: they do not necessarily give influence over policy. Indeed, of all the resources of the national community, only one seems to be 'needed' by the government – the political resource of compliance. The government prefers consultation because shared interests, mutual advantage and agreement facilitate policy-making. If such agreement is forthcoming, if local government complies with the policy, then its reward is a considerable say in the detailed design and implementation of the policy. It is helping the centre realize its policy goals. But in the absence of compliance, and *pace* the other resources of the national community, the government has the option of coercion and it can proceed without the national community. The national community's opposition has an irritant value – it can impose delays – but at the cost of losing its influence on the details of the policy. It may generate a climate of opinion in which its members individually thwart the implementation of the policy. But it is the individual local authority which controls this, local government's, ultimate sanction of confrontation and non-compliance. Unlike a trade union, no association can call a national strike: there is only plant-level action. Whether or not the resources of the national community are commensurate with its tasks (see below), these resources do not allow it to impose binding constraints on the government. The fundamental inequalities in the relationship noted at several junctures are manifest in the distribution of resources.

Any understanding of the changing role of the national community presupposes an understanding of the context within which it operates. The interventions of the national government environment and relations within the national local government system set the boundaries which constrain action by the national community. But not all the constraints are external to the national community. This section has set out the framework for explaining the fortunes of the national community. The next step is to turn the telescope around – to narrow the focus on to the effectiveness of the national community.

CONSTRAINTS AND CLEAVAGES

The purpose of this section is essentially classificatory. At numerous points, individual constraints and cleavages have been discussed. Here they will be drawn together in a systematic fashion. With both an analysis of the context and classification of the contraints, it will then be possible to attempt an overall assessment of the influence of the national community. As before, the discussion parallels that in Chapter 2 and, in this case, Figure 2.2. The classification of constraints and cleavages is given in Figure 10.1.

	Constraints		*Cleavages*
1	Representation generalizing politicization intermediation	1	Type of authority inter-association intra-association
2	Members voluntary NCLG 'closed' alternative access aggregation	2	Political party inter- intra-
3	Organization resources strategic capability internal structure control of joint bodies	3	Urban v. Rural
4	Policy communities issue-scope 'technocrat' v. 'topocrat'	4	Functional diversity
5	National government environment reactive incorporation control – direct indirect factorizing	5	National v. local priorities

Figure 10.1 *Constraints and cleavages within the national community of local government.*

Representation

Under this heading, the cleavage of type of authority and the constraints of generalizing, politicization and intermediation will be discussed briefly, primarily because most of the points should be obvious by now.

First, no association speaks for only one type of local authority and there are marked differences of interests between associations. Agreement within an association can be elusive and agreement between the associations can take on the aspect of a mirage. Presenting one view which encompasses this diversity – generalizing – can prove peculiarly difficult.

The cleavage of political party is of more recent origin. Since reorganization, there has been a substantial extension of party politics. Politicization is now the norm, not the exception, and, in the eyes of some participants, party interests have supplanted local government interests. Indisputably, party politics has served to complicate the internal and external relationships of the national community.

Third, there is the constraint of whom the national community is representing. Because they are *national* organizations, the associations necessarily have close links with other national organizations. This simple fact of life breeds the danger that, rather than representing the views of local government to the centre, they represent the views of the centre to local government and turn diverse local views into a uniform national position. The role of the national community could be described, therefore, not as representation but as intermediation – literally 'coming between' central and local government.

Finally, the constraints discussed so far are further complicated by the cleavage between urban and rural local authorities. Obviously, this cleavage can be seen as another way of talking about the interests of the different classes of authorities, but such an equation is misleading. The different interests of the various classes of local authority could be said to reside in their different range of functions. The urban/rural distinction suggests that, irrespective of the functions of the local authority (be it metropolitan or shire district), they have certain fundamental interests in common. As Sharpe (1978, p. 98) argues, there is a positive relationship between urbanness and the need for public services, and the current distribution of functions is not functionally appropriate. The distinctive needs of urban areas have been articulated very clearly within the ADC, where the demands of the 'big nine' and the 'twenty-two' for a reallocation of functions have been a persistent feature of its political landscape. Such demands have been supported by the ADC, but there has been the equally persistent worry that such support may drive a wedge between large (that is, urban) and small (that is, rural) members.

The distinction between urban and rural also complicates the party political cleavage. Conservatives in rural areas – and independents have not disappeared – differ in a number of significant ways from their urban counterparts. The degree of party organization and discipline in urban areas is markedly greater. Also, the nationalization of local politics is, in many instances, a nationalization in name only. Both the Conservative and the Labour parties have to manage national–local splits. The attempts by the Conservative Party to make organic change a partisan issue were greatly complicated by the support of local Conservative leaders for Peter Shore's proposals. The party leaders on the associations are considerably more vulnerable to such nationalization pressures than their counterparts in the localities.

Members
Although all the organizations in the national community receive many requests for information and circulate a great deal of advice to their member local authorities, none the less its links with them are distant. First, the national community can appear to be part of the Whitehall 'village community' and, therefore, of limited value to the individual local authority. Second, the involvement of individual local authorities in the national community is limited by the latter's lack of resources, leading, yet again, to the adoption of a reactive stance: the associations supply information and advice on demand. Third, the membership of the associations – that is, individual local authorities – do not have systematic procedures for receiving reports from their representatives or advisers. In fact, the only common example of reporting back is that by advisers to their professional associations! Fourth, party allegiance, size and geography have a marked effect on participation. Accordingly, it could be argued that the national community is at best 'distant' or at worst 'closed' – that is, it has developed its own routines for defining and dealing with problems and through such self-absorption it has become unresponsive to the needs and demands of members. The associations are not necessarily the most important channel of communication for individual local authorities. Particular departments can have stronger contacts with their policy community. Large local authorities have their own direct channels of communication with central departments and bypass the national community. In other words, participation in the national community is limited to a few senior members and advisers. Within an individual local authority, the national community is virtually irrelevant for members and officers.

These remarks are not heretical but reflect the basic dilemma for the national community that local government is *local* government. Its actions are legitimate because they are taken by locally elected councillors on issues of local concern. A national community of local government *is* a contradiction in terms. The associations have to generalize when their defence of local government lies in diversity.

They have to develop a perspective on national issues whereas their members' main concern is local problems. Little wonder, therefore, that the national community can seem to be divorced from its members.

Organization
Another class of constraints arises from a group's organization and, here, salvation can lie in the group's own hands. The national community faces some organizational problems.

First, the scale of resources available to the associations is limited. For example, in grant negotiations, the associations have relied upon the DoE for much of the data and most of the analysis underlying the decisions on grant distribution. The effects of the lateness of the DoE's submissions would be lessened if the associations were more self-reliant in obtaining data and analysis. It is commonly argued that the associations are constrained by their lack of resources but, if advisers and the staff of the joint bodies are added to associations' secretariats, the national community seems remarkably well endowed with resources – certainly compared with other pressure groups (see Chapter 3, pp. 95–6 above). However, the national community has an intensive involvement in a wide range of policy areas: its resources may be large but so are its tasks. Second, a substantial proportion of its staffing resources are 'part-time'. Officer advisers are full-time officials in local authorities. The joint bodies are a shared resource which are not for the use of a particular association (see below). Irrespective of comparisons with other groups, therefore, there is considerable pressure on the resources of the associations.

Second, current resources are not effectively utilized. For example, the associations have close contacts with the Houses of Parliament and provide the usual information and briefings for the media. But they have been reluctant to mount public campaigns. In spite of recent improvements in their public relations, and the AMA's 'Keep it Local' campaign, such tactics remain the last resort and are seen as 'second best' to 'normal' consultation. The associations continue to support central departments by providing information and advice on policies with which they disagree. The convict is his own jailer. Constraints are self-imposed.

Third, the internal organization of the associations can hamper their work. For example, the committee system of the associations encourages an over-involvement with detail and a tendency to ratify decisions rather than focus on long-term policy considerations. Just as local government has introduced corporate management to facilitate planning – albeit in many different forms with differing degrees of success – the associations similarly need to develop their capacity to innovate or initiate policies. The strategic capabilities of the existing structure seem unduly limited.

Fourth, the associations can only speak for their members, they cannot commit them. An individual local authority can disregard with almost total impunity an association decision. There is nothing unique in this situation – the TUC regularly faces the problem. However, to the extent that central government is aware of the associations' inability to 'deliver', the latter's negotiating position is weakened.

Central departments have acted to strengthen the position of the associations and displayed a manifest desire to 'aggregate'. These observations suggest that larger associations may well be in the interests of central departments, making the associations better able to respond quickly to central initiatives but contrary to the interests of member authorities. If diversity of needs is a key element in the rationale for *local* government, a *national* representative system which generalizes the interests of local government *and* curtails access for individual local authorities can be seen as a centralizing, homogenizing force. The inability to 'deliver' members is not, after all, a problem for the members but for the associations and central departments. The constraint of organization cannot be divorced, therefore, from the constraints of either representation or the national government environment (see below).

In addition there are a number of organizational constraints arising from the links between the associations and other members of the national community. In spite of the conflict within the national community, the existing links can be accurately described as a 'confederation'. Co-operation is as prevalent as conflict. Ironically, the extent of co-operation poses problems. There are nine joint bodies to be co-ordinated and controlled. It is not surprising that the associations have felt they were receiving less co-operation than their entitlement: hence the associations' attempt to revise the constitution of LACSAB. The joint bodies are an important resource for the associations, but that potential is not always realized.

The problems surrounding the joint bodies do not stem from the difficulties of co-ordinating nine separate organizations. There are more fundamental cleavages. First, a number of the joint bodies serve multiple constituencies. Second, because of their distinct interests, each association wants advice specific to its own needs: they want exclusive access to and control over resources. The distinctive feature of joint bodies is, of course, that they are a shared resource. A number of joint ventures have foundered on the desire of one association for exclusive resources – hence the demise of the joint secretariat of the CCLGF and CIPFA's technical support service. Finally, the larger joint bodies are separate organizations, which have, over the years, developed their own appreciation of problems and ways of dealing with them. Because of their own, often extensive, contacts with local authorities, they feel that they too can speak with authority about the needs and problems of local authorities. Such independence of views, particularly when it appears to be translated into policy decisions, is unacceptable to the associations. These comments apply not only to the officials of joint bodies: the representatives nominated by the associations seem to have a chameleon-like quality of taking on the colouring of their immediate environment. That which has been agreed in an association committee may well be abandoned when the 'hat' of a joint body has been donned.

The national community faces, therefore, a range of organizational problems. Whether or not the associations have limited resources and strategic capabilities depends in part on one's definition of the interests of members. The capacity to respond to central initiatives may be more important to central departments than to individual local authorities. Similarly, the problem of co-ordination is but the problem of multiple interests within the national community in another guise. The key difference about many of the problems discussed in this section is that they appear to be within the control of the national community.

Policy communities

A key feature of central–local relations in Britain is the existence of 'policy communities' which limit the involvement of the national community in any particular policy area. The key actors within the policy communities are the professions and not the associations. A vital resource available to the associations is the professional officer as adviser as well as the various professional associations. The relationship between advisers, professional associations and policy communities is a source of several constraints on the national community.

First, for the 'technocrat', the national community of local government is only one point at which pressure can be exerted. Of greater relevance is the policy community, be it education, fire, police or social work. The constraint on the national community is, therefore, its relatively limited influence on the policy communities and associated professions. For the 'topocrat', the national community is the natural focus of pressure and the problem is to design a more appropriate relationship. Advisers remain full-time officials in their local authority with consequent limitations on the time and energy available for association work. Only infrequently are officers seconded to the associations for short periods of time and only a few officers are able to devote substantial time to association business. Once again, the issue of the exclusive control of resources raises its head.

Advisers of both types, whether in an individual capacity or through a professional association, are potentially valuable resources which remain underexploited, either because the national community is peripheral to, or conflicts with, their interests, or because the form of the relationship is deemed inappropriate.

It could be argued that it is not the function of the national community to exert influence within policy communities. Its function is to represent the general interests of local government. This argument points to an important paradox. Any policy initiative will have repercussions for the finance and staffing of local government. Leaving service policy to the technocratic professions would constrain seriously the national community in carrying out its primary functions. But the national community cannot attend to all policy issues if only because of the lack of time and expertise. And the basic problem of defining the 'interests of local government' remains. The broader the definition of these interests the greater the pressure on available resources. But the narrower the definition, the greater the probability that the general interests will be compromised.

The national government environment

Perhaps the most common criticism of central departments is that they are forever seeking to control local authorities, often adopting conflicting and contradictory stances. Direct control is obviously a major constraint on the national community. But it is equally important to ascertain the extent to which local government, through its associations, *voluntarily concedes* control to central government. Underlying this question, and the issue of control in general, is the conflict between national and local priorities. The furore over grant and the level of local expenditure epitomize this conflict, and it is endemic in central–local relations. If local authorities exist to make and adapt policies to local circumstances and to respond to local needs and demands, the potential for conflict with a central government concerned with the overall needs of the economy is obviously great. The pressure on local government to give priority to national needs can be increased if the national community is overly sensitive to the centre: it could be said to be acting against the interests of localities. In order to explore the extent and effects of such indirect control, it is necessary to examine four interrelated constraints.

The pressure of work on the associations in particular is considerable, their resources are limited and their political leaders have to divide time between the associations and their local authorities. This combination of circumstances, which occurs also for the larger joint bodies, creates the first problem – the reactive stance of the national community. Thus the associations do not establish their own priorities for discussion and negotiation with central government but react to central government's initiatives. At times, everything which arrives on the desk from central government seems urgent, even though an outsider may have difficulty appreciating its significance. The short-term pressure is continuous, and there is the ever-present danger of minutiae swamping both current priorities and the attempt to develop a longer-term strategy.

A corollary of this situation is that central government sets the agenda for discussions between central and local government. The most obvious example is local government finance. Although the national community can influence the implementation of policy, it only rarely takes the initiative – for example, the AMA's work on urban problems and public expenditure. Generally, the content and timing of any policy are decided by central departments and the national community simply accepts them as facts of life. Thus the associations have not pursued issues, such as local income tax, which are potentially beneficial to members.

Third, but related to central government's control of the agenda, the associations' role in national working parties and committees is defined by the centre. Thus, the CCLGF improved co-ordination *between central departments*, suggesting that the CCLGF exists for central government, not local government. A major worry expressed by many local government participants concerned the dangers of co-option – that, by participating in the CCLGF, they legitimized central policy. Even though they may have disagreed with many aspects of the grant settlement, the very fact of participation created the impression that the local government side of the CCLGF was 'selling the cuts to local government'. Certainly, consultation, not co-option, was the major reason for local government's original agreement to participate.

All the foregoing points in one direction – that indirect controls are an important weapon in central government's armoury. Attention is rightly focused on the statutory and financial controls available to central government. But, through its continuous involvement with central departments, as in the case of pay negotiations, the national community comes to share the assumptions of the centre. It accepts that central government determines the level of public expenditure, that it sets the agenda, that it stipulates the terms of reference of consultative bodies, and that their role is to react to and advise upon central government's initiatives. To the extent that this situation exists, it is realistic to talk of local government's 'responsibility ethic' and of control by consent.

The problems which the national government environment poses for the national community are indeed formidable. Adopting a proactive rather than a reactive stance, participating in setting the agenda rather than advising on invited issues, being consulted rather than co-opted, and resisting the subtle pressures associated with indirect controls are not easy transformations. And yet they form an essential part of the attempt to represent members effectively.

It will greatly facilitate the analysis if the interrelationship between the several constraints and cleavages discussed above is briefly summarized. The description of the constraints of representation, members' organization, policy communities and national government environment all had their roots in fundamental cleavages. Thus the problem of representation arose from the divergence of interests within associations and between the member organizations of the national community; from party political allegiances and from the different needs of urban and rural areas. The problem of the national government environment had its roots in the different priorities of national and local governments. Such differences led central departments to minimize variety by co-option and indirect control. The variety of local priorities, coupled with the pressure from the centre for information and advice, led the associations to adopt a reactive posture. The problem of organization also had its roots in the conflicting needs of centre and locality. Central government needs a strong national community capable of responding to its initiatives whereas individual local authorities suffer from the 'generalizing' of the interests of local government such consultation necessarily involves. Moreover, organizational problems within the national community are further compounded by the conflict between controlling one's own resources and sharing them and by the multiple constituencies which several joint bodies have to serve. The problem of policy communities has its roots in the conflict between the service-specific demands and needs of the technocrat which are articulated through the policy communities, and the concern of the national community (and the topocratic professions) with the range of local government's activities. Finally, the problem of members reflects yet again the national–local dilemma of the national community. The national community by definition has to be conscious of the centre's needs and problems, with the attendant dangers of incorporation, whilst the individual local authority has multiple channels of access to the centre and is concerned with local problems. The national community can appear distant to its member authorities.

Bemoaning the self-interest of the associations is almost an industry in itself. But protecting a type of local authority and commitment to party are not examples of myopia or misguided wilfulness. It would be a strange association which did not defend its members and an unprepossessing political leader who was not committed to his party. To criticize the self-interest of an association and to assert the merits of speaking for 'the interests of local government' is to underestimate the elusiveness of those interests and usually to assert that one has the secret key to their definition. The national community inevitably reflects the local government system it is supposed to represent. It cannot change the structure of local government: it speaks for that structure as it exists. Many, if not all, the cleavages discussed stem from the current structure and functions of local government. With these general comments in mind, it is possible to essay a general assessment of the effectiveness of the national community.

EFFECTIVENESS: THE PRICE OF LEGITIMACY

The original discussion of effectiveness identified a range of criteria drawn from the literature on pressure groups and also noted that any assessment of the national community would have to consider the trend towards aggregation based on, and the extent of integration within, the national community. In brief, the effectiveness of, and the extent of integration within, the national community is constrained by the range of cleavages it encompasses, and the attempt to create 'peak associations' has foundered on the same conflicts of interest. But, employing the criteria discussed in Chapter 2, it is possible to offer a number of caveats to this harsh assessment.

Group characteristics and 'operative attitude'
The national community is a legitimate, managerial community: that is, it has a recognized right to consultation on a range of issues, most notably grant, pay negotiations and local government reorganization. This simple fact ensures extensive access to government departments and ministers. Compared with a vast range of pressure groups, therefore, it has to be judged effective: its voice is heard, if not necessarily heeded, at negotiating tables where many groups have yet to win a seat.

However, assessments of influence are notoriously difficult and only relatively easier when analysis is focused on determinate outcomes. The benefits which accrue to a group from continuous involvement can be substantial and yet involve no identifiable changes in policy outcomes. Influence is exercised through the 'rule of anticipated reactions': that is, issues do not form a part of the policy agenda because of the opposition it is thought they will provoke. Similarly, influence is exercised in the selection of items for the policy agenda. If anything, the case studies illustrate the *absence* of this form of influence. Thus, such policies as the Conservative reforms of the grant system were bound to provoke substantial opposition, just as the Labour government's unitary grant proposals had done in 1977, and yet they were introduced. Similarly, central government controls the policy agenda and determines the timing of policy – for example, the timing of the reorganization of local government. However, this form of influence cannot be dismissed. The consensus within educational policy-making serves to limit the policy agenda and the associations are clearly a major, if not the sole, component in sustaining that consensus. If this form of influence is not widely exercised by the national community, none the less its existence in particular policy areas cannot be ruled out.

The discussion of organizational and member constraints is also a discussion of the limits to effectiveness arising from group characteristics. Thus, effectiveness is limited by the voluntary nature of membership, the inability to regulate members, the pressure on resources from the range of demands of both centre and localities and the reluctance to mobilize member authorities.

Characteristics of the policy process

The effectiveness of the national community varies from policy area to policy area and from issue to issue within those areas. Involvement in pay and grant negotiations was more extensive than in other policy areas. Equally, their involvement in other policy communities is more extensive when the issues involve the structure and resources of local government rather than service specific policy. However, these generalizations must be qualified, for involvement also varies over time. Thus, in pay negotiations, the discretion of the national community varied with the government's prices and incomes policy and influence on grant negotiations was more substantial in the late 1960s than towards the end of the period under study.

Such changes hinged on government policy for managing the economy. This policy severely limited the national community's ability to influence outcomes. The asymmetric nature of the relationship between central government and the national community is not unique – the TUC and the CBI operate under the same handicaps to effective influence. The exercise of executive authority and fragmentation are the characteristics of the policy process which limit the influence of the national community.

This discussion of the structural power of the centre courts the danger of overstating the extent of integration between central departments. Conflicts of interest between the Treasury and the service departments (and between the service departments) are not unknown and when they exist central departments can be the allies of the national community, enabling it to affect the final decision. Similarly the varying characteristics of policy communities affect the national community's effectiveness. First, 'departmental philosophies' differ markedly not only between but also within central departments. The potential for influence is obviously greater with departments adopting a consultative style (for example, the DES and DoE) than with those of a more authoritarian, closed disposition (Home Office).

Second, the policy-making process differs between policy areas. At its simplest, some areas have an established policy community (for example, education) whereas others remain highly fragmented (for example, leisure and recreation). Some areas have established institutions and procedures (for example, fire) whereas integration in other policy areas is based on shared ideas, values and knowledge (for example, education). The effectiveness of the national community will depend on the range of legitimate interests with which it has to compete in a policy community; the extent of its involvement in that community – regular or intermittent; and the range of its commitments across a series of policy areas, given the finite resources at its disposal.

The government may have the capacity to manipulate policy communities but central departments are dependent on the national community for information and compliance – a dependence which varies with the stage in the policy process. Central departments are non-executant authorities and they rely on the national community to provide advance warning of, and feedback on, difficulties. At its crudest, therefore, the national community is most effective at the implementation stages of policies for which it holds a monopoly of information. Needless to add, no particular series of events ever fits this formulation. The national community rarely holds a monopoly of information. Alternative sources include the professions and individual local authorities controlled by the same party as the government of the day or, indeed, local authorities which simply agree with the government's policy. And, whilst it is analytically useful to distinguish the implementation stage of the policy process, it has become a truism to note that policy can be redesigned in the course of its implementation. Feedback from the national community can be described, therefore, as an exercise in policy initiation.

Policies not only vary in terms of process, content and stage, but also in the degree of controversy they arouse, especially party political controversy. To the extent that the governing party is committed to an explicit policy and that policy is caught in the arena of adversarial politics, so the limits to the national community's influence increase. Conversely, non-controversial policies, consolidating legislation, regulations on the implementation of a policy and indeed any relatively routinised policy area will be more open to national community influence.

Characteristics of the structure of government

Any distinction between structure and process is artificial. Thus policy communities are sustained by the departmental structure of government and rules such as 'the government's right to govern', and the asymmetric relationships within policy communities are such well entrenched features of British government that they could be described as part of the structure. However, three additional points can be noted under this heading. First, local government interests in the peripheral regions are institutionalized by central structures with concomitant restrictions on the constituency of the national community. Second, the cleavages within the national community have their roots in the structure and functions of local government determined by the government in the Local Government Act 1972 and are, therefore, from the national community's standpoint, substantially immutable. Without a further reorganization of local government, the real difference of interests between types of authority will have to be accommodated: they cannot be removed. Third, through majority party control of Parliament, the government has a monopoly of constitutional resources. This monopoly enables the government to allocate authoritatively functions between different units of government and to change unilaterally the rules of the game in central–local relations, a power which is crucial to the asymmetric relations between policy communities. In short, the government has the option of direction – an option totally denied to the national community in relation to both central government and its own membership.

Aggregation

Four conclusions are, hopefully, obvious. First, during the 1970s, both central departments *and* the national community have attempted to make the associations the 'peak' representative organizations of local government. Second, the creation of peak associations has involved not only the attempt to funnel contact between individual local authorities and central departments through the national community but also the attempt by the national community to reinforce its influence within policy communities (for example, the 'reform' of CFBAC, the abolition of the AEC and its replacement by CLEA, the emergence of ESG(E)). The past decade has witnessed considerable instability in relationships, with the centre 'recruiting' the national community as an ally in guarding the purse strings against the expansive policy communities and then abandoning the attempt in favour of a directive strategy which, in turn, provoked resistance from policy communities. Third, the extent of integration within the national community is severely constrained by the cleavages it encompasses. Finally, the strategy of aggregation and incorporation has foundered on the multiplicity of cleavages within the national community. Whether the example is the CCLGF, pay bargaining, relations with members, or the peripheral regions, the same conclusion emerges: the associations may be 'licensed' by government but they have no 'monopoly' of representation, they cannot 'regulate' their members and they can only 'generalize' when no one interest is directly threatened. The analysis of the limits to the effectiveness of the national community is also an analysis of the limits to the strategy of aggregation and incorporation.

CONCLUSIONS

In short, the effectiveness of the national community is subject to a complex set of interlocking constraints. Indeed, the overall assessment is so negative that it is essential to redress the balance. By focusing on the limits to effectiveness, it is almost inevitable that an ineffectual picture will emerge. It is important to stress, therefore, the first point in the preceding section: the national community is legitimized. A substantial proportion of the matters upon which it is consulted are not partisan, controversial issues. The interests of the constituent organizations of the national community are not so continuously divergent that compromises are impossible. The policy-making process emphasizes accommodation and consensus, not conflict, and this characterization applies to relations within the national community as well as with central departments and policy communities.

The national community has had its successes. Peter Shore was persuaded not to introduce unitary grant. The associations obtained amendments to the first version of the Local Government, Planning and Land Bill and the ACC gained some minor modifications to the final version. The referendum proposal in the first version of the 1982 Local Government Bill was dropped and the proposal of a specific grant for education was withdrawn. The associations were not the only opponents of the various proposals nor were they on all occasions the most influential opponents but, given the aura of doom and gloom which has surrounded them since 1979, it is worth noting that they have had some, albeit limited, influence. And this cryptic balance sheet omits the detailed, almost daily, discussions on the details of a policy. But the issues which command attention – for example, the controversies surrounding central grant – are the ones by which the national community is judged and they are the very issues upon which agreement is most elusive and where the constraints and cleavages have their greatest impact.

The national community is not ineffectual, therefore, but equally it is not a decisive or determinate force: it is a legitimized consultative channel with neither the resources nor, in many instances, the desire to challenge government. Conversely, for the bulk of the period under study, the government sought consultations not confrontation: it preferred action based on shared interests. It may have sought to manipulate those interests but until 1979 it did not seek to override them. In such circumstances, the national community can be seen as a constraint on central departments. The description 'post office' underestimates the effectiveness of the national community just as the description 'part of the constitution' overestimates it. The truth is far more prosaic: it is a domesticated pressure group in a governmental system where executive authority and the interdependence of groups and government are in continual tension. The current assertions of executive authority highlight the vulnerability of group influence in the short term until the unintended consequences of imposed policies highlights, in turn, the dependence of government on group compliance.

Nor can the final assessment focus solely on the effects of the national community on central departments. The discussions of both members and policy communities identified an innovative, rather than reactive, role for the national community *vis-à-vis* local government.

Thus members saw the national community as a forum for sharing experience and ideas: it provided a framework within which an individual local authority could locate its problems. Together the policy communities and the national community constitute a national local government system, which defines the parameters of 'good policy'. Its innovative role may be diffuse, precise attributions of responsibility for specific policies may be elusive, but none the less it plays such a role. As a legitimated part of the structure of government embedded in extensive consultative networks, the national community may not exercise veto powers, it may be vulnerable to the exercise of executive authority, but it has become an established intervening tier of representation capable of influencing, directly and indirectly, both government and its own constituency.

The costs of legitimacy are respectability and responsibility but they are also its rewards. The advantages of continuous access have to be weighed against the need to play by the centre's rules if the access is to be preserved. The national community of local government is not just a contradiction in terms, it is compounded of multiple contradictions. It is both local government's intermediate tier of representation and the flawed institutional network at the heart of centre–local relations. It is the reluctant tool of centre and locality and yet, if governments should seek local compliance rather than control, there would be pressure for some such intermediate tier. Central–local relations over the past two decades have revolved round the tension between executive authority and interdependence, and the national community has mirrored every contradiction and remained *the* legitimated consultative channel for local government. Its survival is the despair of the tidy-minded administrator and a miracle of the imperfections of government.

REFERENCES AND BIBLIOGRAPHY

ADC (1976), 'Evidence of the Association of District Councils', in Layfield Committee, Appendix 2, *Evidence by the Local Authority Associations* (London: HMSO).

AEC (1953), *The First Fifty Years* (London: Association of Education Committees).

Alexander, A. (1982), *Local Government in Britain since Reorganisation* (London: Allen & Unwin).

Allison, G. (1971), *Essence of Decision* (Boston, Mass.: Little, Brown).

AMA (1976), 'Evidence of the Association of Metropolitan Authorities', in Layfield Committee, Appendix 2, *Evidence by the Local Authority Associations* (London: HMSO).

AMC (1972), *The Association of Municipal Corporations 1873–1973* (London: Association of Municipal Corporations).

Ashford, D. (1982), *French Dogmatism and British Pragmatism* (London: Allen & Unwin).

Barnett, J. (1982), *Inside the Treasury* (London: Deutsch).

Barnett, M. J. (1969), *The Politics of Legislation: 1957 Rent Act* (London: Weidenfeld & Nicolson).

Barnhouse, L. P. (1972), 'The impact of local authority associations on local government reorganisation in England 1966–72', MA thesis, University of West Virginia.

Barrett, S., and Hill, M. J. (1982), 'Report to the SSRC Central–Local Government Relations Panel on the "core" or theoretical component of the research on implementation', Social Science Research Council, London, mimeo.

Barzun, J., and Graff, F. II. (1970), *The Modern Researcher* (New York: Harcourt Brace, rev. edn).

Beck, J. M. (1971), 'A history of parish councils and their representative associations 1894–1970', PhD thesis, University of Kent.

Beer, S. H. (1966), *Modern British Politics* (London: Faber & Faber, 2nd edn).

Beer, S. H. (1978), 'Federalism, nationalism and democracy in America', *American Political Science Review*, vol. 72, pp. 9–21.

Benson, J. K. (1975), 'The interorganizational network as a political economy', *Administrative Science Quarterly*, vol. 20, pp. 229–49.

Benson, J. K. (1982), 'Networks and policy sectors: a framework for extending interorganizational analysis', in *Interorganizational Coordination*, ed. D. Rogers and D. Whitten (Ames, Iowa: Iowa State University Press).

Birch, A. H. (1964), *Representative and Responsible Government* (London: Allen & Unwin).

Blackaby, F. T. (ed.) (1978), *British Economic Policy 1960–74* (Cambridge: Cambridge University Press).

Blackburn, J. S. (1979), *Presentation and Interpretation by Local Government of White Papers on Public Expenditure* (Birmingham: Institute of Local Government Studies).

Blackstone, G. V. (1957), *A History of the British Fire Service* (London: Routledge & Kegan Paul).

Blackstone, T., and Crispin, A. (1980), 'Education', in *The Economics of Prosperity*, ed. D. Blake and P. Ormerod (London: Grant McIntyre), pp. 146–71.

Bramley, G., and Stewart, M. (1981), 'Implementing public expenditure cuts', in *Policy and Action*, ed. S. Barrett and C. Fudge (London: Methuen), pp. 39–63.

Brand, J. A. (1974), *Local Government Reform in England 1883–1974* (London: Croom Helm).

Bridges, Sir Edward (1971), 'Portrait of a profession', in *Style in Administration*, ed. R. A. Chapman and A. Dunsire (London: Allen & Unwin), pp. 44–60.

Budge, I., *et al.* (1983), *The New British Political System* (London: Longman).

Buxton, R. J. (1970), *Local Government* (Harmondsworth: Penguin).

Byrne, E. M. (1974), *Planning and Educational Inequality* (Windsor: NFER).

CACFOA (1980), *Whither the Future?* (London: Chief and Assistant Chief Fire Officers' Association).

Cawson, A. (1978), 'Pluralism, corporatism and the role of the state', *Government and Opposition*, vol. 13, pp. 178–98.

Cawson, A., and Saunders, P. (1983), 'Corporatism, competitive politics and the class struggle', in *Capital and Politics*, ed. R. King (London: Routledge & Kegan Paul).

Central Policy Review Staff (1977), *Relations Between Central Government and Local Authorities* (London: HMSO).

Clarke, R. T. (1981), *Personal Social Services Council 1973–80: The Case History of an Advisory Non-Governmental Organisation* (London: PSSC).

Clarke, Sir Richard (1971), *New Trends in Government* (London: HMSO).

Coates, R. D. (1972), *Teachers' Unions and Interest Group Politics* (Cambridge: Cambridge University Press).

Cockburn, C. (1977), *The Local State* (London: Pluto Press).

Connolly, M. (1982), 'Central–local government relations in Northern Ireland', Discussion Paper No. 2, Research Project on Comparative Central–Local Government Relations Within the United Kingdom, Ulster Polytechnic.

Cox, A. (1981), 'Corporatism as reductionism: the analytic limits of the corporatist thesis', *Government and Opposition*, vol. 16, pp. 78–95.

Crosland, S. (1982), *Tony Crosland* (London: Cape).

Cross, C. A. (1954), 'The AMC: a study of its structure', MA thesis, University of Manchester.

Crossman, R. H. S. (1975), *Diaries of a Cabinet Minister, Volume 1, Minister of Housing* (London: Cape/Hamilton).

Cunningham Committee (1971), *Report of the Cunningham Inquiry into the Work of the Fire Service*, Cmnd 4807 (London: HMSO).

Cutler, Sir Horace (1982), *The Cutler File* (London: Weidenfeld & Nicolson).

Dearlove, J. (1979), *The Reorganisation of British Local Government* (Cambridge: Cambridge University Press).

Dunleavy, P. (1980), *Urban Political Analysis* (London: Macmillan).

Dunleavy, P. (1981a), 'Professions and policy change: notes towards a model of ideological corporatism', *Public Administration Bulletin*, no. 36 (August), pp. 3–16.

Dunleavy, P. (1981b), *The Politics of Mass Housing in Britain 1945–1975* (Oxford: Clarendon Press).

Dunleavy, P. (1983a), 'The limits of local government', paper presented to the ANCAN Conference, Queens University, Kingston, 16 March.

Dunleavy, P. (1983b), 'Analysing British politics', in *Developments in British Politics*, ed. H. Drucker *et al.* (London: Macmillan) pp. 253–99.

Dunleavy, P., and Rhodes, R. A. W. (1983), 'Beyond Whitehall', in *Developments in British Politics*, ed. H. M. Drucker *et al.* (London: Macmillan), pp. 106–33.

Dunsire, A. (1975), *Administration: The Word and the Science* (London: Martin Robertson, 2nd edn).

Eckstein, H. (1975), 'Case study and theory in political science', in *Handbook of Political Science*, vol. 7, ed. F. I. Greenstein and N. Polsby (Reading, Mass.: Addison Wesley), pp. 79–137.

Eckstein, H. (1960), *Pressure Group Politics* (London: Allen & Unwin).

Elkin, S. (1975), 'Comparative urban politics and interorganisational behaviour', in *Essays on the Study of Urban Politics*, ed. K. Young (London: Macmillan), pp. 158–84.

Elliott, M. J. (1981), *The Role of Law in Central–Local Relations* (London: Social Science Research Council).

Else, P. K., and Marshall, G. P. (1979), *The Management of Public Expenditure* (London: Policy Studies Institute).

Expenditure Committee (1976), Tenth Report, *Policy Making in the Department of Education and Science* (London: HMSO).

Fenwick, K., and McBride, P. (1979), *The Government of Education* (Oxford: Martin Robertson).

Finer, S. E. (1973), 'The political power of organised labour', *Government and Opposition*, vol. 8, pp. 391–406.

Flynn, N., Leach, S., and Vielba, C. (1985), *Abolition or Reform: The GLC and the Metropolitan County Councils* (London: Allen & Unwin).

Forrester, A., Lansley, S., and Pauley, R. (1985), *Beyond Our Ken: a guide to the battle for London* (London: False Estate).

Foster, C. D., Jackman, R., and Perlman, R. (1980), *Local Government Finance in a Unitary State* (London: Allen & Unwin).

Fox, D. (1983), 'Central control and local capacity in the housing field', in *National Interests and Local Government*, ed. K. Young (London: Heinemann), pp. 82–100.

Geertz, C. (1973), *The Interpretation of Culture* (New York: Basic Books).

Giddens, A. (1974), 'Elites in the British class structure', in *Elites and Power in British Society*, ed. P. Stanworth and A. Giddens (London: Cambridge University Press), pp. 1–21.

Goodin, R. (1982), 'Banana time in British politics', *Political Studies*, vol. 30, pp. 42–55.

Grant, W. P. (1977), *Independent Local Politics in England and Wales* (Farnborough, Hants: Saxon House).

Grant, W. P. (1982), *The Political Economy of Industrial Policy* (Borough Green, Sevenoaks: Butterworth).

Grant, W. P., and Marsh, D. (1977), *The CBI* (London: Hodder & Stoughton).

Gray, C. (1981), 'The new Welsh rate support grant', *Agenda*, no. 1 (Autumn), pp. 65–79.

Greenwood, R. (1982), 'The politics of central–local relations in England and Wales, 1974–81', *West European Politics*, vol. 5, pp. 253–69.

Griffith, J. A. G. (1966), *Central Departments and Local Authorities* (London: Allen & Unwin).

Gyford, J., and James, M. (1982), 'Party political linkages between centre and locality', report to the Social Science Research Council, London, mimeo.

Gyford, J., and James, M. (1983), *National Parties and Local Politics* (London: Allen & Unwin).

Haider, D. H. (1974), *When Governments Come to Washington: Governors, Mayors and Intergovernmental Lobbying* (New York: The Free Press).

Hall, S., and Jacques, M. (eds), (1983), *The Politics of Thatcherism* (London: Lawrence & Wishart).

Halsey, A. H., Heath, A. F., and Ridge, T. M. (1980), *Origins and Destinations* (Oxford: Clarendon Press).

Hanf, K. (1978), 'Introduction', in *Interorganisational Policy-Making*, ed. K. Hanf and F. W. Scharpf (London: Sage), pp. 1–15.

Harris, R., and Shipp, P. J. (1977), *Communications Between Central and Local Government in the Management of Local Expenditure* (Coventry: Institute for Operational Research).

Hasluck, E. L. (1949), *Local Government in England* (Cambridge: Cambridge University Press).

Hayward, J. E. S. (1974), 'National aptitudes for planning in Britain, France and Italy', *Government and Opposition*, vol. 9. no. 4, pp. 397–410.

Haywood, S., and Alaszewski, A. (1980), *Crisis in the Health Service* (London: Croom Helm).

Heald, D. (1980), 'The Scottish Rate Support Grant: how different from the English and Welsh?', *Public Administration*, vol. 58, pp. 25–46.

Heclo, H. (1978), 'Issue networks and the executive establishment', in *The New American Political System*, ed. A. King (Washington, DC: American Enterprise Institute), pp. 87–124.

Heclo, H., and Wildavsky, A. (1974), *The Private Government of Public Money* (London: Macmillan).

Hepworth, N. P. (1976), *The Finance of Local Government* (London: Allen & Unwin, 3rd edn).

Hinings, C. R., Leach, S., Ranson, S., and Skelcher, C. K. (1982), 'Policy planning systems in central–local relations: Appendix C. Central–local planning in education', report to the Social Science Research Council, London, mimeo.

HMSO (1969), *In Place of Strife*, Cmnd 3888 (London: HMSO).

HMSO (1970), *New Policies for Public Spending*, Cmnd 4515 (London: HMSO).

HMSO (1972), *Public Expenditure to 1976/77*, Cmnd 5178 (London: HMSO).

HMSO (1974), *Democracy and Devolution: Proposals for Scotland and Wales*, Cmnd 5732 (London: HMSO).

HMSO (1975a), *Public Expenditure to 1978/79*, Cmnd 5879 (London: HMSO).

HMSO (1975b), *The Attack on Inflation*, Cmnd 6151 (London: HMSO).

HMSO (1976a), *Public Expenditure to 1978/80*, Cmnd 6393 (London: HMSO).

HMSO (1976b), *Cash Limits on Public Expenditure*, Cmnd 6440 (London: HMSO).

HMSO (1977a), *The Government's Expenditure Plans*, Cmnd 6721 (London: HMSO).

HMSO (1977b), *Local Government Finance*, Cmnd 6813 (London: HMSO).

HMSO (1977c), *The Attack on Inflation after 31st July 1977*, Cmnd 6882 (London: HMSO).

HMSO (1978a), *Winning the Battle Against Inflation*, Cmnd 7293 (London: HMSO).

HMSO (1978b), *The Government's Expenditure Plans 1979–80 to 1982–83*, Cmnd 7439 (London: HMSO).

HMSO (1979a), *Organic Change in Local Government*, Cmnd 7457 (London: HMSO).

HMSO (1979b), *Central Government Controls over Local Authorities*, Cmnd 7634 (London: HMSO).

HMSO (1979c), *The Government's Expenditure Plans 1980–81*, Cmnd 7746 (London: HMSO).

HMSO (1983a), *Rates*, Cmnd 9008 (London: HMSO).

HMSO (1983b), *Streamlining the Cities*, Cmnd 9063 (London: HMSO).

HM Treasury (1972), *Public Expenditure White Papers. Handbook on Methodology* (London: HMSO).

HM Treasury (1976), 'Evidence by HM Treasury', in Layfield Committee, Appendix 1, *Evidence by Government Departments* (London: HMSO).

Hogwood, B. (1979), Analysing industrial policy: a multi-perspective approach, *Public Administration Bulletin*, no. 29 (April), pp. 18–42.

Holland, R. C. (1977), 'The Fire Service today', Thirty-Third Pearson Lecture delivered to the Old Scholars Scientific Society at Whitcliffe Mount School, Cleckheaton, 5 March.

Holroyd Report (1970), *Report of the Departmental Committee on the Fire Service*, Cmnd 4371 (London: HMSO).

Home Office (1980), *Review of Fire Policy* (London: HMSO).

Hood, C. C. (1983), *The Tools of Government* (London: Macmillan).

Hood, C. C.; and Dunsire, A. (1981), *Bureaumetrics* (Farnborough: Gower).

House of Lords (1981), Select Committee on the European Communities, *14th Report, Minutes of Evidence, Session 1980–81*, HL 93 (London: HMSO).

Hughes, S. (1982), 'How the AMA works to influence the settlement', *Municipal Review*, December, pp. 149–51.

Humble, J. (1981), 'A foot in both camps', *Municipal Review*, March, p. 249.

Isaac-Henry, K. (1975), 'Local authority associations and local government reform', *Local Government Studies*, vol. 1, no. 3, pp. 1–12.

Isaac-Henry, K. (1980a), 'The Association of Municipal Corporations and the County Councils Association: a study of influences and pressures on the reorganisation of local government 1945–72', PhD thesis, University of London.

Isaac-Henry, K. (1980b), 'The English local authority associations', *Public Administrative Bulletin*, no. 33 (August), pp. 21–41.

Jackson, W. E. (1966), *Local Government in England and Wales* (Harmondsworth: Penguin, 4th edn).

James, P. H. (1980), *The Reorganisation of Secondary Education* (Windsor: NFER).

Jenkins, R. (1971), 'The reality of political power', *Sunday Times*, 17 January.

Jessop, R. (1978), 'Corporatism, parliamentarism and social democracy', in *Trends Towards Corporatist Intermediation*, ed. P. C. Schmitter and G. Lehmbruch (London: Sage).

Jordan, G. (1981), 'Iron triangles, woolly corporatism and elastic nets: images of the policy process', *Journal of Public Policy*, vol. 1, pp. 95–123.

Jordan, A. G. (1983), *Corporatism: The Unity and Utility of the Concept*, Strathclyde Papers on Government and Politics No. 13 (Glasgow: University of Strathclyde).

Keating, M. (1982), 'The debate on regionalism', in *Regional Government in England*, ed. B. Hogwood and M. Keating (Oxford: Clarendon Press), pp. 235–54.

Keating, M., Midwinter, A., and Taylor, P. (1982), 'Central–Local Government Relations in Scotland: The Background', Research Project on Comparative Central–Local Government Relations Within the United Kingdom, Discussion Paper No. 1 (Glasgow: University of Strathclyde).

Keith-Lucas, B., and Richards, P. G. (1978), *A History of Local Government in the Twentieth Century* (London: Allen & Unwin).

Kellner, P., and Lord Crowther-Hunt (1980), *The Civil Servants: An Inquiry into Britain's Ruling Class* (London: Macdonald).

Keohane, R. O., and Nye, J. S. (1977), *Power and Interdependence* (Boston, Mass: Little, Brown).

Kimber, R., and Richardson, J. J. (eds) (1974), *Pressure Groups in Britain* (London: Dent).

King, A. (1975), 'Overload: problems of governing in the 1970s', *Political Studies*, vol 23, pp. 284–96.

Kogan, M. (1971), *The Politics of Education* (Harmondsworth: Penguin).

Kogan, M. (1975), *Educational Policy Making* (London: Allen & Unwin).

Kogan, M. (1978). *The Politics of Educational Change* (London: Fontana).

Kogan, M. (1981), 'Education in "hard times"', in *Big Government in Hard Times*, ed. C. C. Hood and M. Wright (Oxford: Martin Robertson), pp. 152–73.

LACSAB (1978), 'What it is and how it works', *Local Government Manpower*, suppl. vol. 22, no. 5 (October), pp. 11–14.

Laffin, M. (1982), 'Professionalism in central–local government relations', report to the Social Science Research Council, London, mimeo.

Laski, H. J., Jennings, I., and Robson, W. A. (eds) (1935), *A Century of Municipal Progress* (London: Allen & Unwin).

Latham, E. *The Group Basis of Politics* (Ithaca, NY: Cornell University Press).

Layfield Committee (1976), *Report of the Committee of Inquiry Into Local Government Finance*, Cmnd 6453 (London: HMSO).

Leigh, D. (1980), *The Frontiers of Secrecy* (London: Junction Books).

Levinson, H. M. (1971), *Collective Bargaining by British Local Authority Employees* (Ann Arbor, Mich.: Institute of Labor and Industrial Relations, University of Michigan).

Lijphart, A. (1968), *The Politics of Accommodation, Pluralism and Democracy in the Netherlands* (Berkeley, Calif.: University of California Press).

Lindblom, C. E. (1959), 'The science of "muddling through"', *Public Administration Review*, vol. 19, pp. 79–88.

Lindblom, C. E. (1977), *Politics and Markets* (New York: Basic Books).

Lindblom, C. E. (1979) 'Still muddling, not yet through', *Public Administration Review*, vol. 39, pp. 517–26.

Lodge, P., and Blackstone T. (1982), *Educational Policy and Educational Inequality* (Oxford: Martin Robertson).

Lofts, D. (1970), 'Note on the Local Government Training Board', in *Local Government in England 1958–69*, ed. H. V. Wiseman (London: Routledge & Kegan Paul), pp. 92–5.

Lowi, T. A. (1972), 'Four systems of policy, politics and choice', *Public Administration Review*, vol. 32. pp. 298–310.

McIntosh, M. (1955), 'The negotiation of wages and conditions for local authority employees in England and Wales; Part I – structure and scope', *Public Administration*, vol. 33, pp. 149–62.

Mackenzie, W. J. M. (1969), 'Pressure groups in British Government', in *Studies in British Politics*, ed. R. Rose (London: Macmillan, 2nd edn). pp. 258–75.

Madgwick, P., and James, M. (1980), 'The network of consultative government in Wales', in *New Approaches to the Study of Central–Local Government Relationships*, ed. G. W. Jones (Farnborough: Gower), pp. 101–15.

Manzer, R. A. (1970), *Teachers and Politics* (Manchester: Manchester University Press).

Marsh, D. (1983), 'Introduction', in *Pressure Politics*, ed. D. Marsh (London: Junction Books), pp. 1–19.

Marsh, D., and Grant, W. P. (1977), 'Tripartism: myth or reality?', *Government and Opposition*, vol. 12, pp. 195–211.

Marshall, J. (1975), 'Relations between local and central government', *District Councils Review*, vol. 4 (November) pp. 292–3.

Maud, J. (1932), *Local Government in Modern England* (London: Thornton Butterworth).

Meyer, J. W., and Rowan, B. (1978), 'The structure of educational organizations', in *Environments and Organizations*, ed. M. W. Meyer and Associates (San Francisco: Jossey-Bass), pp. 78–109.

Miles, M. B. (1979), 'Qualitative data as an attractive nuisance: the problem of analysis', *Administrative Science Quarterly*, vol. 24. pp. 590–601.

Mitchell, J. C. (1969), 'The concept and use of social networks', in *Social Networks in Urban Situations*, ed. J. C. Mitchell (Manchester: Manchester University Press), pp. 1–29.

Morton, J. (1970), *The Best Laid Schemes?* (London: Charles Knight).

OECD (1975), *Reviews of National Policies for Education: Education Development Strategy in England and Wales* (Paris: OECD).

Offe, C. (1975), 'The theory of the capitalist state and the problem of policy formation', in *Stress and Contradiction in Modern Capitalism*, ed. L. Lindberg, R. Alford, C. Crouch and C. Offe (London: Lexington Books), pp. 125–44.

Office of the Lord President of the Council (1976), *Devolution: The English Dimension* (London: HMSO).

Page, E. (1981), 'Grant consolidation and the development of intergovernmental relations in the United States and the United Kingdom', *Politics*, vol. 1, no. 1, pp. 19–24.

Page, E. (1982), 'Central government instruments of influence on local authorities', PhD thesis, University of Strathclyde.

Page, E. (1983), 'Fiscal pressure and central–local relations in Britain', paper to the Conference on Anglo-Danish Local State Research, Copenhagen, 25–27 September.

Pahl, R., and Winkler, J. (1974), 'The economic elite: theory and practice', in *Elites and Power in British Society*, ed. P. Stanworth and A. Giddens (Cambridge: Cambridge University Press), pp. 102–22.

Panitch, L. (1980), 'Recent theorisations of corporatism: reflections on a growth industry', *British Journal of Sociology*, vol. 31, pp. 159–87.

Pearce, C. (1980), *The Machinery of Change in Local Government 1888–1974* (London: Allen & Unwin).

Perrow, C. (1979), *Complex Organizations* (Glenview, Ill.: Scott, Foresman, 2nd edn).

Pile, Sir William (1979), *The Department of Education and Science* (London: Allen & Unwin).

Plant, R. (1983), 'The resurgence of ideology', in *Developments in British Politics*, ed. H. M. Drucker *et al.* (London: Macmillan), pp. 7–29.

Pliatzky, Sir Leo (1982), *Getting and Spending* (Oxford: Blackwell).

Poole, K. P. (1978), *The Local Government Service* (London: Allen & Unwin).

Prest, A. R. (1978), *Intergovernmental Financial Relations in the United Kingdom*, Research Monograph No. 23 (Canberra: Centre for Research on Federal Financial Relations, Australian National University).

Pugh, D., and Hickson, D. J. (1976), *Organizational Structure in its Context: The Aston Programme 1* (Farnborough, Hants: Saxon House).

Raab, C. (1982), 'Mapping the boundaries of educational policy systems: the case of Scotland', *Public Administration Bulletin*, no. 39 (September), pp. 40–57.

Ranson, S. (1980), 'Changing relations between centre and locality in education', *Local Government Studies*, vol. 6, no. 6, pp. 3–24.

Redlich, J., and Hirst, F. W. (1958), *A History of Local Government in England* (London: Macmillan).

Regan, D. (1979), *Local Government and Education* (London: Allen & Unwin, 2nd edn).

Rein, M. (1976), *Social Science and Public Policy* (Harmondsworth: Penguin).

Rhodes, R. A. W. (1979), 'Research into central–local relations in Britain: a framework for analysis', in *Central–Local Government Relationships*, Appendix I (London: Social Science Research Council).

Rhodes, R. A. W. (1981a), *Control and Power in Central–Local Government Relations* (Farnborough: Gower).

Rhodes, R. A. W. (1981b), 'The changing pattern of local government in England: reform or reorganization?', in *Local Government Reform and*

Reorganization: An International Perspective, ed. A. B. Gunlicks (Port Washington, NY, and London: Kennikat Press), pp. 93–111.

Rhodes R. A. W. (1982), 'Final Report on the Local Authority Associations in Central–Local Relationships', Social Science Research Council London, mimeo.

Rhodes, R. A. W. (1983), 'Can there be a national community of local government?', *Local Government Studies*, vol. 19. no. 6, pp. 17–37.

Rhodes, R. A. W. (1984), 'Continuity and change in British central–local relations: the "Conservative threat"', *British Journal of Political Science*, vol. 14, pp. 311–33.

Rhodes, R. A. W., Hardy. B. H., and Pudney, K. (1981), 'Public interest groups in central–local relations in England and Wales', *Public Administration Bulletin*, no. 36 (August), pp. 17–36.

Rhodes, R. A. W., Hardy, B. H., and Pudney, K. (1982), *'Corporate Bias' in Central–Local Relations: A Case Study of the Consultative Council on Local Government Finance*, SSRC Central–Local Relations Project, Discussion Paper No. 1, March (Colchester: Department of Government, University of Essex).

Rhodes, R. A. W., Hardy, B. H., and Pudney, K. (1982b), *Public Interest Groups in the National Community of Local Government: A Comparative Study*, SSRC Central–Local Relations Project, Discussion Paper No. 2, June (Colchester: Department of Government, University of Essex).

Rhodes, R. A. W., Hardy, B. H., and Pudney, K. (1982c), *Patterns of Resource Exchange within the National Community of Local Government*, SSRC Central–Local Relations Project, Discussion Paper No. 3, July (Colchester: Department of Government, University of Essex).

Rhodes, R. A. W., Hardy, B. H., and Pudney, K. (1983a), *The Reorganisation of Local Government and the National Community of Local Government: A Case Study of 'Organic Change'*, SSRC Central–Local Relations Project, Discussion Paper No. 4, January (Colchester: Department of Government, University of Essex).

Rhodes, R. A. W., Hardy, B. H., and Pudney, K. (1983b), *Local Government Pay Negotiations and the National Community of Local Government*, SSRC Central–Local Relations Project, Discussion Paper No. 5. February (Colchester: Department of Government, University of Essex).

Rhodes, R. A. W., Hardy, B. H., and Pudney, K. (1983c), *Constraints on the National Community of Local Government: Members, 'Other Governments' and Policy Communities*, SSRC Central–Local Relations Project, Discussion Paper No. 6, March (Colchester: Department of Government, University of Essex).

Rhodes, R. A. W., Hardy, B. H., and Pudney, K. (1983d), *'Power-Dependence' Theories of Central–Local Relations: A Critical Assessment*, SSRC Central–Local Relations Project, Discussion Paper No. 7 July (Colchester: Department of Government, University of Essex).

Richards, P. G. (1975), *The Local Government Act 1972: Problems of Implementation* (London: Allen & Unwin).

Richards, P. G. (1980), *The Reformed Local Government System* (London: Allen & Unwin, 4th edn).

Richardson J. J., and Jordan, G. (1979), *Governing Under Pressure* (Oxford: Martin Robertson).

Riverdale Committee (1938), *Report of the Departmental Committee on Fire Brigade Services*, Cmnd 1945 (London: HMSO).

Roberts, L., and Hodgson, P. (1978), 'Local authority associations', *County Councils Gazette*, November, pp. 231–4.

Robson, W. A. (1966), *Local Government in Crisis* (London: Allen & Unwin).

Rose, R. (1982), *Understanding the United Kingdom* (London: Longman).

Royal Commission on Local Government in England (1967a), *Written Evidence of the Association of Municipal Corporations* (London: HMSO).

Royal Commission on Local Government in England (1967b), *Written Evidence of the Ministry of Health* (London: HMSO).

Royal Commission on Local Government in England (1967c), *Written Evidence of the Department of Education and Science* (London: HMSO).

Royal Commission on Local Government in England (1968), *Written Evidence of Professional Associations* (London: HMSO).

Royal Commission on Local Government in England (1969), *Report,* Cmnd 4040 (London: HMSO).

Royal Commission on the Constitution (1973), *Report*, Cmnd 5460 (London: HMSO).

Saran, R. (1973), *Policymaking in Secondary Education* (Oxford: Clarendon Press).

Saunders, P. (1980), *Urban Politics* (Harmondsworth: Penguin).

Saunders, P. (1981), *Social Theory and the Urban Question* (London: Hutchinson).

Scarrow, H. A. (1971), 'Policy pressures by British local government: the case of regulation in the "public interest"', *Comparative Politics*, vol. 4, pp. 1–28.

Schmitter, P. C. (1979), 'Still the century of corporatism?', in *Trends Towards Corporatist Intermediation*, ed. P. C. Schmitter and G. Lehmbruch (London: Sage), pp. 7–52.

Schmitter, P. C. (1982), 'Reflections on where the theory of neo-corporatism has gone and where the praxis of neo-corporatism may be going', in *Patterns of Corporatist Policy-Making* ed. G. Lehmbruch and P. C. Schmitter (London: Sage), pp. 259–79.

Sedgemore, B. (1980), *The Secret Constitution* (London: Hodder & Stoughton).

Self, P., and Storing H. (1962), *The State and the Farmer* (London: Allen & Unwin).

Sharp, E. (1969), *The Ministry of Housing and Local Government* (London: Allen & Unwin).

Sharpe, L. J. (1978), 'Reforming the grass roots: an alternative analysis', in *Policy and Politics*, ed. D. Butler and A. H. Halsey (London: Macmillan), pp. 82–110.

Sharpe, L. J. (1979), 'Modernising the localities: local government in Britain and some comparisons with France', in *Local Government in Britain and France*, ed. J. Lagroye and V. Wright (London: Allen & Unwin), pp. 42–73.

Simeon, R. (1972), *Federal–Provincial Diplomacy* (Toronto: University of Toronto Press).

Simon, H. A. (1960), *The New Science of Management Decision* (New York: Harper & Row)

Simon, H. A. (1970), *The Sciences of the Artificial* (Cambridge, Mass.: MIT Press).

Smith, G. (1981), 'Michael Heseltine – the most disastrous Environment Secretary', *Local Government Chronicle*, 3 July, p. 685.

Social Science Research Council (1979), *Central–Local Government Relationships* (London: SSRC).

Stanyer. J. (1973), 'The Redcliffe-Maud Royal Commission on Local Government', in *The Role of Commissions in Policy Making*, ed. R. A. Chapman (London: Allen & Unwin), pp. 105–42.

Stevenson, B. (1982), 'De-controlling the Fire Service', *Public Money*, March, pp. 21–2.

Stewart, J. D. (1958), *British Pressure Groups* (Oxford: Clarendon Press).

Stewart, J. D. (1977) *Management in an Era of Restraint and Central and Local Government Relationships* (London: Municipal Group).

Stewart, J. D. (1980), 'From growth to standstill', in *Public Spending Decisions,* ed. M. Wright (London: Allen & Unwin), pp. 9–24.

Stewart, J. D. (1983), *Local Government: The Conditions of Local Choice* (London: Allen & Unwin).

Stewart, J. D., and Jones, G. W. (1982), 'The Layfield analysis applied to central–local relations under the Conservative government', *Local Government Studies*, vol. 8, no. 3, pp. 47–59.

Stewart, J. D., Leach S., and Skelcher, C. K. (1978), *Organic Change: A Report on Constitutional, Management and Financial Problems* (Birmingham: Institute of Local Government Studies).

Tadpole, Peter (1981), 'A view from the gallery: Michael Heseltine', *Sunday Times Magazine*, no. 76, 15 February, p. 76.

Taylor, J. A. (1979), 'The Consultative Council on Local Government Finance: a critical analysis of its origins and development', *Local Government Studies*, vol. 5, no. 3, pp. 7–36.

Taylor, R. (1980), *The Fifth Estate* (London: Pan).

Thompson, A. W. J., and Beaumont, P. B. (1978), *Public Sector Bargaining: A Study of Relative Gain* (Farnborough, Hants: Saxon House).

Tivey, L. (1982), 'Nationalised industries as organised interests', *Public Administration*, vol. 60, no. 1, pp. 42–55.

Truman, D. B. (1951), *The Governmental Process* (New York: Knopf).

Vickers, Sir Geoffrey (1965), *The Art of Judgement* (London: Chapman & Hall).

Wade, E. C. S., and Phillips, C. C. (1977), *Constitutional and Administrative Law* (London: Longman, 9th edn).

Webb, A., and Wistow, G. (1982). *Whither State Welfare?: Policy and Implementation in the Personal Social Services, 1979–80*, RIPA Studies No. 8 (London: Royal Institute of Public Administration).

Wildavsky, A. (1975), *Budgeting: A Comparative Theory of Budgetary Processes* (Boston, Mass.: Little, Brown).

Wildavsky, A. (1980) *The Art and Craft of Policy Analysis* (London: Macmillan)

Williams, G. (1981), 'Education: evolutionary change in a harsh climate', in *Government Policy Initiatives 1979–80: Some Case Studies in Public Administration*, ed. P. M. Jackson (London: Royal Institute of Public Administration), pp. 181–99.

Wilson, H. (1973), *Democracy in Local Affairs* (London: Labour Party).

Wilson, H. (1974), *The Labour Government 1964–70* (Harmondsworth: Penguin).

Wood, B. (1976), *The Process of Local Government Reform 1966–74* (London: Allen & Unwin).

Wright, D. S. (1978), *Understanding Intergovernmental Relations* (North Scituate, Mass.: Duxbury Press).

Wright, M. (1977), 'Public expenditure in Britain: the crisis of control', *Public Administration*, vol. 55, pp. 143–69.

Yin, R. K. (1981), 'The case study crisis: some answers', *Administrative Science Quarterly*, vol. 26, pp. 58–65.

Young, A., and Sloman, A. (1982), *No, Minister: An Inquiry into the Civil Service* (London: BBC Publications).

Young, K. (1977), '"Values" in the policy process', *Policy and Politics*, vol. 5, pp. 1–22.

Young, K., and Mills, L. (1980), *Public Policy Research: A Review of Qualitative Methods* (London: Social Science Research Council).

SUBJECT INDEX

AUTHOR/NAME INDEX